The Planet's copy.

WE'RE ALL IN THIS TOGETHER

Kirsten Brydum
Franklin Udall Lindsay

Front and back cover art designed by Frank Lindsay.
Graphic design engineering for front and back covers provided by the master Einar Berg.
Back cover photo of Kirsten Brydum taken by Frank Lindsay.

First published by Dog Ear Publishing
4010 W. 86th Street, Ste H
Indianapolis, IN 46268
www.dogearpublishing.net

ISBN: 978-160844-470-0

This book is printed on acid-free paper.

Printed in the United States of America

❧ ♡ ♡ ♡ ❧

Written for Mothers, Fathers, Sons, and Daughters who believe there is a time and a place for everything under the sun, and the time for war is now done. We have but one blue planet...time to share and practice the Peace of abundance so the children have a future to look forward to.

we're all in this together

Peace to you in all you do ~

Acknowledgment

This collaboration of intent could not have been possible without the Grace that put so many good people into the life of amazing. To a father, who supported without judgment and loaned his life so that this work could be produced. His support is a rock on which strength is drawn. To a daughter that needed to know what, why, when, and where the life of a father had gone. Her love another rock on which to draw strength. She was always there in a time of need. To a brother who was the rock of backup and the author of plan "B". He turned the tide of doubt into support. And to a very, very special friend who believed together we can, inspiring from beginning to now, with the flow of that which I stumble to articulate accurately. She is the rock of kindred spirit. There are never thanks enough I could return. Know that this thanks is embellished with great reverence from the heart.

Then there is the cast of colorful people that individually shared themselves so this life could be as full and as rich as intended. Here I mention a few. Mary Brydum/Bell aka Mamie Page, your patience with the dinosaur, your toxic humor, your unshakable friendship, is incredible testimony to your faith in this project. You edit with a knife that would make an attorney proud. You're the mother to the daughter we call Madam President; you earned the right to first read. Kris, you forced open the mind at just the right time and allowed a book to flow. Thank you for sharing your song so others may sing. Karen Epifano, you stopped the pain of hard work more than once, healing with the touch of care from your island of wise. You inspire stewardship of this planet we call home. South Whidbey Island is a very lucky place to have you. Care of my home provided by Cindy Zimmerman and daughter Sabrina, with the ever breeding pair of loveable little dogs, Tiger and Lilly. Linda Rawson, the roommate who provided home in Hawai'i and her sister Jan Frazier-Sherman, who provided pickup for the overflow computer entry from her home in Fairbanks, Alaska. Lenny Puma, the man who provided the heart to care for my business in my absence. Lenny, you are 1 in 7 billion. And Marie Dadisman, whose ever encouraging words as I approached a final product helped lift the workload from the perspective of fresh eyes. Again, there is never enough thanks to express my gratitude to you all.

The best is last, although she was mentioned as very, very special at first, yet merits a second nod. She is an incredible little bundle of photons from the Universe inspiring one's mind to move at speed c. She lives the walk of Spiritual awareness, the real change others can only talk about. The future of our planet is bright with the Grace residing in this soul of someone so fair. Thank you for sharing your guiding spirit, a place in your heart, and always an open door for me to rest and replenish my weary soul. I will be forever in your debt Kirsten Brydum.

So in your journeys should you cross paths with this feature of Grace, wrap your arms around her and say thanks again for me. Listen for her wisdom in the journey home.

FORWARD

Told from the perspective of the normal every day from someone who might not be considered normal every day, forced to live tortures of stupidity while waiting for the world to change. The fine line of sanity lived by humans, opened for inspection as you watch one human's run for the roses. Drawing from insight that speaks from common ground, you'll be challenged to participate in the openness of truth. Cliché written to satire, the human lives out that which is laughably innocuous, unbelievable, yet true. This is not based on a true story…this is a true story. He is all characters in the drama of life.

Deeply you will delve into another perspective from a man 'dealing with it'. Nothing special really, except the nature of the help he receives. That's where the story really lies and might have us by the end of the journey suggesting that there really is a different way to approach the problems we all face. This is a work of story lived that is intended to convince you of that peace. Aggression in problem solving will be rested, the antidote for addiction will be administered in dosing that everyone can tolerate. Deep down you will understand that all people desire the same, and that there is only one blue planet that we share. It is suggested that we all learn to share; using the uniqueness of a story you've not likely heard. An attempt has been made to provide a tool to attain our goal to share the abundance of life on earth. If we don't, our search for all that we hold common will never be realized.

The tale will take you back to child. To the simple human life of the child within, that yearns to free the force that creates. Crafted to build feeling, much like the energy in arts and crafts class when we were young, bursting at the seams to get busy. That energy giving food for thought that nourishes creation may be sparked in your heart as well. A self-help book for the planet in delectable little portions of everyday that is easily digestible. Some sweet, some sour and then there are those that are lived in love. All brought to you in the living color of life so that you too can consider the box. By journey's end, you may be ready to step out of that box and onto the path of real change. Real change that needs to be made now, for our planet to survive as home. We all feel deep down that the road currently traveled by humanity may not be the one that leads us to that harmony of that home.

Thought-provoking stimulation that may have you asking, if our tax dollars have been funding a Department of Defense for a hundred years, why can't we fund a Department of Peace. The defense we use to provide the illusion of security has succeeded in only making the image of America that of a bully. And the 'bully syndrome' only gets you Columbine. You may decide you don't want your government creating Columbine. The divisions we draw and the walls we build will have you asking, "Chip everyone?" We hope when you reach the end that you too are ready to become ambassadors of humanity setting the bar to 'do no harm'. Practice 'FREE', if we do not we will know that "Evil triumphs when good men do nothing."

By the end we hope you are wondering...

Anarchist Heart
Tyson Ayers

CONTENTS

CHAPTER 1

THE LITTLE GIRL IN A WHEELCHAIR

This time was so much different than the first; now at least he had arms, not just legs, yet nothing could have prepared him for the heat. Even the ice vest was of minimal help. He was soaking wet from the sweat he had generated on the mile long parade route. As he rounded the last corner and headed for the Chamber of Commerce office, all he could really think about was getting out of his costume and pounding as much cold bottled water as he could hold. The success of what he had accomplished in the concept, design and production, as well as the personality he had brought to life in this oversized happy clam had not occurred to him yet. All he could think about was water.

In the final few hundred feet to the office he found it difficult to see as the sweat poured profusely from his forehead. The constant rain of salty droplets streaming into his eyes was stinging so bad he had to squeeze his eyes closed tight, then shake his head to try to attain some relief. The costume modification that had provided armholes was a great safety factor in case he should fall, but provided no ability for him to wipe the sweat from his brow. The sweat that now was continually streaming into his eyes at this point.

"It's like opening your eyes underwater in the ocean" he thought, trying not to run into anyone on the crowded sidewalk because of his fuzzy vision. The sidewalk was busy with families making their way to the festival and he greeted a few more folks with a quick handshake hello. The door to the office was in sight, which meant relief from the relentless heat and thirst, when he saw a family with the Dad pushing an overstuffed wheelchair. For a fraction of a second he thought about trying to hustle up and slip through the door before they could intersect his path, but what the heck one last greeting couldn't hurt.

He remembered the warning he had been given by the costume maker regarding the response of some children to a costumed character. "They might become frightened," she had warned so he approached cautiously. The family slowed and stopped. His voice from within the costume delivered his greeting, "Welcome to the Clam Festival folks," and he extended a white-gloved hand for a quick handshake with the Mom. He watched closely for the reaction of the young autistic girl that was semi-reclined in the heavily padded wheelchair, noticing she was motionless with her eyes transfixed on him. The look in her large brown eyes was a look of inquisitiveness, so he bent down slightly taking her little hand in his and gently shook it as he spoke again, "And hello to you. Welcome to the Clam Festival, have a fantastic day and enjoy the sunshine."

With that her eyes widened and she began to react with a flailing of her arms. Her head turned from side to side with her voice uttering sounds that he could not understand. Her eyes remained fixed on him even wider now; he feared he might have frightened her, and he withdrew his hand. "Have a great day folks," he offered as he backed away quickly to calm any fears excited by the gaudy costume. He hand gestured with a big 'thumbs up' then disappeared through the chamber office door for some relief from the heat and much-needed hydration.

The day had started in a light fog at 3am for Frank. Assisting with preparation of the festival grounds followed by three hours of semi-controlled chaos as the vendors arrived to claim their booth space, unload their vehicles and set up. By 9am the fog, which is typical for Pismo Beach in the summer, had rolled back to reveal a glorious October morning. Fall in Pismo can be spectacular.

Unfortunately he knew that this stellar weather, meant the debut of this costumed character he had named Sam might be a little warmer than anticipated. He had hoped to find someone to put on the outfit and take on the role of Sam D. Clam, but had found no takers. So this first run for the city mascot was up to him to pull off. As a director for the Chamber board he had made a commitment to develop the costume. He had spent a year coaxing his in-law Sue, who worked in the costume department at Knott's Berry Farm, into building the costume for him. He lodged overnight with Sue and her husband Paul on his periodic Los Angeles freight runs for his business, pestering Sue for construction details on each visit. Finally in her frustration she said she should just build it for him. He jumped on that opportunity to ask how much it might cost for her to do that; when she responded with an amount he said he could guarantee payment. Sue agreed and with that Sam the Clam came into being. Now it was up to him to develop the character.

Sue imparted many details as to proper code of conduct and procedures for a costumed character which he followed to the "T", except the part about no talking. Being a Chamber / City representative, Sam could not pass up the chance to promote this beautiful town and Frank figured that one day Sam might become a valuable tool for marketing Pismo Beach. He was not one to pass up opportunity, and he was a dreamer. While suiting up for this first parade his mind raced with what he might do or say to bring Sam's character to life. The costume had to have a fixed identity that could always be worn by whoever played the role, so "happy" was the chosen personality to adopt.

Another rule Sue imparted for a costumed character: if the head was covered the rest of the body must be covered so as not to show any skin. This consideration did not mesh well for sunny warm weather. The soft foam costume shaped as an oversized Pismo Clam had to be raised over the head and lowered down over the trunk of the body. The person going inside then guided their arms under the adjustable support straps and through the armholes. The costume came down to the knees and a foot over the head. Extruding body parts meant the arms had to be covered with a long-sleeved shirt and the legs covered with a leotard. White gloved hands and the feet adorned with what became Sam's trademark size 13 bright red Converse All Star high topped tennis shoes. Sam was good to go, but the body inside was unable to vent excess heat. The ice vest he wore he figured could address that issue. The issue now was how to convey the character.

He had to figure out as he suited up what type of animated movements he might perform to add a friendly loveable feel to Sam's "happy clam" personality. He was winging it, flying by the seat of his pants and he noticed he had sweaty palms as he pulled the white linen gloves onto his hands. This was it 9:45am, time to head for parade line-up and Sam's big show. Frank, a 39-year old businessman with no prior acting skills to draw on other than life itself, could feel the pressure mounting. He always said he'd try anything "once." The outcome of this debut was to determine if this was to be his "once" inside the buffoon-like costume. Marshalling a large dose of "OKAY here goes," out the backdoor of the Chamber office he went with his chaperone Rebecca in hand.

Sue had also told him, "Because you never know what people may do you need to be chaperoned at all times to prevent costume damages or physical injury from aggressive kids." Not to mention the fact that the visibility out of Sam's black screened teacup sized eyeholes sucked! He could only see what was directly in front of him and only about eight to ten feet out. This could have been a disastrous situation when it came to curbs, planter boxes or small children that should wander into his path. Had he not had Rebecca to guide him to his place in the parade line-up, he might have never made it. He felt fairly confident that negotiating the city street parade route could be accomplished on his own, so he and Rebecca agreed she'd walk the route on the sidewalk available to assist in case of emergency.

Taking up his position in front of the Judkins Middle School marching band all he had to do was wait in his foam-lined sauna, which now was approaching 100 degrees inside. Sue had warned of overheating. It was an uncommonly warm 75 degrees at 9:30 on the sunshiny Pismo day. As he heated up the question of "What the hell am I doing here" struck first. "Where was the fog?" was second. He could have really used some of that fog to cool things down. "Oh well, it will all be over in an hour or so," his only thought to comfort.

Ten o'clock start time came and went. Finally at 10:30 the parade line participants jolted forward and the party was underway. Already he had exceeded Sue's suggested twenty minute time limit, recommended by the big boys at Disneyland and Knott's for a person to fill a full body costume at any one stretch. The temperature inside was now 100 plus and although the ice vest he wore provided minimal relief, the sweating had begun as he began the parade trek. Immediately, almost by instinct, he began to portray Sam's personality through exaggerated hand movements and strides, waving to the crowd with an occasional "thumbs up" or big "OKAY" hand gestures from white-gloved hands. The marching band's drums and brass elements drove Sam forward, providing a cadence he could match with his huge red feet. The march of the comical clowning clam was a spectacle as Sam approached the first turn and the parade announcer's booth, manned by the Chamber's Executive, Bill Awson.

"Now welcome for the first time ever Sam the Clam. Sam is the mascot for the City of Pismo Beach… Clam Capital of the World." was announced by Bill to the overflowing crowd that packed the sidewalk lining the parade route. With that pronouncement a cheer went up from the onlookers. Sam stopped to take a bow, wave to the crowd and enjoy the moment only to hear the announcer say, "Sam better get moving or he'll be run over by the marching band."

A quick glimpse sideways out of the eyehole revealed the band was within a few feet, coming on strong, and they had no intention of slowing down for Sam! He was about to be trampled into chowder. Half turned he had to sidestep very quickly to put some distance between himself and the onslaught of youth. The size 13 shoes made nimble foot movement nearly impossible and he just about lost it when he slipped in a pile of horseshit which had been deposited by a previous parade participant. "So much for Sam's 15 seconds of fame" he mused with just a touch of disappointment as he stumbled onward. The crowd had not been disappointed however and applauded the poo-tripping recovery from disaster.

Now it was all about catching up to the rest of the parade, as well as occasionally turning around to walk backwards for a visual check to insure he maintained a safe distance from the marching machine behind him. The temperature inside by now had to be 110 degrees and he knew he would have to muster his Arizona desert conditioning to complete the parade course without passing out. Thirst beckoned to be quenched.

That's why the door to the Chamber office had loomed large as an oasis. As soon as the door closed Frank struggled out of the bulbous costume, his soaking wet long-sleeved crewneck T-shirt, then made a beeline for the water cooler. He fell into a chair in front of the cooler while slugging down cold water as fast as he could swallow. Rebecca and other staff members concerned about his well being asked repeatedly if he was alright. He wasn't sure himself. Several minutes later he noticed his face was still beet red. As he splashed cold water onto his head from the restroom wash basin his thoughts turned to finding a replacement. The heat he was radiating was beginning to subside, his thoughts of ever finding someone to endure this physical abuse just short of torture bordered on impossible. "Maybe creating Sam wasn't such a good idea after all" crept into his thoughts.

Being that there was no script to what duties and functions were to be performed by Sam the Clam, Frank assumed that the job of Sam was done for the day. Then an incoming call via hand-held walkie talkie radio to one of the Chamber staff from the Chamber executive lent some direction. Bill reported that folks coming into the festival grounds were asking to see Sam the Clam. Bill was calling to see if Sam could come down for awhile and greet the crowd streaming in through the festival gates. Despite a weakened withered state he reluctantly agreed to don the suit again to make an appearance. After all he had committed to being Sam for the day and saw this as an opportunity to promote, which was the whole reason for Sam's development anyway. So back into the suit he went and with Rebecca in tow they headed out for the block-long walk to the festival grounds.

Upon arriving Frank stepped into the character of Sam and positioned himself at the main gate entrance. He began to greet the incoming waves of festival-goers with hand shakes and verbal greetings of "welcome to the clam festival, we're glad you're here," "have a wonderful day," "enjoy the food and sunshine." This was a much less physical task which made the heat factor tolerable and he actually started to enjoy the clowning.

Over the course of about two hours he greeted hundreds of people, many of whom wanted photographs taken of their family members with Sam the Clam. Eventually he was joined by the beautiful contestants from the scholarship pageant, including the crowned Clam Festival Queen. Rounds were made strolling amongst the vendors' booths greeting folks and posing for hundreds of pictures. It was a great visual watching a crowned queen with entourage escorting the jumbo-sized clam. The colorful troupe really elevated the festive spirit of those they came into contact with and the PR benefit was paying big dividends. He began to visualize the role Sam could play in the future. Now if he could just find someone to play the part. Success of the concept had been achieved: Sam was lovable, a hit with kids and adults alike. It should be easy to find someone willing to take the spot, he speculated.

Sam broke away from the entourage, heading back to the chamber office for more rest and water. Back at the office and out of the costume he sat exhausted. It was about 3:00pm and it had already been a 12-hour day. Another call came in from Bill stating that someone was needed for traffic control at the corner of Pomeroy and Cypress streets. Short staffed as usual for volunteer events, Frank agreed to fill the assignment for awhile. His body was tired, but his mind was racing thinking about the possibilities for this newfound "Happy Clam" promotional tool. The traffic control was a no-effort responsibility that allowed him time to daydream about new roles for Sam to engage. He took up his position with radio in hand and began to reflect on the days' accomplishments while dreaming into the future. All was well, feeling a bit refreshed and relaxed for the first time that day knowing the brunt of his responsibility was done.

From out of nowhere a dark cloud of 'what if' injected its venomous negativity into the bliss of an otherwise perfect day. 'What if' someone was to find out about his drunken indiscretions from long ago? It would ruin everything. That thought momentarily turned his stomach. He pushed the nightmare out of his mind, returning to the positive thoughts of success achieved during the day. But, because of the brush with 'what if' he focused more intently on finding someone to take over the role of Sam.

Finally a relief person arrived to take over traffic control at about 4:30. He gladly handed off the radio so he could head back, gather his things and go home to rest. He was mentally and physically exhausted, he had been on his feet for the past 15 hours. Somewhat dazed as he headed out to return to the office he finally realized someone was calling his name. He looked around to see the Chamber executive waving him over to the sidewalk.

Oh crap, what does he want me to do now? he thought.

He made his way over to where Bill was standing, issuing directions to a couple of other volunteers. As they departed Frank asked,

"What's up?"

Bill turned with what Frank perceived as an insistent, somewhat concerned look asking,

"Did you greet a family today pushing a little girl in a wheelchair?"

His heart sank. For a split second he thought that he had scared the hell out of the little girl. Had the family lodged a complaint with Bill?

"Yes I did. Did I scare her? I'm so sorry, I didn't mean to!" Frank stated apologetically willing to accept the chastising he was sure he was about to receive.

Bill looked at him with a long-day face and said,

"Well no, not at all. The family came to me about an hour ago; they wanted to say thank 'you' for that greeting. They said it was the happiest they had ever seen their little girl. Sam's attentions brightened her whole day. They wanted me to thank Sam for making their little girl's day joyous."

What an emotional roller-coaster. Fear of frightening the little girl turned to elation knowing he had gifted her and her family with an exceptional experience. His heart soared. He knew at that moment that this job of playing Sam D. Clam was to be his for a long time to come. If he could bring such joy being Sam, then it could be a vehicle for him to pay forward for the darkness in his past. "Okay... thanks." was about all he could stammer.

That caught him totally off guard; deep emotion from the wellspring of heart grew, and he turned to walk away. He did not want to let anyone see the mist of emotion in his eyes that this unexpected praise evoked. Like an epiphany he really felt as if he had found an avenue for his own personal atonement with the Universe. It felt right to be engaged in an endeavor that was a win-win for so many and paid forward with interest in healing for his soul. As he walked back to the office a peace transcended the fear of 'what if' as he personally accepted the task of creating a character out of Sam. A character of joy, a character destined to elicit a million smiles that for him was to fill the void left from never having been able to say "I'm sorry" to the one he had wronged. The two block walk back to the office was supported with the high of success even though he was exhausted. Despite his daze he managed to thank the Grace of the Universe for this new direction in sacred task. A task gifted from the joy of one little girl in a wheelchair.

~~~~~

We are all colorful string woven into a tapestry of life that becomes who we are. It takes many strings to complete this wonderful work in which we are all encouraged to contribute our parts. This weaving is a tremendously intricate pattern of interconnected events that is each one of us. We each play a role in the completion of this grand picture called life. How that role is developed is the choice we are all gifted. We are now going to look at one string of that tapestry and a journey lived to the fullest extent intended in the gift. We all share in the responsibility of co-creating what we have, and from this weaving we will see the commonality of what we all want. All we have to do is just show up and create. Enjoy this story of how one string contributes to us all.

CHAPTER 2

MULTIPLYING CLAMS

The product supply runs Frank made to the Los Angeles area for his growing little business in Pismo took about three hours each way. He could stay overnight free at "cousin" Paul and Sue's and be back in Pismo the following afternoon for about $30.00 in gas. Those runs where a savings of about $200.00 in freight charges. He looked forward to these runs. They provided a little time away from the daily routine of running Genesis Water, as well as a substantial monetary savings for the business. His business was a retail water treatment facility, soon to be bottling facility that was open to the public sixty hours a week. Time away was rare and coveted.

During these treks he could devote time to planning and dreaming about his various projects. It was on one of these trips, shortly after Sam's successful debut, that the thought of a storyline marketing plan for Sam lit him up. Up until this time he wasn't quite sure what he was going to do to promote Sam and how to keep the character fresh, alive and interesting to the people in the community. His thought: why not create a family; make them real everyday people, entities that everyone could identify with just like the folks next door. The storyline could be a progression of joys, dramas and other life events that could be highlighted every year at the festival. A story people could follow. Sam and how about a girlfriend - Pam - then maybe they could get engaged and then marry. Then maybe Pam might get pregnant, having a clamette or two or three. His mind spun with wild ideas to capture community interest.

"Wow" he thought "this might work." All he had to do was sell this idea to the Board of Directors, convince Sue to build the costumes, and find people to fill the roles to be played. This storyline could take years to play out and would be a fantastic PR tool for Pismo's Clam festival. Plus he figured it might be a good way to include his daughter in his chamber service some day. He was always looking for ways to spend quality time with his only child.

The plan was proposed at the next board meeting and accepted in part to proceed with the building of the second entity, Pam. Sue agreed to build the costume to the specs provided by Frank and he again guaranteed payment for her work. The 'Pam' costume was delivered a few months before that year's Clam Festival and he proudly presented the new addition of the clam family to the Board. The question was asked, "Who is going to fill the costume to play the part of Pam?" to which Frank replied he had not found anyone yet.

At that moment a hand went up from amongst the board membership and a tiny little voice said, "I'll do it." It was of all people Judy Earn. What a surprise! Judy was a petite little lady in her fifties, standing about five feet tall with an absolutely effervescent personality. Judy and her husband Hardy had lived in Pismo for over forty years and she had been on the Chamber board for at least ten of those years. She was an incredibly busy lady being an owner of a large hotel and other properties, as well as a board member at Hearst Castle just up the coast. Judy was not who he expected to have volunteered to play the part. He was soon to find out she was absolutely perfect for playing the role of Sam's main girl.

Pam E. Clam was a much smaller costume with decidedly feminine features. She had larger wider eyes with long eyelashes, Betty Boop ruby red lips, a dainty bow on top of the head finishing with a pink feather boa draping around the back and over the arms. Judy fit the outfit perfectly. She brought her own flamboyant additions of high-class boots, formal silk gloves and to top it all a hand-held parasol which changed in style and color on each outing. She was the perfect compliment to Sam's masculine image. Sam was a rather plain basic clam shape with a big broad black smile, much smaller eyes and of course the size 13 bright red Converse tennis shoes. What a pair; it had to make you laugh when they were seen hand-in-hand walking down the street.

Judy and Frank strategized on how best to promote Sam and Pam and when the word got out that Sam had a girlfriend the offers for newspaper, radio and television interviews began to roll in. He convinced Judy that the best way to make Sam and Pam real was to keep their personal identities secret so that no one would know exactly who was inside the costumes. This was suggested by Frank in part to quell the 'what if' that nagged him from time to time. The press, board members, friends and family also complied with that request of anonymity and their identities for the most part were never revealed. As time went on the question of who was inside did pass, except for the young inquiring minds that tried to peer through the eye screens trying to figure out who or what was inside. The costumes were always put on and taken off out of sight of the general public. Their identities could only be discerned by their voices which most folks couldn't figure out and if someone did the request for confidentiality was honored.

On another beautiful October morning, Pam E. Clam was introduced along side Sam to an overflow crowd attending the festival parade. The enthusiastic response of whistles, cheers and applause invigorated the pair as they walked side by side waving to the responding smiling faces. They eventually split up, taking positions on either side of the street, shaking hands and inviting all to join them at the festival. They really had a ball playing up their roles. After the parade they greeted folks coming into the festival grounds, posing for hundreds of family photos. Even the foreign visitors, many of whom couldn't speak English, insisted on family portraits. Japan, Korea, Germany, Spain... these images went around the world. Giant clams, what a kick.

Their enthusiasm was contagious and that year the receipts from the festival gate revealed a substantial increase. Success! Judy was hooked and would continue to play the role of Pam for the next ten years until the clams' retirement. Frank's passion for the project burned with even more intensity and the plan to move forward with his storyline of an engagement, wedding and babies was implemented by the board. For him the ability to give away such happiness to all the smiling faces, especially the kids, was an amend that made his soul soar and kept the gut wrenching dark cloud plague of 'what if' stress at bay.

Over the course of the next year Sam and Pam marched in the Grover Beach Holiday Parade, Arroyo Grande Harvest Festival Parade, and did radio and television interviews in preparation for their announcement of their engagement to be married. The engagement was announced at that year's Clam Fest and the date for the marriage was set for the following year. The wedding was to be the theme of the following festival. As festival time approached he was amazed at how seriously everyone was taking the event.

Holy crap, it was set up like a real marriage. A top hat and cane for Sam, a veil head dressing and a really, really big ring for Pam. A Maid of Honor, Bridesmaids, Groomsmen, Best Man and a huge marriage certificate. Flowers, invitations, corsages, and stage for the chapel, reception room, food, organ and organist for the wedding march ... this friggin' thing was out of control!

Local actors enlisted to play the various parts alongside one television personality Andrea Barber, who played Kimmy Gibbler on the ABC television sitcom "Full House," was to be Pam's Maid of Honor. Hell, the whole damn town had a part or was assisting in some way to help pull off this "Wedding of the Century" as it was being billed. "What the heck," he thought, "Isn't this what community festivals are all about?" The community was involved, excited and participating. He figured that this aspect in and of itself was a success, as he had not seen this much excitement around the Clam Festival in all the time he had been involved. This was sweet, but definitely out of control. He felt as if he was truly getting married again and shit he already had a wife and a child! What a rush. Judy felt the same and she had a husband! How the two kept up with their real lives as business owners/operators, parents, and other projects they were involved in was truly Herculean.

The big day came. Another beautiful fall day greeted a massive crowd. Frank and Judy stepped into costume and character at about 9:45am; it seemed they were in character for the rest of the day. Frank again had arrived at 3:30am to lay out the festival grounds, guiding the volunteers through the chaos of vendor set-up; he now was the lead man for the process. A quick pastry with a cup of hot coffee was all he had time for before a band of volunteers and concerned citizens whisked him away from his set-up responsibilities, making sure he was at the chapel on time.

In the parade Sam and Pam had to ride in a float specially prepared for the soon-to-be- married couple. This change they were not fond of, but acquiesced as the adornments to their costumes made the brisk walking pace of the parade just too hard to handle, especially with Sam's big top hat, the weight of which pulled the rest of the costume if he bent. Having to keep an upright stance made it virtually impossible for him to see anything shorter than about 5 feet tall. So ride they did, waving and gesturing to the masses lining the streets. More people than they had ever seen.

You wouldn't have thought that a fictitious wedding of two costumed characters would draw so many people from so far away. People had come from Fresno, Bakersfield, Modesto, Visalia, some of them traveling hours just to see this event. This brilliant, small stroke of inventiveness was nothing but fun, resting a smile on his face. The rest of the day was pretty much a blur, except one part.

He'd never forget what he saw out of his eyeholes while the organist played the wedding march and Pam came to his side. Hundreds of people streaming up off the beach and out of the shops and stores that surrounded the festival grounds, pushing up to the barricades so deep with people that he couldn't see any spaces left to fill. It was truly amazing. When the organist stopped and before the preacher began there was this uncanny silence, all eyes were directed at the stage. Even the vendors stopped what they were doing and stepped out to watch. All that could be heard was the gentle wash of the waves over the sand and a seagull crying its approval as it soared overhead. You could have heard a pin drop and then the preacher began, "Dearly beloved." It was an unbelievable day. What was more unbelievable was that years into the future, as Sam and Pam greeted folks coming through the festival gates, many commented on having been there for 'the wedding'. How cool to have given someone a fond memory that they might remember long into life.

The following year PR releases informed folks in their community that Pam was with child and that the delivery date would be shortly before that year's festival. This really excited fans again and a contest was initiated to name the baby clams. It had been reported in a humorous newspaper article that Pam's ultrasound had shown not one, not two, but three baby clams. Entries poured in from everywhere. Three was going to be a challenge for Frank to find an additional two kids to fill the costumes that Sue was already making. He had one filled and that was to be his daughter Elise. She was ten years old and because she was his only child she was automatically enlisted into projects Dad participated in. This was one of those enlistments. She had a great personality; being somewhat of a ham, she would compliment the group perfectly. Now the challenge was to find two more. The gender of the babies had been determined, two girls and a boy. This was rough, as Elise demanded to be one of the females. In all of his contacts around town he knew of no one with kids that same age group that was even remotely interested in being a clam! Boy or girl! His belief that Grace provides in all good things was his only hope after months of searching without any success.

His pleadings to the Universe were finally reinforced when the vacant home next door to his was occupied by a family with kids. The Rockwood family had just relocated to the area from Orange County and lo and behold they had two daughters, Kylee and Devan. Kylee was Elise's age and Devan a year older. The girls were soon good friends. Joanne and David were friendly outgoing people whom Frank had met through a business related query. The new neighbors were soon enlightened about the Clam movement and within days Joanne had volunteered her kids to help out, at least for the initial appearance. Kylee jumped all over being the second female clam which left Devan holding the bag playing the male. Devan reluctantly accepted playing the male role when reassured no one would know her identity and that none of the babies had to speak. Anonymity was really the only way the kids would participate. At this age for the girls, if their peers found out, it would have surely meant severe humiliation. That would have been intolerable. Anonymous was good.

With the completion and fitting of costumes, along with the building of the baby carriage float in which they were to ride, the girls actually started to get excited about playing their parts. First up: Harvest Fest parade, Sam and Pam actually pushed the babies to a second-place trophy in the novelty category. Quite a sight to see Sam and Pam pushing the giant baby carriage down the street with three very wide eyed and lovable little clams inside. The kids ate up the attention, so it was a no-brainer that they were on board for the biggest event the Clam Festival. Clam Festival parade was a smashing success and a first-place trophy. Hundreds of photographs snapped and the girls felt they were stars. The third and final event was the Grover Beach Holiday parade with another first place. The girls were stoked. The costumes were delightful and the girls made the baby thing come to life. Needless to say Sam and Pam were proud doting parents with a handful to look forward to.

Frank had been looking forward to that festival a year prior and began working to secure an interview of the Clams on a Los Angeles news station. The City of Angels was largely an untapped market for tourism trade to Pismo. Pismo's Convention and Visitors Bureau's focus on tourism at that time was concentrated in the inland valley cities of Modesto, Fresno, Bakersfield and Visalia. If he could land an interview in Los Angeles he could introduce five to six million people to the Clams and their beautiful town of Pismo Beach.

He zeroed his efforts in on the morning newscast he liked the most, KTLA. He secured the name of a production staffer and went to work pitching the idea. A few weeks after initial contact, Sumi the production assistant called him back to discuss the details of what might be presented so she could pitch the idea to her production manager. He suggested bringing the reigning Chowder Cook-off Champs, Splash Café, to serve up some of their award winning clam chowder along with the hilarious bunch of costumed clams. The song and dance routine "Macarena" was hot at the time and Frank suggested that the baby clams could perform this routine live, thinking that alone would surely have the viewers smiling. Sumi laughed at the prospect and asked about timing the interview a few days before the actual festival for maximum benefit. Frank responded that would be perfect. Sumi said she'd see what she could do and get back to him. Frank was excited. A live morning news broadcast in Los Angeles with the Pismo Clams was one decision away from becoming reality. He informed the Chamber Board as well as the Splash Café owners of the positive contact. Everyone was quite surprised that he had made such headway and now the wait was on.

Life goes on and Frank's business was starting to really take off along with the one other volunteer project that he had chosen to stay involved with. His days were incredibly busy with his retail business and bottling facility along with the Price Anniversary House restoration project. It was easy for him to burn 70 hours a week devoted to these projects and as the weeks turned into months only a glimmer of hope remained for the interview to be secured. Divine timing prevailed however and one morning at 7:30 as he unlocked the door to his shop the phone rang. It was Sumi, confirming an interview! A live interview featuring Splash Café and the Pismo Clams three days prior to the festival, it just didn't get any better than that! He was instructed to have the entourage at the studio in Hollywood at 6:00am for the interview at about 6:30. His heart was pounding as he hung up the phone. Thank you Lord! He said it out loud. What a score the Clams were going to Hollywood and with just a few weeks to prepare he went into overdrive to pull it together. Game on!

Frank and Joanne left with the kids a day and a half early to travel down to Hollywood to take in the sights, sounds, and smells of the LA area. The day prior to the interview included a visit to the La Brea Tar Pits followed by lunch and shopping at the Farmers Market over in the Fairfax district. They then decided to drive up into the Hollywood hills to look for a suitable location to put on the costumes and photograph the whole Clam family with the Hollywood sign as backdrop. They drove many narrow twisting turning roads nestled amongst the vast estates and bungalows lining the Hollywood hills. The area reeked of money and security, Frank began to doubt they could find a suitable location for the shoot. Besides, there where five of them and five costumes to fill of which Joanne had agreed to don the Pam costume to pose as Pam, so who would take the photo? Periodically they caught a glimpse of the Hollywood sign, but none of these spots lent itself to the intended scene. The road they had been traveling came to a dead end at which point they were practically at the base of the sign, but the angle was too steep for the right shot.

Turning the car around and heading back down the road Frank figured this part of his plan was not to pan out. Then abruptly, almost as if another hand was pushing the wheel, he veered left onto an insanely narrow street. At first glimpse it looked like a driveway. He proceeded slowly as the road wound its way upward. If they were to have encountered another vehicle they would for sure be forced to stop and back up, there was no way two vehicles could pass one another in this gorge of rocks and homes. As they mounted the crest in the road it flattened out and 'bam' there it was, a perfect spot of open space. A manicured grass plateau about 150 feet long and 80 feet wide with large lush trees lining the cliff, with a 30-foot wide opening offering an unob-structed view of the Hollywood sign dead center! It was perfect, a little oasis of undeveloped land amongst the sea of homes and roads that covered the hazy rolling hills. What a find; not a soul around.

Frank smiled, aware as he parked the car and they all exited with such excitement that it probably looked as if crazed alien tourists' had landed to anyone witnessing their arrival. The group walked over to the fence-lined cliff to take in the view. He scoured the surrounding homes for signs of life, hop-ing to find a person to enlist to take a photo or two. With no one extra in the entourage to take the photo he and Joanne decided that they should take the "missing Dad photo because he is behind the camera" family picture. They strolled back to the car to suit up, when up the hill from the same direction that they had just traveled appeared a convertible with two occupants.

Seizing the opportunity as the car halted, Frank hurried over to ask if they might take a moment to assist in photographing the Pismo Clams. It did not help that this young couple in their mid-20s were German tourists on vacation and out only for a leisurely drive, not a close encounter. With the kids in costume and running around like kids do and Frank approaching in the tights from his costume, the look on the man's face said it all too clearly. "What in the hell is going on?" "What are these strange people doing?" "Are they dangerous?" "I've heard stories about people like you," all flashed in a split second through the young German's eyes. Frank felt the fright emanat-ing from their eyes and slowed way down. Approaching the couple peaceably and taking a moment to explain in a broken English conversation, they then happily agreed to lend a hand.

With the kids and Joanne in costume Frank posed them. Before crawling into Sam's costume he took the camera to pick the best angle from which to capture the moment. He gave a few points of reference to the German gentlemen along with the camera, climbed into his suit, took up his position, telling the young man to shoot at will. The shutter of the camera revealed through the noise it emitted that many photos were taken. As he gazed through the eyeholes back at this lovely couple from Germany, he noticed their huge smiles as they watched the scene in front of them. Happy exaggerated animated colorful Clams. What had seemed potentially life threatening just minutes before had turned into a comedy playing out before their very eyes, melting their fear and turning this moment into a happy laughing memory of their trip to LA. The Clams had a way of doing that to people. Frank wondered if the stories they told to their friends back home in Germany would be believed. Without photographic evidence he speculated that might have been a difficult story to sell.

Back in the car and heading down the hill, it was agreed that they'd return to the hotel for a quick dip in the pool for the kids. Frank could touch base with Judy and Hardy as they were due in, together they could set plans for wake up calls in the morning. He found Judy and Hardy in their room, discovering Judy had come down with a terrible case of the flu. The poor little gal was bedridden. Only the second hitch in the plans, the first being his daughter's broken arm that was in a cast from wrist to the elbow. Not too bad for a plan with logistics as complicated as this. The show must go on however, so his attention was immediately focused on convincing Joanne she'd have to play the role of Pam, live, to some four million plus viewers of the morning news. Not an easy task, but after the initial shock wore off, Joanne the trooper that she was, agreed to do it with more than a little trepidation.

That hitch settled and the kids out of the pool, the kids requested a trip to Hollywood to find a place to have some dinner plus see the sites. Adults concurred. Bad call! What a culture shock. Down amongst the t-shirt shops, tattoo parlors and adult bookstores with sidewalks conveying everything from the flamboyant to the vagrant, a diner was finally found to satisfy the appetite. Joanne and Frank whispered their desire to bail out as soon as possible, but the kids had other plans. Three against two... the adults lost the war of will. For the next hour as twilight set in and the lights of the boulevard radiated to life, the old ones followed the young ones from store to store as the girls searched for that perfect memento commemorating their trip to Hollywood. Back in the car with all accounted for, it was back to the hotel for the rest they needed as the 4:30am wake up call was going to be on them in no time.

The hotel's wake up call blistered the serenity of sleep soon enough. Frank was already up and began to make the rounds to make sure everyone else was up and on target for their 6am arrival time at the studio. He had already reconned the route they would take, ensuring they were on time and everything went as well as could be expected of three groggy, hungry kids.

At the security gate entrance to the TV station they were issued passes and directions to studio "C." Sumi met them at the security door to the studio, showing them around and where they could suit up for practice. The adjacent studio to where the live broadcast was taking place was huge. The studio was much larger than any they had ever been in and provided ample space for the kids to rehearse the ridiculously funny act of synchronized flailing called the Macarena. Ross and Joanne from Splash Café had already arrived.

The plan was relayed to Ross and Joanne to set up the Splash Café staging just off camera next to the Mrs. Fields Cookie interview staging, which the Pismo troops were to follow. The Clams were to be positioned just off camera left of Mrs. Fields' set-up. There they were to wait until Mrs. Fields and Mark Kriski, the weatherman / interviewer, were done with their segment. When the station went to commercial break, the Fields interview set-up was to be wheeled out, the Splash Café set-up wheeled in and the Clams placed for the interview segment. This had to all be accomplished before the commercials were done and the newsroom came back to live cameras. No room for error. The call to prepare was to be at about 6:45 so with time to relax Frank assessed the condition of the troops. Ross and Joanne were dialed in and ready. Hot fresh clam chowder filled the air and was beginning to make folks hungry. The thought of clam chowder for breakfast is not what might appeal to most folks, but most of the people in studio had probably been there since 3:00am so this might have been close to their lunchtime.

Joanne Rockwood dressing as Pam was visibly nervous, Frank again reassured her she was going to do just great. All she had to do is gesture a simple hello when introduced and then just stand there. Frank dressed as Sam was to be the only one miked, he was to be the only Clam asked to respond to questions. The kids were raring to go, cocky with teenage attitude and confident that their synchronized dance routine would make them stars. Simple the kids thought, all they had to do when the background music of the Macarena started was to stand in place and do their routine. They could do it – they were stars after all. Great he thought, that was the spirit they needed to go on live TV and make it work. The call came at 6:44 for everyone to get into place, Ross and Joanne stage left with the Splash props and the Clams stage right of Mrs. Fields Cookie demonstration platform.

Now Mark Kriski the station's meteorologist is somewhat of a playboy and Frank wondered why he had been chosen to do the cookie mixing and fixing with Mrs. Fields, who Frank was sure had to be an elderly well accomplished pastry chef. After all the brand had been around for a while and it seemed you could find Mrs. Fields Cookies in all the major supermarkets. To have that kind of wide spread exposure he figured she had to have been around for awhile and hence a few grey hairs. Wrong! When Mrs. Fields stepped out to take up her position he was floored to see that she was in fact about a 35ish stunning blond bombshell with a take-charge seductive attitude who was dressed to kill. Mark was in seventh heaven.

When the station was about to go live quiet was called for, the lights came up, cameras came on, and all hell broke loose. The mixing of ingredients was meshed with heavy sexual innuendo, and the flour for the mix was flying. Mark was having a difficult time taking his eyes off Mrs. Fields' breasts as he tried to keep his shit in the mixing bowl as it spun. Mrs. Fields was having as much difficulty trying to direct his endeavors, and began to play along. Frank forgot exactly where he was and that silence was required. He almost laughed out loud at their shenanigans of squeezing and kneading raw cookie dough as if it were erotic parts of one another's bodies. There was flour, dough and eggs everywhere, the segment went on and on. After all this was good stuff and the anchors at the news desk, Barbara Beck and Carlos Amezcua, found it hard to stop laughing as they announced the upcoming interview with the Pismo Clams. The floor director yelled cut as the station went to break and the lights came down.

Game on! Stagehands wheeled the Fields platform away and rolled Splash's into place. Show time! Stagehands positioned the Clams in front of the beach backdrop that the prop department provided stage right of Ross and Joanne. With final positioning adjustments from crew, Frank gave a final word of encouragement to the troops then took his position. They were all now facing the news desk with three of the four large dollied cameras facing them. The huge bank of stage lights that were currently off looked as if they were twenty feet tall and wide hanging about 12 feet off of the stage floor. Carlos was to be the interviewer and he positioned himself next to Sam, as Sam was to be the first to be interviewed followed by Ross and Joanne. Frank saw the floor director turn towards them and begin to speak, ready to gesture the countdown back to live feed from his right hand.

"Okay folks, we are back live in 5, 4, 3," and then you could hear the electrical breaker being thrown and the hum of electricity as it surged its way to the light panel. Wham! Lights flashed to full on with what felt like a million candle power causing temporary blindness and heat you could feel through the costumes. Frank glanced to the right and could tell the kids had frozen. All their bravado had melted under the glare of hot lights and daunting stare of camera lenses. "Oh shit, don't choke now" he thought. From the floor director 2 was verbal, and 1 was in the form of the final finger of the floor director's right hand closing to a fist. They were live and millions of viewers in the LA area were now looking directly at the crew of Clams from

Pismo Beach. Franks palms were sweating like they had the first day in that first parade. He prayed he could keep his composure to answer the questions he was about to be asked. Carlos began, "Well folks we're back with some interesting visitors from Pismo Beach, Sam and Pam the Pismo Clams and their three new kids. Welcome Sam what brings you and the Clam family to Los Angeles?"

"Thanks Carlos," Sam responded then continued, "Well we have come down on behalf of the Chamber of Commerce to invite the folks in Los Angeles to come up and see how folks in Pismo Beach celebrate community."

"Great and you've brought the whole family I see," Carlos stated hurriedly.

"Yes Sir," Sam responded.

"Now since we are running short of time let's go over and see what Chowder Champs Ross and Joanne from Splash Café have been cooking up for us," Carlos announced as he walked to where Ross and Joanne were standing waiting for their grilling and to serve up some hot chowder in the traditional sourdough bread bowl. Funny, how men seem to gravitate to beauty. Carlos did and his first question was directed to Joanne, a very pretty lady with that California 'beach girl' look.

"So what have you prepared for us today Joanne?" Carlos inquired.

Meanwhile, Sam held his position turning slightly so he could hand gesture to the kids without the cameras picking up his actions. The Macarena was beginning to play in the background, as of yet there was no movement from the girls who seemed to have turned to stone. Sam knew (hoped) his microphone would be off by now, so he took the liberty to do some low level verbal coaxing. Finally the girls began. Within a few seconds they had synchronized their movements with one another and the music. Rough start but all good now he thought, then redirected his attention to Carlos and the Splash Café setup. By now Carlos and Barbara had full chowder bowls in hand and were sampling as Carlos' continued questioning Joanne asking,

"So how did the Clam Festival get started?"

This was the one question Joanne did not know the answer to, Ross stepped in to cover. Splash's entire interview was flawless, Ross' articulation of the festival beginnings brought laughter. With that Carlos announced the tease for the next segment, the floor director yelled "cut!" and the lights went off. The whole of the interview was about four minutes. Frank felt a little discouraged that they didn't get more air time as they had been scheduled for ten minutes, yet all were relieved it was over. A quick Clam photo with Barbara and Carlos, then out the studio door into the now risen sun they went. The cool of the dawn in Hollywood and some breakfast calmed the adrenalin rush of live TV.

Driving back to Pismo with Elise asleep, exhausted by the pace of the trip, Frank weighed the events of the day in an effort to gauge the success or failure of the trip. On one hand he felt smug in the success of gaining the interview, on the other hand he felt a little disappointed that the group had not received more time to shine as bright as they could have. He decided not to come to any conclusions until he heard from the folks who had seen the show and recounted what they thought. All he knew for sure was that he had been able to give the kids, himself and Joanne an experience that would be remembered fondly the rest of their lives and, really, wasn't that what it was all about. He thanked the Grace that truly had made this good thing possible. No dark clouds today, 'what if' but a distant haunt that did not invade the moment.

Two days later on center stage at the Clam Fest the naming of the Clam babies was announced. Digum, Sandy and Pearl were now the kids' official names and the crowd applauded approval. The two girls bickered a bit about who would be Sandy and who would be Pearl, but that's what kids do.

The girls played their roles well for a couple of more years until they pretty much outgrew the costumes. The outings were always robust as the girls really played up the sibling rivalry thing. Kylee and Devin moved away when the Rockwood family took up new work and residency in Napa Valley. Elise became a member of the Judkins Middle School marching band, the same band that had almost put an end to Sam D. Clam in his first parade outing. In 2000 Elise would be crowned Miss Teen Pismo Beach in the Clam Festival's scholarship pageant. Good kids, good sports, Frank and Judy were happy to have worked with them. Their commitment to the task they sometimes bitched about was greatly appreciated. There were other kids who filled the bill from time to time, but none played the roles quite as well as the original three. Funny, how originals always seem to be the best.

~~~~~

We all like to leave others with fond memories as we weave our way through our experience on the planet. Our intent sets our stage from which we play out that, which in turn reveals the answer to our question of what is the purpose of our life. Intention following what has been spoken through purity of heart, creates unique lives that flow with commonality toward the finished picture of life's purpose. That full picture we all will see at some point. When may depend on the purity of our intent. Resonating from this part of our chronicle, the string we follow weaves with purity of intent with another string in life's tapestry, its contact leaves indelible colors of memory for others to behold long after. We are all color.

CHAPTER 3

RIGHT, TRUE, FAIR OR NOT

"You either do it right the first time or you die," Frank could remember his father saying. At the age of five or six that had stuck becoming one of the philosophies he lived by. Interesting what sticks with importance as we grow up. This one was one of those things. He had also grown to know that in this effort of trying to 'do it right' you couldn't really count on anyone other than self, family and close friends. You usually learn this one the hard way and it then sticks.

Effort it was. At about this age, his Mom had recounted to him years later, doctors had told her that her son would probably never read. Something was making it difficult for him to learn, he struggled to get a grasp on the reading and writing thing. His attempts in school were often met with failure except on the playground. He had a terrible time with reading, writing, math, but boy could he play a mean game of kickball. Grade C work was about all he could muster in the classroom, but all A and B work in the field.

With two sides to every coin however Frank also had the 'I'll try anything once' thing going on. This unfortunately led to a lot of bangs, bruises and the occasional gouge requiring stitches, but miraculously no life-threatening injuries. Broken bones somehow were narrowly avoided; cartilage was another story…broke his nose on his first attempt at surfing.

In 'trying anything once' there was always some risk involved, which as with any first-time endeavor usually ended in sweet success or painful failure. He learned to weigh options and if there was any doubt of success he usually avoided the pain of failure. The thinking process did not always present the full gamut of options as fast as his desire to push the envelope for bigger, harder, faster, and sometimes the failures were huge. It took years and countless failures for the 'do it right or …' and the 'anything once' to temper one another. He wasn't stupid; it was just occasionally he did stupid things. He may have not been considered to be the brightest coin in the drawer at times, but he was perceptive and had the ability to put the pieces of the puzzle together on occasion.

He also had a developing drive to know the truth and the desire for things to be fair. Not that in pushing the envelope he always told the truth or was fair, he sometimes felt he needed to stretch the truth or expand the rules to fill his need to be equal to everyone else. Even when he would rage in fits of anger he never acted intentionally to hurt anyone because in truth that would not be fair. These angry outbursts took years for him to get a handle on as he learned that they brought pain not only to the recipient of his rage, but also to himself. His perceptiveness and desire for truth led to one more discovery at this early age, that lesson was that some truths can cause confusion.

While living in Waco, Texas at the age of five, he had wondered out loud to his mom and dad why he and his brother Robert had three sets of grandparents. All the other kids he knew had two. He watched as his mom and dad shot looks of concern at one another, then he was told "we will talk about it later." That "talk about it later" thing was always a red flag meaning the folks hoped he'd forget about the question. He didn't. One night after posing the question again, he overheard his dad say to his mom that he'd take Frank to his office tomorrow and tell him. By the tone of their conversation he felt as if he was going to receive some treasured information that was reserved only for the privileged. He had not been able to figure out the answer to his question himself and his persistence to having an explanation was finally going to be addressed. He felt special by the importance that seemed to be placed upon the imparting.

This was special. He wanted to know why when he saw Grandma and Grandpa in Holbrook, Arizona; they had taken him around saying "This is where your dad grew up, this is where he went to school" and so on. Then when he visited Grandma and Grandpa in Oakland, California they too would say the same thing. "This is where your dad grew up, went to school" and so on. Then in Prescott, Arizona Grandma and Grandpa would say the same thing about mom. What... did he have two Dads? He was about to get the answer he sought.

The next morning Jim took Frank down to his office on the air base. Jim was a kind man, big in stature and Frank loved the time they spent together. He loved the wrestling and rough housing together on the living room floor. Jim almost let him win those wrestling matches, then telling him if he ate his spinach he might win next time. He always ate his spinach!

A cool haze filtered the sunlight as they drove, Frank noticing that Dad was uncommonly quiet. He could not quite understand the silence especially if Dad was about to impart some big news. Big news usually meant a lot of conversation so why not this morning. This was the first time he could remember going to his Dad's office ever, this had to be really big news. He felt pretty special and about to explode with anticipation, but because his dad was so quiet and solemn he kept his usual motor mouth of questioning silent as well.

When they pulled into the parking lot, the only sound to be heard was the crunching of the tires on gravel as Dad parked. They got out and Dad said, "Follow me." Frank was one step behind. They entered the building and walked down a very long hall. Looking down as he walked he noticed the hallway floor was so slick and shiny that he could almost see his reflection in its shine. He heard the hallway echoing their footsteps as they walked. No talking, just walking. Then through a door to the right at the end of the long corridor that led into an office that was full of cold steel desks and chairs without anyone in them. They made their way to one particular desk where Dad stopped, gestured with an implied pointing saying, "This is my desk."

Jim picked him up, sitting him on the right side of the desk then sat in his chair so that they were eye to eye. Frank couldn't read the look on his dad's face. The expression was strained with compassion yet all business. He began to think that this expression which he had never seen before might mean that bad news was imminent.

"Frank, I don't know quite how to explain this to you, but I'm not your real father." Frank looked at his dad with twisted bewilderment not comprehending, not even remotely, what he had just been told. What did 'real' mean?

"Your dad was an Air Force fighter pilot like me, but he was killed in the Korean War." Jim furthered. Frank's look was now totally blank as his brain was on overload with too much unrecognizable information. "Killed... what did that mean exactly" he wondered silently?

"His name was Franklin Udall and these are his medals that I am sure he would have wanted you to have," Jim continued as he opened the top center drawer to the desk. Frank looked down to see several medallions attached to brightly colored ribbons placed neatly in their individual velvet boxes.

"How was he killed?" Frank asked as if he really understood the finality of what 'killed' meant. After all he didn't want to appear stupid.

"In a plane crash" Jim responded.

The questions Frank had where cascading through his mind only and not out of his mouth. "What did 'real dad' mean? Wasn't Jim his 'real dad'? What exactly did 'killed' mean? If it was an airplane accident, why didn't he bail out? Had this dad not done something right?" The questions became a blur as he picked up the medals one at a time to feel the relief stamped into cold metals of bronze, silver and copper. No tears, just dumb confusion.

The rest of the day for the young man was spent in the clutter of uncertainty about the meaning of real. The one thing he had found out for sure, truth could be confusing. The truth was given for clarity, but he was far from clear. Amongst other things it was hard to understand why his real and present dad seemed to be upset. Frank's sense of loss he felt about his lost dad he saw in his present dad's eyes. Afterward he'd always have a heightened sense of anxiousness whenever Jim went away on duty. He had lost one dad and he didn't what to lose another. He remained vigilant in asking God to take care of his dad while his dad was away. In time he began to believe those meditations worked, that was real. After all, who else did you know to ask for that kind of help when you were that age? So that working relationship with the Universe afforded him the feeling of having some influence or control on outcome.

So in these early years the need to be comfortably in control to 'get it right the first time' had been woven into the fabric of his personality. The need for control pushed him to 'take charge' in his endeavors, if he felt he couldn't control a situation he would simply remove himself from participation. After all, bailing out was better than dying. Bailing out however was also associated with being a quitter. He hated being called a quitter as that meant the inability to complete a given task, which was failure. Confused...he often called to the God he had come to know for solace through those times of failure. Another important thread of 'real' woven into the colorful fabric of his life's truths collected to sustain the young soul.

Ability to complete a task was also a thread of this woven fabric that became who he was. His picking and choosing of situations to be involved with, coupled with a need to command for control, made it difficult for him to get along with other kids. He often found himself alone. Alone, meant reduced risk of failure that could be noticed by others. That was reduced risk of ridicule. That was comfortably in control. He found that by busting out on his own he could risk pushing the envelope. If he failed to complete the task, that was okay because nobody would know and he didn't have to deal with the negative energy of feeling inadequate.

Just like us all a small piece of Frank's self esteem died each time he was informed of failure, and then restored to life with the positive energy of praise received for his successes. The early years were a constant struggle between his life and death quest for equal footing, which was rarely attained in his scholastic endeavors. He searched constantly for a 'book of truth' that might teach him to 'do it right.' No different than anyone else. This was the same search that we all enjoyed, or hated, depending on one's successes. As years went on the peace and joy of 'doing it right' and knowing 'truth' were but fleeting moments in his arduous trek through life. The discovery of the Bible with the 10 rules to live by offered a ray of hope for his inquisitive mind, only to be diminished by the discovery that other competing beliefs existed and practiced with equal fervor. Confusion persisted.

Many years later he realized that even our Constitution wasn't embraced as truth by the very folks that wrote it. Not to mention the current climate of interpretations. "These truths we hold to be self evident," why then did we need a high court to interpret their meanings? Truth should be simple, self evident and freely shared he thought. Shared so all might enjoy the peace truth has to offer. However some things we do as humans he found can embarrass these Bills of Rights and that didn't seem to be fair to the truth. Fair was shaded and jaded by the confusions of interpretations that did not emanate from real truth. He was beginning to figure out that the 'reality' of life was that not everyone on the planet seemed to engage the same knowledge of what was true, right and fair. He yearned for positive reinforcement so he could remain hopeful knowing he was 'doing it right.' A daunting task for a little man, answers were slow to manifest and hope faded in and out.

Resigning to popular status quo warped the young mind into going with the flow to get it 'right', true or not, was the only way for a young idealist to attain some semblance of normalcy. After all, all he really wanted was to enjoy the peace of normal just like everyone else. He had however; found a couple of things to be true, right and fair. Do unto others as you would have them do unto you. That was fair. That was true. That was simple, if you continually poke someone in the eye with a sharp stick; they are going to poke you back and that hurt. This was one of those hard lessons he had to learn, the other was much easier. If you love a puppy, treat it kindly the puppy will love you in return... unconditionally, always. That was right. Throughout the next many years he had many puppies and a few cats too. The love always felt better than the pain of a poke in the eye. That was probably a universal perception he thought and tried to live the love rather than the pain.

~~~~

We all have intimate details from the distant past that help set base color to the string to be woven. This detail is important to the color we become.

CHAPTER 4

FULL

Frank had been in Pismo Beach for about six months and was heavily involved with making his new business a success. He had purchased a small retail water store, moved his wife Linda and their daughter Elise from Lake Havasu City, Arizona in June of 1991. Upon arriving he had quickly ascertained the need to promote the business affordably as his shoestring budget didn't supply a lot of extra cash. Using the tight budget marketing reality, common ground that most other businesses in the shopping plaza stood on, he organized a successful low-budget pamphlet advertising campaign. That campaign caught the eye of the Pismo Chamber of Commerce Executive director Bill Ausen.

Bill had been directed to Frank as the developer of this marketing plan, after discovering the imaginative piece of advertising circulating in the community. Bill intercepted Frank on the sidewalk in front of his store, introduced himself and began to inquire about the development of the fun, cartoon-like announcement of goods and services offered by the plaza's businesses. Bill was impressed with Frank's ability to organize a majority of the plaza's twenty-five business owners, producing a creative advertising tool that was working to bring in needed revenue and exposure for the new plaza. Bill was also intrigued by his philosophy of including the businesses in the pamphlet that had not been willing to pay to participate.

Frank explained he had convinced the paying participants that objected to this policy that it was okay to give it away, arguing that if successful, next time those holdouts just might be willing to get involved. Based on results that strategy had paid off, three holdouts had already asked about the next run. The two men talked at length on many facets of business in the plaza while basking in the morning's warm fall sunshine bathing the sidewalk. Frank broke away appropriately from time to time to attend the needs of clients as they arrived, soon to return to the exhilarating conversation. Little did Frank know that he was actually involved in an interview that Bill was covertly conducting on the sidewalk. Bill evidently was satisfied that Frank was an articulate businessman with some exciting fresh ideas in his marketing approach; he then revealed the underlying reason for his contact with Frank and posed his request.

"Would you like to fill a recently vacated seat on the Chamber of Commerce Board of Directors?" Bill asked.

Frank was astounded, honored and humbled all at the same time by the importance of the position and the responsibility it required. He questioned Bill on the responsibilities associated with the acceptance. He wanted to assess his ability to fulfill those responsibilities successfully before making a commitment to accept the position. He wanted to make sure he wasn't getting in over his head. Not one to say no when opportunity came knocking he agreed to sit and serve if the Board so desired. He saw the position as a vehicle to subtly, and without cost, market his business while representing the desires and concerns of the business owners of Pismo's newest shopping district.

"What an honor," he stated as he accepted the consideration. The two parted with an exuberant hand shake.

Frank immediately phoned his wife Linda to inform her of this fantastic new avenue of possibilities to grow their little business. He was so engrossed with regurgitating the details of the potential he saw, he failed to hear the reluctance Linda was exhibiting in the tone of her responses. He was that way at times, too caught up in his 'own thing' to notice input that detracted from the excitement of the moment. He didn't hear Linda's concerns that were being communicated in her cool toned response. This in Linda's thoughts was just one more thing to take from the family's time together, time that was ever so precious to Linda and Elise. He didn't hear the message of family time importance, he only heard the do or die drive to produce a successful business. In his mind the survival of the family was dependent on the business doing well. He was prepared to work a hundred hours a week if needed, blinding him to the needs of his wife and daughter. Good businessman... yes. Good husband... questionable. Excel... yes he did.

On the following Tuesday morning of the regularly scheduled Chamber Board of Directors meeting Frank was received, reviewed and approved to fill the Board vacancy. Over the course of the next five years he was to be reelected twice by the Chamber membership. He really endeared himself to his constituents with his honest scathing comments on the Chamber sponsored fireworks show. His insistence that the fireworks purchased for the show be put out to bid put the Chamber in the position to gain bigger more exciting shows for the same amount of money. This created positive changes that led to rave reviews of the summer's hottest event. "We got a bigger bang for the buck," he would say with a chuckle at the clichés' fit.

He was a hands-on guy who believed in leading by example. His constitution was to never ask someone to do something he was not willing to do himself. His involvement was prolific. From Board committees to liaison for the plaza, he was able to bring about some good, positive promotional programs that enhanced local business, including his. When no other Board members raised their hands to volunteer to help for the 3:00am setup of the

Chamber's biggest money maker, the Clam Festival, Frank did. His refinement of that task over the years lent to a savings of time that meant they wouldn't have to start that program until 4:30am. His talents did not go unnoticed and he was considered for the position of Chamber Board Vice President with the Presidency sure to follow. The Pismo Beach City Council also nominated him to serve on the Planning Commission. That was a last straw.

With growing disharmony in his marriage he realized his plate was too full and he needed to relinquish some of his responsibilities. He needed to work on family skills. So he pulled back to regroup, thanking the council for their consideration and the Chamber Board for theirs. He wasn't a quitter; he just finally learned to say no to more responsibility. He did keep his position on the Chamber Board as well as continue to be lead man for festival setup and of course his role of Sam D. Clam. He also kept his position with FOPH, one other special project that he felt complimented growth through service. More on that later. All in all though, the plate was still full to overflowing.

With his thriving business and a family with a growing daughter, he had plenty to keep him busy. His story line marketing program success with Sam, Pam and Baby Clams eventually won him the honor of being named Pismo Beach Chamber of Commerce "Director of the Year." The recognition of his good work within the community bolstered his image of self, blinding him to the needs of family. He was feeling a sense of achievement in rebuilding his life that had been shattered years earlier after his first marriage fell apart. Rebuilding from destruction so complete that the thought of recovery was remote and death was felt but a heartbeat away. But by Grace he had been able to pull himself from that abyss, that truth reminding him to be humble. Humble yet unaware, that the success of the business was depleting the bond of his second marriage.

~~~

We all can succumb to the perception that a full plate is needed to sustain our survival. What cost is paid when the string is stretched so thin that its true color fades when overextended?

CHAPTER 5

GIFT OF TREASURES FOUND

The phone rang and Frank picked up on the second ring "Genesis Water, Frank speaking," he announced. He had a three-ring policy. Answer the phone by the third ring so folks know you were attentive to their inquiries. Also announce where they had called and to whom they were speaking, just a good business practice he had learned over the years. He had also found that this was a good way to screen telemarketers, as 99% of the time the salesperson on the other end was not paying attention always asking, "Can I speak to Frank?"

This phone practice then afforded two opportunities: one, a quick way out of a potentially long protracted extraction from a sales pitch and two, a brief fantasy vacation to some far away exotic location. The second always left him with a smile on his face as opposed to the first which always made him feel he was wasting valuable time in a useless conversation. He never bought anything over the phone. When, after the telltale moment of silence of call transfer, the caller on the other end asked for him by name after he had already announced to whom they had reached, he would respond, "Oh, you just missed him, he just left on a month's vacation to Maui, [Bora-Bora, Fiji, Tahiti...etc.] to write a book, can I take a message and forward it on?" The voice on the other end usually responding "Oh, that lucky dog," or "Man, it must be nice, I'd like to go there," then asking "Is there anyone else that can make a decision on ...." "No," Frank would respond. Conversation over! Quick, easy and as he hung up the phone he could dream for a few moments of actually having the opportunity to fulfill the fantasy travel. Great fun!

This time however it was a legitimate call from a new-found friend. It was Suzy Ormond, a bubbly, effervescent gal from the Chamber of Commerce whom he had met a few months prior when he had taken his position as a board member. Suzy had witnessed that Frank was a hard-working guy, and she had called to see if he might be interested in helping out on a clean up day at the old Price Anniversary House. This was intriguing, he thought. A potential diversion from the six day a week schedule he worked at the shop.

"What's the Price Anniversary House, and how old is it?" he asked.

"It's where the founding father of Pismo Beach used to live, and it's 100 years old," Suzy reported.

Man that might be cool to see, he thought.

"What time?" he inquired.

"Starts at noon and lasts till about three," Suzy reported.

What the hell, he figured. He could have time to go to church and then cruise on out, get a little workout and learn some local history.

"Sure, why not, anything I need to bring and how do I get there?" he queried.

"Maybe some gloves and some water." Suzy informed him, then continuing,

"Just get on Frady Lane and follow it out under the freeway. Pass the baseball fields and the wastewater treatment plant. Go through the gate and onto the dirt road that goes under the railroad tracks. Just keep going, you can't miss it, you'll run right into it."

Simple enough, Frank surmised,

"Okay, I'll see you there," he promised.

"Thanks so much," Suzy reiterated twice before hanging up.

Frank's thoughts transported him back some 20 years to his Anthropology 101 class in college, recalling the useful tidbits of information about where the best places were to look for artifacts. Maybe he could find some neat trinkets of yesteryear. "A treasure hunt, how fun is that? A little bit of work with the potential of finding treasure, this was going to be a fun diversion," he speculated with a bit of thrill.

Up early off to church then back home for the traditional Sunday breakfast with the family. Exuberant tones of discovery laced his conversations at breakfast. Sunday mornings had become the only morning Frank could share breakfast with wife and daughter. Any other day he was usually out the door, off to work before that part of the morning ritual was prepared. Sunday was a family day shared doing, or going, together on some sort of an adventure. This Sunday was a little different. Linda and Elise begrudged the fact that they were not included on this Sunday's outing.

That was okay though, the two ladies had made plans to do other 'girl things' for that afternoon. Dad's confidence in finding treasure however soon had Elise pleading to go along. Elise loved adventures with Dad and the certainty of finding treasure made it much more appealing than doing 'girl stuff'. Dad had to reassure his daughter that old buildings were far too dangerous for young ladies to be crawling around and under, besides he'd be bringing the treasures he found home to share. Elise satisfied that she really wasn't going to miss much quelled her incessant pleas, then telling her Dad to "find a lot of stuff" as she loaded him into his truck with a big kiss and a wave good-bye.

Driving slowly down to the beach in a heavy late summer fog on the Pacific Coast Highway, Frank finally found Frady Lane. As he turned on to the narrow roadway he thought it looked a lot like an alley instead of a road. How could this be right...? It looked as if it dead ended a few hundred feet ahead at the railroad tracks. Approaching the end he found it made a hard left-hand turn to parallel the tracks. Okay he thought as he made the turn, the road was headed in the right direction, but he still thought it a trifle far from the Canyon where the house was supposed to be located. As he finished the turn he observed the 101 Freeway overpass and beyond through the foggy haze he could see the baseball fields in the background. So far so good, so on he pressed. Winding around the ball fields and past the city maintenance yard the road stopped at an ornate old iron bridge that straddled the Pismo Creek. The bridge was old and had barriers to prevent vehicle passage; that's when he noticed the bridge's steel girders looked like Swiss cheese, sporting holes eaten through by the salt air. "I must be getting close, that bridge looked a hundred years old," he reasoned. He noticed an open gate just to the right of the bridge with a dirt road dropping down and under the railroad bridge that spanned the creek.

He assumed he was going the correct way, turned and drove down the tiny road that paralleled the creek. Willow trees dropped out, over and in some cases onto the dirt one-lane road that wasn't much more than a glorified footpath. He passed a large rock outcropping that caused the road to narrow even more as it pushed against the tree line that exploded up and out of the creek's channel. The large rocks began to back off to the right allowing the road to widen as it entered into a clearing framed by a shear cliff dotted with large overhanging Coastal Oaks to the right and the Willow-lined creek to the left. The expanse of field that greeted him as he pulled through the narrows was in full production. Neat straight rows of squash, heavy with ripening fruits, covered the expanse of flat land as the road curved to the left and tucked up tightly to the tree-lined creek.

He was amazed at the contrasts shrouded in the foggy mist. Farmland ran up to the Oak strewn cliff that was lined at the top with million dollar homes. At the end of the field the road broke away from the creek line, rose slightly and carved left again following the foot of the gently rounded golden grass covered hills flowing gracefully down to the base of the canyon floor. As he rolled along, the vista expanded as the fog cleared to reveal the canyon's half-mile wide flood plain.

On the opposite side of the canyon the rise of the coastal mountain range jutted sharply skyward. This canyon boundary of mountain rising swiftly off of the oceans' beach was also covered with expensive homes with great views. The homes went all the way to the top of what had to be a thousand foot crest. The road meandered, dipped and rose again to reveal another large field fully cultivated. A couple of hundred yards in the distance at the end of the sea of green, he could see a two-story structure that might be his intended destination.

Hugging the foot of the hills the road flattened out as it passed a small white 10'x12' building with a gabled roof. Then he passed a faded dark red barn type structure that was maybe 15'x 30' just to the right of the road. Approaching the two story L shaped house he could see it was enclosed by a chain link fence about 15' to 20' away from the structure, topped with razor wire. The building did not seem to warrant such heavy fortification as its state of disrepair was evident. No paint remained on the faded grey siding that faced the ocean. The thresholds to the two doorways in the pocket of the L on that side of the building were two feet off the ground. That suggested that a porch that may have been there was now gone. Every window had broken glass and a few had no panes at all. The dead weeds that were waist high inside the fence perimeter indicated no attention had been paid to the property since at least early spring.

Hooking left around the back of the house he saw a few parked cars and a large open gate with a pathway beaten through the high weeds to a porched entry. This side of the home was in a little better shape with at least some very faded paint remaining on the exterior. As he slowed to a stop he debated whether or not to just keep going. His gut told him that this was going to be a big job. To just clear the weeds and brush inside the fence line would take a few hours. At that moment two more cars pulled up from behind with a few occupants, one of which was Suzy. Trapped now by vehicles, the escape route was cut off and he'd at least have to stay for a little while. Stepping from his truck he was introduced to the other folks emerging from the vehicles. En masse the group made their way through the high brush and weeds to the dilapidated steps of the home's back porch. They carefully climbed the four precariously flexing steps leading up onto the covered porch, devoid of railings of any sort. Two more individuals emerged from the back door to greet them and invite all inside.

One of these individuals was a breathtaking sandy blonde with green eyes and perfectly proportioned figure which captured Frank's attention straight away. She ushered everyone into the dining room of the home, thanked everyone for coming and introduced herself as Betsy Arnette, the acting secretary for the Friends of Price House. Betsy laid out the goals for the day, dividing the manpower between the inside and outside projects. With the amount of work to be done Frank wondered if he'd have any time left in the day to treasure hunt the booty he had promised his daughter. Frank was impressed with Betsy's prepared structure for the day's activities and lack of wasted words. She ran a tight ship he thought. Betsy was a treasure, but not the kind he had promised to return home with!

He chose to work with the outdoor crowd as it was sure to be the most physically demanding. After four hours of hard work the waist-high weeds and brush had been reduced to a few large piles just outside the fence enclosure. The place looked much better inside and out with the risk of fire greatly reduced. At about 3pm Betsy called an end to the day, thanked every-one for contributing and dismissed the crowd. Most of the twelve to fifteen people headed for their cars to return home for a hot shower and well-deserved meal. Frank took this opportunity to engage Suzy and Betsy in some more conversation to gather detailed information about this group with the funny name. He wanted to know the goals or visions they entertained for this place called the Anniversary House. The information he received was almost endless.

He was told the Friends of Price House was a group formed to take on the task of restoring the Anniversary House to its former beauty when con-structed in 1894. The house was on a four-acre parcel owned by the City of Pismo Beach, leased to the FOPH for the renovation effort as well as the development of a park plan to surround the house. The Friends of Price House were in the process of applying for 501c3 Non Profit status to facili-tate easier fund raising and grant money acquisitions. The group was in its infancy with Suzy as the acting President. Betsy as it turned out was actually the head of PB City Parks and Recreation division, but worked as a non-paid volunteer on this project even though it was city property. The house was a registered National Historic Site, which had saved it from being used for fire practice when that had been suggested by a former city Fire Chief. The house was said to have been given by John Price to his wife Andrea as a 50th wed-ding anniversary gift. The elderly couple moved into the home on or close to their wedding anniversary date, from the adobe home where they had spent the previous 50 years, hence the name Anniversary House.

John Price was born in Bristol, England, went to sea as a young man and ended up in California virtually penniless. Eventually settling here in the canyon to start his family, by the end of his life he owned most of the coast-line and mountains that are now known as Pismo Beach. The history in between was incredible. FOPH was entrusted with the telling. This was an all-volunteer effort and of course they were looking for new members. Frank was invited to the next scheduled meeting as they locked the gate to go home. He said he'd consider the offer.

Processing all the information received, his thoughts reeled as he headed back down the dirt road toward the gate that allowed him to rejoin the 20th century. The group needed help, and at least he could provide their most needed commodity, water. That would be easy as he owned a water company, and the exposure might provide some free select marketing. Great..... He was already speculating as he rolled out onto Frady Lane. Mother and daughter were not going to be happy if he chose to participate.

The location was amazing. The setting felt as if one was far out in the country when in reality one was only a little over a mile from the beach and a full blown 20th century. The summer fog was upon him again as he passed through the narrows heading for the gate when he realized he had found no treasures to return home with. Or had he ... maybe the real treasure was the house and park. After all, how often does someone have the opportunity to help create a park? Real treasure is a gift to be shared, not to be hidden away. Real treasure you give away. Building a park was a perfect way to share that treasure. That was his thinking.

He only briefly considered the wife's feelings. Maybe he wasn't really thinking. He attended that next meeting of the Friends of Price House. He found the group to be a collection of local citizens willing to share their diverse talents in this effort to save a piece of local history. Organized in the late 1980s FOPH had already assembled key professional talents that were essential to the cause. He was the next to join their ranks. Only heaven knew how long he might stay to serve with the others in shared vision.

One of those involved was Dave Atson, a former Pismo Beach City Manager and current FOPH treasurer. Dave was a robust gentlemen who when speaking exhibited incredible knowledge of city planning and protocol. Dave's intimate relationship with city staff and council, coupled with his vast knowledge of planning procedure, was key in guiding the group to the successful fulfillment of their cumulative vision. Dave was a family man with two kids his daughter's age and Frank knew instinctively that Dave was to be a mentor with a tremendous influence in his life.

FOPH had already been gifted with other key individuals one of whom was Rob Nessaly. Rob was a civil engineer; his talents were to be absolutely vital in a foundation-up restoration of the Anniversary House. Rob's willingness to give freely of his talents had already produced foundation plans approved by the PB City Planning department. Another key was Irby Bordon, a local attorney who had taken on the project of preparing and filing the necessary paperwork to secure a 501c3 non-profit status for the group. Joe Ollen, a licensed General Contractor, was on board to facilitate the preparation and implementation of Rob's foundation plan work and security measures for the home. Suzy Ormond, the President of FOPH, was a former Parks and Recreation Commissioner with a vast array of connections in the business community as well as with current Commissioners.

An indispensable entity of crucial significance was Mrs. Jean Ubbard, a historical writer for the local paper and board member of the South County Historical Society of San Luis Obispo. Jean was a genteel soft-spoken lady in her mid-sixties who wrote a column on local history with such insight and flavor of the past you could taste it. Jean's column was filled with the most fascinating information giving the reader a real sense of the South County's early days. Jean was considered to be the guru of local history

Then of course there was Betsy, a dynamic lady of boundless energy and attention to detail. Betsy volunteered her lunch hour to act as secretary, taking meticulous minutes that arrived via mail within a week of the previous meeting. These minutes contained bold type **ACTION** items naming the person who had agreed to produce results on any particular item. This was an absolutely perfect system for producing results. A commitment you may have made at the recent meeting hit you in the face a week later, reminding you that you had committed to getting something done for the 'cause'. Betsy was the catalyst for moving the group forward on task.

Frank was extremely impressed with this collection of folks. He viewed them as being on the cutting edge of a vision for a park that might ultimately be the gem of the city's park system. The concept and people involved could not fail he figured. The feel of the energies involved that had assembled these talents felt as though it was being guided by another Hand. So he threw his hat into the ring and offered up his service. His ability to at least provide water for the volunteers whenever needed and his assistance in any other capacity he was able to fulfill might help in some small way. Besides, he gambled, maybe he could get some exposure for his business and of course hunt for artifacts. Mother of Daughter was definitely not happy when informed of her husband's desire. Linda again reluctantly surrendered to his wishes.

With that a second career was launched. Over the course of the next year he played with enriching his involvement. He built a memorabilia fund raising program. Fun projects like the development of a framed square head nail. Nails extracted from some of the original construction of the adobe's wooden exterior that had been destroyed by fire in 1987 provided the buyer the chance to own his own piece of early Pismo history. A white ceramic tile and wood-mounted brass plaque depicting the original 1894 photograph of Mr. and Mrs. Price on the front porch of the new Anniversary House, the porch that was missing entirely on the existing structure. Limited production numbers encouraged sales. He worked with Joe Ollen upgrading electric power boxes along with devising and installing secure coverings for all openings to the home. This was a must to prevent invasion from the local homeless and thrill-seeking teenagers. Unfortunately a creepy old house out in the middle of nowhere was an enticing draw to bored teenagers.

Joe taught Frank structural upgrading of the old home's underpinnings with some real gritty work performed under the home. All work done under the house was performed under the inquisitive gaze of well-embedded families of really large rats, mice, reptiles and spiders. Some of the reptiles looked like they had just stepped from the movie 'Jurassic Park'. He learned the art of design and construction of foot bridges built over the Pismo Creek to provide access for folks attending open house events. The whole endeavor was a giant learning experience for him. He loved every minute yet failed to find time to treasure hunt.

The Friends of Price House board of directors had been pleased with his ability to create, develop and follow through with new ideas. He worked hard as a team member, many times going beyond the call of duty. The board gave him a position on the board, encouraging him to keep the Chamber Board up to speed on the progress and needs of the FOPH project. When Suzy began to experience overwhelming personal difficulties and had to resign her post as President of the board, Frank was asked to take the position. He was surprised by the board members' insistence that he was the perfect choice for the office and despite the momentary dark clouds of 'what if' he agreed to serve. It was to be an office he was to be re-elected to for the next twelve years. They just wouldn't let him go.

Early on, his voracious enthusiasm for the project grew, and by the time of that year's big community awareness event was held, Linda and Elise had become involved as well. Linda had resigned herself to the fact that if she wanted to spend more time with her husband, then she would have to become involved with his outside activities. His involvement with Friends of Price House was bringing in more clients to their business as he had thought it might, but Linda really didn't see that. All she knew was that the City of Pismo owned the property and she felt that her husband was just working free for the city. He was. Linda thought that he should be paid for all the work he did and this was a source of some considerable friction in their marriage. Nevertheless, at this point in time she put on her happy face and lent some support. She couldn't be involved in the Chamber Board, so Friends of Price House was her only chance to keep tabs on her husband, whom she suspected was having an affair. He wasn't.

Elise on the other hand was happy to be included in anything Dad did. Elise had become a Campfire Girl and her group was invited out several times to participate in various activities at the Anniversary House. The girls enjoyed each adventure as they encountered wildlife of all sorts. The deer with their baby fawns elicited the motherly ooohs and aaahs from the group and the snakes had them squealing in fright. Their contribution of artistic endeavors to paint all the window coverings to look as if the windows had curtains hanging gave the girls a sense of pride and accomplishment. The troop felt so connected to the house that they chose to hold their year-end closing ceremonies at the home. They all cried as they parted and Frank knew that they all had created memories that would last a lifetime. This was the first group to enjoy the house and surroundings but it would not be the last. After all that is why a park is created: memories.

A huge event to heighten public awareness entailed months of planning and coordination by the twenty or so volunteers. All participants were bent on producing a successful open house encounter for the general public to enjoy and learn. The days prior were loaded with last minute preparation that kept everyone jumping. Friends of Price House had run publicity ads that invited the general public out for a peek at the park. Donations accepted! There was to be a horse drawn buckboard ride that would take attendees from the lunch and program site across the creek and out to the house. There were drawings for door prizes and a raffle for commodities, contributed by local businesses, memorabilia sales, and tours of the Anniversary House. Enjoying music from the turn of the century played by a thirty piece band, or a chance to meet and talk with descendents of the Price family, provided diverse entertainment possibilities.

All this had been planned for 100 attendees, close to a hundred and fifty showed up. Volunteers were all dressed in period attire which lent well to the overall feeling of a turn-of-the- century experience. Frank had been asked to help emcee the event through the lunch service and giveaways; he had become known for his gift of gab. In top hat and tails he was quite the sight, provoking smiles from ear to ear as he looked like Halloween a few weeks early. After the lunch he took up his position on the straw bale lined buckboard, narrating the early history as each wagon full of attendees enjoyed the half mile trek out to the Anniversary House. Upon arrival at the home the passengers would disembark, then treated to tours of the home by more costumed volunteers. Returning passengers were thanked for coming on the free ride and reminded that this all-volunteer effort was being supported by their voluntary monetary contributions. "Don't be afraid to feed the kitty," he coaxed as he helped the passengers unload.

Their success was measured at the end of that very long day by the six hundred or so dollars received from the donation bucket and raffle ticket sales, as well as the enthusiastic comments received from those who attended. The icing on the cake was the discovery of two full-color front page photographs in the county's largest newspaper. One photo was of the buckboard loaded with smiling faces as it plodded down the dirt road to the Anniversary House, the other of a tour group inside the home. Accompanying the photographs was a very complimentary article covering the event and its event staff 'Friends of Price House'. This was the publicity the group had hoped for, identifying the project, its goals and the group that was leading the charge. The fourteen hour day had paid off big time and the accomplishment was even noted by city council members. The snowball of recognition for the project was beginning to roll down hill and picking up a considerable head of steam.

Frank's responsibility and dedication grew. He had made the board aware that security was going to be an overriding issue for the project and early on he was given a key to the gates. He made quick runs to the house a few times a week trying to heighten the on-ground presence. The effort to deter the unknown visitor/visitors who kept cutting holes in the fence and attempting to enter the house was a challenge. Whoever was trying to get in had gone so far as to use a shovel and pick to blast their way through the three-quarter inch thick plywood security covers that he and Joe had installed. The individual that kept trying to get in was making his attempts under the cover of darkness, so he and Joe installed motion detection security lights, only to return and find the lights broken out with rocks. This pissed Frank off to no end and he began to put together a program to find a care-taker to fit their needs.

He had become familiar with the ebb and flow of folks willing to volun-teer. He had come to know that the right folks came along at the right time, as if a divine clock was ticking out the cadence. He chatted up the Price House project to many of the regular clients to his store; he saw this as an avenue to acquire new volunteers. One such individual who had shown some interest was a tall, pony-tailed character with steel blue eyes named Glen Ray. Glen had been stopping by once a week or so to fill his water bottles and to Frank he seemed to live out of the 1950s International Harvester milk truck he drove around. The old milk truck Glen called Millie had a message printed on its side that pretty much sized up Glen's philosophy on life, "Bikes not bombs."

Glen was an eclectic treasure to say the least. He was often dressed in attire that didn't match whatsoever, right down to the different colored socks that adorned his feet if he was wearing shoes. Glen's sturdy build backed up his claim of having been a marine, although the long hair gave Frank some doubts. Glen was well tanned year round which seemed to validate his state-ments about teaching volleyball to a regular troop of girls at a local beach. He was a very good looking man in his mid forties and his boyish playful con-versations had Frank thinking he was probably a successful ladies man. Glen never mentioned working for a living. Frank speculated he was attached to a girlfriend that might be taking care of his monetary needs.

As Frank divulged his concern over security at the Price House he noticed that Glen began asking some very intelligent questions as to how he might be expecting to solve this problem. Frank explained that a full-time caretaker was needed to live on the property. This individual was going to have to have their own self-contained RV and be able to supply all the necessities for com-fortable living, as the Price House had no facilities at this time. Glen listened with interest. The Price House could supply electricity however, and the cost would be paid by the Friends of Price House in exchange for the caretaker's work at the property.

A week or so later he was questioned by Glen in more detail as to what the responsibilities might be and how long he thought this person might be needed. It was apparent that Glen might be considering the position, although he wasn't quite sure if Glen had the right look for the job. A few visits later, Glen revealed that he and his current girlfriend were not working out. Glen then suggested if the board was in agreement he would gladly take the position. Frank eagerly took that offer to the board.

He worked with the board to weigh the pros and cons and to discuss the terms of an agreement with a clause to rescind. He warned the board that Glen looked a little rough around the edges, but assured them that Glen had what it would take to make the situation work. The board agreed by unanimous vote to bring Glen in as the on-site caretaker. Breathing a sigh of relief, he now had a comrade in the game of battling the elusive intruders. The security game was on, so let the games begin.

Boy, did the games begin. Glen borrowed a friend's camper to provide comfortable accommodations for his new home at the park. The unit was parked in close proximity to a power box that provided electricity to the Price House with an extension to the rolling home. Glen settled in to his accommodations and began reporting to Frank daily on the small projects he was working on to secure his space.

At the end of the first week Glen flew himself north to Santa Rosa, California to see his parents for their annual family reunion. Glen was not only a pilot, he was also a certified aircraft mechanic capable of working on everything from jet engines to helicopters. The more Frank got to know Glen the more he was impressed with Glen's credentials and capabilities. Glen indicated prior to leaving that he would only be gone for a few days. Frank agreed to drop in and check on things while Glen was gone. The Friday and Saturday visits were uneventful. When he arrived on Sunday morning however, he found the front gate wide open. Pulling out and around the house he found the RV gone, initially thinking that Glen had returned early and had driven to town for provisions of gas, propane and food. Driving up to Millie the milk truck he noticed the front windshield was broken and the red flags went up. He exited his truck so fast that the truck had not even come to a complete stop. His brain reverberated a line from a movie he had seen as he began an intense survey of the site, "Houston, we have a problem."

Instant visual information revealed that all of Millie's windows had been broken. A ground inspection of the location where the RV had been parked yielded more bad news, broken glass on the ground around the proximity of the driver's door. "Oh shit Houston, we have a really big problem" ran through the brain as his usually tempered demeanor exploded and he actually yelled "fuck" at the top of his lungs. Jumping back in his truck he raced to the closest phone and called the police to report what appeared to be a stolen vehicle and vandalism to Millie.

Returning to the site to wait for the police to arrive, he struggled with what and how he was going to tell Glen. When the officers arrived further investigation found the vehicles tire tracks in the dried grass were headed north up the canyon. That would be a dead end as he had been up that direction before and knew there was no outlet in that direction. He and an officer jumped into his truck and followed the lead, hoping to find the vehicle abandoned somewhere up the ever narrowing road. No luck, but returning they did find evidence that the RV had turned around. The officers took more information and a check was done of the Anniversary House. No damage to the house. At least that was some relief.

Frank called Glen and gave him the bad news. Glen returned to file the proper reports, both figuring they would probably never see the RV again. Much to their surprise the vehicle was found three days later in a parking lot at the State Park just up the road. The most bizarre part of it all was that all of Glen's belongings were still inside. The only thing missing was Glen's wine collection. This was the end of the beginning to the security battle. The issue of security was going to be a wild long ride into the future. At least at this point Frank knew that his new career journey with Glen and the Price House was going to be entertaining.

He may not have found any artifact treasures up to this point, but the prolifera of treasures he had found in the people, the place and the events that had been gifted through his participation was undeniable. The intention to find treasure was being fulfilled in a vastly different perspective, opening his mind to awareness that the flow to these unique gifts was a flowing of Grace. The right people at the right place at the right time to make things work was timing that was not of his hand. These flashes of insight, although brief, were at least small understandings that managed to stimulate observation of the spiritual journeys connection to the life he was leading and that was the biggest treasure of all.

~~~~

We all look to enrich the journey by connecting with others that share common vision. We may not always be aware at the time all contact is made that they are, and we are right where we need to be. This is part of the tapestry's picture we don't always see because of the furious pace that we weave our string into the fabric. When we slow to observe, the narrowed focus reveals the beauty of the expanding picture and the Grace filled hand that gently guides our string.

CHAPTER 6

HOPE, FAITH AND GRACE

There is a force that champions the greater good. The search for a connection with that energy is a path that most of the human race travels at some point in time. At least that was Frank's speculation. This quest for connection leads in a multitude of directions for the billions now on the planet. He was no different. The hope of finding this connection was in the faith of Its existence. He found for himself that hope spawns faith that spawns an intimate personal journey of discovery for connection to that energy he called Grace. The intensity of these discoveries brings peace, which breeds more hope, which breeds more faith. Faith in the personal discovery of and walk with this Grace is an ongoing process for him. Faith in Grace has no timeline, no set schedule and he had to remain patient knowing Grace guides. That's the journey of his spirit that is centered by his faith anyway.

Frank had headed down many different wide roads during his dark days of hopeless wandering. We all have those days to a greater or lesser degree. The path he had finally found had narrowed. He came to understand that the energy of Grace provides for the greater good and he learned to be patient never knowing exactly where that hand of Grace might appear. He understood that if any given idea was going to work he could not direct it to happen. He found if he removed 'self' from the equation the greater the chance of success. He enthusiastically includes other peoples input into project concepts, knowing Grace facilitates the best of the best. He knew that 'self' would screw it up every time. Being successful in following this path that excluded 'self' he discovered he would always be rewarded with unforeseen riches. By pursuing goals for the greater good, Grace will pay dividends in abundance. So Frank learned to pick good projects and 'just put it out there' knowing Grace provides. That was his faith anyway.

As Frank walked to the bank of mailboxes that served his portion of the block where he lived, he noticed his neighbor from three doors up en route to retrieve his daily mail as well. As neighbors they had seen one another occasionally, waved hello, but had never met face to face. Arriving at the mailboxes, the two exchanged the customary hello then to introduction with exchange of names and then they began to chat. Frank brought the conversation quickly to the Price House foundation project. That was his focus at that time on the project and he relished talking of its progress. The large man of almost six-foot-three named Jack Straw acknowledged a familiarity with the project, showing an interest in the current activities.

Frank had developed the ability to request assistance in Price House projects in everyday general conversations with whomever he was conversing. His enthusiastic, positive attitude toward the project occasionally prompted an inquisitive response from the person with whom he was conversing. After some spirited conversation Jack suggested that he just might stop out and take a look. Frank knew if an individual stopped out for a look the bug of inspiration would either bite or it would not. He never pushed the individual for their involvement, he left that up to Grace.

Prior to ending their extended conversation, Jack inquired when the work party might be out at the house again so he could bring his wife Lee out to see the progress. Little did Frank know that this man in his early seventies who walked with a slight limp would eventually become the Friends of Price House Vice President, his right hand man and good friend.

Jack and Lee showed up on the next workday and Frank was astounded by their contrast in size. Jack was six three-ish weighing two hundred twenty five-ish pounds to Lee's barely five foot one hundred pounds soaking wet. It was apparent to him that they were an inseparable pair as they strolled around the site, inspecting preparations being made to lift the house off of its current pier and beam foundation. Jack recounted his earlier years of being a concrete man, prepping and pouring thousands of foundations in Orange County, California during the building boom of the 1950s through the early 1970s. Jack and Lee confessed to having been involved in the first Price House committee in the late 1980s but had phased themselves out as the project lacked direction and progress. Now they were excited that real work was underway with clear goals. They were so excited by what they saw they joined on the spot.

This cute couple of synchronized energy absolutely exploded to life much like a dormant volcano with years of pent up magma pressuring the earth's crust for release. They blanketed the community with their white hot enthusiasm, generating volunteers, commodities from local businesses and large amounts of money. Jack and Frank would belly laugh together as they spoke of Jack's fundraising technique.... size matters. Jack's large stature with an inability to take "no" for an answer, simply had business owners squealing "yes" when they saw him approaching their front doors. Lee was the record keeper of the team, the folks who did not commit the first time around found themselves on her 'hit list' for Jack's return visit. Jack was good! Frank affectionately referred to him as Guido.

His fondest memory of Jack was impressed during the initial stages of the foundation work at the Price House. The house had been lifted off the ground about thirty six inches on the low side of the gentle slope the house had set on for the previous 100 years. The footing trenches had been dug and form boards were being staked in around the perimeter. Jack had given Frank direction on the proper way to stake and form a pony wall under the house and Frank had headed under to execute the work. Frank requested some additional information shouting from under the house. Hearing no response he turned around and was amazed to see Jack crawling toward him on his belly, hammer in hand and a half dozen nails hanging out of his mouth. It was like watching the Cavalry arrive. Jack was truly an old school concrete man with a hands-on spirit and a heart of gold. Jack and Frank became inseparable.

The magnificent work of preparing for the foundation concrete pour did not go unnoticed. The volunteers had worked through the summer months and into early fall. Work days had originally been scheduled for Wednesday, Saturday and Sunday afternoons, but by the end of August the schedule had morphed to Wednesday, Thursday and Friday afternoons 4:00 pm to dusk, all day Saturday and most of Sunday. Although crew sizes varied Jack and Frank never missed a day. Jack's guidance produced a stunning completed work of forms strung with steel and topped with foundation bolts, ready for inspection by the City of Pismo's building inspector. An inspection was called for on a Friday morning with concrete scheduled to be poured by the volunteers on Saturday morning. The two intrepid volunteers were a little nervous as they were never sure how many volunteers might show, eleven plus yards of concrete is way more concrete than two guys with a concrete pumping crew can pour and finish. Somehow Frank just knew the Universe would deliver.

Construction had been slow in the five cities area in the early 1990s and a contractor by the name of Tim Prichard had volunteered a lot of his time to help on the foundation preparation. Tim met the city building inspector Friday morning to field questions and start any corrections needed. Frank arrived at his business at 7:00am to take care of needed activities and planned to get to the site by 1:00pm, after Linda arrived to relieve him. The inspector had arrived at the construction site at 7:30am and had invited a friend along to see the impressive work the volunteers had done. It just so happened that the inspector's friend owned a local concrete contracting business. At 8:00am the phone rang at Genesis Water and Frank picked up. It was Betsy. She was calling from city hall to inform him that the inspectors' friend was so impressed with the volunteers' work, they were volunteering to do the concrete pour for free, but it had to be done that morning.

"What should we do?" Betsy asked.

"Call and order the concrete!" He responded in a heartbeat.

A free crew of professional concrete men, you just could not pass that offer up. Game on! Frank went into a frenzy of activity calling Jack, calling

Linda in early, calling clients to reschedule appointments and then out to the site by 10:00am as the first concrete truck arrived. By noon the second truck pulled away, the last of its load having been pumped into the new 20th century foundation for the gem of local history. By 1:30pm the last of the finish crew had cleaned their tools and were on their way to their next job. The forms had held and a tremendous amount of work scheduled for the following day was already done. Somehow that energy of the Universe Frank was so confident in delivered big time.

By 3:00pm when Betsy arrived, Frank and Jack had begun some selective stake and kicker removal from the forms. Betsy, Jack and Frank had become a tight team on the project and they decided to sign their names in the top of the concrete of the front porch foundation wall. They knew that no one would ever see those signatures, but the little kids in them came out and they just had to do it. What a day! The following day when the volunteers arrived to help, all there was to do was remove the forms and beam with pride at what they had accomplished.

That year at the Pismo Beach Parks and Recreation Department's annual awards banquet, the award for "Volunteer of the Year" was co-conferred upon Frank and Jack. Frank was beginning to notice that his willingness to give of his time and talent was beginning to pay dividends for the family and the business. His identity within the community was being established as a kind, giving person able to lead. Becoming known as a man who could be trusted to get the job done was good for the business that provided the livelihood for the family he loved so much. By Grace good things were happening, he could feel that energy.

Jack and Lee were an amazing duo of that Grace. Jack, Lee and Frank spent a lot of time together over the next few years dreaming up ways to make progress on the Price House on a shoestring budget. Jack and Lee also became big fans of the Pismo Clams. Whether building floats for the Clam Family or organizing Price House fundraising events, Jack and Lee were always there to help. Their friendship extended far beyond just the projects. During Frank's deeply depressing days when Linda filed for divorce, drained the bank account, left with Elise and moved to Orange County, Jack and Lee were there to see him through the despair of divorce and separation from his daughter. Frank in turn was there for Jack when Lee died from cancer a few years later. Lee's passing was just after their 50th wedding anniversary and Jack was devastated. Frank wept with Jack over his loss, weeping again a couple years later when Jack died from a broken heart.

Good people come and good people go, it was the ebb and flow of life. Frank felt great sorrow in the passing of these two wonderful people who treated him like a son. Their passing did afford him some peace though. During their years as friends the dark clouds threatening shame grew from his 'what if' past. Knowing he'd never have to explain those dark days to his friends softened the pain of their passing. The dark clouds of doom that swirled around the 'what if' in his life had grown despite 'official' promises made. The rain of destruction the dark clouds promised for his life could not now disable the friendship that he, Jack and Lee had enjoyed. By that Grace he was eternally grateful.

~~~~

We all wonder why and how the path we forge is directed. Is it simply individual effort? If that were so, it would take but a single string to complete the picture. We all are aware that it takes more than one. We are also aware that the unexplained has a place in the picture as well. We all develop a hope and faith that this energy which we cannot fully understand extends favor. Unexpected pleasant events are gifts reinforcing that faith and we journey forward hopeful for more connection to that Grace. The story of the string we follow has had a glimpse of both the pleasant and the grievous, observing both to be guided. How and why didn't matter, gratitude did.

CHAPTER 7

LOVE OF TRUTH LOST AND THE FALL INTO THE ABYSS

Keeping things simple was important to Frank. It made life easier to nego-tiate if any popular belief could be traced back to a basic known princi-ple. Basic principles known by everyone on the planet, a universal knowledge if you will, that could be considered universal truths; building blocks of truth, simple for all humans to understand. Simple truths like, "killing is not a good thing!"

Understanding was important to him. He tried throughout his life to keep all things basic and simple to avoid the fog of confusion. It was a gru-eling task keeping truth in perspective. The more life as he knew it was extrapolated out from the basic and simple, the more prone it was to be per-verted from truth. Kind of like the belief that 'the killing in war can eventu-ally lead to peace'. The further the extrapolation was extended, the easier it was to create new perceived truths. Once one accepts these new truths the easier life becomes to exist within the parameters of new popular beliefs. Each system or society adopted its own set of perceived truths designed for its own survival, thusly division became acceptable. Universal truth was being abandoned and new truth accepted to serve the self-interest. He often won-dered if he was the only one on the planet to walk in this fog of confusion.

Slowly but surely Frank began to let go of his quest to stay in simple truth. He became complacent. Sucked into the easier way, he was willing to go with the new flow. The flow seemed so wrong at times, but what could one do, singing the song of alarm only fell upon deaf ears. Keeping simple, keeping basic meant keeping it to yourself. Trying not to think about what was going wrong in the world around him was the only way for him to stay calm, so he partook in diversions in an attempt to avoid further mayhem in his brain. It became addictive trying to avoid the confusions of life.

In the time of transition in the teenage years he fumbled his way through the discoveries we all encounter. In the discovery of love and affection he tried to hold on to what was considered normal and right. He fell in love, or so he thought, with a beautiful young lady named Cindy Levan and they dated as a steady item throughout their high school years. He remained rigidly true to their relationship even while separated half a world away.

Cindy's father had taken a position that transferred their family to Taiwan, China, and he wrote to her several times a week. He missed her fiercely. Cindy was two years younger than him and their separation took place as she entered her junior year and he his senior year of high school. Frank's Dad was transferred from the Pentagon in Washington DC, to the Air War College in Alabama, and at that point in time Frank had made it clear he did not want to leave his last year in high school to start all over new somewhere else. His 'true love' had left and he wanted to at least stay in familiar surroundings for his last year. He didn't like the prospect of change and stood firm in resistance. He devised a plan that provided an acceptable alternative to the disruption of moving, satisfying the addiction to resisting change.

His family had become close friends with the Rains, another Air Force family who lived across the street from their Champ Springs, Maryland home. Arrangements were made for him to live with the Rains for the ensuing year. Frank was close with Allan, the next to oldest son. They surfed together, ran an apartment pool together, even had a band together. He spent that school year going to class during the day, working at a men's wear store in the evening, saving his money and making plans to go to Taiwan to see his beloved Cindy after graduation.

He was good at making detailed travel plans, after obtaining a formal invitation to visit from Cindy's parents. Cindy was the love of his life and he felt sure they were meant to be together for the rest of their lives. This summer-long trip to the island formally known as Formosa challenged his ability to remain faithful to his convictions of true love forever, as Cindy eventually revealed an unfaithful liaison with another boy from the school she attended. After the numbing of this revelation subsided, he confided to Cindy that he too had established close relationships with other girls, but had never allowed these contacts to become intimate. Frustrated yet proud of his chastity... then on to learning other lessons.

He and Cindy discovered the power of forgiveness together that summer and the peace it brought. His disdain for personal failure allowed his mind to expand the realm of possibilities, within reason, to preserve the trust he had placed in Cindy. Unfortunately, 'within reason' meant strings or conditions to protect self. Conditions had been attached to this forgiveness by Frank and agreed to by Cindy in her attempt to keep their love for one another steadfast. His understanding of human nature was beginning to grow, he was learning to manipulate for benefit. Not the best path to follow, attaching strings for benefit. At least his tolerance for others expanded as he absorbed the different culture of Taiwan and dealt with the unexpected wrinkle in his relationship with Cindy.

That summer of 1971 was spent exploring life and reaffirming their commitment to one another. He returned to the DC area content to wait for Cindy's return. After several more months of separation, Cindy's family did return to Washington and she finished her senior year of high school while he finished his first year of college. The relationship grew stronger and Cindy entered the University of Maryland. College life was out of control with new found freedoms and both struggled to keep the grades up. Frank had completed four semesters and Cindy two when Cindy's family was again transferred, this time to Louisville, Kentucky.

The separation was more than the two young lovers wanted to handle, so plans were made to marry and relocate to San Diego, California. Frank was done with the long distance commute to ride waves, grey skies, cold winters and sticky, nasty summers. Cindy was done with the slow, seemingly backward ways of the Kentucky lifestyle and being stuck under Mom and Dad's roof and rules. A formal church wedding was followed by a reception, as tons of family and friends came from far and wide to shower the happy couple with at least forty pounds of rice. Frank found some of that rice twenty years later while doing some deep restoration to the Porsche, which they and their dog Toroko had driven to their new life in California.

The electricity of their new adventure began to dim as the reality of life's demands set in. Frank made many mistakes in his personal direction and began to feel inadequate as a provider. He had fallen into the water industry, after discovering that his employer at the printing and mail distribution house he had worked for was ripping off his clients. The money was better, but never enough. When Cindy became pregnant they were concerned that they might not able to care properly for a baby. In his more frequent stupors of drunkenness an abortion of the pregnancy was discussed. The father's inability to cope was more pressure than Cindy could handle and the baby was lost. The baby's soul refused to be put in harms way. This was a blow that hit them both very hard, yet unable to speak about. This act broke a basic truth that they both believed in, "thou shall not kill." Truth had been perverted and sadness remained in their hearts for a life not given a chance. Life lesson learned ... killing hurts. Pressure kills.

Cindy procured a better job with the phone company and they relocated to Huntington Beach, California. Frank was able to transfer with his company and the future seemed brighter. A year later Frank decided to finish his last hours needed for an AA degree and pursue a law degree in order to be a real provider for the family. He applied himself to a 12 hour curriculum and graduated on the Dean's list. The law exam didn't go as well, his squeak-by score was a disappointment. Wrapped up in self and personal failure he failed to see that he was not providing Cindy with the attention required to keep their love ablaze. Then one night, in another drunken stupor, he saw Cindy having a conversation with another man and imagined infidelity. They had attended a party that evening, and upon returning home he exploded in confrontation. Self-absorbed, he did not hear a word of what Cindy had to say and physically manhandled the woman he loved. Cindy left that night never to return. She was smart. He didn't fare as well.

Truth had become; love had strings. The fog of that confusion was going to take a long while to lift, with a ship under sail that had no compass. The spiritual journey was failing to see any light as the journey of self sat in the dark seat of failure, having no ability to plot a course to restoration. That night life changed. He began the dismal spiral downward into the abyss of drug and alcohol induced decadence and depravity that would haunt him the rest of his life. It was a year before he could speak civilly with Cindy, all the while wanting desperately her understanding and forgiveness. He was sick, very sick and he turned to alcohol, drugs and sex to deaden the pain of failure. He was desperately seeking connection with another human who would listen to his woes and offer understanding without judging his continued failure to be a decent productive person. He withdrew from life seeking comradery in local beer bars and cocktail lounges. These places he could go after work, get a buzz and a smile with an occasional one-night stand. Life had turned very dull. His only grounding was the pair of Lhasa Apso dogs he retained from the divorce. He remained loyal to their care, they in return greeted him nightly with loving enthusiasm no matter what time he arrived home.

The quicksand of the abyss was swallowing up life; his blinded lifestyle produced only despair. He was shutting down and did not know it. His work was mundane, repetitive sales that he was good at. He declined offers to take on more responsibility and move up the ladder. The work was simply there to provide the means to deaden the pain.

The continuing search for that perfect someone was not too successful in the haunts of his nightly ritual wanderings. This elusive, idealized someone he could almost visualize seemed like a faded memory of someone he had met in the past, but his scattered brain could not recall for sure. He had turned from the help of God as he knew him, because he was questioning his faith in truth and his only hope in God was for some sort of forgiveness at death. The peace of spiritual connection was dismissed in favor of the human connection that was touted to be the 'happy ever after'.

Spiraling ever downward into a cesspool of depravity the 'try anything once' became a sick mantra driving him closer and closer to self-destruction. Eruptions of self-pity punctuated a life that was floating from high to high into madness. Wake up calls of a drunken driving arrest and a detention by authorities for a 72 hour suicide watch/evaluation, did nothing to alter his plundering lifestyle. The sun had set for faith; the dank darkness of 'never happy' was smothering the flickering flame of hope. No return was an option ...only to a lost soul.

~~~~

We all want to know the truth woven into the heart of the fabric. We compromise when conflicted, twisting truth to fit need, to quell confrontations that threaten. A diminished spirit results, running to addiction to hide its shame. We all suffer, we all teeter on the edge, some fall into the abyss. The string we follow has abandoned spiritual connections and is falling too, lost out of love. Again the past provides detail to the color of the present in the string we follow.

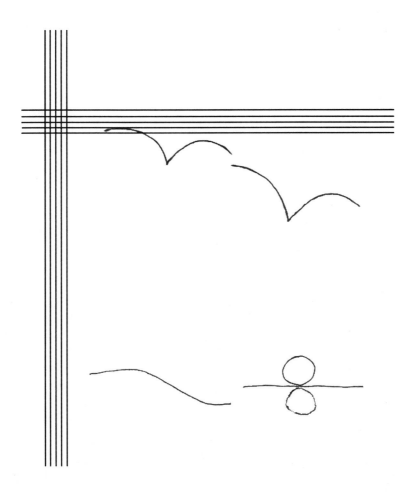

CHAPTER 8

DREAMS, NIGHTMARES AND
THE LURKING 'WHAT IF'

The dream was like nothing Frank had ever experienced before. It was a level of consciousness with indeterminate fuzzy borders of reality. A feeling of being somewhere else, yet knowing here. Here being blurred by there. A sense of urgency here, mixed with the calming peace of being there. He felt he knew this long lost friend that was there, able to see, smell, hear and the peace of touch as if she was here. The calm of reconnection was rushed by the reality of how brief the encounter of theirs was to be. Duration seemed critical. Each moment was treasured to the heart, elongating the stay. And the color, beautiful color. The brilliance was breathtaking yet soft. The time had come to go and he held on for dear life. He was not prepared to go as abruptly as he had come. He wasn't sure how he had gotten there, but he didn't want to go! He didn't want to go! He didn't...

He was jolted abruptly awake shaking from the experience, but his mind was as sharp as a tack. The bright morning sun streaming through the window and the clean air he inhaled deeply, posed instant recognition that he was in the here and now. He immediately tried to recall and relive every detail of the dream he had just lived. This was not some drug-induced phenomena or a hung-over detox illusion. This was a visitation at another level of consciousness that had occurred during a good night's rest that had accompanied a pretty tame previous day.

The experience was so vivid it shook to the soul with its intense message of remembrance. The dream's intensity stirred his heart, riveting the mind in its reverent recollection for three days. His demeanor had brightened from the extraordinary reunion with this dear friend and he wondered if somehow they might have connected souls. Hope had rekindled and her name was Hana Lisa Joi. He loved the sound of her name. Her voice in the dream had ushered in a calming peace to his spirit, previously immersed in turmoil

Hana Joi had been to Frank one of those people you meet, blend into harmony with and discover a level of friendship that might possibly never be attained with another. If you are ever so lucky to find this special bond, you know it can never be broken. He was amazed that it had been so long since he had thought about Hana, three days of remembering the dream encounter prompted a desire to try to find her.

It was 1978 and had been six years since he had spoken to Hana. He felt compelled to at least try to find her, as a sense of need for his assistance hinted too by the dream lingered in his thoughts. He tried time after time to secure a phone number for her, or even her brother Stefen whom he had lived with in his first year of college. Directory assistance operators in the DC metropolitan areas worked on his requests, all to no avail. As time moved on the denial of success took away the urgency and ultimately the hope of finding her. This girl he held dear in his heart now was being let go again. Time and the abyss were sucking away the peace she embodied, sucking away at the memory almost to never. This beautiful girl was only to be remembered in the far distant future as Grace afforded. He resigned to helplessness, eventually asking God, who he rarely talked with anymore, to take care of Hana Joi. Briefly the spiritual dialogue had welled from the depths. And back into the abyss he fell.

Into his black hole he descended. Deeper and darker each return trip. Actions so shocking that he finally faced a cause for remorse. If anything might turn him around it would be an action that caused him to weigh his value as a human with disgust. This event occurred and he had a heavy price to pay. This price he willingly accepted for even he knew he had crossed the line of decency, feeling obligated to take responsibility for his actions that are considered heinous even by the most hardened. Paying for one's faults is a far better price than a life lived in total disgust of self. That recovery he was to learn walks the thin line of sanity.

Stopped mid-stride by the hand of justice, he became aware that his life was out of control. His desire to climb out of the abyss was harnessed to the dictates of the court. Frank made strong agreements with the court, to follow exactly their dictated requirements that would release him from further penalties or disabilities associated with his crime. He served his time in jail and fulfilled probation requirements faithfully. He was granted a change of plea to 'not guilty' with a dismissal of charges, the court's record to be sealed and expunged in October 1982. The end of his five years spent under the court's direction did not end his personal shame he had in himself. He would always have a heavy heart for his indiscretion. Remorse would be felt forever and he would struggle with that demon from his past as he tried to rebuild his life.

We all have demons from our past. We all look for doors to put them behind. Once one makes a concentrated effort to leave them behind and shut the door, the process of restoring self-worth begins. Changes are made to help one forget and with luck those memories fade. Forgiving self, the door is closed, never to be opened again. However the remorse one feels never fades. It is there as a vivid reminder that we are less than perfect. In some cases much less than perfect; reminders to keep us humble and grateful for escape from the darkness. If our actions have left victims in our wake, remorse is the reminder to pray for their recovery and the fading of any memories that interfere with their happiness or joy in life.

With the doors closed to the past one goes on to rebuild what has been destroyed. Changes occur over time and by avoiding the traps that pull us down we make progress. We keep the events of our past to ourselves in an effort to prevent our new friends, family and co-workers from judging us on our past. If we were to wear our past deeds of misdoing on our sleeve we might rarely have the chance to be evaluated on who we have become after closing the door to the past. We all have a desire to be accepted and liked by those around us. Posting the past to potential new friends in initial greeting sets the stage for negative judgments and pretty much closes the door of opportunity to expand any relationship. Delivery of negative facts of the past disables someone's ability to be accepted for whom they are now and that is why we close the door to those facts and move on. We have all done this with something from our past, unless we have led a perfect life. His intention was to move on.

During his court-directed years he had been able to keep his job with the water company, moving from sales to production and eventually into route work. A back injury from the age of five years old laid him up from time to time and he moved into the office to help staff while recovering. He was developing a pretty clear picture of the bottled water industry, choosing to stay with it despite its provocative perception by the general public. After all, what really was the need for a bottled drinking water? Our government was telling us the water from the tap was safe to drink. He had developed his own ideas about that and his personal experience was telling a different story.

A few years prior when he had started working with Silver Springs Water in San Diego, one of the perks of the job was free water to use at home. He took advantage of that offer and found the product to be much more pleasing aesthetically. The bitter taste and smell of chlorine was not present. He found he was actually drinking more water. He also discovered it produced a much better cup of coffee. Whether at work or at home, he always had a supply of bottled product. Within six months he was never going to the faucet to draw water for consumption. That choice was to be reaffirmed in no uncertain terms.

When his friend Jimmy, who lived in his apartment building in Ocean Beach, suggested a weekend trip to San Jose to see an old Army buddy, Frank was up for that. Affording a 'boys out' weekend was agreeable to the wives and the men left on a Friday morning for the nine hour drive. Upon arrival the beer drinking began, as they drifted back through the stories, good and bad of the Vietnam War which had just ended. Frank had been vehemently opposed to the war and had drawn a high enough draft lottery number so as not to be drafted. He had a few close friends who had not been so lucky and he recounted some of their horror stories as well as his own involvement in the anti-war protests. The stories and beer flowed until 1am when they all finally dropped into bed. At 4am Frank awoke with party mouth and a burning desire for water, the alcohol his body was processing had dehydrated him and thirst had to be quenched.

Opening the refrigerator in the bachelor pad revealed only beer. No juice, no milk, no water. He figured the beer wouldn't get the job done of quelling thirst, so he opted for a tall glass of tap water. The water foamed a bit as the glass filled, the smell was pungent and it tasted muddy as he slugged it down then returned to bed. Around 5am he awoke to a violent stomach. It was all he could do to get to the bathroom sink before the contents of his stomach were heaved forward in massive, successive convulsions. After five or so minutes of gut wrenching he returned to bed figuring the worst was over, except the dizzying headache that throbbed in his head.

Sleep came and went and at 6:30am he again headed to the restroom to sit on the stool to empty the liquid mass from his lower intestine. That event threatened to wake the rest of the household with sounds of noxious gas release. The ensuing day's activities revolved around close proximity to the bathroom, as cramping dictated further need for release. The following day he remained queasy for the entire ride back to San Diego. Forty eight hours of questioning the cause of this uncomfortable occurrence produced only one conclusion. It was the water! This was not a hypothetical answer, it was an answer produced after the recall of similar events he had experienced. Coming from a military family they had moved about every three years, and every time they arrived at their new location this occurrence of upset stomach and diarrhea hit. The family affectionately referred to these occurrences as the G.I.'s. He had finally figured it out; it was the water. So if water could produce such a violent reaction from the body rejecting the water's contents, how safe could it really be to drink... especially long-term?

Frank now had gathered some evidence suggesting quality might be of concern. Of course water being one of the three basics to life on the planet; he decided to stick with the industry as a career. He now felt some validity in what he had chosen to do for an occupation.

We are not taught much in public school about water other than the basics. Most people know that the earth's surface is seventy-five percent water, but what most folks don't know is that only two percent of that total is fresh water. Of that two percent, eighty percent of that fresh water is locked in the polar ice caps. We do not seem to appreciate how precious little of it we have to work with, or how unmanageable it is to protect our water from the belching contaminations of the 21st century. Water is known in the scientific community as the universal solvent; anything it touches it tries to pick up and take along for the ride. Water supports life, and many dangerous microbiological contaminants will thrive in a water delivery system if unchecked. We dump other contaminants such as chlorine or chloramine into our water systems to keep these undesirable bugs at bay. How good could that be to ingest?

Awareness of these thoughts seemed to be more prevalent in Southern California during the mid 1970s. Statistics showed that eighty percent of the bottle water being produced in the nation was being consumed in Southern California. Good industry potential he thought. He settled in to learn all he could about what worked and what didn't for the industry. It didn't take him long to realize that the water industry was worldwide.

He recalled that when he was in Taiwan, the water they consumed was brought to them by a little Chinaman. The little man of about five foot brought six-gallon round glass bottles to the back porch, two at a time. The bottles were removed from a horse drawn wooden cart and placed in separate hemp rope cradles at opposite ends of a stout bamboo pole about eight feet long. The slight man of maybe ninety pounds then lifted the pole from the middle to take up the slack in the rope baskets that held their weighty cargo. Climbing underneath the pole with a padded shoulder, he would lift and head out for the intended destination. The pole that was balanced on his shoulder bent and strained at the weight from both ends, flexing softly as he walked. An amazing site and he could have kicked himself for not having taken a picture of this unique mode of delivery. It sure would have been a good conversation piece to show to his friends in the industry. A worldwide trade that had been going on for hundreds if not thousands of years and will continue well into the future he surmised. A sound trade, that if he wished could take him anywhere in the world.

It had been a while since his eyes had seen anything but the abyss. Now at least the horizon was exposing a new vista of hope through work, even though the search for the old friend had been futile. Liquor was still the medication of choice he sought to kill the sting of loneliness from the lack of human companionship. Adrift in short term relationships that he tried to sustain always led again to more liquor. He just couldn't go deep or real, afraid the 'what if' from the past could rear its ugly head to destroy any connection he made.

The bottle was his only friend. 'What if' was never a problem with that friend. The friend in liquor knew his past and came around anyway, despite the past, whenever asked. He thought he could control his crutch by periodic short-term bouts with sobriety. Three days maybe a week, then back for more medication. He thought he was better than before, now he could put together a few days of stone sober now and again. He did notice that when he did return to the medication the start of the trip took longer, longer to get to the dead place of numb and dumb. ...Control? Fat chance!

Work was going well but the social life sucked. No wonder, his social time was spent at home hibernating with his bottles of bliss. Going out was out of the question, his condition by the end of the night put himself and others at risk. At least that truth stuck. This at-home party put a severe damper on his ability to find a willing female to share her charms. Release while flipping through the pages of a magazine was just not even close to the real deal. So when a couple of his friends suggested a trip to Las Vegas to gamble and score hookers, he was more than ready to jump on that train.

Rich, Rick and Frank were good friends. Rich had recently started rooming with Frank and all three worked together. A trip like this was certainly to be a contest of machismo amongst the three. A plan was set, the three strutting cocks were to leave the day after Christmas and return four days later. This timing gave them three glorious days in Vegas doing whatever their hearts and dicks desired. Three crazy guys hell bent on one thing – girls! Sick goals that could be satisfied in sin city, the trio could barely contain their enthusiasm as Christmas Day came and went painfully slow.

Frank was half lit as he piled himself into the back seat of Rick's car. A half pint of Wild Turkey was already flowing through his veins, another pint for the ride close at hand. The 9am departure time from Rick's house in Riverside would put them in Vegas by early afternoon and the party could begin.

Begin shit, Frank was already well underway and that was a dangerous thing. His personality had two directions when drunk, either a party fun guy or a raging lunatic. Party fun guy was just that, the life of the party with a million jokes in his repertoire. If the joke man was on he could keep people laughing for hours. Raging lunatic on the other hand was not a pretty sight. His loud, foul-mouthed, bitter ranting degraded everything from government policy to women's motivations. His obnoxious verbal crap led more than once in the past to a blind siding fist to the jaw. That raging lunatic really screwed the party up, not to mention the cuts and bruises he couldn't remember how he received when he awoke the following morning. He was not in control of the personality that might manifest. It was a coin toss on who might show up to the party. This day was no different.

The car was full of testosterone driven anticipation. By the time they had reached Barstow the lunatic had arrived and Frank was beyond control. Rick and Richard had enough, issuing him an ultimatum to tone it down or get out. So while the others shopped for travel munchies and filled the car with gas, Frank's "fuck you" attitude took him in a different direction. Instead of sticking with his buddies for a mellow trip to Vegas, he picked up more alcohol and disappeared.

Wandering into a grove of trees down by railroad tracks, he sat down and cracked a couple of cans of mixed cocktails. Pounding the drinks down as if they were water, he sat and thought what his next move might be. Home or Vegas? After weighing the options his 'I'll show them' attitude brought him back to the northbound highway on-ramp. Even in his stupor he managed to hitch a ride towards Vegas, only to be let out at the next off-ramp a few miles up the road. Even though he wore clean attire gifted for Christmas the day before, it could not mask the stink of drunk. Thus the invitation from the nice folks in the RV to seek another ride left him roadside, to stick out his thumb to try and snag another Good Samaritan headed in his direction.

All plans are subject to change. When the black and white California Highway Patrol cruiser rounded the corner to get on the freeway he knew his plans were about to change. The officer pulled over and questioned him as to why he was hitch hiking on the freeway. He fabricated and told a story of trying to get back to his car that was left broken down somewhere up the highway. Requested identification was produced and after a wants and warrants search was run he was informed that hitch hiking on the freeway was illegal, he would have to find another way to his 'broken down vehicle'.

Well okay, what next? First things first and down to the small store/gas station located not far from the freeway on ramp. Grabbing a gallon of cheap wine he headed down a dusty dirt road that led to railroad tracks that paralleled the freeway. Downing half the bottle of disgustingly sweet wine while sitting in the shade of a Palo Verde tree pondering his situation, boredom set in. Noticing an open bulkhead at the top of a railroad grain car that sat on the tracks in front of him, he decided to do some exploring. Just a minor distraction he thought, then he could resume the quest to reach Vegas.

Climbing to the top of the massive steel rail car, he planted his feet firmly and bent down to look inside the cars dark innards through the car's open hatch. The speed, at which he bent in his drunken state, caused his right hand to miss the handrail around the bulkhead. He caught the opposite side handrail with his left hand which caused his body's momentum to shift a bit to the left while still heading downward. Natural reaction to regain control was about to become successful with the pulling of the body toward the secure steel rail. The speed of no control began to slow and downward motion had just about reached its stopping point. His brain was beginning to send the message that every thing was going to be okay. Then the unexpected...Bam! From out of nowhere his right eye cavity came into hard contact with cold steel. The shot of pain stood him straight up. The little exploring he had decided to do was going to hell in a hand basket ...quick!

He brought his hands up to cup the eye he wasn't sure was still in its socket. He staggered backwards and the back of his knees hit the knee high railing behind him. Momentum continued backward. Frank realized he was going over the edge as his knees buckled. "Shit" was the first thought, as it's a long way down to a landing he could not see, and "**NOT GOOD**" raced through his muted brain cells secondarily. "This was not going to be pretty!" "Hit right or die!" was his brain's next report, as he started a slow motion backward flip to a certain hard landing. Somehow the brain shot an order to roll with the momentum to hopefully create a flat, spread eagle landing, face up! Letting go and letting Grace handle the calculations for that perfect landing, was the only explanation he came up with days later.

The landing was very hard. Legs, arms, head and back hit the inch and a half granite gravel rail bed all at the same second. Instant deceleration forced all the air from his lungs. Pain reported to the brain from every corner of his body. "Lay still, don't move" was his only thought as he faded to black. Unconscious for how long he didn't know. His next conscious interaction with reality was to hear what sounded like a police radio call. Eyes still closed, he heard the voice say,

"Blah blah blah to base."

"This is base." the radio responded

"Yeah base it looks like we got one down and hurt, over." the reporting voice expounded.

With that Frank opened his one good eye to see a crew cab railroad vehicle. A gruff burly face hanging out the driver's side window looking at him with mike in hand was the face of the voice that talked. The radio chatted back,

"What's the condition, blah, blah, blah?"

Frank knew if he wanted to avoid problems he needed to respond, so he did,

"Hurt, I'm not hurt!" as he struggled to stand and fake normalcy.

"What are you doing here then?" shot the gruff stern voice from behind the wheel.

Frank focused his good eye that had been blurred slightly by the pain of standing. He saw a cab full of railroad workers' faces focusing their attention to his bloated right eye. The eye was already swollen shut.

"I was just resting." Frank responded with feeble sincerity.

"What happened to your eye?" the driver demanded.

"Oh, I got into a fight" he said trying to smile and shrug off real concern.

"Base to blah, blah," the radio solicited.

"Hold on base," the driver responded.

"Are you sure you're okay?" the burly face asked again in stern questioning.

"Yeah, Yeah I'm okay." Frank responded.

"Okay you shouldn't be down here so get the fuck out of here!" the driver commanded in no uncertain terms.

"Yeah... okay no problem." Frank responded as he walked in front of the truck to put some distance between himself and authority, trying not to limp as he made his way toward the dirt road.

His body had taken a tremendous blow, all movement was excruciating. Making his way toward the road he heard the other workers in the truck commenting on how bad he looked. He thought to himself that he was probably hurt, but not that bad after all he was walking. After walking far enough up the road to satisfy the driver that he wasn't coming back, the truck pulled away. He turned around returning to the bushes where he had stashed his bottle of wine prior to climbing the train and taking the big dive. Grabbing the half full bottle he retreated far into the bush to medicate the pain and inspect his injuries.

Sitting down hurt! Standing hurt! Walking hurt! Shit, just breathing hurt! The lower back and left leg were especially bad. He opened the bottle and took a couple of long, deep, warm hits of the sickeningly sweet wine. It stung to get his lighter out of his front pants pocket. Both his hands had several small bleeding cuts on the back of them. He got a cigarette out, lit and inhaled deeply. As he exhaled he thought to himself, "I think I may have a problem with drinking." ...*Ya think* "I should really think about quitting," as he raised the bottle to again drink deeply. *...I guess you can muster the courage to quit if you're having a drink.* He pulled up his sweater sleeves to inspect more bleeding puncture wounds, covering the top of his arm from wrist to the point were the sleeve concealed the rest of the arm. With the way his back and the back of his legs felt, he suspected they too were covered with a fair amount of these same wounds.

He watched through the bushes for the return of the railroad patrol truck. He didn't want to be discovered as he tried to medicate the pain and try to figure out what he was going to do next. Vegas, girls, booze, that would make him feel better he concluded. *Wow... that's clarity.* Now just how to get there? The sun was telling him that he had to make a decision soon as maybe an hour of sunlight remained. Vegas was north. The sun was at his back as he sat looking at the railway in front of him. That seemed to mean the direction north would be left. How far? He didn't know. Shit, he didn't even know where he was. As he gazed north up the tracks the thought crossed his mind that walking was out. *...Brilliant!*

Hitching another ride was out with the way he looked, but what about the train? There were several sets of tracks and at least two of them had trains sitting on them. He could see an engine about a dozen cars to the north and he speculated that it was headed in the direction he needed to go. Should he try to jump on if it starts to move? Frank questioned the wisdom of a move like that as he finished off the last of the bottle of sweet anesthesia. *...Wisdom?*

No time for pondering that decision any longer. The train sitting in front of him suddenly lurched to the left, slamming each car's coupling as they engaged consecutively in a giant chain reaction of motion. Vegas or bust he thought! A quick survey right and left to check for patrolling personnel and the dash began. Lucky for him the forward motion of the train was slow as molasses in its forward acceleration. The tonnage in tow made it possible for him to match its speed despite his almost crippled left leg. Grabbing hold of the handrails that bordered the steps up to the deck of the grain car, he was able to pull himself up and gain footing. He was on! Moving toward his goal of Sin City he hoped! Positioning himself at the end of the car to break the wind, he sat to think about how he was going to feel once the wine buzz wore off. *Act first, think second...Again...Brilliant!*

The sun set and the winter desert air began to chill quickly. Soon it was damn cold. The train was rolling along at fifty to sixty miles per hour and he was being chilled to the bone. "Boy, this was a bad idea" ran through his mind. *Again...Ya think!* It was just about dark when from the left side walkway appeared a railroad worker. Both were startled by the unexpected meeting,

"What the hell are you doing here?" blurted out the railroader.

"I needed a ride." Frank stammered sheepishly.

"You can't be here!" the rail-man said in disbelief.

"Follow me!" he commanded.

Frank stood and complied. The journey forward was an exercise in pain management. The chilled traumatized muscles in his body did not want to cooperate. Making their way forward required traversing rocking rolling train cars, his body recoiled in pain with each step. Hands so cold they barely felt the steel handrail. After reaching the engine, a door was opened and he was motioned in. Closing the door the rail worker told him to wait there. He nodded compliance.

The engine room's roar of horsepower was steady and the heat generated was a welcome reprieve from the freezing exterior. Returning, the rail worker ordered him to the back of the engine room and into a small control room with one seat. Lined with gauges, dials and levers he was instructed to sit down and not to touch anything. He nodded in understanding and the worker left closing the door behind him.

Frank sat contemplating his predicament as he watched the desert roll by on the now moonlit night. The drone of the engine and the pain now pounding in waves soon had him on the floor looking for the relief of sleep. He fell asleep on the engine room floor breathing the thick oily smell of diesel fuel, grateful to be warm again. He awoke a while later to the sound of a more labored drone to the train's diesel motor. Was the train slowing? He labored to get up off the floor and back into the chair. The whole body was stiff with pain. Looking out the window he could see the headlights of cars on a freeway about a mile off to the left side of the train. Looking northbound he saw a cluster of lights a few miles ahead. If he was going to get out of this predicament of a certain grilling by authorities, he would have to get off this train before it reached civilization. He checked and found the exterior door was unlocked, but the train was moving too fast to bail right then. He'd have to wait and hope for the train to slow down a bit more before he could even think of making an exit that wouldn't incur more injury.

The train's engine cadence became more labored, and yes in fact the train was slowing. He figured they must be going up a grade as the decrease in the train's speed was becoming more discernable. The train's forward motion had slowed to maybe ten miles per hour. That small cluster of lights was now straight off the left side of the train and at the closest point to the train they would ever be. It was now or never! He stood his racked frame up, opened the door and slipped out closing the door behind. Down the steps as far as he could go he watched the desert roll by for a second or two, took a deep breath, then the leap. ....*Inject any comment you want to....*

The legs buckled immediately upon contact with the ground and momentum threw him forward for several violent rolls before his body stopped its uncontrollable flailing. Frank laid on the desert floor for a minute or two trying to assess his condition and taking inventory. Wallet, cigarettes, money wad, arms, legs. "All here!" was his assertion. ...*Yeah right.* "Okay, can I stand up after this latest beating," he wondered.

Real effort to stand was a good indicator that his body had taken about enough abuse for one day. The limp was worse. The left leg at the hip just couldn't take much if any weight. It was an arduous trek across the desert floor to the cluster of lights that represented refuge. The cold of the night set to the bone again as he traversed the long mile to civilization. A couple of hundred yards out he began to see what made up the cluster of lights. A gas station, a couple of small buildings, one larger building and several trailers illuminated by two street lights emitting stark white light, displaying the village that stood in the middle of nowhere. Light coming from the windows of the larger building indicated activity and hopefully food. He could see cars parked around the exterior and he really hoped it was a restaurant. Approaching from the black of the desert was at the back side of the largest building. It wasn't until he rounded to the front that he discovered he had hit the jackpot. The sign protruding over the front door announced Jean Nevada Bar, Grill and Casino open 24 hours. Wow what a score, food, booze and gambling! All that was missing were the girls.

As he opened the door to walk in he remembered how bad he must have looked, so he approached the bar with his head down trying not to show off his pulverized eye. Taking up a stool away from the other patrons he ordered up his first round of medication.

"Shot of Wild Turkey and a draft beer please." he asked of the bartender.

"Sure." the bartender said, setting a shot glass on the bar and filling it.

He grabbed the glass, lifted it to his lips and threw the burning liquid down the back of his throat. Returning the glass to the bar he motioned for one more, as the bartender delivered the drawn draft. The second shot went down as quick as the first, followed by a long, cold swirl of draft. He lowered his head, leaned against the bar, anticipating the relief the alcohol would supply from the body ache and pounding in his right eye.

"May I ask what happened?" asked the bartender as he wiped down a glass.

Frank knew he would be telling 'this story' frequently so it was time to come up with a good one. The truth was embarrassing to tell, with the listener coming to one obvious conclusion... 'This guy's got a drinking problem'. So manufacture he did.

"I was jumped." Frank responded, figuring expansion of the story was to come as needed.

"You okay... Are you sure you're ok?" the bartender asked with genuine concern.

"Yeah, the eye hurts, but I'll be okay." he delivers with confidence, not really wanting to talk about it in any further detail.

"Is the restaurant still open?" Frank questioned wanting to change the subject.

"Sure, 24 hours." the bartender confirms.

Wishing to avoid protracted conversation he threw down one more hot shot, downed the beer and limped off to get something to eat. Eating was a chore, but a chore that had to be done. Nutrition had been limited to the carbohydrates found in the alcoholic beverages consumed in the previous 24 hours. With nutrition and hydration ordered he went to the restroom to clean up.

He had not urinated all day and that urge led him to a urinal as a first stop. Release was difficult, the pain that stretched across his lower back made relaxing tedious. Flow finally started, he gazed down to see a blood red stream of urine passing into the bowl. This sight frightened him. Continuation to fruition was impossible as waves of pain again reached his lower back with the pushing required to empty the bladder. "Oh boy, something was really wrong. Blood in the urine was not a good thing." was his astute observation. ...Astute is laughable!

He zipped up his pants, hobbled to the sink to wash up and for the first time saw his face in the mirror. He was not prepared for what he saw in the reflection looking back at him. Prolific black and blue bruising of the eye socket area; the eyelid had a small cut and so did the cheekbone. The eye socket area, from the bridge of the nose to the temple, and from the eyebrow to the cheek was swollen out to the level of the points. He could not force the eye open with facial muscles. He pried the two lids apart gently with index fingers of both hands, to inspect for damage to the eye itself. As the lids parted he noticed he could see out of the eye, which at least was good news. The white of the eye however was completely blood red with eye movement labored but viable. The cold water clean up felt good, making him wish he had a cold compress for the damaged eye.

Returning to his café booth he ate his meal and hydrated with several glasses of iced tea. Abort Vegas was his final decision. Return home to seek medical attention, was the first good decision he had made in the past 24 hours. Returning to the bar he order more medication and asked about transportation available that could get him back to the Riverside area. The bartender indicated that the Greyhound bus stopped right in front of the bar at six thirty in the morning. He glanced at the clock, 12:30am it read. Okay only six hours to wait; now if he could just find some place to lie down. The body demanded rest. Then a tap on the shoulder. Frank spun around on his barstool to find two uniformed sheriff's officers standing in front of him.

"Sir could we speak with you?" the one with the most stripes asked.

"Sure," his response as they escorted him to and out the front door.

Outside the grilling started and the lie took on a truth of its own. Frank wove a tale of an unprovoked attack by one or maybe two people, as he exited a restaurant somewhere between Barstow and this place. When asked how he ended up in Jean, he improvised a very different train ride. Indicating he had been rendered unconscious by a blow to his face from what he thought was a wooden club, then to wake up in a box car that was traveling at a high rate of speed, he continued the ruse. He speculated the motive was robbery as he found his wallet missing, but still had his money and ID because it was in his shirt pocket under the sweater he was wearing. When asked if he needed medical attention, he indicated that his intention was to return home on the bus in the morning to see his own doctor.

Leary but satisfied, the officers left and he returned to the beer he had left at the bar. He finished the beer with one last shot of Turkey to keep the pain at bay. Glancing at the clock he read 1:45am then began a search to find a place to get some needed rest. The facility was just about deserted, the gambling area had a few dark corners where he found a place behind curtains that masked a table and chair storage area. Lying down well hidden, he hoped to wake up in time for the bus that was due to arrive in four hours. No wake up call available here.

Sleep was attainable as long as he didn't move. Movement nailed pain spikes into any portion of his body that stirred. Then the sound of air brakes discharging spent pressure hastened his mind's acknowledgement that sleep was over. His groggy mind reported the arrival of the bus. What time was it he wondered, as he unfolded his stiff aching body, forcing it to stand. Limping past the empty bar, a glance at the clock revealed 6:20am. Emerging from the building into the cool morning air helped to dislodge the nasty stale carpet odor stuck in his nostrils and on his clothes. The large Greyhound bus parked in front was a welcome sight. Contacting the driver, he purchased a ticket that could get him as close as possible to Riverside General Hospital. Once there the emergency room staff could evaluate his injuries and let him know if he was slowly dying. He felt like it.

One last trip to the restroom before boarding, the blood in the urine he passed was vivid red and the pain points had magnified in intensity. The alcohol had worn off, but the thought of more to dull the pain turned his stomach. He cleaned up the best he could taking note his entire face had a rounded bloated look. He made his way back out and onto the bus, seating himself as far away from the rest of the passengers as possible. The nearly empty bus pulled away on time.

He nodded in and out of sleep as the southbound trip progressed. Not many new passengers were gathered as the bus pulled in and out of various stops along the way. That was good; the seat next to him remained empty, and the need to explain how he looked didn't arise. The Victorville stop however filled the bus to capacity. While the bus was filling the seat next to him remained empty right up to the very end. No one was willing to sit next to the guy who looked so bad. The unlucky last passenger to board was an exquisite Latin girl with long straight dark hair, dark brown eyes, and perfect figure. Frank could sense the compassion from all the other passengers as they watched the young lady discover the only seat left was next to the most undesirable passenger on board. He felt sorry for her as she reluctantly took the seat.

Frank apologized for his looks to ease her apprehension, then turning back towards the window to ride quietly down the grade into the basin. On any other day he'd have engaged conversation, in an attempt to gain the phone number of such a pretty girl. Not today however. His stupidity over the previous thirty hours left him in muted reflection, concerned for his physical well being. She parted their silent company at her intended destination, wishing him well and hoping he'd be okay. The tone in her voice indicated her appreciation for his reserved nature during the ride, making him feel he had finally done something right. Sober was coming.

Exiting the bus at the Riverside terminal, he quickly hailed a taxi and was delivered to the emergency room entrance at Riverside General. On-duty staff quickly admitted and triaged him to determine needed testing to evaluate the severity of his injuries. The concocted story he was sticking with prompted a call to and a visit from the Riverside police. The interview conducted between the full body x-rays and the iodine scan resulted in a dead end case with no need for further investigation. The ruse that had no definitive details as to who, how or where worked again. The battered body was the only evidence that something extreme had happened. The mouth that had spoken from that body managed to keep his ass out of jail anyway.

The doctors on staff wanted to keep him overnight for observation; he declined. Finding out that his liver and hip had been damaged but would heal, and the eye was not permanently damaged was good enough for him. Death was not imminent. He took the prescriptions for needed medications, checked himself out and began the mile or so limp back to Rick's house where he had left his car just thirty some hours before. After arriving at the car his mind set was to fill the prescriptions, get back to the house, and get into a real bed. As he drove home to Corona, he promised himself he wouldn't drink again, well anytime soon anyway. ...*Okay! We'll see.*

Pulling into his driveway wrapped him in the warm blanket of security of home. The nightmare was over. Walking through the front door was like a reunion of long lost friends as his dogs, Kimmie and Toroko, welcomed his return with joy and concern. The dogs knew something was wrong and inspected him from head to toe as he greeted them with loving embrace. He fed them an extra hardy meal, took the prescribed medications and dropped into the bed that had been calling his name the entire journey home. The dogs immediately joined him. Standing watch over their friend, their concern comforted him as he dropped into deep sleep.

He awoke twenty-four hours later to the dogs barking at the return of his roommate and intended travel partner to Vegas. Rich and Rick entered the house, were stunned by his appearance, but relieved to find him at home. The expected barrage of questioning started and he again told his fanciful tale to the concerned audience at his bedside. He got out of bed briefly to take more medication and shift the conversation to details of their trip. He listened to their recounting of looking for him, finally giving up and then trying to enjoy the intended nature of their trip to Vegas. He apologized for ruining the trip and returned to bed hoping for physical recovery needed in order to work the following day. That was not to happen.

It took a full two weeks for him to recover enough to handle his delivery route on his own. Owning his own bottled water route in Downey and Pico Rivera did not provide any time off for injury. He had to scramble to keep the operation running according to schedule. He did manage to stay sober for those two weeks, which in turn faded his previous realization that maybe he had a problem with drinking. Thinking he had control he fell off the wagon, but this time he tried to tone it down, not wanting to ever have a reoccurrence of that longest day in his life. ...*We'll see.*

~~~~

We all stumble. This part of his story is told so you can understand how much abuse one can inflict upon oneself when you look up and you only see bottom. The abyss is a dreadfully deep place when you fall. What is woven from this place is only destruction. Rays of hope flickered, spirit touched for a moment, but with no connection the string we follow lies dormant in dark isolation of medicating addiction. The tapestry's creator can only weave with string that can connect to compliment the color of the elegant picture to be produced. None of us can add our color to the picture from isolation. Like a boat on the ocean with no rudder or wind to fill the sails, life goes nowhere.

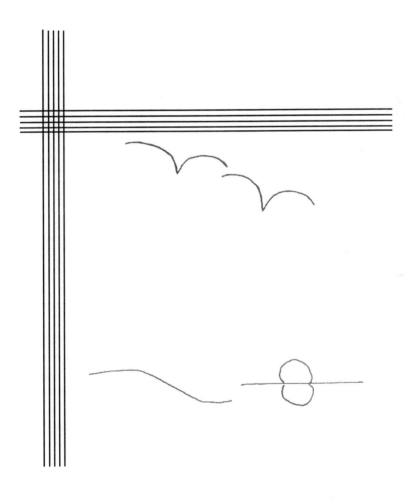

CHAPTER 9

DOORS CLOSE, DOORS OPEN AND
A HEART FAIRYTALES TO HAPPY EVER AFTER

Frank's move from Huntington Beach to Corona was made after two violent confrontations with a neighbor in an adjoining unit. The two unprovoked attacks on him were made by the neighbor in an attempt to inflict bodily harm. It was some sort of vigilante type retribution, after Frank had openly confided to the neighbor about the act for which he had been prosecuted. Fortunately for Frank his ability to defend himself saved him from major injury. His crazed neighbor's attempts to inflict harm made it abundantly clear that the truth about what he had done in his past could cause a violent reaction from some people. He now knew the past would have to remain secret. He must hide the past to avoid future outbursts of rage from those that could not accept that decadent episode of his past, it was not who he was now.

The move to Corona was perfect for him as he was building a water route in a rural community adjacent to Corona. Besides basing him closer to his route operation it also removed him from his old environment of nightly haunts in the bars around Huntington. The house he occupied provided room to breathe and focus on his business. The succession of roommates he had also provided companionship that was missing in his old abode. The only connections that remained alive from his former environment were the Pacific Ocean and his ex-wife Cindy.

He and Cindy had managed to rebuild their friendship after a contentious divorce. Frank had realized that Cindy was really a friend and not a foe. He came to understand the reasons for her leaving. Eventually agreeing it was the best thing for the two of them in the long run. Friendship remained strong and when Cindy married Jimmy Logan, Frank was the photographer for their wedding. Good friends are hard to come by and Frank remained on his best behavior whenever visiting. Cindy and Jimmy eventually bought a house in Riverside not far from where he lived, helping to keep them closely connected. Cindy and Jimmy's happiness represented hope that he too might one day find a match.

His camaraderie with several of the other owner/operators at Silver Springs Water flourished. There were about five or six of the top producers that had developed a little breakfast club to which he had been invited to join. Their early morning gatherings set a jovial motivating tone for the day and he absorbed the best of their knowledge to improve his business operations. He ran a clean operation, avoiding the pitfalls encountered by others that lacked the business sense needed to really be successful owner/operators. His periodic encounters running company clean-up operations over the years also provided valuable business insights. He was regarded by the breakfast group as one of the best salesmen at the Orange branch and was welcomed into the tight band of buddies. He was also known to have an incredible knowledge of water, earning him the nickname "doctor of drinkology," Doc for short. He fit and it felt good.

This morning breakfast retreat also provided one other crucial benefit for him, the chance to flirt with a beautiful young gal that was the hostess on the morning shift at the restaurant they frequented. This was a fringe benefit he looked forward to. Months of teasing and testing culminated with Frank finally asking her out. The first date of dining and dancing led to a second date and a third.

Her name was Linda Scanlon. Her long brown hair, brown eyes and vivacious zest for life soon had him anxiously awaiting their weekend get-togethers. They grew close fast. Linda too shared deeply in their attachment. Discussions delving into their thoughts on the future revealed like-mindedness in the search for the elusive happiness. He had fallen head over heels for Linda. Within a month he had asked her to move in to his home and Linda agreed.

Thus began an amazing partnership on a road to ever happy. They made a comfortable nest with the possessions they had. He at twenty-nine felt able, capable and willing to provide for his twenty-three year old companion. The sync in the relationship was immediate. A deep love was soon flowing, within a few months the fanciful talk of marriage and family became more serious. He was weighing the pros and cons in his own mind. Most of his gut reaction indicated he was ready to commit again. One reservation he harbored was that all this had come about lightening fast. Shoot, his first marriage was started after years of courting. This romance had happened all in the course of less than six months.

"Well," he thought to himself, "I've done the long road; maybe the short road is the ticket. I'm not getting any younger" was the echoing drumbeat in the back of his mind. He felt a sense of urgency, lucky to have found such a sweet lady full of energy willing to experience the world with him. It had been seven years of stalled progress on the road of life since Cindy had left. Linda rekindled the hope of moving forward. A normal life beckoned; all he had to do was commit to "until death do us part." The only other reservation he had was when his gut wrenched at the thought of 'What if'. Keeping the darkness of the past behind a locked door was imperative to him in order to keep this new door to happiness open.

A gorgeous day spent in the sun and surf in Newport Beach set the stage for engaging in the bonding ritual. Late lunch and drinks at the Beach Ball restaurant, watching the crowds walk by topped the afternoon off. The 'if we got married' questions that were interjected from time to time during conversation energized spirits. On the return trip back to Corona, Frank was quietly contemplating asking Linda to marry him. The rush of last minute questioning racing through his head had been resolved. He was enthralled with her beauty, enamored by her spirit, enchanted with the connection. The only matter to decide was how and when to ask. The only unknown factor, whether or not Linda might accept.

The Universe answered that question. Frank's nervous inner thoughts reached a conclusion, he'd pop 'the question' when they returned home. That was only a mile or so away. The Universe did not wait. Linda, turning in her seat to face him with fire in her eyes asked,

"Frank, do you want to get married?"

He was stunned. Uncertainty had vanished in a heartbeat. Pulling the car to the side of the country road they traveled, he turned and responded,

"Yes, of course! But I thought I was supposed to be the one who asked?"

Breaking into laughter they hugged from the heart, overwhelmed with the bliss of mutual validation. The rest of the ride home was surreal as the enormity of their agreement kicked their thoughts, hopes and dreams for the future into overdrive.

Linda phoned her mother and sister straight away to share her joyous news, Frank set about creating a ring to show his sincerity. He wanted to do it right on bended knee, but the ring thing he had forgotten all about. While Linda gushed with joy talking to her mother and sister, he quickly fashioned an engagement ring of macramé twine. When Linda had finished speaking on the phone he took her gently by the hand leading her to the living room. Kneeling on his right knee he asked Linda to marry him and slipped the ring onto her tiny finger. Linda's eyes filled with tears at this deeply romantic overture and crying "Yes" she embraced him to the soul, awash in the glow of love.

The subject of where and when of the wedding had created incredible energy. The sense was sooner than later in regards to when, both anxious to take the oath of commitment. The tremendous romantic excitement of where was to be talked about for days. Planning for a short romantic getaway, to be celebrated with a small contingent of family and close friends proceeded with the same synchronicity familiar in all their endeavors together. First of May, Lake Tahoe, on a boat, in Emerald Bay was the exciting conclusion of where and when. This fit the small amount of time and budget available for a wedding holiday.

The gathering in Tahoe was smooth and exciting. Even with only a two-week notice Frank's mom, dad and brother were able to attend. That first night in Tahoe, Frank introduced his nervous bride-to-be to his family at supper. The dinner and recreation they shared late into the night was topped with a soft snowfall and luck at the gaming tables.

The following day of family gathering with preparation for the big day was interesting to say the least. Linda's mother Pat ran the planning with her customary tight fisted Portuguese style. Pat's matriarchal role in the Scanlon family was a real show. The outfits Pat wore on her robust five foot Portuguese frame were just too bright and way to tight, she was a sight to behold. Checking and double checking all the details for "Linda's day" was Pat's way of contributing and showing her joy in seeing her daughter happily married. They were lucky to have Pat, she was a gem, just a little rough around the edges. Lady Luck was with them again that night before the wedding when Linda and Frank hit the gaming tables. Money fell into their bucket like the snow falling again. It was looking as if the stars had aligned.

Pat's prodding's paid off though. The following morning all arrived, and the boat left on time. The men had been banished from the cabin as all the women prepared Linda for her magical trip. Pat even laid out logistical details of the on board wedding event. The couple was to be taking their vows on the flying bridge of the vessel facing the group of well wishers at the stern. Pat had all the movements choreographed to her desires.

Frank however defied the gods and changed the plans after talking with the preacher who was to officiate the nuptials. It had been understood by all early on that the ceremony was to be carried out on the boat. The rules of docking and disembarking at the castle located on the shore of Emerald Bay, required a permit issued by the Native American Tribe, who were now the stewards of the land. Not having the permit meant not getting off the boat according to the Captain. Preacher Jim however convinced Frank that a brief docking and walk to the castle that stood nearby should not offend the spirit of the land or the tribe. He and the Preacher then asked the Capitan to make the docking, reasoning that this early in the season with snow to the waters edge no one would be there anyway. So the Captain agreed and a docking was made.

As the men began to leave the yacht, the Captain informed the women of the change in plan. Momentarily all hell broke loose as Pat charged the groom demanding answers. This was not part of 'her' plan, she was furious with Frank for not consulting with her on changes. This froze the troops in their tracks. He thought fast for answers that could turn the tide in his favor. He needed to disarm the armed and dangerous tongue of the little Portuguese woman charging his direction, before she actually got a hold of him. He was able to placate Pat with the enticement of an even more romantic setting for her daughter's wedding and the disembarking was allowed to resume.

Men helped the women down the slippery snow-covered plank to the beach without a fall to record. A short walk through the trees to the clearing in front of the stone castle revealed wonderland scenery enchanting enough to win even Pat's approval. Frank saw forgiveness for changing the plan in the eyes of the fiery little Portuguese he was to soon call mother-in-law. Pat surveyed the scene while squealing her approval, drawing laughter from the crowd, and the party was on.

The virgin white snow accented the emerald green water of the bay and the grey stone of the castle. The dark green pine that encircled the clearing stretched snow-sprinkled bows into the broken gray/blue sky above. Linda was breathtaking. Frank was burning her image deep into his mind; he could not recall seeing anything so beautiful! Linda's small frame complimented by the lace-appointed white gown flowing to the snow covered floor was an angelic image. Linda looked as if she was floating as she approached to stand by his side in the chapel provided by nature. The faux white rabbit fur jacket with fawn colored collar she wore for warmth added a soft rounded touch. Linda's long, dark brown hair exquisitely framed her olive skinned face with piercing brown eyes and cute nervous smile. When she arrived at his side the beam on his face told everyone he was the luckiest man alive. The storybook union lifted spirits skyward as Preacher Jim invited God to bless the new couples' vow 'till death do us part'.

The pronouncement of man and wife was followed by a loving kiss with soulful embrace and acclaimed by cheers from those gathered. The fusion of soul elevated the couple to a dreamlike state. Their eyes locking in a communion of love was only briefly interrupted by the crush of congratulatory hugs from the envious attendees. The division intolerable the couple drew together again in short order. He lifted his companion's body and soul into his arms to carry her back to the boat. His sure-footed stroll along the snow-covered beach allowed Linda to fall away to never never land. Eye to eye they whispered romantically while making their way back, leaving only a single pair of footsteps behind in the snow to evidence their total union.

Corks popped the cold champagne to life as the love boat pulled away from its mooring. A leisurely cruise around the island in the middle of the bay provided a dreamy launch from the winter wonderland marked in their hearts forever. Only cheers of salute to toasts made broke the silence of the vast wilderness that surrounded them, the two at one with the Universe, as a wafting snow intermingled with rays of sunshine streaming through holes in the broken sky. The unscripted nature of the day's events only added to the fairy tale movie feel of 'happily ever after'. He and Linda ended that day wrapped in peace as they drifted off to sleep in the warmth of being one.

The peace and continuity in their relationship remained strong. His personal peace however was to be tested shortly after returning home, when the beast of 'What If' raised its ugly head. That part of his past he had chosen not to reveal to Linda. That was not who he was and he feared the negative energy and destruction such information might cause to Linda's unwavering trust. What he had done was not who he had become. His intent was that what he had done remain buried to all except him. His comfort from those ugly thoughts was in knowing the door to that closet was closed and tightly locked. Or so he thought. Fortunately the visitations of 'What If' up until then had been few and far between. Soon enough that was to change.

~~~~

We all need a gentle nudge from the Universe from time to time helping create change that is good. Sometimes those nudgings are not so gentle. Movement forward with our weave is not always what we expect. Isolation in the abyss of self is sometimes forced into change when rocked by rude events. But, even the rude events are Universe-inspired calls to connect. No matter how much fear has shut us down, heart opens for help. We open just enough. We reconnect and begin the journey out of the abyss. The tale of woe transmutes to a tale of growth. We open a little more and amazing gifts are afforded. We keep darkness locked away to preserve the light we again weave with. We thrive when accepted for who we are. The string we follow in this prose is no different

CHAPTER 10

LIFESPRING TO FATHERHOOD
THEN ON TO RECOVERY

Direction of intention is always subject to change. The Universe has a propensity of throwing you a curve ball now and again. Frank knew the simple white envelope bearing the return address of the Orange County Superior Court contained positive energy for him. He also knew that once opened by anyone else, the letter could release a firestorm of negative energy that could test a person's capacity for compassion.

Feeding on the positive energy of closure the correspondence represented, he had left the letter out, the occasional glimpse reminding him that he had followed through and that ugly chapter of his life had been closed forever. A week after his first date with Linda, wishing to avoid any negative energy, the reminder was squirreled away to the bottom of his top dresser drawer, forgetting its existence as he courted his wife to be. His assumption was that his private space would bury any key that might open the door of 'What If' and he forgot all about the letter. He should have thrown away the key! Linda found that key and opened that door, unleashing the storm he had so feared.

Returning home from work one evening he was not greeted with Linda's normal loving embrace. The glare from Linda's eyes and a broken disheveled look suggested a big problem, he asked what was wrong. Linda produced the letter, shaking it in her right fist as she demanded to know what 'THIS' was all about. For the first time 'What If' had become 'What Now'. Frank's heart sank. His first response was that of rage at the breech of his privacy. This was a vain attempt to make that breech of privacy the bigger issue. That didn't fly. The bridge he had not wanted to cross was now the only path he could take to avoid impending doom. Linda, his love, was at critical mass and it was up to him to comfort her mind with honest, open details of this horrible chapter in his life. They worked together for hours. He answered every question posed by Linda, at times in painful detail. Frank, exhausted from the emotional toll of the event, broke down and wept. He implored her forgiveness for his failure to fully disclose his past. She needed time to feel the answer she could live. All he could do was wait.

His remorse for the pain Linda was suffering had him leaning on alcohol again to mask his pain. He waited days in a muted drunken stupor before finding out that their bond might endure. Linda was willing to move forward letting the past be the past. She was fairly confident that that piece of paper was not whom she had married. A toll had been exacted but repair had begun and trust grew from honest communication.

The best thing Frank had done was to introduce Linda to his former wife Cindy. Early in their relationship he had accepted an offer of dinner with Jim and Cindy at their new home in Riverside. He had informed Cindy of his growing affection for Linda and Cindy's invite was extended to both. He almost foiled the formation of a tremendous friendship that was to grow between Cindy and Linda; he didn't confess that Cindy was his ex wife until the two were on the way over for that diner. This maneuver gave Linda no chance to back out, she didn't appreciate the entrapment. Once introduced, however, Cindy and Linda bonded instantaneously. Cindy and Linda's relationship flourished, adding insight and understanding for Linda into Frank's character as Cindy knew all to well of his sordid past. The relationship also served as refuge from the cataclysmic emotional storm that had been unleashed from the 'letter event'.

As time progressed, Cindy's unique ability to inject positive energy into any given situation provided comfort for Linda's times of trial. He had been told by all his friends not to make the introduction of the two, it could be a 'very bad thing' they warned. He dismissed their misgivings. Knowing the unique place Cindy and Jim occupied in his life dictated inclusion of anyone he was serious about. The decision paid off big time. With Cindy's help Linda's trust in Frank was restored. He and Linda moved on from that episode of hurt. By Grace they moved back to the joy of family planning and warmth in healing.

During the healing the couple attended a personal training program called Lifespring. Frank had done both the Basic and the Advanced Interpersonal Experience trainings a few years prior to meeting Linda. The first level Basic training program was a week long journey of removing road blocks in your personal life that hindered personal growth and happiness. The positive energy created during the training; brought to its pinnacle by Sunday afternoon graduation ceremonies, leaving attendees on a level of harmony with the Universe that is difficult to explain. Convincing Linda to go was a challenge, but worth the struggle. He wanted Linda to also have the tools for living that was offered in that Basic program. He encouraged her to go by offering to attend with her. She agreed and by the Sunday night graduation Linda and Frank's soulful union had reconnected on its highest level. The romance they enjoyed together that evening was culminated with passion that set the night on fire.

The couple had been trying for months to create a baby, once they had decided to grow the family. They really enjoyed their efforts. Those efforts no matter how often attempted never seemed to accomplish the task of creation they so desired. Frank became the brunt of jokes from Linda's side of the family. Pat constantly, playfully, accusing him of "shooting blanks." However, on that March 26th 1984 graduation night from the Lifespring experience, romantic energy hit a fevered pitch! A month later the couple rejoiced with positive results that conception had been achieved. The news spread like wildfire to friends and family.

The buzz of expectancy motivated many changes to established routine. The crush of changes fueled some old doubts in Frank's mind. He reviewed in quiet retrospect the wisdom of bringing a child into a world he viewed as out of control. His perception of what might be in store for this new baby really agitated him. His mind saw a world sinking deeper into chaos and strife. The deceptive ranting of hypocritical authority kept real truth well hidden. His brain could not visualize a way to create real peace on earth and he was fearful that a life of happiness in peace might not be attainable for his child to be.

He kept these thoughts to himself not wanting to interrupt the joy experienced by the new mother-to-be. These deep complex analogies compiled from millions of bits of information did not fit conventional rationalizations. Over the years of argumentative discussions with his dad, who was at the other end of the spectrum, he had been dismissed time and again as a crazy liberal radical being taught by Communist puke professors. If he was wrong, only time would tell. He was unable to articulate his reasoning because of its complexities, he felt alienated from the mainstream truthiness.

Frank always remembered one heated dinner discussion with his dad. He had made a statement with conviction that "the USA's defense budget was a bullshit boondoggle." Going on to say, "no military force on the planet in their right mind would ever try to invade this country." He was willing to bet that even the Pentagon's claim that Russians had a first-strike capability was crap and would probably be revealed to be inaccurate intel by the Russians themselves years in the future. He finished by stating that "our only real enemies are terrorists and they were not coming in the front door they were coming in the back." No hard cold facts to present, just his intuitive gut feelings, again to be dismissed as liberal lunatic crap. That discussion took place in the fall of 1972.

Now, his choice to escape from this negative vibe was simple; drink. The world gone wrong feelings of hopelessness, were only quelled by his weekly church attendance and nightly alcohol. As Linda's pregnancy progressed the stresses increased and so did his drinking. By mid summer of 1984 Linda had had enough. She turned to her friend Cindy for help.

Cindy was Linda's sanctuary. Their deep level of friendship permeated all levels of the female psyche. The sisterhood that had developed had become a rock of retreat that each could rest upon. Their weekly get-togethers eventually became weekly trips to Palm Springs for poolside sunning and lunch. Linda always returned home energized. The women's face-to-face contact was eventually broken when Jimmy took a contract to program for the Bart Transit System in San Francisco. In the fall of 1983 Jimmy and Cindy moved to Moraga, California just outside of Oakland. Linda was devastated that her best friend had moved, but the phone contact kept the sisterhood alive.

Frank and Linda traveled up in the spring of 1984 for an extended weekend to see Cindy and Jimmy's new house and share the joy of Linda's pregnancy. Little did Frank know that Linda and Cindy's camaraderie had led them to develop a plan to save the marriage that Linda could see was floundering. Linda did not want to bring her child into the world and under the same roof with Frank if he continued to drink. The potential for her baby to suffer the abuse that she had suffered growing up was just too great. By July, three months into her pregnancy, she was ready to put her foot down. Actually, both feet down, she was ready to walk.

Arriving home again from work with the glow of alcohol on his breath, Linda confronted him again with his need to quit, which sent him into a rage. The ensuing argument only inflamed his anger and diminished his control. After a devastating raging episode that left the kitchen in shambles, he announced he was leaving and headed down the hall. Linda sped through the living room to intercept his retreat at the front door. With an outstretched hand to his chest she announced that he was not going anywhere. He lost it. With a two hand blast, one on each shoulder, he pushed Linda backwards propelling her backwards and through the front screen door.

Frank watched in slow motion horror as Linda hit the ground hard on her backside. He didn't realize he had pushed her so hard and immediately assisted her to her feet. With profuse apology he asked if she was okay as he helped her inside. Linda broke away from his help, heading inside without saying a word or even looking back. As the screen door closed he realized he had really fucked up. He figured he'd only make things worse if he went inside so he turned and walked away.

He spent hours in a dive bar at the end of the street trying to numb remorse. After dark he headed back up the street to check on his wife. He knew that he shouldn't go inside, not wanting to chance an eruption of rage again. Instead he peered through the window to make sure she was okay, deciding to sleep off his intoxication in a vehicle parked on the side yard.

Sheepishly he reentered their home the next morning. He had to go to work and he needed to get ready. Linda had worried about him all night, but said nothing the entire time he was readying for work. He remained silent as well. As he was about to walk out the door Linda said simply, "Either you quit drinking or I am leaving." He looked at her and could tell this had been the last straw. Saying nothing he hung his head in defeat and walked out the door.

He returned home that evening to find Linda gone. The note left behind stated she had gone to her mother's house for a while until he figured out what he was going to do. He went to the liquor cabinet, grabbed a bottle of vodka and removed the cap. Taking a long warm swill he swallowed hard and winced from the burn in the back of his throat. One more to steady the nerves and he picked up the phone to call her.

Linda took the call screened by Pat. Linda's low firm tone sent the message that she wouldn't return if 'he' did not get some help to quit drinking. He reluctantly agreed that he needed help, remembering the 'train ride' that had solidified the message 'he had a problem'. Not having insurance that covered recovery treatment programs though, put him at a loss as to what he could do. He wasn't just looking for another excuse to prolong the inevitable. He did want to change, but the payment for the help wasn't in the accounts.

Money was an issue. Always was. They didn't have the money to pay for a recovery program out of their own pockets. Linda said she was making some inquiries and they should talk the following day about it. He agreed to keep an open mind. He apologized again for his actions, stammered out an "I love you" as emotion choked in his throat. Hanging up the phone he took another long hard hit of Vodka to deaden the pain of self-examination. He needed help and he finally knew it. His unborn child deserved better than this. The more he thought, the more he drank with his ever faithful dogs as his only companions. He drank himself into quiet oblivion, passing out in the late night hours. The abyss was calling, he knew he was falling.

Linda returned home two days later with information in hand. Frank was stone sober to greet her. Linda left her belongings in the car, ready to bolt if things turned ugly. After a brief cool hug Linda got down to business. Laying down several brochures she had received from Cindy, Linda explained the options available. The expense plus time required by most of the institutions was far more than they could arrange. One however caught his eye.

The name of the place was Duffy's of Myrtledale, located in Calistoga, California. They offered a one week detox/recovery program for four hundred dollars. Cindy and Linda had also identified this same one as a possibility. The girls had already called to find out that the next available opening was on July 18th just two weeks away. Cindy had offered accommodations at their house for Linda, as the institution was just north of their location. Frank was in a daze as the pressure was on to make a decision. 'All about me' kept him from realizing that the day open at Duffy's was two days after his wife's birthday. Sober was the best present he could ever have given, if he could only afford the price.

He could credit card the money. He could get the time away from work. Could he bolster the commitment to be successful? He wasn't sure he could until he looked into Linda's eyes. "Is THIS the one you'll do?" she fired with ultimatum firm in her voice. The look he saw made him flash back to a few days prior and the slow motion fall with the look in her eyes as she hit the ground. "I never want my child to see me that way" was in his gut. "Yes," he responded, "let's make the reservation."

He did not find out for a few years that if "yes" had not been the answer Linda would have left, never to return. He also found out the reservation at Duffy's had been made by Cindy and Linda well in advance of his decision. He had no idea what he had agreed to, he only knew he was about to start one of the greatest challenges of life. Learn a new lesson. To beat addiction had to be lived hand in hand with Grace. He just didn't know that part yet. Really he didn't know much.

~~~~

We all experience bumps as we weave through the tapestry. The hand of the tapestry's creator gets our string through the grind. The string we observe is creating space to hand in hand.

CHAPTER 11

SECOND THOUGHTS, ONE LADY IN THE NIGHT AND AN EARLY BEGINNING TO AN END

The 5 freeway is a hot road through the interior valley of California in the middle of July. Making their way to Moraga, Frank and a three month pregnant Linda were glad to be in an air conditioned car. Clicking off Bakersfield, Fresno, San Jose, the ride was quiet, the two didn't talk much. He was wired with thoughts on challenges to be faced in just five short days. Linda was apprehensive that he might bail on the plan and not follow through. She was holding her breath just hoping to make it to 'check in' at Duffy's.

Arriving in Moraga at about dusk, the two silent weary travelers were greeted warmly by Cindy and Jimmy. Quickly pairing off, Jim took Frank aside to see how he was doing; Cindy probed gently into Linda's state of mind. The two men smoked a little herb together and Frank shared his thoughts and fears. Jim tried to reassure him he was going to be alright. He really respected Jimmy, always had, so he listened. Jimmy looked like Paul McCartney, played guitar exceptionally well, and had a soft demeanor. Perfect for Cindy, and Frank valued his insights regarding the world in which they lived. However on the subject of addiction recovery, Jimmy had to admit the subject was not his forte. Nevertheless Jimmy offered total support.

The group enjoyed a great barbecue; Frank managed to keep his beer intake down to reasonable, despite feeling he was in deep shit. The dinner conversation was about anything but recovery programs. It seems everyone was on the edge of their seats in regards to his commitment. Even Frank! Especially Frank! Second thoughts did creep into his thinking process from time to time; he never said anything to Linda about those spasms of fear. On a lighter note, plans made at dinner to visit the City the following day to lunch and sightsee managed to ease the tension somewhat. They planned to take the new Bart train from Orinda station to the Embarcadero, browse Fisherman's Wharf and lunch downtown at Jimmy's favorite Japanese restaurant.

All rising and readying for a fun trip into San Francisco was overshadowed terribly by Frank's tense demeanor. After sharing some cannabis to take the edge off they headed out for the Orinda station platform. The sleek train arrived with the group choosing the front unit to ride in, the view over the engineer's shoulder was the best view by far. Frank and Jimmy talked about the programming of system operations as they watched the operator guide the train of coaches from stop to stop. Jimmy was proud of his involvement in the programming that made the system work. Frank was secretly proud he hadn't had a drink to calm his nerves yet. His 'program' kept resonating with the pending bending, able to facilitate change that could put him back on track.

He forgot all about the pending doom of the recovery program as the train approached to shoot the tube under the SF Bay. He wondered why anyone in their right mind would build a tunnel under the Bay, knowing the geologic sensitivity of the area. As the train dropped in, the speed accelerated and so did his heart rate. He lifted up a quick request to Grace to hold off on any tectonic movement for the next few minutes. Reaching the bottom of the decent, the train leveled out and he watched the LED readout of speed climb to 72 miles per hour as the train rocketed toward San Francisco. Lifting up and out to be greeted by sunshine, he breathed a heavy sigh of relief. He also had the thought that a good shot of whiskey might taste real good about now. Anything would do to settle the nerves that were beginning to fray.

Sunny San Francisco is always a pleasure. Bouncing from site to site brought back a lot of childhood memories for Frank. He was amazed at the changes in Fisherman's Wharf since the early 60s when he had visited often with his grandparents. His otherwise pleasant visit around the town was being interrupted more and more by agitating thoughts though. The unknown territory of not ever drinking again was to be encountered in a few short days. His brain was having a difficult time trying to imagine seeing the world from sober eyes....forever! His nerves were fried. His withdrawal from conversation was a signal to the others that something was up. Nobody wanted to suggest a drink, but they knew he was craving one. By the time they arrived at the restaurant for lunch he was mute to the outside world. The virtual world of trying to guess the future's outcome swirled in his brain like a witches brew. His mind kept saying to him metaphorically that the world of a man with a broken leg and no crutches for support was going to be a cold place.

As they were seated he was only able to refocus into reality long enough to order a Tsing Tao beer. The numb hum of agonizing over the unknown was gradually replaced by the restaurants reality of muffled conversations mixed with the ting of utensils tapping porcelain plates. Barely back in reality he poured a glass from the bottle of beer that had arrived. He lifted and drank from the glass deeply, but in a dignified manner. This was a top of the line fine dining establishment and guzzling beer was not part of the ambience. Linda, Cindy and Jimmy only wished this wasn't the start.

The party ordered from their server who was dressed in pressed black pants, jacket with tails, starched white shirt and white linen gloves. Really 'uppity up' Frank thought. Rather tense conversation followed as the rest of the group felt his demeanor was about to change. The first course arrived and as they prepared to dine Linda asked if there was any ketchup. Frank responded rudely abrupt, "In this kind of place they probably don't even know what ketchup is," then ordered, "Don't even ask."

He continued offering thought that such a request might go so far as to be considered an insult by the staff. Linda inquired anyway. The staff person winced in misunderstanding then bent slightly to Linda in an attempt to clarify her request. The waiter unable to understand the request left to seek help from other English speaking staff. The fuse was lit; all Frank did for a moment was stare at Linda in disbelief. His whole life for the past week had been orchestrated by others. Now a direct request had been disregarded. He exploded. Taking two twenty dollar bills from his pocket, he threw them on the table telling Jimmy, "That's for lunch." Standing up so fast he knocked the chair he had been sitting in to the ground while announcing very loudly, "You bitch!" he turned and stormed from the restaurant.

First stop, a bar for a well whiskey and draft then up the hill to China-town and another bar. Jim Beam straight up and another draft and Frank settled in for some serious medication. He switched to Wild Turkey for a few more doses prior to leaving. He then headed out to find a bowl of good Chinese noodles before the good part of the buzz kicked in.

The large amount of alcohol consumed on an empty stomach was having the desired effect. Finding an open courtyard off an alleyway off the beaten path, he sat down to his bowl of steaming noodles. This vantage point gave him a good view of the oriental culture that unfolded before him in the high rise buildings that surrounded the open space where he rested. Mild stupor was settling in on his brain as he viewed and listened. Odd smells wafting by thick with spice. Every window seemed to display color, every balcony having laundry hanging to dry. A small car being driven down the alley between a telephone pole and a metal gas meter guard pole getting stuck drew his attention.

This comedy of the car soon had a crowd of young men. He watched as they tried to maneuver the car out of its precariously tight position. Failed attempts brought the sing song of their Asian language to fevered tempo and pitch as their arms flailed directions to one another while scurrying about the vehicle. This amounted to free entertainment for Frank; he chuckled as he watched the little Chinamen's frantic attempts to dislodge the car.

Frank set his bowl down, got up and went to survey the situation. After seeing the car was less than an inch from the steel pole, he offered his summation of the situation to the only one who could speak English. He suggested that if they wanted to proceed forward they would have to pick the front end of the car up and move it over a few inches toward the telephone pole. Otherwise he explained, the cars angle would surely cause scrapping of the rear quarter panel. Offering to assist, he positioned himself at the front bumper and the group followed suit.

"One, two, three, go" he directed and nothing happened except his exertion. His nuts just about hit the ground. It took him a second or two to recover. He then tried to initiate another go at coordinating the group. The second cadence count to go and they all got it, despite the language barrier. The car moved an inch. Two more lifts and the driver was able to free the car from its predicament.

With gestures of "thank you" the young men piled back into the car smiling, teeth beaming their success. Frank too smiled back with a big whiskey grin, but his grin was generated by the thought he had just participated in a real Chinese fire drill. Great fun he thought, now off to another bar to celebrate. He forgot all about his bowl of noodles.

A time gap in memory ensued and he found himself down on Broadway in the X-rated district. Fully buzzed he wandered from shop to shop enjoying the decadence. Door barkers at the numerous bawdy strip bars and sex shows tantalized interests, he eventually entered one. The two drink minimum at twenty bucks a piece and poor show soon had him back out the door. As night fell and the lights of the City began to glow his buzz was beginning to dim. He took up a seat on the steps of a building to watch the blur go by when a voice from his left seemed to be addressing him. Turning he discovered a cute, petite brunette all of 21 or so sitting just up the steps and behind him. "Where had she come from?" his brain flashed.

"Are you talking to me?" he asked.

"Yeah," she responded matter-of-factly.

"Are you looking for a party?" she asked with a questioning stare.

What? She couldn't be a hooker he thought, so he asked.

"Are you a hooker?" blurted out of his dumbfounded mouth.

"What are you a cop?" she shot back in question.

"No," he said.

"Good, let's party" she offered up almost joyously. "What the fuck is happening?" he mussed to himself. "Have I just been propositioned by a party angel?" crossed his mind. This would be a first! He had thought about paying for it before, he had just never had the opportunity.

Details get sketchy, but bottom line Frank ends up somewhere in the City in a hotel room being undressed by the soon to be naked little nymph. The flashing neon light outside only accentuated the unreal surreal scene inside, adding pale blue strobes of light as the little fox devoured her prey. Any request was granted...for a price. Amazing feats of sexual prowess performed for the pleasure of both, generated sweet tones of ecstasy from the two one-time lovers. No rush to finish as the passion of the flesh played out. It was an amazing gift of erotica between two strangers. The business of their arrangement long forgotten in leisurely after glow conversation that followed.

"What time is it anyway?" He sighed.

"Ten-forty" she responded as she watched him dress from the comfort of her pillow.

"Do you know what time the next BART leaves going towards Orinda?" he asked of the little vixen.

"BART...BART shuts down at 11:00" she said, startled that he didn't know!

Panic gripped him as he realized three things. One, he had no idea where he was in relation to any BART station – lost! Two, he had spent the entire $200 in his pocket, most of it gladly given to the passionate little play thing – no cash to buy a ticket! And three, no wallet full of credit cards, he had left it in his wife's purse – you're screwed...no way home. All this information forced Frank to sit down on the edge of the bed, head hung in dumbed disbelief.

"Man, I've got a problem." he said turning towards her with a stunned look on his face!

"What's wrong," she asked as she drew herself closer, kneeling in front of him in all her naked glory. With quite some embarrassment he laid out his plight as quickly as he could; hoping for mercy, pity...something. He swallowed his pride and asked,

"Do you think I could borrow enough cash for a BART ticket from you?"

Her hands shot to her mouth to hide the smile that peeled across her lips. Her eyes twinkled in glee as she reclined backwards onto the pillow, her soft shoulders twitching the laughter that her hands held back. She pulled her hands down and tried to speak,

"What... what you need to borrow money from me?" she stammered.

Frank's eyes locked on hers, pleading for mercy.

"Sure, sure" she said as she rolled slightly to retrieve her purse from the night stand. "How much do you need?" she asked.

"I think about six bucks" he responded with relief washing over his face.

She giggled a bit as she looked down into her purse. Extracting fifteen dollars she proclaimed with the sweetest of smiles,

"Here, I had a really good time" and handed the money to him.

Frank thanked her profusely.   Agreeing it had been an incredible encounter as he finished dressing. Receiving quick directions, he then took her face in his hands and lifted it gently so their eyes could meet one last time. His deep sincere look said he was going to remember this experience for the rest of his life. He bent, kissed her softly on the forehead and whispered,

"You're incredible, thank you."

Reaching and opening the door he turned around one last time, drinking in her naked magnificence kneeling at the end of the bed. He didn't want to leave but he had to go. They each raised a hand in farewell, bidding good bye simultaneously. He shut the door quietly, then realized as he dashed down the hall to the outside world that he never asked her name. Nor she his.

Hitting the deserted street lined with fog shrouded high rise buildings that were not familiar, his brain struggled to recall and follow the directions the angel of adultery had given. Somehow he found the BART station. 10:52pm the clock read. He hoped he wasn't too late. Purchasing a ticket with the money he had borrowed he entered the deserted underground train platform. The robot like voice that echoed over the loud speaker announced the arrival of an incoming train. "I'll be go to hell" he said with relief under his breath, the train was headed in the right direction. He might just make it home that night.

Exiting the train in Orinda he set about finding a ride towards Cindy's house. It was a long walk if he couldn't hitch a ride. Traffic was nil but occasionally a car passed going his direction, yet no takers for the outstretched thumb attached to the stumbling. Finally snagging a ride from a kind soul that was about as inebriated as he, he arrived to a darkened house well after all had retired. He had to knock to arouse the sleeping household, and a check of his civility was done before access was granted. He assured everyone that he was under control. Few words were spoken before retiring, and he slept that night very distant from his wife.

The following morning the household was on pins and needles as he emerged from the bedroom. Was he bailing on the recovery plan or not was the question to be answered. During the course of the day they learned that he was still willing to follow through at least right now. Side bar pow wows between Jimmy, Cindy and Linda had them asking the question whether or not they should wait three more days before checking him in. A call was made and a confirmation given that an early check in could be done. Now all they had to do was to convince him to go early. With cunning maneuvering the brain power of three managed to plant the seed of an early start to the rest of his life. Early in, means early done they reasoned for him. That rationale worked to their favor. The shock of Frank agreeing caught them all by surprise. He had one stipulation to which they reluctantly agreed; he required a fifth of Wild Turkey for the ride to Calistoga. ...Go figure!

The next morning at about 11:00 he entered Cindy's car with a fifth in hand and suitcase in the trunk. Cindy drove, Linda rode shotgun, and Frank in the back, Jimmy was off to work. Cindy and Linda prayed to make the two hour ride without loosing the maniac in the back of the car. He was in rare form as they approached Napa Valley. Then it dawned on him, Calistoga was in the middle of Napa Valley. A little slow, but then he yelled from the back seat,

"How fucked up is that? I'm going to a place to dry out in the middle of wine country!"

He had polished off about half of the bottle and his blood was boiling. Cindy and Linda prayed harder.

Reaching St. Helena he began to get aggressive. He stated in no uncertain terms a second demand, overtones indicating that if not granted he might just call the whole thing off. Cindy and Linda reluctantly agreed and prayed even harder. The girls did not want to stop the car, but had to, to satisfy his demand. Pulling into Christian Brothers Winery parking lot the girl's worst fear set in, "if we let him out will we ever get him back in?" Rolling to a stop in front of the wine tasting room they resigned themselves, each asking privately to themselves, "Oh God help us."

Grace prevailed. Frank's Uncle Laurence had been a friar at the winery through the 60s. He wanted to stop, revisit, taste some wine and select a few for purchase. Mementos for his parents he claimed. "Sure!" the girls thought. "Stash for after getting out," they suspected. He did reluctantly reenter the vehicle to resume the journey. As the door shut behind him he knew it was now or never if he wanted to bail. He stayed in his seat and sank into quiet desperation, swigging generously from time to time from the Wild Turkey clutched securely in hand. The girls silently wondered if Duffy's would accept him in his drunken state. Fear was growing that they might have to keep him! They prayed even harder.

Intensity grew making Cindy stiffen. The car careened down the road as Cindy's foot involuntarily pressed down on the gas.

"Hey, slow down. What's your hurry." he yelled from the back seat, shattering the silence which released the muscle spasm push that gripped Cindy's power foot. Reduction of speed soothed the beast in the back as they wound their way through downtown Calistoga. The left turn by the airport put them on the home stretch and the speed increased as intensity increased. They rocketed the last two miles.

Cindy had to brake the car sharply in order to make the turn into the driveway of Duffy's. Frank swore they were in a four-wheel drift as they rounded onto the dirt road entrance. The maneuver was so abrupt that he ended up lying on his side. Cindy locked up the breaks, skidding to a stop in front of the facility's main reception building, rolling Frank to the floor.

Cindy stayed in the car with Frank as Linda exited. Linda's near panic state was calmed when told that 'yes' they would accept the mangled package they bore in the back of their car. Two husky gentlemen accompanied Linda back out to the car to assist in coaxing the removal of the drunk on the floor. Still reclining on his elbow he looked out as the door opened, focusing beyond the trio and onto the building's front porch. Rocking chairs on the porch full of people rocking back and forth were his first visuals of Duffy's. Must have been twenty or more rocking rockers framing the entrance of the building.

"This must be hell." he thought as he now became aware of the outstretched hands offering help out. He hesitated for a moment, looking down at the almost finished bottle he held in his hand. "This is it. This is for my marriage. This is for my child. This is for me." he surrendered to himself and laid the bottle down.

Climbing out of the car, refusing the assistance, he staggered a bit then stood tall. He hugged and kissed his wife, hugged Cindy, picked up his bag and said,

"I'll see you in a week" then walked away.

That was it. He was here. Now the real work could begin.

~~~~

The tapestry's string woven to a point of fray, not sure of intended course. The weaver's hand indulges a winding course knowing the path will straighten after the last hurrah of addicted self. The final days of colorful lusting for self indulgence brought to an early end by surrender.

CHAPTER 12

SURRENDER INTO THE POTTERS CLAY

After check-in at Duffy's, including an initial evaluation, Frank was escorted to his temporary accommodations in a building having a dorm-like setting adjacent to the main gathering hall.

"Four hundred dollars for this" he scoffed.

"I had a better room two nights ago for a lot less" he said out loud as his agitation was beginning to show. Shown where he could rest, he threw his bag on the bed. An invite to come and meet some of the others was met with resistance, indicating he only wanted to rest. The two fellas that provided escort said no problem they would return in about an hour and a half to get him for dinner. He scowled,

"I'll probably sleep through dinner." The men smiled and left.

He awoke to hear someone speaking his name while shaking his shoulder. Not wanting to be awakened he told them to go away rather rudely. They said they would when he got up for dinner. Pissed off, he shot up out of bed and demanded to know why he had to go to dinner.

"It is the rules," one man explained.

"Fuck the rules!" Frank snorted.

Finally able to calm him, they eventually got him to go along with the program for the moment. He reluctantly put his shoes on and followed, telling himself the only reason he did so was so he might quench his terrible thirst.

Entering into the main building was a scene. The porch was still occupied by all the rocking people and inside was full as well. Not rockers, but big plush couches and chairs full of people. Escorted through the massive living room and through the ornate double pocket doors on the opposite side, he was shown the dining hall. At that point he was told that he should get to know some of the other people; dinner would be announced in about half an hour. After asking if he had any questions, he indicated he didn't, they left him alone. He had forgotten he was thirsty.

"Okay here we go," he thought as he surveyed the room. Numb from the booze and groggy from the sleep, he was in no mood for conversation. Visual inspection was good enough for now as he worked his way toward the front door. Scanning the crowd he noticed the diversity. There were young, old, angry, happy, quiet, loud; what a mix. Looked kind of like a bar scene, glasses of liquid in hands of those that casually chatted, the haze of tobacco smoke hung thick in the air. Then an astounding sight; a gal with a tray full of drinks appeared from a side hallway. She looked like a damn cocktail waitress. He watched as she searched out certain individuals then handed them a drink. That looked good as he remembered his thirst. But what the hell was going on? This was getting more bizarre by the moment and he made a beeline for the outdoors to catch a breath of fresh air.

Popping through the front door he made his way to the porch railing. Taking a deep breath he tried to comprehend all the visual information that was contradictory to his impression of a recovery program. This wasn't making sense and he turned his attention to the scene on the front porch. Huge covered porch, 10x50 at least he figured. The vista was impressive. Scattered buildings on a manicured plot of ground with jutting mountains in the background, very nice he thought. He then looked down the row of rockers rocking and shook his head. Every rocker had a body rocking back and forth. Must be a slow life here he assumed. Right then the 'cocktail waitress' appeared from the front door with one full drink still on her tray.

"Frank, Frank Lindsay." she called, while searching the crowd for acknowledgement.

"Yeah, that's me," he reported, now even more confused.

"Yeah Frank I have your drink" she announced as she approached.

"What, what drink... I didn't order a drink... I'm here to quit... what is this?" He rolled out in one continuous question.

"It's a Hummer and it's for you," she answered.

"What's a Hummer, what's in it?" he demanded.

"Whiskey and water." she responded.

"I'm here to quit. I don't want it" he retorted with a wrinkled befuddled look on his face.

"It's okay, everyone gets one when they first arrive." she consoled.

"I don't want it. Take it back," he demanded.

"No, it's okay. Everyone who arrives intoxicated gets one. It's to help you detox slowly."

"This one is for you." she repeated.

"I don't want it. Give it to someone else." his response now showing agitation at her persistence. He noticed that all the rockers had stopped rocking and all eyes were all fixed on his exchange with the 'waitress'.

"Please just take it," she pleaded.

Fed up with endless bicker, he picked up the glass and emptied it onto a bush on the side of the porch.

"There you go!" he said returning the glass to the 'waitress' tray.

She turned without responding and walked away.

Frank noticed as he had emptied the glass that a half dozen of the people sitting in the rockers lurched forward slightly as the drink emptied onto the bush. "Were they that desperate?" he wondered. "Will I be that way too?" shot fear into his mind. It was fixed in his mind that his program had started. By throwing that drink out he'd also thrown out the self that now knew to surrender. Surrender self and become the clay to be molded. No more drinking, that's it! He hoped desperation could be controlled. He wasn't sure, but he knew he'd soon know. Fear had to be met head on.

He threw himself headlong into the program. The twelve step guided program was met with very little resistance on his part. The AA stigma quickly transformed into the AA family. The tremendous amount to learn in a week had to last a lifetime. From time to time he ran into those individuals that stated, "A week at Duffy's won't be enough for a guy like you," adding, "You'll be back." This served only to solidify his resolve for success. The Grace of reconnection with a Higher Power served as the rock for him to draw that strength from. He opened up with honesty about his affliction. When the time was right his tales into the abyss provided insights for others to draw from. He mostly listened though. The depth and horror of the abyss was relived time after time as others recounted their stories. A lot was to be learned from listening. Many tales went far into the reaches of the abyss, none going quite as far as he had been, so he decided not to open the door to the worst of the worst. That demon stayed locked away as he had already experienced the unpredictable reactions that story could produce. That honesty might only cause pain. Locked away the only pain it could inflict was to be to him in the form of 'What If.'

The days marched by structured and confined to the twenty or so acres the old estate occupied. Contact with the outside world was strictly forbidden. Towards the end of his week long stay he was allowed a single phone call to his wife. He asked her to assist him in gaining required information on the nearest locations and times of AA meetings. He then tried to convey the elation he felt from the progress he had made. He was feeling confident, but Linda wasn't. Her tone of 'seeing is believing' was not the emotion he was expecting. He was filled with remorse that he had destroyed Linda's trust in him so completely; it was futile to try and convince her otherwise over the phone. He told Linda several times how much he missed and loved her before hanging up. Feeling alone, he wept alone.

The thirty meetings in thirty days mantra loomed large the final two days at Duffy's. It was just one of many tasks to practice on the road to recovery, probably the most important though. Fear of the outside world, away from the safe supportive family at Duffy's, also loomed large. He knew the key to survival was to find a family 'out there'. 'Out there' was coming soon.

When Cindy and Linda came to retrieve Frank on checkout day, they had no idea what they might find. Phone conversations with staff members gave some hope for continued progress. Staff had done what they could with just a week to work with. The two girls knew it would be a miracle if he could make it for a week on the outside 'sober'. Shit, they hoped he could make it one day. Truth is so did Frank. All the hard work was about to be tested.

When the women arrived at Duffy's they pulled in much slower than the first time they had arrived. Seeing the girls' pensive faces peering through the windshield, searching the crowded front porch looking for any sign of him, revealed they were more than a little uneasy. They didn't see him right away. When the visual search ended they had found him sitting in a rocker gently rocking, smiling a hello as eyes made contact. Rising, he walked down the steps and hugged welcome to both. Extra special warmth and love flowed through the hug he gave to his wife. Linda felt it! Cindy felt it! So did half the crowd seated in their rockers rocking. The trio walked up the steps to meet with staff and Frank was pelted with encouragement from several he had befriended that stood amongst the crowd.

"That a boy Frank!" "We're going to miss you man!" "Good luck buddy!" On and on through the living room and into the office to check out, his pending departure was acknowledged with encouragement. He had made a lot of friends in a very short time and they wished him well on his journey because his light had touched theirs. Linda could feel it! Cindy could feel it! Even Frank felt it! Hope was in the air. By Grace the road to recovery had started.

~~~~

We all are given second chances as we weave our way. How we approach them is choice. When we surrender to change we find we can do our best work for the greater good of the tapestry we are all involved in creating. The string we follow is gifted by Grace through surrender, another chance to light up the colors he was meant to radiate. Just how he shines is choice.

CHAPTER 13

RETURNING PEACE TO SLEEP

Pulling out of the driveway of Duffy's, Frank looked back one last time. The safety net was disappearing out of the rear window and a jolt of aloneness swept over him. It lasted only a moment as he returned his attention to Linda and Cindy. Conversation was light. Cindy and Linda were feeling him out for hints of stability. He was feeling Linda and Cindy out for hints of reestablished trust. The apprehensiveness of being out on his own was keeping his verbosity fairly muted at this point.

He was doing okay until they got to Napa. As they left the city limits a huge roadside billboard stuck a knife in his heart. Visually filling the entire passenger window it read, "Go Wild! Wild Turkey" with a full color picture of a full bottle of his favorite elixir. Hit him so hard he could taste it. "Boy, that's fucked up," he murmured to himself. He needed a meeting and he needed it now! Making a joke with the girls at what he had just seen helped stifle his first test against craving. He was only an hour out! How many times a day was he to be tested? Unsettling was an understatement.

Back at the house in Moraga he readied to go to his first 'outside' AA meeting. The girls brought Jimmy up to speed on what they thought; they did express a glimmer of hope. The girls had prepared a schedule of meetings and directions to each location. He had chosen to go immediately to one that was about to start at a bank building nearby. Jimmy, Cindy and Linda were amazed by his choice to go so soon to a meeting, they had not expected that. Shoot, they really did not know what to expect. He left vowing to return 'sober' in a couple of hours. They all prayed he could.

He found the bank parking lot. Pulling in he noticed a parking lot filled with nothing but high dollar cars. He wondered if he was in the right place. Porsche, Mercedes, Jaguar, Corvettes, etc... this couldn't have been the parking lot for the drunks anyway. He parked well away from the wealth and began the search for the right room. He found an open door that read "meeting room" stenciled in gold, walked through and immediately knew he was in the wrong place. The high back plush leather seats that surrounded the massive boardroom table were not AA sanctioned seating he concluded. The men seated in the chairs had fifty-dollar hair cuts and though casually dressed he figured it was an after hours bank meeting.

"Oh sorry," he said as he turned to leave.

"Can we help you?" said a voice from the head of the table.

"No, I think I have the wrong place." he said, almost out the door.

"What are you looking for," persisted the white-haired man seated at the head of the table. "Oh Shit," he thought, "I don't want to have to tell him I'm looking for a low life AA meeting." He was trapped by a direct question that demanded an answer. He could have been rude and just kept going. But he didn't.

"I'mmm... looking for the AA meeting." he stammered while trying to swallow his pride and hide his embarrassment.

"You're here," shot the commanding voice with white hair.

"Come on in and sit down we're just about to get started." the white-haired man beckoned. Frank about shit! Stopping him dead in his tracks in disbelief, he practically had to close his mouth with his hand.

"Who are these guys?" Frank wondered as he settled into one of the plush chairs. He felt like a little kid as the chair swallowed him. The smell of fine leather filled his nostrils. The crunching sound of leather made him feel important. "Who are these guys anyway?" he asked himself again. He soon found out. Doctors, lawyers, bankers and he was sure there was an Indian chief somewhere in the room. Power People! They all had one thing in common, they were all sick and needed help. Welcome to AA.

His first AA meeting was an incredible adventure. The movers and shakers had accepted who he was and offered him help in any way they could. Help given away at no cost, no strings attached with only one request: just don't drink. His mission became so much clearer in that one meeting. The strength they helped him to realize dashed the fear of beginning his recovery on the 'outside'. The men shared their family. He thanked them for their insights, regretful he might never see them again. "What a bitch'n way to start" he thought. Leaving energized he rushed home to tell his story of his first AA meeting sober! Sober, and that felt free. His excitement spilled over to the trio awaiting his return. They saw the change in his face and heard it in his voice. They shared a late supper filled with laughter and light heartedness. Retiring to bed Frank held Linda in bliss. He saw hope glimmer in her eyes as she felt the returning of the man she loved. They all slept peacefully that night for the first in a long while.

Jimmy and Frank arose first the next morning. Jimmy headed out to work, Frank settled in with coffee on the veranda to read his Big Book he had won at Duffy's on bingo night. The girls slept in, they needed it. When they awoke he served them coffee. They chatted about the activities of the day. The girls included him in their destinations, not wanting to leave him home alone. His only request was a dip in the pool at the clubhouse and an AA meeting at some point. The trip to the pool was first.

The water felt good as he did a few laps in the Olympic size pool. To test endurance he did a couple of laps underwater. Using the diving boards provided some thrills. Hopping out he joined Linda for some poolside sun. The L-shaped pool was large with a lot of deck all around. The diving board area was quiet, at the far end away from the lifeguard shack and snack bar. He and Linda sat at the diving area and talked uninterrupted by the kids at the other end of the pool. As they chatted he occasionally scanned the pool as old lifeguard skills and habits die hard. It felt good that he and Linda had alone time. He felt as if he was introducing a whole new person to his gorgeous wife. Linda seemed to have the same giddy excitement of meeting a new handsome hunk for the first time. The conversation felt connected, alive and full of hope.

Suddenly, queerly, Frank sensed panic. Not his or Linda's, but panic coming from somewhere within the pool. He could smell it. Shooting up out of his chair, he turned to face the pool. Scanning for the source of the adrenaline emitted by someone in a life or death struggle, he inventoried the pool and surrounding deck. Instantly he spotted a young lady just off the end of the diving board at the deep end who was in the throws of panicked thrashing trying to keep her head above the waters surface. Her wild fight for survival couldn't be seen by the lifeguard standing on the deck, talking to someone at the other end of the pool. The lifeguard hadn't yet sensed the adrenaline the young lady emitted. Frank broke into a sprint towards the distressed girl. The eyes of her smaller companion, standing petrified at the pools edge, met his begging for help. Linda shouted, "What's wrong?" as she sensed the immediacy in his actions. He didn't answer.

From a full run, he broke a cardinal rule of lifesaving by diving into the water without first looking for a land based rescue device. He then surfaced at the distressed girl's side. Grabbing her wrist firmly, he pulled up to prevent her head from sinking below the surface again. She gasped for air. He pulled her to the side of the pool and gave her support as she coughed, choking up and out the water that she had swallowed. Her companion and Linda were at their side in seconds inquiring if she was all right. The young Asian girl was shaken but okay. He waited until she had regained a normal breathing rhythm. He stayed by her side until he determined she had regained enough composure, then helped her from the pool, adding a cautioning word to her about the deep end. The young lady and her friend thanked him for the assistance.

Frank had only rescued two people in his short career as a lifeguard. This was number three and he wasn't officially on duty. ...Or was he? After all, aren't we all on duty for one another as we journey through life... sober? Linda wanted to know how he knew that she was in trouble so quickly; she had not realized it until it was almost over. He couldn't really explain it. "It was just a sense that you develop after hours of watching out for folks at a pool." he stated trying to explain the phenomenon. Linda beamed at her hero. He had showed a side of himself she had never seen. It made her feel proud and safe, made him feel pretty good too. This is who he really was and he was back. The talk at dinner that night was full of accolades for what he had done. He admitted to having done nothing special.

Cindy and Jimmy were thanked for all their help, hospitality and patience over the previous two weeks. The trip that was to mark his start to recovery might not have been possible without the Grace of their love and support. He and Linda were eternally grateful. Frank hit another AA meeting that night, returning home to fall romantically into bed with his wife. They all slept again in peace, especially the mother-to-be that now had a restored confidence in the man she had married. He and Linda left to return home to Corona the following morning. They were to return to the Bay area several times over the next couple of years to see their dear 'City' friends.

~~~~

We are all able to shine; when we do we all can do anything. When we do, we all benefit. All we have to do is weave our string into the tapestry, shining with a heart of Grace. Then we all sleep in peace.

CHAPTER 14

CREATING CHILD BORN

By mid August Frank had thirty days of sobriety under his belt. He was awarded a 30 day chip as a token of his accomplishment from his nightly AA meeting group. The group in Corona was a diverse cross section of society much like the group experienced at Duffy's. From the former Mayor of the city to the farm laborer along with the court's appointments, a group he hadn't encountered at Duff's. The court-appointed attendees were always a super unhappy lot. Unlike Duff's, the court-ordered were not there on their own volition and they brought a whole different energy he found interesting. Like Duffy's, the group had become his safe haven from the pressures that might lead him to drink. Every meeting had something of value for him to hear, even if he had not wanted to attend. It was an every day of the week job to stay off the sauce, at times a minute-to-minute struggle.

His work environment had become his biggest challenge; all of his friends had been drinking buddies too. The nightly offers to buy him a beer at the hangout next door tested his resolve. One old timer at Duffy's had revealed his key to successfully overcoming the desire that an invite like that would elicit. He would simply say, "Not right now thanks, maybe later." Frank had found great value in that single response needed to resist the temptation. He used that response a billion times in the effort to stay the course.

By mid September he received a 60-day chip for sobriety, which at times was hung on to only by Grace. He had not divulged to his buddies at work the true nature of his avoidance of their nightly requests. Yet his good friend, breakfast partner Lou Paul had his suspicions and asked him what was up. Responding, he revealed for the first time that he was an alcoholic to someone outside the program. Friends stick around no matter what and Lou did. The information Lou passed on to others quietly trickled down, and up, and soon the invites for drinks ceased.

He was finding the road of recovery a morphing challenge, with increasing periods of serenity between shortening periods of suffering. Linda was in utter disbelief as day after day ended with a sober husband. She never knew the intensity of the struggle. Day to day encounters with near disasters was not recounted by Frank in the nightly rundown of the daily activities. His daily victories he did share, so Linda too could feel the success of their cooperative effort. He wanted to keep it that way; her pregnancy was doing well and showing big by mid October. Linda's trust in her husband was growing.

Any negative energy was left at the AA meetings he attended. The 90-day chip felt sweet and he set his sights on six months.

The extra stress of being forced to move, the house they were in had been sold, was handled well. He didn't crumble when told they had to move. Moving was something he really didn't like doing. Linda found a cute, much newer house up the hill in Corona, and move in was complete by early November. This was to be the house they were to bring their new child home to. Linda's passion became the design and preparation of the nursery. 'Dad to be' looked for something special to do for that nursery as well.

Boy or girl they did not know, the ultrasounds never revealed the baby's gender. Linda was being told by everyone it was probably to be a boy. Her mother, her doctor, her sister, they all thought for one reason or another that the child would be a boy. Frank was on the fence in that matter. He really didn't care one way or the other as long as the baby was healthy. His gift for the baby was to create a wooden baby cradle, which the child one day could be proud to pass down as an heirloom. It had to be of special design and the highest quality wood. This cradle made by his hand was to be his passion for a month and a half prior to the child's birth.

The clarity of sobriety had restored his creativity. The cradle project was bigger than his scope of knowledge in woodworking and he took a risk in enlisting help from Alfred, a friend and former drinking buddy. This was a huge risk, Linda knew it. Frank knew it and tried to quell Linda's reservations as the project got underway. The first few nights he worked at Alfred's, Linda wrestled with anxiety until his sober return. He wrestled as well, fending off Alfred's repeated offers of a cold glass of Port wine. Alfred soon came to understand his resolve and his offers ceased. Frank would work, Alfred would drink and direct. It made for an unusual pair working in a symbiotic relationship to create a very unique piece. Alfred was a master woodworker with all the tools and knowledge to create beautiful furniture. Frank was grateful for his help. Cutting, gluing, clamping, sanding, followed by more cutting, gluing, clamping and sanding. It took two weeks to prepare the knotless white oak stock for assembly.

The cradle design they came up with was a cross between Pennsylvania Dutch and Amish. Plain, functional, elegant. The angled sides of the cradle were twelve inches deep at the foot of the bed. Two thirds of the way to the head of the cradle started the graceful curve of the side. The curve rose twelve inches which provided the perch for the rounded top to sit. The graceful curved top with its four inch overhang all around was the crown to the gem of workmanship. The cradle rockers with a rounded ball foot on either side provided a smooth soothing rocking motion from side to side. The assembly completed, the seemingly endless hours of finish sanding began. A labor of love for Frank, he worked nightly after meetings as time drew near for Linda's delivery.

In early December the cradle was finished in a golden oak stain and brought home for Linda to see for the first time. She was astounded by the work. With motherly approval she had him place the cradle in their bedroom, on her side of the bed. Linda arranged Cindy's handmade bedding and bumpers inside and they fit perfectly. The loving detail provided by Cindy added the perfect warmth to the security of the solid oak. The last detail to the perfect piece was to be the baby.

Linda said she didn't care, boy or girl; she was going to be thrilled either way. One day out of curiosity 'Dad to be' asked if she'd like to try an old folksy ritual that was touted to be a sure fire way to reveal the sex of an unborn child. Having fun she was up for, participating in an old wives' tale... couldn't hurt. "Sure, why not. What do we do," Linda gamed. He helped her lay down on her back on the floor in the warm sunshine. Tying a one foot length of string to Linda's wedding ring, he dangled it above her plump ever-so-expectant belly. It was said in days of old, by holding the string with ring perfectly still about three inches over the abdomen it would begin to move on its own. How it moves reveals the sex of the baby, straight line back and forth...boy; around in a circle...girl. They were skeptical, but what fun!

He held the string perfectly still. The wedding ring dangled, sparkling in the sun streaming into and onto the floor where 'Mom-to-be' lay. Both watched intently and the fiery stone began to move. At first, kind of a slow back and forth motion that then morphed into a strong circular pattern. "Girl" he announced, delighting his wife's hidden dream. They laughed, hugged and played that afternoon. Linda was having fun and her husband was sober. Sober Frank was having fun too.

The baby was due on Christmas day by the doctor's calculations. Frank felt it could be sooner. Linda was ready for it just to be over. La Maze class kept them busy preparing for natural child birth. In mid December he agreed to work a Saturday to run a day of water deliveries for his buddy Lou's route. For some reason Lou was behind and Frank could help get Lou caught up, plus make a little extra dough for the soon-to-be-three family. While away he wore a pager for the 'just in case' call of 'baby coming'.

That day was a horrible delivery run; a massive winter storm had descended upon the Los Angeles basin. It was a very cold day with lots of rain, snow level in the mountains down to just 1500 feet. He had to stop at a Laundromat twice that day to dry his clothes and gear. Long day and he drove home after dark in the pounding rain. The warm shower broke the chill, the warm dinner soothed the soul and the sound of the rain put him to sleep early that night. His sleep was restful but attentive. He knew when Linda got up to go to the restroom during the night, he didn't always know when she returned. That night he fell back to deep sleep before Linda had returned from one of her bathroom excursions.

"Oh my God, something's wrong" bolted him to consciousness. Focusing, Frank could see Linda sitting up and trying to inspect the bed sheets. He headed for the lights.

"I can't stop peeing" Linda said as the lights went on.

Groggy assessment revealed Linda's water had broken, that meant the baby was on the way soon. At 2am pre-rehearsed plans worked like a charm except for the rain part. They stayed fairly dry loading into the car just as the sky opened up to pound rain again. They made their way very slowly to Corona's Circle City Hospital. He couldn't help but notice the ferocity of the downhill torrents of water crossing their path on the journey to the hospital. Some intersections had so much runoff that the torrents were able to move rocks the size of volleyballs across their path. Reaching the hospital, the sky finally let up long enough to get the pregnant little mother-to-be inside.

Their shoes squeaked as they walked down the corridor to the admissions desk. At the desk the attendee expressed surprise they had not called ahead. Luck was on their side the Alternative Birthing Center was available. They were directed down a hall and through two double doors to the left, which they were told would put them at the location they needed to be. Dad-to-be thought he had the directions right. In his excited state of 'getter done' not all info was processed with total coherence.... even sober. Frank guided Linda carefully down the hall and through the first set of double doors on the left, which put them in an open-air courtyard. He thought that was odd. Something must be wrong he surmised as he spun to catch the door. Too late, it clicked shut and locked.

"Oh crap!" he said as he headed to the doors on the opposite wall.

"This one better be open or we are in deep shit." he summed up for Linda, he could hear another cloud burst coming. Reaching the doors he grabbed the knob and twisted. Locked!

"Son of a bitch!" shot forth. He had managed to trap himself and the mother-to-be in an outside courtyard at 2something in the morning with the pounding march of another approaching deluge almost upon them. Frantic, he tried again. Locked!

"Damn it!" 2am or not he began to knock very loudly on the door. Desperation set in as the sky opened, he pounded on the door. This was not a good way to gear up for labor he reasoned. His flurried fisting of the doors surface began to drown out the noise made by the pounding rain.

The door was opened by a nurse, finger to lips, shushing him as she questioned,

"What are you trying to do, wake everyone up? People are trying to sleep!"

"Trying to get out of the fucking rain," Frank stated, ushering his wet wife thru the door.

"We were given the wrong directions and trapped by locked doors," he continued in his defense.

"What are you looking for?" the nurse quizzed.

"Maternity. My wife's having a baby." he responded pointing to Linda's protruding stomach.

"Okay you found it, just the wrong door in...follow me," the nurse directed.

During the drive down, Linda had only a few minor contractions and the nurse informed them it might be a while before 'real' labor gets underway. About then a 'real' contraction hit and Linda needed to be peeled off the ceiling. She was taken into the exam room and paperwork started. The part Frank thought was ironic, Linda's personal doctor had left for vacation the day before telling Linda not worry he'd be back in time for the delivery. Frank knew the Doctor's due date estimation was wrong, the bad news was that Linda now had a new doctor attending her first time through labor. Good news from the nurse was that the birthing room was available. More bad news, the attending doctor who was to be doing the delivery was known as the C-section king. "He isn't tolerant of natural child birth because it takes so long," the nurse informed much to the dismay of the parents-to-be.

So the process began. Linda was admitted with the contractions about 20 minutes apart. The two 'almost parents' got down to the business of finding Linda's focal point and breathing pattern that worked to alleviate the discomfort. Between contractions, Frank slipped outside occasionally to call friends and family to inform them of progress. By 6pm that evening he asked if he could go back to the house to feed the dogs and shower. Linda agreed, telling him not to be long. The dash home and back was not quick enough. Linda blasted him upon his return. He should've known. Serious contractions were coming about every ten to fifteen minutes and while he was away Linda had lost her focus. She let him have it hard, both barrels from her shot gunning verbal lambasting. The nurses smiled as they assisted in calming her down. He apologized profusely.

By midnight Linda was exhausted but in control. She was able to doze off occasionally for brief respites as pain subsided, Frank staying right by her side. He was right there encouraging focus and breathing as pain of the new contraction would wake her from the brief reprieve of slumber. When Linda reached a dilation of eight centimeters she was wheeled into the ABC room with husband so close at her side he was almost part of the gurney.

The ABC room was a whole different world from the stark sterile setting of the rest of the hospital. Warm calming earth tones adorned the two large beds, walls, curtains, and rocking chair outfitting the room. Mirrored dressers and artwork on the walls made the room feel as if it was a master bedroom in a high dollar hotel. A very comfortable place to bring in a new life Frank thought as he attended to Linda's refocus in the new surroundings.

At 2am the contractions were coming every four or five minutes. The fetal monitor was in place reporting the baby's condition; Linda was elevated into birthing position. Linda's mom and her entourage waited for word down the hall. The contractions were coming even faster as Dr. C-section King made his grand entrance. Demanding his stool while berating the lack of room to work, he positioned himself between Linda's gaping legs. As he scooted up close another severe contraction spasmed through Linda's body. Groaning hard, she defecated causing the doctor to retreat backwards on his rolling stool. Not the welcoming Dr. C-section King had wanted and this set him off even more.

"Clean that up," he demanded.

"Wasn't she given a suppository?" he growled.

"Yes sir." one of the nurses responded.

A quick clean up and Dr. 'I don't have time' moved back in for inspection. Linda had felt what had happened, she and Frank tried to contain the humor they saw in the scene.

Over the course of the next half hour the two maintained phenomenal control of the pain that racked Linda's body. They were an in-sync team. The doctor started asking Linda to push as the baby's head was nearing position for final delivery. She pushed with all her might and the doctor would ask for more. After about the fifth or sixth push ordered, the doctor looked up and saw fetal distress indicated on the monitor. Immediately he ordered that Linda be transported to the operating room. Dr. C-section had spoken. Within thirty seconds Linda was being wheeled down the hall in a rush. Her mother gazed troubled from the window of the waiting room. All Frank could do is shrug his shoulders as they passed Pat's ever watchful eye. He was not going to leave Linda's side for a second to explain, Linda needed him close. Once in the operating room, the monitor report showed more stable signs of the baby's condition. Dr. C-section King decided to give Linda one more chance to deliver naturally. An episiotomy was done and again Linda was told to push. She pushed with all her might. One, two, and three more times she pushed, Frank holding her hands and counting out the breathing cadence with each attempt.

"Okay, here we go now push real hard." the Doc sparked up.

"I have been!" Linda screamed back while pushing and emitting guttural noise that sounded like something from a horror movie.

"Here comes the baby," the doc announced and Frank watched as the head emerged.

"Good going," Frank comforted as he returned to coach Linda's next push. One last push and the baby delivered out and into the hands of the doctor.

"It's a healthy baby girl," the Doc announced after quick inspection.

"What?" Linda asked in disbelief?

"It's a baby girl?" Frank stammered in as much disbelief!

Mom looked back at Dad in twisted bewilderment. She had been so convinced it was supposed to be a boy; she could not believe what she was hearing.

"Really?" she questioned.

"Really," the nurse said, as the new baby was held up and shown to Linda. Linda radiated. The pain and pressure gone, normal breathing restored, Linda looked at Frank and said,

"Well, that wasn't so bad."

Frank tried to rationalize what he had just heard Linda say. The hours of agonizing contractions all forgotten as the nurse presented the new baby to her mother. Linda beamed as she inspected the newborn. Frank was handed surgical scissors and shown where to cut the umbilical cord. Both were high as kites from the exhilaration of the birthing event. His focus on his wife's well being through the ordeal was highlighted when Dr. C commented to the nurses that Frank had been "the best damn La Maze coach he had ever seen." The nurses concurred. Linda too agreed and dismissed him to go and inform the anxious family of a perfect birth. He then took a break for nicotine; a celebratory whiskey jolt was only a passing thought.

Linda was returned to the ABC room. Frank met her there with a small portion of family in tow. Pat still didn't believe they had delivered a baby girl and wanted to see for herself. Linda proudly displayed her newborn, glowing as she accepted the crowd's adulation. The family's short stay was curtailed by the attending nurse, who ushered all but Frank reluctantly to the door. The two new parents began their bonding with their new daughter. The attending nurse showed the exhausted couple proper handling procedure for the new bundle of joy.

The biggest question that had not been answered was that of the new baby's name. A name had been chosen months before in the event a girl was to be born, then all but forgotten as 'baby boy' had reverberated in all subsequent baby conversations. Reaffirming their agreement that the name was perfect, they confirmed their choice to the inquisitive nurse. She would be named Elise. Elise Elizabeth Lindsay, to be precise.

Dad was handed his child for the first time. Emotion he had never felt welled from his heart. He rocked gently in the wooden rocker, and touched her face with affectionate awe. He spoke softly to her while cradling her in his arms and as he held the miracle of life, he whispered to her from deep in his heart.

"Hello Elise, its Dad. Welcome to the world."

He lifted up thanks to the Grace that had provided him sobriety, vowing to do his best as a dad as he rocked his baby girl to sleep.

The euphoric energy abounded as the two new parents shared an amazing meal in the comfort of their room. It was not your typical hospital ration, this meal had been specially prepared for them in the hospital's kitchen. With Elise asleep close by, they dined and chatted, glowing in the joy of being new parents. The nurse returned afterward to administer light medication for Linda's discomforts. She returned later to take Elise to the nursery for overnight care so the drained parents could get a good night's rest. Frank made sure Linda had all that she needed before climbing into his bed to retire. He watched as Linda drifted into slumber with a peace etched on her face he had never seen before. He wondered if she realized that two miracles had taken place that day. Two miracles of new life. One was Elise, the other was a sober dad. Linda knew. Her face reflected her gratitude in that peace.

At 6am the following morning Frank was up and ready to go when the nurse returned with Elise. He held Elise and marveled at her full head of dark hair. Elise also had the olive skin of her mother and he guessed the two would look a lot alike. Linda readied for nursing and Dad laid Daughter at her mother's breast, watching as Elise took nutrition. He was amazed at how fast a newborn learns where the food source is and how to retrieve the sustenance. Excusing himself, he left the room to find the administration office to do final paperwork for checkout.

He was directed to the accounting office, a problem with the insurance carrier had been discovered. The staff person pulled up the file and explained that their insurance carrier had refused to pay for the labor and delivery, based on their assumption that Linda was in fact pregnant before coverage had taken affect. Normally he'd have gone ballistic, but he didn't. He was upset with himself for not getting written assurances nine months prior when he thought the timing was suspect. The verbal assurance he received over the phone from the Blue Cross agent could never be proved. Disgusted with the news, he asked a bit indignant,

"How much?"

"Nine hundred seventy one dollars" replied the sympathetic staffer.

He was somewhat relieved, he had envisioned a much larger bill. He opened his wallet and produced a credit card. This episode so incensed him that he vowed to never buy health insurance again. Frank returned to the ABC room in an agitated state. Linda sensed something was wrong and asked. He calmed himself telling her what had transpired as he collected and packed their belongings. Linda remained quiet not wanting to fuel his agitations.

Bags in hand Frank was walking out the door as the nurse entered and inquired,

"Where are you going?"

"Home!" Frank replied matter-of-factly.

"Well, you can't leave yet. I've got to do a birth certificate and the doctor has to sign the release forms," she whined.

"How long will that take?" he snapped.

"Not long, providing the doctor thinks Linda is ready to go," the nurse replied with some authoritative indignity.

"Is there anyway we can speed this up?" Frank asked anxiously.

"I'll see what I can do," the nurse replied with a little compassion.

Frank left to retrieve some more coffee from the cafeteria, returning in time to meet with the doctor. Linda was fine, the doctor commented, then stating he'd send a nurse to the house in a couple of days for a follow up check up. Cleared to go, the nurses took the new baby to the nursery to ready her for the trip home. Linda was placed in a wheelchair for the trip out the front door to the waiting car. Frank had gone outside to position the car for Linda and the baby. He had not been outside for twelve hours and was stunned by what he saw. Returning to Linda he kept to himself the surprise of what awaited outside.

The nurses returned with Elise and a surprise of their own. The nurses presented Elise to her mother all wrapped up snuggly in a giant Christmas stocking! All laughed at the sight of the tiny baby's face peeking out of the way oversized red and white velvet stocking. As they wheeled to the front door, Frank asked how much it might cost to fill that stocking as it hung from the mantel at Christmas time. They all laughed as they speculated at the cost to fill the stocking's three-foot length might easily have taken a months salary. The speculation made the new dad shiver and it wasn't from the chill of winter.

Wheeling into the lobby toward the front doors, the smiles on the faces of all the onlookers added to the festive farewell. Frank and Linda watched for Elise's reaction to her first trip outside as they wheeled through the front door into the crisp air of winter. She grimaced slightly at the blast of chilled air that rushed across her face. Linda gasped at the surprise of the vista that greeted her. A crystal clear sun shiny day that was cool and crisp. Directly across the valley in front of them stood the tall mountains of the LA basin's transverse mountain range, the surprise was the blanket of stark white snow that covered them top to bottom! It was a truly beautiful sight, the likes of which most people living in the basin never see. Snow halfway down those mountains was rare, all the way to the bottom was once in a lifetime.

Bidding a Merry Christmas farewell, the now family of three pulled away to return to their home on Fraser Circle. Their house sat close to the top of the housing development that reached up the flanks of the mountains behind the hospital. Those mountains too were covered in snow. Frank and Linda speculated excitedly if snow would be at the house. Arriving a few minutes later they discovered the snow line was just a couple of hundred feet higher up, but still marveled at the winter wonderland views surrounding their home. Mother Nature had gifted a beautiful welcome home. It was an absolute delight.

The new family sauntered up the walk from the car to the open front door where Pat awaited. Entering to Pat's welcome they soon were engulfed in a tumultuous welcome from the dogs. Frank lifted Elise carefully from Linda's arms and sat on the couch so the dogs could get a better look at the special package they had come home with. All three dogs knew this was something special. Toroko and Blizzard inspected quickly, sniffing carefully, then returned to the floor. Kimmie's inspection was more thorough as she had been a mother five times herself. Kimmie's introduction was culminated with a licking kiss to Elise's forehead. Pat came unglued.

"Get that dog away from her," she demanded.

"Dog germs are not good for babies." she howled!

Frank returned Elise to Linda with no comment on 'dog germs'.

Dad noticed Mom had a shadow from that point on. Kimmie was that shadow. The dog followed Linda wherever she took the baby.

Following an abbreviated feeding the sleeping child was taken to the new cradle in the bedroom. Elise's tiny frame fit with plenty of room to grow. With Elise sleeping soundly, mom and dad returned to chat with "grandmother" Pat and "grandfather" Herb. Kimmie stayed behind. Frank watched from the end of the hall. The dog gently lifted her front legs up onto the cradle railing and peered down at the sleeping baby. Satisfied all was well, the dog lowered herself back down and found a comfortable place to sleep next to the cradle. Kimmie was still there two hours later, not leaving until Elise was gathered up for another feeding. Elise would grow to love that dog, she would cry when Kimmie passed and was buried.

In January the family celebrated four events. New Year's, Frank's birthday, Elise's first month and a six month chip of continuous sobriety for Frank. The year was off to a good start full of positive energy. Elise was beginning to sleep through the night. God really did answer prayers. Frank was a doting dad and he even did diapers. He was never able to convince God that he should be taken off that duty.

That spring Dad and Daughter could be found at the pool at the end of the street. Linda looked on in concern as Frank took Elise into the pool for the first time. If she could have prevented it she would have, but she couldn't. Dad just wanted to waterproof his kid and Mom was real resistant. Dad won. Working in short intervals he soon had the six month old child holding her breath while doing her frog-like swim. Elise became totally comfortable in the water with her dad. Linda became totally comfortable with his teaching methods, eventually looking forward to Dad and Daughters hour long jaunts to the pool. Dad and Elise could bond and Linda could have some time to herself.

July rolled around with two milestones to celebrate. Linda's birthday and Frank's first year sober. It had been a year that had been minute to minute at times. The cold clammy hands of the abyss were relinquishing their grasp on Frank and Linda's souls. Life was peaceful and growing for the most part. He did however have a major confrontation with his 'demon behind the door' that brought him to his knees. The confrontation was in thought only, but never-the-less the thought had ugly overtones. Frank's covenant was to keep the door to 'What If' closed to his daughter forever. It was only to be an issue if someone else was to open the detestable door. He surly wouldn't. The thought shook him white. The destructive wedge that could be driven into the heart of the bond he and his daughter were developing would be shameful. Why anyone might do something like that was beyond his ability to understand or control. He knew that Grace only might provide peace from that concern. He struggled to let that be.

~~~~

We all are delivered into the tapestry of life in the same way. We all come from the womb of Mother. With our first breath we begin to weave connections in love and trust without fear in our world. This is a gift we all enjoy when we first arrive. It is peace and we spend the rest of our journey yearning to return to that place. The string we follow is no different.

CHAPTER 15

WINDS OF CHANGE FILLING SAILS OF ENLIGHTENMENT

Elise turned one, then two, then three years of age in peace. Frank, by Grace, celebrated a second and third year sober. Linda and Frank celebrated a third and fourth wedding anniversary in trust. Frank's idealism had tempered into conformity of the everyday hard working Joe. His adamant concern for world stability and peace had melted into concern for the stability and peace of the family he had been entrusted with.

With the cloud of the liquor stupor gone, the clarity opened a myriad of doors. The winds of change began to mean opportunity for growth for him. Positive energy was given at the break of each new day that became manna he fed from every morning. Spikes of negative energy were to be bathed in Grace, transforming chaos to calm.

Each discovery of peace that came to him he tried to forward, passing on that gift to others in need. If he could help bring peace to turmoil in someone else's life he was happy to give that peace freely. This became his way to pass on the Grace he had come to know as repayment for the Grace he had received. One recipient was his close friend Lou Paul. Louie and Frank had worked alongside each another for years. As breakfast club members they shared many of the same attributes respected by the management who shared breakfast with them. When Brother Lou began to deal with the demons that haunted him, Frank's help was sought. Frank's commitment continued long after the start of Lou's recovery was well under way. Theirs was a symbiotic friendship in recovery, with the success of one feeding the success of the other.

Suppressing the rattling vibration of temptation was jokingly referred to by the duo as 'keeping the wing nut tight', the imagery coming from the sight of a wobbling wing nut of an automotive air cleaner rattling loose as the screaming motor raced. A tight nut meant a smoother performance; a loose nut meant certain rough running. The program of keeping each others' wing nut tight provided the brotherhood with repeated success over the course of many years.

Clear purpose and objectives motivated Frank's willingness to give when he could. As long as he could perceive a successful outcome to his input he didn't hesitate becoming involved. He was coming to the realization that by giving he received. Not that he expected anything for his efforts. The right effort always seemed to pay a dividend. He never knew what the dividend might be and gladly accepted whatever Grace granted.

There was one calling however which perplexed him. The message had been received once before, years earlier, a dream-induced communiqué from Hana Lisa Joi that was sensed deep in his heart. The second dream was again vague in clear purpose or objective and was again over-toned with a strong sense of a compelling need to connect. Once again the message received in a powerfully vivid dream awash in radiant love from the sender was demure in specific detail. The image was so powerful it jolted him awake and lingered with him for days.

Frank didn't try to explain the dream to Linda, just the person behind it. He felt a strong need to tell his wife about this experience. He told her of his friendship with Hana and how he felt compelled to try and reach her because of the dream. Linda was concerned about the effect this dream vision had on him and the jealousy it stirred within her. Yet, she did agree to his request to try and locate Hana, despite the fear she had that he might actually succeed. Linda sensed his concern. A more modest search was done to no avail and he moved on to other tasks of kindness.

Doctrine had become, if he couldn't figure out how to save the world he could at least help to save one. If a need was there he did whatever he could to fill it. Even for complete strangers. This attribute was part of his core going back many years. His instinctive response to assist those who could not help themselves, at times putting his own life in danger, was part of 'what it was all about,' at least to him. Whether it was running through downed live power lines to assist accident victims, entering the water to save a drowning victim, or verbally disarming a pistol-wheeling gunman at the critical point of shooting, he was willing to lay down his personal safety to assist another. Act without fear. He had become complacent to general principles accepted as norm, but never let the paranoia of liability deter him from acting to prevent suffering. At least he'd try with Grace, without the fear of someone suing him. If he could do something responsible and good then he would. His compassion for humanity was something Linda never fully understood. He hoped he could pass this on to his daughter Elise.

When Elise turned four, the winds of change blew the family eastward. Frank took a management position and the family relocated to Lake Havasu City, Arizona. The responsibility he took on in the business he was asked to direct, expanded his tolerance and compassion for others. It too tested his sobriety as it reawakened his awareness of social injustice.

Aztec Water was a small family-owned and operated business that supplied bottled water products up and down the Colorado River. From Laughlin, Nevada to the north and Parker, Arizona to the south, Aztec was the biggest distributor servicing the area. A financial backer of the operation, Joe

Ragier, had sent Frank in to reestablish order to chaos. A tumultuous divorce of the couple who co-owned Aztec, Kate and Richard, left the company languishing without a leader or clear direction. Joe had entrusted his financial investment and company leadership to Frank. Frank worked it like he owned it.

He officiated as the company moved through wild times. Drugs, in-fighting, lack of equipment, vehicle accidents, employee accidents, logistics, nepotism...you name it, he had it thrown at him. All the constraints placed on him by owners and the web of interactions in all the 'family' problems enhanced his ability to improvise as well as tolerate with compassion. Kate and Richard's two sons, Mike and Chris, ran two of the routes, and when Richard passed away suddenly, Frank had a whole new role to play. He became a friend as well. Through compassion he transformed his leadership and that was enlightenment.

He found being a friend accomplished more than being a boss. Working ones way through problems involved a lot of interactions with a lot of different people at Aztec. Staying in a peace keeping spirit of friendship, he tried and avoided the negative energy of confrontation. Negative energy breeds negative energy and does nothing to realize peace. We all know this truth. This experience at Aztec plainly showed him that truth. Keeping the peace amongst the families, business partners and friends was challenging. At times he was placed in situations that made him very uncomfortable. By treating each person with dignity and respect in these encounters, peaceful solutions were usually realized. By Grace he learned, affording dignity, respect and compassion while working forward to peaceful resolve, moved success. He was learning good things.

Peace however is not on everyone's agenda. Somewhere in childhood the act of revenge or retribution for harm inflicted is discovered. The addictive sickness of that action can lash out at any time and peace is not its motive; malice is its only intent. No dignity or respect there. The vindictive act of revenge can be played out easily when hidden behind the cloak of anonymity. The ugly device of accusation anonymously has become accepted practice in society and was eventually perpetrated vindictively on Frank.

This act of vengeance opened his eyes to the Gestapo-type methods that we as Americans have allowed our elected representatives to enact. He saw for himself how we now allow authorities we employ through our taxes to trounce on basic human dignities. Guilt is now presumed, innocence has to be proven. No dignity or respect there. He was reawakened to his passion for rights and his desire to undo wrong. Idealism reignited. Effort to right wrong even in a small way took every ounce of energy he could muster. His hope: to make a difference, to effect change and by Grace not to fall back into his abyss in defeat.

It was 110 degrees outside that day and Frank had spent most of the day in Needles, California doing pick up work for one of his route salesman. Arriving back at his office at Aztec he changed hats and began paperwork for the remainder of his day's activities. It was about 3 in the afternoon when the phone rang and he was summoned. He picked up. It was Linda on the phone, an inanimate confused tone in her voice as she asked if he was alone. He said yes and Linda began to regurgitate details of what had transpired over the previous five hours.

"At 9 this morning Child Protective Services and the Lake Havasu City Police picked Elise up at daycare and are holding her for examination by a doctor," Linda started.

"What? What for?" Frank interrupted.

"Because someone called in anonymously saying you were molesting her," Linda replied.

"What!" Frank retorted in disbelief.

"Who did?" he demanded.

"I don't know, they won't tell me." Linda said in frustration.

"Where is Elise now? I'll get to the bottom of this." he snapped, boiling to anger.

"I don't know they won't tell me," again was Linda's drained reply.

"What the fuck! Where are you?" he shot.

"At the police department," Linda responded.

"I'll be right down and I'll get to the bottom of this!" he exploded.

"No, they don't want to see you right now." Linda cautioned.

"What?" he screeched in confusion.

"They want to ask me some questions before they talk to you." Linda informed.

"What the fuck!" he yelled, as he approached rage.

"They said they'll call you when they want to talk to you." Linda relayed.

"Fine, they know where to find me," Frank screamed as he slammed the phone down onto the receiver totally enraged by what he had just experienced. "What If' reared its ugly head. What he was about to experience was to enrage him even more.

He was white hot with anger as he slumped back into his chair to evaluate the situation. His basic summation, the people we pay to protect and serve, had abducted his five-year old daughter. These people were now holding his daughter, subjecting her to what he could not imagine. He and Linda were being threatened with immediate permanent removal of their daughter from their family. The dignity of first coming to them with this absurd, viscous accusation had not been afforded. Their rights as parents and as Americans had been trounced upon with no hard evidence of any wrongdoing; guilty until proven innocent.

To him this all added up to actions you might find being used in communist countries. To be more to the point, this is what one might expect to find in Hitler's Germany with the Gestapo-like tactics employed to intimidate with no respect for human dignity. To him these actions struck at the very core of what America, the Constitution and Bill of Rights were all about. This was America and he was going to fight and fight hard to see that this type of abuse of power was quashed. An abusive America was not the America he had grown up to believe in.

First and foremost he was going to secure the return of his daughter. How was the challenge? White hot anger led him to confront the attacker head on. He went directly to the offices of Child Protective Services to find out who was accountable for this gross evasion of moral protocol. He entered the building with fire in his eyes, seeking out the individual responsible for initiating the morbid chain of events. Finding her within seconds of entering, he began his search for truth with shaken composure. His discourse with this individual started with dignified inquiry for answers. His query was stymied time and time again by the stink of the anonymity barrier. Anonymity laws that had been erected to evade accountability, to protect the accuser and the Gestapo-type tactics of the CPS robots involved. The lack of progress was intolerable to him, his composure was unable to sustain her sub-human level of consciousness and actions perpetrated by the organization she was working for.

Having reached his limit for the ingestion of putrid, unfulfilling dialogue, he unleashed his pent up rage. Abruptly standing with a laser-like lock eye to eye with what he now considered an enemy to justice, he vowed to bring down the Gestapo-like organization she worked for by whatever means possible. Fury had taken over and he lashed out in his own moral decay. Bending slightly to be as direct as possible, in a fierce tone uttered through gritted teeth, he questioned the true motivation and conscience of the person to whom he was speaking. The fury seen in his eyes suggested danger and the social worker backed away in fear. He left to pursue the now personal crusade against this evil, cooling down only slightly when he stepped into the intense part of the day's 115 degree heat. Exiting the parking lot, he lifted his heart for strength through Grace. He had come close to doing harm and that was just not tolerable. He apologized for sinking into the madness of the negative; he sought guidance from Grace in a silent meditation.

Led back to his office in a numb buzz of festering rage he began a search for help. In short order he was given the phone number of an attorney with the advocacy group VOCAL. This group had coagulated into formation as a direct response to the abusive power being wield in the guise of Child Protective Services nationwide. That conversation led to the deeper understanding of the loss of rights and the struggle to be faced. Frank enlisted his personal help for the cause, promising to immediately turn over any factual information to bolster the case against this sanctioned criminal behavior. Hanging up the phone, he was not encouraged by what he had learned. This was going to be hardball and he waited in a disturbing state of agitation for the police to call.

Call they did and he flew to the police station. With reserve of emotion, resolve to uncover wrong, he ventured into the hornets' nest. The consistent sting of accusations was met with consistent denial and request for proof. When threatened with video tape made of Elise confirming guilt, Frank lost it. Slamming his fist down on the table he demanded they "produce the fucking tape." The show of unequivocal denial of guilt caused the accusatory detective seated across from him to recoil from the display of fury.

Frank then noted a diversion and skirting to the request to produce and show this supposed evidence. Further incensed by weaker and weaker evidence diminishing any need to continue the witch hunt charading as legal protocol, he summed up his growing contempt for what was being perpetrated, inviting the questioning detective to draw close as he was now going to impart to the detective something of importance. Leaning forward the detective indicated he was ready to field this information. Frank asked if the detective knew what his middle initial in his name stood for. The detective said no and asked to be enlightened. Frank imparted that name and confirmed that he was related to this very powerful Arizona political family. He concluded his brief dissertation in saying that if he didn't have his daughter back by the end of the day, he could ensure that the wrath of this influential family would come to bear on all involved in this ludicrous abuse of power. His calm matter of fact delivery of his stated goal caused the interrogating detective to sit straight up in his chair, speechless. It took a moment for truth to process. Rising to his feet, the detective excused himself, informing with apology he'd return momentarily.

Returning, the detective now announced that the doctor's findings had conclusively proved that Elise had not suffered the abuse the anonymous caller had claimed, and she was currently enroute to be reunited with her parents. Elation with relief swept the emotions, disturbed only by the revelation of the doctor's examination procedures that had been performed on his daughter. Abuse of his daughter under questionable legal protocol, masquerading as a pretense for protection of the child in question, inflamed him. Again, he demanded to see the video tape that the lead detective had said contained evidence of guilt, prompting the doctor's molesting exam. The detective avoided the request by changing direction of conversation as Linda was led in to reunite with Frank.

Within a half an hour Elise was back in the loving arms of her parents. Frank lifted a small silent prayer of thanks to the Grace that had provided the success of truth. As he and the family left the stink of the police building, Frank was asked aside by the interrogating detective. The detective offered his apology and an offer to make the video tape available to him the following day. Frank accepted the apology, indicating he'd be back at the start of the detective's shift to pick up the video. The almost secretive tone of the offer suggested to Frank that the offer was probably a break in official protocol.

Well after dark on the short ride home, Dad and Mom searched for signs of Daughters mental condition after a day spent with invasive strangers. To their relief Elise seemed in good spirits, happy to be sharing the happier details of her day, a bowl of ice cream sweetened the days end. He and Linda never asked her to reveal her feelings or details about the physical invasion of her body. The parents prayed that any memory of that part of the nightmare might fade as time facilitated a return to normalcy. No provision by the State to provide mental aftercare for the hideous shelling of the family's dignity suffered that day at the hands of the State. No acceptance of wrongdoing acknowledged by the State at all. The system was broken and broken badly.

The State may have failed to see the atrocity that had been committed, but Frank didn't. As soon as Elise was tucked safely into bed he was on the phone to the VOCAL attorney. He described in detail the horror of the afternoon and was applauded by the attorney for the unexpected return of their daughter to their custody. Frank transmitted the information about gaining access to the video taped interview that had been done with Elise, sparking a fervent request by the attorney to procure a copy. The VOCAL attorney then went into detailed descriptions of how to spot illegal, manipulative questions directed to Elise. The coercive tactics during questioning of minors, using anatomically correct dolls, would be a direct link to illegal interview procedures. The prospect of a smoking gun that could be used to prove the victims rights organization's claim of coercive illegal tactics excited them both. Frank went to bed that night with a sense of relief and renewed sense of purpose. Relief to know his daughter was home safe, and relief he did not drink to deaden his rage. His purpose now was to provide a tool of truth to be used as evidence of a system gone wrong in a veiled attempt to do right. The door to his demon of 'What If' had been closed as abruptly as it had been opened. The video's value as a tool of fear in the interrogation room was quashed by the power of truth. His purpose now was to provide the video as a tool of truth to quash a wrong that brings so much suffering and pain when used as a tool of revenge. The system unable to stop itself once started in motion. "Shame on us for building such a system and allowing it to exist" was his summation before drifting into unsettled rest.

Six thirty the following morning he met the detective at the prearranged location. Frank was asked not to mention receiving the tape as it was handed off. The return of the tape that day was requested and only to the detective. Frank agreed. Returning home he plugged in the tape to watch a horrendous display of manipulation enacted upon his daughter by two so called psychologists. He counted a dozen or more denials by Elise to the psychologist's attempts to elicit responses designed to incriminate her dad. By the end of the tape Elise was agitated and wanted to know why they were asking so many questions about her dad's penis. He was infuriated, but he had the smoking gun.

Frank rushed the tape to a local video reproduction outfit, ordering two copies, one for him and one for the VOCAL organization. He then rushed to his office to phone the VOCAL attorney to inform him of what he had found. The VOCAL attorney was jubilant to be getting a copy of this damning evidence and gave Frank the address to send it to. That afternoon he had his copy, the VOCAL copy in the mail and the original back in the hands of the detective. A week later he took a call from the VOCAL president extolling appreciation for the most valuable tool he had seen to date for their efforts to effect change. Frank felt proud to be a party to that change. He lost interest in his pursuit of a lawsuit against the State for the damage the intrusion had caused his family. He did not want to dwell in negative energy. His copy of the tape went into his bottom dresser drawer where it remains to this day.

The stress of that malignant day lingered for months to come. Added stress of Aztec Water being sold to Hinckley and Schmidt signaled a time for change. He had worked for Hinckley and Schmidt when they purchased Silver Springs Water in southern California. He had never cared much for the Chicago based H&S company philosophies and eventually left his 12 year employment with Silver Springs, after tolerating a year under the new ownership. H&S valued their trucks more than the employees that drove them; that drove Frank up the wall.

By choice and with Grace, Frank quit his lucrative position with H&S and became a stay- at-home dad. Between three small, part-time jobs for him and Linda's full time venture into the working world, the family was able to enjoy their life on the river. Boating, camping, fishing, swimming, the family had time to play together and that was nice. Elise learned to swim like a fish, ride her bike without training wheels and cast her fish pole with amazing accuracy. Linda learned what it was like to be the bread winner. Although she wasn't too impressed with his cooking ability she didn't complain too much when he produced the evening meal. The family was ready for anything and everything that came their way. And the winds of change did fill their sails, blowing them by Grace westward to the California coast.

~~~~

We all experience rude. It rubs us the wrong way on our weave for peace. We act to right wrong. We connect with responsibility, and create for the greater good. From fearless selfless gifting of assistance to those in need, the Universe smiles and returns the gift in abundant portion. Change happens and we move on to weave another day. The string we follow is no different.

CHAPTER 16

PHENOMENAL INDOMITABLE POWER

Frank's desire for fairness abounded in all aspects of life including business. His philosophical differences with corporate America produced a free-thinking, successful, small-business person. He did not tolerate the notion that machines were more important than the employees that ran them. Leaving Hinckley & Schmidt again meant he did not have to compromise his values. Not having to compromise what you believe was so satisfying. Building a satisfying life is probably a goal that everyone on the planet shares. Frank and Linda were no different.

After leaving the corporate environment, the couple set out on a search for new opportunity. The desire to live back on the Pacific Ocean brought them to the mid California coastline. Half way between Los Angeles and San Francisco was a truly unique area that inspired investigation. While Frank interviewed with local water companies, Linda searched the newspapers. On a particularly beautiful fall day he returned to the hotel room to report his progress. The report was not very encouraging when he recounted the morning contacts. Linda however had a bit of exciting news and handed him the classified ads she had been perusing. Circled in red at the top of the page was an ad under 'Businesses for Sale'. Reading the ad, his spirit lightened. The ad was for a business which he had dreamed in concept years before, a retail water store. If he could afford the cost, this opportunity could be the perfect launch point for building a dream he had harbored for a long time.

Contact was made with the sales agent and a meeting was set for that afternoon. Unlike the other interviews he had attended, where he sensed he had been perceived as over qualified, this one felt perfect. Hand in glove stuff, you know. He was the exact 'right guy' for this business he overheard the agent tell the seller and a meeting was arranged with the owner immediately.

The anxious couple hurried over to meet the owner and see the operation. Walking through the door they were greeted by a little Italian man with bright cheery eyes and a huge smile. His name was Lenny Puma. Lenny approached with his outstretched hand, Frank noticed he appeared to have a labored crippling walk. As they shook hands Frank felt a positive happy energy from the exuberant little man. "Lenny is Italian what do you expect" he thought. Lenny just seemed to be happier than most. Lenny's firmly grounded positive energy blended with his, and within minutes they felt like old friends.

The meeting lasted for quite awhile. Discussions about the business, family and ideals went into quality detail. Lenny's physical condition was the motivator for Lenny wanting to sell the year old business. Lenny had been born club footed and the dozen operations he had endured over the course of his childhood had left him virtually crippled. He just couldn't handle the physical nature of the business any longer. Humping fifty pound bottles of water out to customer's cars was killing his feet, legs and back. You would've never known he was in so much pain. Lenny's positive attitude and broad smile never hinted of his daily struggle.

He and Linda were jazzed at the prospect of purchase, but honest that the price asked was more than they could afford. Frank passed on some helpful suggestions for improvement to the water production end of the business while talking on the many different subjects of mutual interest. Upon parting the two men exchanged phone numbers, Lenny promising to keep Frank posted should he drop the asking price.

Feeling somewhat let down, the couple packed up and headed back to Pat's house in Carson. Elise had been staying with Grandma and Grandpa while Mom and Dad had gone up the coast. This was the first time the parents had ventured from Elise's side for an extended period and the reunion was a thrill. Packing up and heading back to Havasu provided a sense of return to routine normalcy for the trio, the fantasy of owning their own business fading.

A few days later Lenny called to inform Frank that an offer had been made and an escrow opened for the business. Frank was disappointed but happy for Lenny. They talked for a while, Lenny thanking Frank for suggestions he had made that Lenny had already implemented. Frank thanked Lenny for keeping him posted, reiterating a desire to be informed if circumstances warranted. Lenny agreed in his robust positive Italian disposition. A month or so later Lenny called again, relaying to Frank that the first escrow had dropped out, but a second offer was now in the works. This time however the price had dropped a bit. The price was still more than Frank thought he could muster, but asked Lenny to keep him posted anyway. The jovial little Italian agreed and life went on.

The winter of 1990 in the Arizona desert was beautifully dramatic. a customary warm up to 80 degrees, followed by a snowstorm. Snow in the desert is an unbelievable sight. That year's snowstorm had left two-mile wide by five-mile long swatches of white, painted at intervals across the desert floor. The blue of Lake Havasu sparkled like a gem on the background of tan and white that surrounded their desert home. The snowstorm was a fitting finale to a spectacular winter season. Spring warm up generated a reawakening of spirit that was exemplified by the soft green tones blanketing the desert. Dreams of moving to the coast had become a distant fantasy. Linda and

Frank began to revise their thoughts about leaving their desert community and that's when the lightening struck. Curve balls always come when you least expect it, don't you know?

Frank's parents had just left from their week-long stay. Frank's mom, Elizabeth had just celebrated her birthday, enjoying her first grandchild Elise. Grandpa Florida was pretty proud as well. Grandma and Grandpa Florida, that's what Elise called them because they lived in Florida. The visits were always fun but too seldom. At about the time their RV trip had come to a close back in Florida, Frank's phone rang. Much to his surprise it was Lenny from California.

This time Lenny's tone was a lot different. Instead of the happy-go-lucky Lenny it was a downtrodden defeated tone that resonated in his voice. Lenny informed Frank he was closing the business. It had been six long months since they last talked and Lenny was at the end of his rope. Three escrows had opened for the business purchase, and all three buyers backed out at the last minute. Lenny's physical condition just could not take the daily rigors anymore and he was throwing in the towel. Frank listened carefully; he felt Lenny's pain. Lenny and his wife Judy had decided to close the business, take their lumps, and move on.

Frank tried to stick to the positive, encouraging Lenny not to close down the business he had worked so hard for. After all, he told Lenny, there was value to the client base and that base needed the service the store provided. He asked Lenny to sit down with Judy, come up with a rock bottom price for the business and let him know. Maybe, Frank suggested, if the price was do-able they might be able to make the deal happen. Lenny agreed to hold off closing the store and consult Judy. With a lighter demeanor generated by hope, Lenny was glad to give it one more shot. The only contingency was that the deal had to be done by June 1st when the lease was up for renewal. Frank agreed to a short escrow, cash deal, no backing out at the last minute. The spirits of both men soared as they hung up, the light of hope burning bright for both again.

Lenny called 24 hours later with an offer Frank could not refuse. Now that's Italian. Frank then phoned his dad to run a loan proposition by Jim. Jim requested a business plan which Frank worked on until the wee hours of the morning, overnighting that plan the following day. A phone conversation a day later clarified the plan details and by Grace a funding loan from Dad was secured. Frank phoned Lenny 72 hours after their initial conversation. A gentleman's agreement was reached and the ball was rolling.

It was phenomenal how the huge amount of details that facilitated this major move fell into place. Two and a half months after the deal was made the family was settling into their new home in Pismo Beach. Frank was becoming more aware that an extraordinary power directs when positive energies are humbly sought and followed. He knew this indomitable power had manifested throughout this process that he could not have pulled together himself. He also sensed this remarkable Grace flowing through the spirit of his newfound friend Lenny. Lenny's incredible willingness for giving was a kindred nature that bonded the two into an indestructible friendship. Lenny Puma was one in a billion and Frank was grateful for his kindness. The friendship was to see the best and worst life offers up, each standing by the other's side no matter what was to be shared. That's Grace.

~~~~

We all like to see dreams fulfilled as we journey. Sometimes we dream a dream, time slips by, and the dream fades only to be thrust back into the light and gifted to fruition. We ask ourselves, "How did that happen?" The string we follow is no different. Now, however, he is aware that some dreams have an extraordinary energy woven into the tapestry by Grace.

CHAPTER 17

EASIER, HARDER, SURRENDER

So opened a new door down the path of 'happily every after'. The soft cool blue of the Pacific Ocean, rolling in to greet oak-dotted rolling hills shrouded occasionally in fog, was a welcomed change from the stark hot Arizona desert. This was the place he and Linda wanted to put down their roots to raise their daughter. Elise turned six that year and begin first grade. Frank celebrated his sixth year without liquor, grateful that path had become easier. Linda celebrated 29 and began to dread the big '3-0'. A happy, normal family excited in their pursuit of the 'American Dream'.

Twelve to sixteen hour days spent creating for success had become common place. The main focus was the business that was expanding by leaps and bounds. Plans for the water bottling plant had been approved by the State and construction had begun. This upgrade to the facility was worked in conjunction with upgrades to the retail facility; most of the work had to be done after closing. It was not uncommon for Frank to return to the office after a dinner with the family and work until 11 or 12 at night. He took advantage of the hours the retail end of the business was closed and most holidays too were spent on facility upgrades.

Linda too was busy. She was Frank's right hand person, handling the retail operations when he was out, as well as being Elise's doting mother. Frank's approach to growing the business relied heavily on Linda manning the office, their tight budget was not yet able to afford an employee. The business plan was to expand from just the retail outlet into bottling and delivery, as well as treatment system service. Linda's help was crucial.

Frank had developed a beautiful logo for Genesis Water which he had embroidered on all his casual work shirts. The logo had become the main advertising vehicle for the business. He figured this pleasant image, displayed on various items associated with the business, could provide a recognizable image of stability as over time it disseminated into the community. Quietly, subtly, the logo was being recognized as a sign of quality and the trust of the growing consumer base affirmed his approach. Quality products and on-time service at a fair price also helped to establish the company's solid reputation that began to garner the best advertising of all, word of mouth!

His outside projects were beginning to have a positive impact on the business as well. His work with the Plaza Promotions Group, Chamber of Commerce and Friends of Price House was building a web of interconnected contacts that furthered the success of his goals and aspirations. The time involved to fulfill his obligations to each organization was growing and some days he had no room for wasted motion. The ballet of tasking to accomplish a given day's goals was truly epic at times. A sun up to sun down dance with logistics and the clock amazed even him at the end of the day he had been able to get it all done.

He also saw the value of this volunteer sacrifice and the dividends it would pay for the business. Linda however was not so convinced that all of his efforts [without pay] would ever reap reward. Linda was beginning to resent these outside commitments, and the debate about their value was beginning to undermine the tranquility of family life. Frank had become a workaholic and Linda didn't like it at all. Building and running a small business is tough on a family, especially when the limited budget could not afford additional employees. A one-man one-woman show to handle a six day a week concert of obligations drummed out a hectic daily beat. He could handle the demands; he only hoped Linda could too.

His daily routine always had him back at the shop to relieve Linda by 2 or 3 in the afternoon. His activities after returning were subject to the flow of retail customers, sometimes providing quiet time to plan and strategize for the dream. Daydreaming was the short word for it. Planning and strategizing just made it sound so much more productive to him. Daydreaming to him was an escape to the positive realm of the Universe where just about anything is do-able, we have all been there.

On one of those afternoons in July of 92 his thoughts had wandered off to his old days back in Maryland. He wondered about his high school and whether or not they did reunions. It had been twenty years, the year prior, since he had graduated. He had heard nothing regarding the class of '71' having had any such event. Of course, he had moved away soon after graduation and had no contacts who knew of his whereabouts, so the lack of notification was a given. In a moment of daydream stupor, also known as inspiration, Frank decided to call Maryland directory information to get the phone number for his old high school. He hoped they might have a contact number for someone who might have handled the 20-year event. The thought of possibly getting placed on the roster for the 25th reunion was a pleasant distraction and he made the call.

Getting the number for the school was easy, but too late in the day to make a connection. The left coast, right coast time difference put the call off for a day. At some point in time during that evenings slumber, Frank had another visitation from his dream-state friend Hana Joi. Brief, crisp and to the point Hana, said hello, beckoned contact from her heart and then she was gone. That hello echoed in his memory when he awoke. It dawned on him that connection might be made if reunions where held. If the school has a reunion committee contact person, he might find the number for his long lost friend Hana.

Hopeful of satisfying this reawakened desire to reconnect put a spring in his step throughout the day's duties. He was back to the office early to relieve Linda and further his two-fold phone mission, of which he had not mentioned anything about the effort to his wife at this point. Once the retail traffic in the store had died down he made the call to the school. The call was quickly routed to a staff member who had a name and number to the previous year's reunion committee. The name sounded familiar, but he could not put a face to the name. He immediately called the contact. The conversation was robust and full of delightful information regarding the 20 event, but no information as to the whereabouts of Hana. He took a handful of numbers of other friends that were still in the area, hoping one of them might be able to shed some light on his quest. He also had his name added to the notification list for the upcoming 25th reunion on the outside chance he might be able to attend. He called several of the numbers and talked to old friends, ultimately finding that no one had seen or heard from Hana in years.

Then his first big break came on the last number he had on his list. Frank's good buddy from senior year Carl Arquette, gave him the number of an upperclassman, Bobby Cadwell, who might have information on Hana's brother Stefen. He made the call to Bobby and once again hit pay dirt. Bobby knew Hana's dad's first name and confirmed he was still living on Bent Island in Maryland. Bobby also confirmed he had seen Stefen within the past year, but did not have any information on Hana. Pressing on he dialed information and within seconds received the phone number for John and Gina Joi, Hana's mom and dad. He was now so close to success he could taste it and immediately dialed the number.

As the phone on the other end of the line rang he wondered if John would remember him. He did not have time to give that much thought as the phone was answered on the second ring. He asked the male voice that answered if he was speaking to John Joi and the voice returned, "No this is Stefen." "Unbelievable," ran first through his mind then out of his mouth. It was Stefen his former roommate and Hana's brother. He rushed with the thrill that he was seconds away from finding Hana and he informed Stefen to whom he was speaking.

Stefen was astounded that it was Frank on the line. The former roommates laughed as they reminisced briefly about a few of their exploits from so many years prior. Frank then changed the conversation to Hana. Stefen was a wealth of information. He revealed that Hana and her son lived a short distance away, she was well and doing great. He also provided that elusive phone number Frank had been seeking for years. He thanked Stefen for his help indicating he'd call him back soon so they could catch up more fully on the past twenty years, but his mission was to talk to Hana and he apologized for being so rude. Stefen was okay with that, telling him he knew his sister would get a kick out of hearing from him. Hanging up he noticed his hands shook as he looked at the elusive number he had searched so hard for and now held in his hand.

He was a bit dazed as he looked down at the number. He couldn't believe he was eleven digits away from final contact with a person he felt so compelled to talk with. Would this connection finally provide some answers to the heartfelt visitations he had in his dreams? Would Hana feel the same heartfelt joy of being reconnected? Would she even care? He didn't know, but he was about to find out. That scared him a bit and he tried to calm his racing mind and pounding heart.

He decided to hold off making the call to Hana until the shop was closed. If he was to have full attention given to his friend, he didn't want any interruptions from the outside world. During the final hour before closing he marveled at how all the phone calls to old friends he had made had been answered. "What was the chance of that." he thought. He also wondered where the conversation might lead if Hana was to answer the call he was about to make. A strange sense of calm replaced the daze of disbelief felt when Stefen had given him Hana's number. He closed his eyes to bask in the calm emitted from the peace of knowing he was about to fulfill a task that beckoned for completion for so long.

Locking the front door to the shop, he noticed the heart rate picked up as he headed to the phone. Ten seconds later the numbers had been dialed and the phone on the other end began to ring. On the third ring the receiver was picked up.

"Hello," said the unmistakable voice spoken in the dream from a couple of nights before.

"Is this Hana Joi?" Frank asked, knowing full well to whom he was speaking. He knew Hana's voice with its unique blend of tone. Smooth, rich, with a hint of insecure sarcasm and a slight Maryland accent the likes of which he had never heard from anyone else on the planet.

"Yeah," Hana responded.

"This is a blast from the past. Guess who this is?" He stated with inquiry.

"I really don't know, who?" Hana retorted with only slight curiosity.

"Frank Lindsay," his response.

"Oh my God, you've got to be kidding!" Hana shot in shocked response. Frank reassured her that it was really he and his conversation cascaded into a pool of preserved memories.

As he talked, he sensed a bit of distance in Hana's voice. It was as if she really didn't have much time to talk, she didn't elaborate on topics covered.

He told of the anguish he had felt over their loss of contact, which drew an only slightly reciprocal response. He didn't reveal the unusual visitations that had prompted his search, only the fact that he had a strong desire to find her over the years. Hana acknowledged only wondering occasionally of his whereabouts. He asked if she might attend the 25th high school reunion and offered to take her if he could get away to attend. Hana said that might be fun and she'd think about it. He was doing most of the talking when he asked if she was seeing anyone. Hana answered 'yes' and in fact he was sitting on the couch waiting for her to return. He suddenly realized he was intruding and apologized profusely. Pledging to not lose contact again, he ended the conversation, telling Hana that she was special to him and to call anytime if she'd like to chat. He wished her well, said goodbye and hung up the phone.

Now more perplexed than ever, he sat back and wondered why he had felt so compelled to make that contact. None of his questions as to why had been answered. Hana's reserved tone in the conversation did little to stimulate any excitement over the reconnection he had been so keen to reestablish. Feeling somewhat diminished, he began to think that this crusade was not to fulfill any need Hana had, just a need he had. After all Hana was fine. She had a significant other, a house and a son. Her needs seemed to have all been met. He was perplexed that he felt his hadn't been. Little did he know Grace had another plan.

By the end of that year Genesis Water's bottling operation was up and running and the first delivery days of the route operation were being built. Chamber of Commerce was going strong, Frank chairing two committees and sitting on two others. Elise was seven years old and growing up fast. She was now in second grade and wanting to work the cash register at the store. Friends of Price House were making headway with Anniversary House foundation work and fundraising. He still had not found any time to hunt artifacts at the old house.

Linda and Frank had celebrated their tenth wedding anniversary and he passed a seventh year milestone without a lick to drink. Linda was growing more agitated about having turned thirty as well as the time she had to invest at the store. Frank's time spent on the volunteer projects didn't help ease Linda's agitation.

Sam the Clam had made his first appearance without any arms, and Sam's picture showed up in the local paper. Sam's second appearance was in that year's Clam Festival parade. Through the joy of one little girl in a wheelchair at that event came the inspiration to commit to the long range storyline of Sam, Pam and Baby clams. Sadly though there had been no call from Hana and the conversation they shared had become a distant memory for Frank.

The following year just got busier. Frank was amazed he made it without turning to 'the sauce' for escape. Success was all around him in everything he did except at home. Linda seemed to be unhappy and growing distant. His feeble attempts to pay more attention to Linda's needs failed most of the time making him feel inadequate and unhappy. He had lost his romantic touch in his zeal to be successful in all the other commitments he had made. He felt the success of the business meant success for the family, but something was wrong and he tried to put his finger on it.

The trouble seemed to be money. The things he'd do for nothing seemed effortless and filled with positive energy that made good things happen. However, the quest for the dollar always bore the drag of negative energy that stymied the free-flowing joy of being alive. Success had come to mean money and he resented having to slave to such an idol in order to attain the elusive tranquility we all desire. Consumer-based tranquility seemed an oxymoron. This felt like such a wrong direction. He was searching for something different that could surmount the negativism money holds on the soul. This was a paradox in simple thinking, yet it weighed on his simple mind.

Everyone likes to be comfortable in the system we have allowed to organize, that takes enough money. Unfortunately not all have enough to be comfortable, and that bothered him. Money had enslaved the planet into a droned cycle of life, complacent to the few that actually controlled the money. The zesty joy of real living in giving had all but disappeared in daily life. Money always seemed to have conditions or strings attached and that was a negative emotional drag on his daily peace. Whereas real giving had no strings and that nourished the flow of peaceful existence. Money seemed to have no peace. A struggle or conflict always seems to hover close by when money was around. Unfortunately daily survival seems to require it. Money seemed to be the major snag to real peace, he could do nothing about the destruction money and its pursuit brought to the peace in his family's life. The inflationary spiral of ever increasing costs for survival that our economies are based on was killing the chances of ever having a stable, predictable, peaceful planet for family oriented life. There seemed to be no way out of the cycle and that bothered him.

So where is the comfort in this grind he wondered? For him the comfort was in the joy he experienced in the positive success of the work he gave away. That joy was not shared by Linda, and their union was growing apart. The almost poverty level income, was just enough to get by, and that was severely straining the marriage. Frank tried to increase the income hoping more would bring peace, but it never seemed to be enough. Something was always there to snatch up the extra, producing the need for more and it just seemed to be a vicious cycle. Cycling to nowhere.

Frank had been watching the inflationary spiral destroy more and more. More and more had less and less. Basic daily survival was becoming less comfortable or affordable. The spirals inflation rate for cost of goods or services far outpaced the average man's wage inflation and that was true for him as well. He was beginning to see that at some point in the future, only the well to do would have enough to buy the goods or services offered and there would not be enough of them to keep that type of economy afloat. He could see a collapse of the economic system coming. Even though his business was growing, the inflationary spiral was eating up all the new money generated. His hope of ever getting over the hump seemed distant, and he only hoped Linda could wait. That is if it might come at all. Cutting back on the family's expenditures had become the way to stay flush but was hugely unpopular with his wife.

By the time that year ended, Frank hated Christmas and most of what it had come to stand for. Money ruled. How sick was that? Watching American corporations exploiting slave labor in third world countries, just to keep the bottom line up so the CEOs could get their million-dollar bonus didn't sit well with him. The disease of profit now controlled dignity, to which the human race was its fodder. Frank figured this wasn't a good thing. "The people on the planet are going to see this some day, and boy are they going to be pissed," he thought. He disagreed to this treatment of people, and the whipping they were receiving on an annual basis. Then he recalled the words of Gandhi, "Be the change you wish to see in the world."

Frank vowed to try and never raise prices if at all possible. He knew that if change is going to happen it had to begin with him. He felt that if he was trusted and the products or services he offered were good, he could grow more income through increased clientele. His plan was working, but slowly. He rested at night knowing that the Universe always provided. He was sure that the money guys with the other ideas were surely going to have to answer for their deeds one day. That wasn't going to be pretty. He wondered if everyone on the planet would have to suffer along with them. He suspected they would; when was the question.

So '93' rolled to a close on a somber but sober note. For the most part positive energy was propelling all projects forward. Even though the overall economy was dull and lackluster, the business was growing. He could be grateful for that and other success afforded. The foundation at the Price Anniversary House had been completed. The Universe supplied and FOPH had been blessed with a newcomer to the project. Mike Fairbrother was a master carpenter and was rebuilding all the double-hung windows in the grand old house. Committee work with the Chamber of Commerce was effecting positive changes to the annual fireworks show and Clam Festival. The City sign ordinance review committee that he chaired was well entrenched with many community players attending and offering up valuable input. The Plaza Promotions committee was beginning a new television advertising campaign that was slated to start in mid 94. Sam D. Clam now had a girlfriend, Pam, and they marched in a trio of local parades. The delightful duo announced their engagement, and the storyline marketing of Pismo was beginning to roll. He had his irons in a lot of fires.

Highlights for that year had to include Frank and Jack Straw becoming a driving force behind the Friends of Price House with several projects already underway for the little park they were helping to build. Elise had convinced Dad to train her for the cash register operation at the store. He taught her to count back change and cut her loose. Even he was amazed as he stood back, monitoring Elise's capability. Elise's third customer really tested her composure when he threw down a fifty-dollar bill for $1.65 worth of merchandise. She wasn't rattled at all as she counted back the customer's change with the bravado of 'I've been doing this for years'. She nailed it. The cash register job was Elise's whenever she was in the store and Dad had no worries about her capabilities.

He also heard from Hana Joi that year. The contact came in the form of a wedding invitation. Hana and her boyfriend Raul were getting married and Frank was happy for her. He was unable to attend, but sent a card of congratulations. He filed the invitation with Hana's phone number, intent on keeping his promise not to lose touch. He lifted up a personal appeal to Grace for the new couple's well being. Had he not been married he felt possibly he might have felt jealous. That felt strange.

He also achieved a higher level of connected awareness with an Exquisite Energy that escorted him on his personal journeys through life. After smoking tobacco for twenty some years he had been able to quit. His numerous attempts to quit on his own had failed miserably and in shear frustration he fell into a deep plea from the soul asking for Grace to remove the monkey from his back. That early morning request followed the previous day's attempt to quit. That attempt resulted in a cigarette twenty minutes after his determined swearing off of tobacco forever. So much for his will power. He wasn't sure how long it had taken to open heart as he knelt in plea, but when he opened his eyes he felt something was dramatically different. Surrender. Two hours later, the craving monkey that usually climbed up one side of his back and down the other had not even shown its face. Linda insisted he put on a nicotine patch before he left for work just in case, but he knew there was another force at work in this program. His spiritual journey was beginning to recognize that force more frequently. Three days later the monkey was gone and he was shown again, by Grace we go.

Another demon had been rendered almost non-existent. These demons behind the doors of 'that's what's past' only occasionally rattled his serenity; he was grateful for that. Even the demon behind the door of 'what if' had been quieted to only infrequent rumblings. He still struggled with the paradoxes of life, but he wasn't searching the bottom of a bottle for the answers and he was doubly grateful for that. All in all it had been a very interesting ride to this point.

~~~~

We all experience grateful from time to time. We all experience money. We all experience concern. We all yearn. Success, failure, easy, hard, surrender and change, we all share in the journey's weave. The string we follow connects to all that we share in collective experience. Yet in the examination of the paradoxical, serenity is gifted as the weave continues.

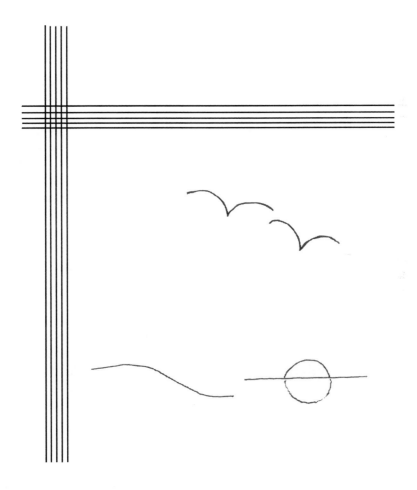

CHAPTER 18

SHAKEN

1994 rumbled onto the scene from deep within the earth providing Frank and the business an opportunity to be gifted reward for good works. His freight pick-up runs to Los Angeles had increased in frequency as the business grew; and he had another run scheduled for Monday, January 17th. The plan was to leave on Sunday afternoon, drive to and stay with cousin Pauly and Sue for the evening. Then an early a.m. wake and jaunt around the basin picking up products needed, returning to Pismo that afternoon. On the Friday before he was to leave he decided to change plans and push the run back to that Wednesday. His week had been particularly exhausting and he wanted that Sunday to rest, recuperate and spend some much needed time with the family.

At 4:31am Monday morning Frank was awakened out of a dead sleep by his internal motion detectors. A split second from dead sleep to wide awake announcing in a stern authoritative way, loud enough to be heard by the neighbors, "Earthquake!" Within seconds he, Linda and Elise were standing in the backyard in their night clothes, pitch dark as the earth quivered under their feet. Frank's brain was sizing up the energy release in an effort to determine size, proximity and potential for larger ground motions. As the event subsided he told Linda it was either a small local event or possibly a much larger event with an epicenter much further away.

Elise and Linda were somewhat used to this drill. He had taught them to be aware of Terra Firma's propensity for unannounced dramatic movements, running this evacuation drill with the family several times before. He learned of the tremendous power the earth could unleash from his structural geology classes he took in college. He preferred to evacuate a building if possible during an event because the view was much better from outside. Not to mention less chance of something falling on you. This of course was contrary to 'official directions in the event of earthquake'.

Frank was pretty good at picking up on the P waves of earthquake energy release. This usually afforded a few extra seconds before the destructive S waves hit, causing problems with personal movement to safety. Elise and Dad had practiced the drill about a year before during the Yucca Valley/Big Bear events. They had been staying the night at Grandma Pat's in Carson and the two made it outside to watch the last fifteen to twenty seconds of the first event that rolled them out of bed at 5:30am. He loved this stuff and his disaster preparedness exceeded that of most people who lived in California. He knew it was a matter of 'when' not 'if'.

This event was so early in the morning that not much could be seen. Frank had the girls crawl into bed together for comfort; he headed upstairs to check the television for news of the event. Black screen with audio only was all that the Los Angeles stations could muster. As he listened he was able to discern that damage had occurred in Los Angeles, which meant a substantial event had taken place close to the basin itself. By the time he was ready to leave to check the shop, a preliminary magnitude of 7.2 was being reported with the epicenter being approximated to the Northridge area. Finally incoming visual images were making it clear that his Wednesday freight run was going to be difficult if not impossible to accomplish.

He was at the shop by 6:30 to prepare for what was sure to be a monster day. Power had flickered on and off during the early morning event. If power was out to the rural areas, there would be droves of people in to pick up water. This wake up-call from Mother Nature would also have the procrastinators in to purchase disaster preparedness supplies. The day was huge water volume wise, the general public showed up continuously throughout the day to secure water provisions that had been neglected prior to the morning's event. It was an exhausting day.

Just before six that evening the phone rang; Frank picked up. It was the Red Cross and they were calling to ask for assistance in providing water. It had been a long day and he thought he had misunderstood their request because of his fatigue. He hadn't. Thousands of people had been displaced to shelter sites and many of the sites had no potable water. He listened while they made their pitch, which included payment for any product he could deliver. He couldn't believe that they were calling as he was three hours north of the affected areas. He asked if they knew where they were calling, he figured there had to be some mistake. He was informed that there was no mistake; licensed bottlers outside the affected area were the only ones picking up their phones.

Frank told the Red Cross representative that he was scheduled to make a run to Los Angeles and he'd be leaving the following afternoon. He agreed to fill his truck to capacity with packaged water and deliver it wherever they needed it... no charge. He was told to deliver to Royal Oak High School in Simi Valley. He confirmed an 8 or 9pm expected time of arrival for his delivery. It wasn't going to be much, but he'd be there. To him that's what you do to help those in need.

He then called a friend at the local paper to inform them of the request, suggesting it might make a good story on local efforts to help out the folks in need. The following afternoon as he loaded the truck with the donation cargo a reporter showed up to get the details of the story. The reporter snapped a few photos as well and Frank took off to make the run. It felt good to help even if it was only a drop in the bucket.

Arriving at the appointed drop site, Frank added his cargo to their dwindling supply. He was astounded to see the frightened, dazed, zombie like condition of the refugees housed in the high school gymnasium. Most seemed lost and confused at their plight as they huddled quietly with their families; he felt sympathy for their displacement. He was thanked for his assistance as he headed out for Sue and Paul's.

Up early as usual. After his early morning supply run he stopped in the San Fernando Valley to do some video documentation of the damage caused by the now dubbed Northridge earthquake. The scenes he captured from some of the locations he had delivered water to years prior confirmed his theories on true building safety. The original 7.2 had been downgraded to 6.9 and still the damage had been cataclysmic in some locations. Driving through Sherman Oaks, Van Nuys, and Northridge and eventually through the true epicenter of the event, Reseda, he captured the aftermath on video for the family to see. Then back to Pismo.

Two days later he received what money can't buy. Front page center color photo with a story on Genesis Waters' effort to help in the earthquake recovery. He was proud of what he had done and grateful for the exposure. It was a big boost to the good name of the company. Giving with Grace had paid big dividends. He knew it was 'just what you do' when called upon to ease the suffering of other human beings. Above and beyond, "No" he would state, "anyone else would have done it."

The year had started with a bang and ended with a bang. In between life was pushed at roaring grind. Huge ups and downs rocked the house that Grace built. The news of his mom being gravely ill caused him much concern. The distance that separated him from his family only allowed for one last visit between Mother and Son. They laughed hard together one more time.

The giving was receiving, but Frank's ability to give to the marriage had all but shut down. Daily and nightly battles with Linda had worn him down to the point he was avoiding Linda's attempts to communicate. The relationship was shaken to the very core and he was feeling a tug from the abyss. Most other aspects of his life were going so great, he wondered why he couldn't make his marriage as good.

The pace and success in all the projects he was involved in made the year blow by. Sam and Pam's announcement of wedding plans for the following year really had sparked the crowd's interest to follow the Clams' story. All the other projects combined had not brought as many smiles of joy as the sight of the two happy clams bouncing down the streets in local parades. This joy of that giving was only to be followed by a huge low when Linda abruptly moved out and served him with papers for divorce. He didn't see that coming, guys never do.

That day his world shattered. All he had been working for came crashing down, his brain went into escape mode. The doors of doom were rattling hard as he struggled to cope with loss. He came close to grabbing a fifth of vodka as he found himself in a liquor store that first night spent alone. "Nobody would have known," he thought. He could have gotten drunk, but that would've only been a temporary fix and do nothing to improve his circumstance. By Grace he decided not to throw away his eight years of struggle. Pulling back from the edge of the abyss he chose nicotine and an A.A. meeting instead.

Linda took Elise, moving to her sister's house in Anaheim Hills, separating Dad from Daughter by four hours. Without an employee it was all he could do to handle his obligations of six days at the store with after hours and Sundays for everything else. Everything else did not include turn-around trips to Anaheim Hills. Work, eat, sleep, over and over again was the remedy for the heartache of separation from his only child. That year holidays were spent in deep depression. He missed his little girl so much. Their weekly phone contacts were the only source of hope to lift his spirits. Only Blizzard, his last remaining pet, filled the void of silence in the empty home he returned to each night.

That year the core of all he had known had been violently shaken. Shaken to the point, that escape from its rumblings was found only in the faith that the Universe won't give you any more than you can handle. His search for that handle was grounded only by the Grace that he struggled to understand, he felt overwhelmed in the aloneness of one who repeatedly asked for an answer to 'why'. For better or for worse, at this point he felt he was alone in the worst. By choice sober.

~~~~

We gain, we lose. We have all been shaken. We all have asked why. We have all felt alone. The strings that had woven as one are now two and the string we follow continues his weave, alone again. He was holding onto responsible by a distressed handle of faith that better days had to lie ahead.

CHAPTER 19

WAY DOWN TO THE WAY UP
THE MAIL DELIVERS

In 95 a year began again that tested perseverance and stamina. Perspective for a positive future was under the gun from the start. Obstacles to the personal joy of living, tempered early on with the return of his daughter to the area in which he lived. That was huge. Elise reenergized his resolve to head to the top of the mountain. Taking the high road is so much harder, but when you reach the top you have a much better view... Or at least different as one embraces understanding that an Elegant Energy guides the spiritual journey on which we have all embarked.

By Grace he had found the perfect new employee to help with the business operations. His name was Steve Denneen. They were a perfect match for one another. Steve did not want much and Frank couldn't afford much. He knew Steve was a compliment to the business from day one. Steve, however, probably had his doubts. The comedy of drama that played out on that first day was to be laughed about for years.

Late in 94 before Elise had moved south with her mother Frank was in a quandary. He had water deliveries to make and no one but Elise to watch the store. Linda had already divorced any notion of working at the shop, leaving him on his own. Elise was dropped off at the shop in afternoons after school to help out, but she was only ten years old and that was a bit young to be left alone for three hours while Dad ran deliveries. He was in a fix. He had been taking applications for two weeks and just before closing on Saturday night took one last application from Steve. Steve was supposed to have come in the previous day, but the swell had picked up and Steve had gone surfing instead. Frank could relate. He had those same priorities in his younger days.

Steve had his share of bad work experiences and really didn't want to work. Steve's dad Bill, a respected local environmentalist, had just by chance – Grace – talked with Frank the week before. During that conversation Bill revealed his wish for someone to give his son a chance with a job. By that Monday morning Frank was willing to take the chance. At about 9am he picked Steve's application out of the pile and made the call. Steve's mom Carol answered the phone then asked Frank to hold as she went to get Steve.

"This is Steve" came the slightly groggy announcement.

"Hey Steve, what are you up to?" Frank asked, realizing Steve had just gotten out of bed.

"Just waiting to hear what time you want me to start." Steve responded partially awake.

"How about right now?" Frank questioned in earnest.

"Right now!" Steve retorted in sleepy disbelief.

"Yeah, as soon as you can," Frank implored.

"Okay," Steve replied and hung up.

An hour later Steve showed up on deck ready... for what he didn't know.

Stevie was casually nervous as he received basic instructions from Frank. This was a large chunk of responsibility with loads of information for the free living surf master to take on, all in one shot. Frank reassured Stevie that his daughter Elise was to be at his side to help get through the next several hours as she had that Monday off from school. Just before leaving to make his deliveries, Dad instructed Daughter to roll up the coin from the vending machine. Dad knew she needed the busy work to keep her out of Stevie's hair as he began his new work challenge. Elise became the real challenge.

Frank returned a few hours latter, noticing right away that Stevie had a strangely stressed look about him. Unloading the truck he made small talk with Stevie going over the details of the day. From what Frank could detect from the flow of conversation, everything seemed to have gone fairly well. When Frank began to talk future and they began to discuss scheduling Stevie interjected, wishing to ask one more question with more than a little trepidation in the voice.

"Sure, shoot Steve what's up?" Frank asked.

Stevie's face had a conflicted but determined look as he posed the one question that was sure to make or break this deal of working at Genesis Water.

"Do I have to take orders from your daughter?" Stevie asked with a conflicted tone.

"No, ah...why?" Frank responded inquisitively.

"Because she told me I had to roll the coin from the vending machine and that I had better get it done before you returned," Stevie said in a tone that hinted, "I'll quit" if that's the case. Frank almost choked and then almost laughed as his vocal cords tried to translate the jumbled message misfiring from his brain. If this was supposed to be humor... it was working.

"Why that little bit... of course not Steve." Frank choked out with only minimal restraint from the laughter trying to escape from those same vocal cords. The air movement through the throat was similar to the pattern experienced when any fluid in the mouth might be forced out through one's nose, while drinking.

"She's got a lot of dues to pay before she'll be giving any orders around here." he shot!

"I'll speak to her right away and we'll get this crap cleared up right now!" Frank finished.

"Whew, that's a relief!" Stevie replied, the stress now gone from his face.

"I really think I'd like it here, but I'm not taking orders from any little girl!" Stevie offered in totally rigorous honesty. They both laughed hard. And with that a brotherhood had begun that is still alive.

As 95 rolled in and along Stevie grew with the business. His unique personality was a charm, helping to grow the retail end of the business automatically. Working was a big step for Stevie, his ten hours a week maximum was all he managed to handle. His vagabond free living lifestyle of surf safaris up and down the California coast took a while to reset. He even had difficulties sleeping amongst the roar of civilization, but with time was able to assimilate. Stevie was a great resource and a great kid. Frank was grateful to have him. He did have words with Elise regarding the coin rolling incident. Stevie and Elise eventually became good friends.

That year was going to be full of sweeping, reaching changes. The chaotic pace of life was becoming more and more bearable as Frank found even greater success with the projects he had come to love. He even found success in the divorce project that he really hated. Only with Grace could that project find any good end. At least Linda and Elise had returned to the Pismo area. He had been overjoyed by that change; it really lightened his load of the daily grind. Linda had ultimately agreed that Los Angeles was not where Elise should be raised. At least the two adults could agree upon that if nothing else.

The Price House was cranking in a wild array of directions. Frank was beginning to pull together bits and pieces of historical information that eventually exploded the scope of the project. It was now becoming clear that Price Canyon where the Price House was located may have had a significant role in many of California's important historical events. The trail of evidence led him to the discovery that Portola, the mission Friars and De Anza Settlers had all used the canyon as a transitional pass. Between Los Angeles and San Francisco a transition from the coast route to the inland route had to be made for ease of passage. Price Canyon was the place for that transition. According to what he found when the Rand McNally maps of the major trails used in the course of California history were overlaid, Price Canyon was the only place all the trails crossed on common ground. This made perfect sense as the trail through the canyon provided fairly flat terrain and water, while avoiding a steep mountain passage at the north end of Pismo known as Shell Beach. Undoubtedly the trails followed were those of the native Chumash and the village of Pizmu that had been located halfway up Price Canyon. This was good for the explorers and settlers but bad for these peaceful indigenous peoples who had lived in the canyon for thousands of years, maybe as long as ten thousand years. Here comes the white man…there goes the neighborhood.

All this information now meant that the scope of work for a historical park had to expand. To cover all the different stories of the canyon's history was going to take a lot more than just four acres of land. Frank went to work trying to find more. And the park master plan that the Friends of Price House had begun to work on was filling up with all kinds of new ideas. All the while Frank was personally doing the removal of damaged plaster from inside the Anniversary House. The guy was nuts with the desire for progress. His mantra became 'daily progress'. Still no time had been taken to look for artifacts though.

This was the year of a divorce and at the same time the year of 'the wedding'. Sam and Pam the Pismo Clams became 'one,' Frank and Linda became 'two'. It must have been strange gearing down for the divorce of a union and at the same time gearing up for a massive wedding with all the bells and whistles. Emotional highs and lows of dramatic proportion were part of the package marking the beginning and end of '95. Rapid fire blasts of emotional extremes confused him, making him wonder who was writing this script of unrehearsed realities. Only by Grace was he able to hold on to the wagon as he bucked and bounced his way through another year without falling off.

Recovery from the despair of the holidays was hastened by the return of Elise to Pismo, only to be followed by the call from his dad that his mom had taken a turn for the worse. February began with his award of "Director of the Year" from the Pismo Chamber followed within days by the call from Dad that Mom had died. His short trip back to Florida for his mom's funeral only provided the chance to say goodbye at her funeral. He felt unprepared for the loss and carried a heavy heart for not being able to be by his mother's side at her time of transition.

The movement through grief back to joy was achieved by the caring love from daughter Elise and the demands of the projects that consumed his time. The year's goals for progress for the Price House and Sam and Pam's storytelling immersed him back into an intense daily stride that left little time for self. By early fall the fruits of this labor manifested despite the process that had dissolved his union with Linda. The division of assets from the marriage only served as a catalyst to harden his resolve to never marry again. The realization that the union of two hearts through Grace had been reduced by man to a civil contract called a marriage license that pitted one against another materially, that was a conflict to true harmony. "That sucked," he thought and his mind wandered looking for a way to solve that harm.

Learning to 'give it away' was a life lesson that had begun when Frank became a volunteer. 'It' (time and talent) was easy for him to give away. 'It' ($) always seemed to carry a lot more weight when 'it' was tied to the material world's dollar sign. Giving 'It' away when money wasn't involved was a joy. Giving 'it' ($) away in the divorce was miserable. As part of the divorce agreement, Frank had to quitclaim the house they had purchased together in Havasu and that hurt. The divorce process as a whole took the understanding of what it meant to 'give it away' to a higher level. Even though giving away the house meant giving up financial security, 'It' also served to promote harmony in the divorce process. 'It' had another positive aspect, relief from being a landlord from 450 miles away. The lessons were good, but hard to swallow as the expectations for the marriage were put asunder. What he was beginning to learn about 'giving It away' helped to preserve his sanity in the years to come.

Expectation was another of the emotional attachments he was beginning to understand. He had already found that when you truly 'give It away' you expect nothing in return. "Funny how you always seem to receive more than you had given when you expect nothing in return," he thought. The more you expect in any given effort the more apt you are to be let down, had been his experience from time to time Now he understood the less the expectation, the greater the reward. However there are events that demanded an expectation to be attached, lived up to and fulfilled. Sadly this year he realized that wasn't always the case and a promise made wasn't always a promise kept. He learned this lesson had many facets, each shining light in its own way.

A rose was sent by Frank to his mother's grave for Mother's Day that spring. That July he surpassed the eleven year mark without having a touch from the bottle of relief. By August Frank and Jack began gearing up to paint the Anniversary House exterior, leading the City of Pismo Parks and Recreation Dept. to honor the two with a co-conferred award of "Volunteer of the Year". Then November rolled around.

The holidays were not one of the happiest times of the year for him. He rarely could be with family, but at least this year he'd have his daughter close by. It looked as if the end of the year was to go out on a fairly good note, lots of highs through the year to be proud of. He was too busy though to pay much attention to lows that were going on in the rest of the world. He tried to pay little attention to the ache in the heart for the loss of his mother. He paid enough attention to know that the planet was shrinking with the onslaught of electronics. He failed however to pick up on the assaults being made on personal freedoms and human dignity. That reality was now to invade his world.

It was a cool gray autumn day about 2pm when Frank stopped by his house to grab a quick sandwich before returning to the shop. Before going inside he stopped to retrieve the mail from the box. Scanning as he walked, sorting junk from real mail, he was pleased to see that the stack of bills was fairly small. He tossed the piles on the kitchen counter then began to make a sandwich; he was famished.

Finishing the making he began the munching as he fanned the mail for quick review. Standing at the counter to eat was standard bachelor practice while multi-tasking the mail priorities. One piece of mail stood out as unfamiliar and he pulled it from the pile. It looked like a form letter with a bad letterhead of faded ink that was slightly crooked. Probably some sort of form solicitation he thought and moved it to the junk mail pile.

As he was eating he slit open the envelopes from both piles, quick inspection of the bill pile revealed nothing out of the ordinary. Moving on to the pile of junk mail he smiled at the number of credit card offers he had received. Seemed like every day he received at least one offer of a 'pre-approved' credit card 'waiting just for him'. Having good credit was filling the mailbox to choke with offers. Reaching the bottom of the stack he came to that piece of mail with the faded letterhead. He looked closer and found the piece had a Department of Justice logo which made him curious as to what was inside. He slipped the single page letter from the envelope and began to read its information.

Within seconds his world was plunged upside down. The information he was reading made his face flush to pale, his heart flutter like a butterfly, stomach turn, appetite vanish and legs falter. Feeling lightheaded he felt his way to a chair as he reread the letter in disbelief. Sitting dumbfounded he could only think that some sort of a mistake had been made. He reread the letter for a third time trying to absorb the accusation and directive that the letter contained. The numb of pending doom forced him to remain seated as his brain tried to reconcile the information that was in direct conflict with the 'court's dismissal' that had been ordered thirteen years earlier.

The buzz of doom was slowly accompanied by growing anger that he felt as he was being forced to deal with a situation that should have never been an issue in the first place. Somebody at the Department of Justice had made a huge mistake and that mistake was now jeopardizing everything he had worked for. 'What If' just became 'What Now' and a major issue to survival. Dredging up a cold dark past was not an energy he wanted to expend at this point in his life. The past was the past and not relevant to here and now in his opinion. The past was not who he was, it was what he had done, that mistake he had paid for, according to the Superior Court for the State of California. His anger began to subside as he thought the error was to eventually be discovered by the DOJ personnel who had generated the letter. He decided to wait on taking any further action on the letter's directive, not wanting to open any can of worms that was not necessary to open. The elevation in heart rate experienced as he had read the letter was proof enough that this issue could kill. He took a few deep breaths trying to calm the heart.

Returning the letter to its envelope he remained positive that it would all work out without having to really do anything. Surely the DOJ should catch the error and the nightmare of the past would not have to be relived. Finally able to stand, he stowed the letter in a safe place just in case, then returned to the shop to complete the day. Powerful tugs of negative energy regarding the letter haunted his thoughts the rest of the day, also making for a restless night of sleep. That long-closed door to 'WHAT IF' was threatening to be reopened in a vile, disgusting manner and that was eroding any semblance of peace he was looking for in life. He tried to remain positive that the 'What If' would not become the 'What Now'.

One week later a certified letter from the Pismo Beach Police Department confirmed that the nightmare was to continue. Forcibly and not to be ignored was the request for contact regarding the Department of Justice letter. Blood pressure was on the rise, the face flushed, numbing buzz returned as Frank dialed the detective that had sent him the letter. The detective didn't pick up and instead got a voice mail prompt. He left his name, phone number and returned to his work at hand. Heart was pounding and sinking.

Early the next morning prior to the shop opening he again phoned the detective. This time the phone was answered by the detective and the inquiring began. He spent well over half an hour explaining the situation as he understood it to the detective. His demeanor was calm, but his heart raced. To the relief of his overloaded heart muscle his clarity on the issue was good enough to warrant understanding from the officer. The agreement the two men reached was that Frank was afforded a reasonable amount of time to collect evidence to prove his contention that an error had been made by the Department of Justice. He thanked the officer for his understanding.

He was relieved to feel he had an ally in his efforts to keep the door to 'What If' closed. Fortunately the detective had his original case number as Frank had no records of that entire ordeal from long ago. That case number could pinpoint the documents from the two agencies he now needed to be contacting. Dredging up this past was not something he wanted to do; it was now something he had to do to protect his reputation and ultimately his survival. This he feared was going to be a nightmare. The almost nightly dark dreams afflicted sleep.

The search began with inquiries to information operators to retrieve phone numbers for the two agencies that held the keys to the truth. Orange County Superior Court Records Department and the Probation Department were to be the starting point for this search. Phoning the court records department supplied the address and protocol needed to receive copies of the court record. He immediately sent off his request for any and all documents associated with his case. A blank, signed check was included to pay for the copies requested.

The next call was far less fruitful. Making contact with the Orange County Probation Department records division revealed records to his case had been destroyed a few years earlier and his probation officer had retired some years earlier. That was not good news, yet he felt confident that court records alone should be sufficient enough to dispose of any further need to traverse the road of doom. Within a couple of days he was able to phone back the Pismo PD's detective to inform him of the progress made. Now all they had to do was wait. The officer was satisfied Frank had made a reasonable effort to satisfy the officer's requests.

Pending doom had been put on hold and Frank returned to his survival routine trying not to dwell on the negative energy that surrounded any thoughts of the past. Thanksgiving came and went and was a bit of a downer. The holiday had been spent working and alone. As Christmas approached Dad was informed he was to be alone again as Elise and her mother were to share the holiday with Linda's family.

That was okay with Frank. He was really starting to question the season's true designs, he wouldn't have been very good company anyway. Between the agitations of the letter from the DOJ, the lie surrounding the season and being alone, the tide of emotion was pretty low. A week out from Christmas, one candle in the window was all the spirit he could muster for the season. It was to take an extraordinary power to turn that minus tide around.

A typical evening of television escape prior to turning in prompted thoughts of his friend Hana Joi. A television movie 'tearjerker' that told the story of two long lost friends reuniting sparked his desire to know how she was doing. With their contact suspended, Hana hadn't called, it was but wishful thinking on his part. Wishful thinking aside, he still wondered why he felt so connected to this girl of the past. Fanciful, with little chance of fulfillment as the thoughts of reunion might have been, at least they lifted his spirit for a few moments before he drifted off into a deep rest that had eluded him for weeks.

Same drill following day and home for lunch about 1pm... the run to the mailbox to check for a response to his record inquiry... still nothing. The unusually large stack of mail was fattened with Christmas cards. Even though he had not sent cards out in years he was still receiving them. The junk mail was thick as well and the pile was planted on the counter in a heap.

He slit open all the envelopes as he ate, then began a re-review to make sure he hadn't missed anything important. Once again he found no response he was anxious to receive, so he decided to look at the Christmas card return addresses. A quick peruse revealed one shiny label that caught his eye. The name line read "Dream It." He thought that was a bit unusual. Looking down at the town and state, he just about dropped his soda. It read Bent Island, Md. Only one person on the planet that he knew lived on Bent Island... that was Hana Joi! He couldn't believe his eyes. It couldn't be true. Or could it? He raced to extract the contents. Yes, it was a card and the front was a glossy photograph of a Tiger crouched lazily in the grass. Christmas card or what? No ribbons, no Christmas trees, no bells or angels. Was this a Christmas card or what? Opening the card he searched for a signature as to who it was from. There it was, right under the bold red Merry Christmas...Hana. Penned on the opposite page was a simple note that read, "Hey Frank, this year's the twenty-fifth reunion. Are you going?"

Frank's heart did a back flip and the spirit roared alive. He now had an address he could respond to. How unreal the whole thing seemed having that card arrive the day after seeing that stupid movie. "Whose timing was this of? What moves this enigmatic clock," tumbled in his muse. Now time to find the perfect card to respond with became his mission of focus. He was amazed at how fast and how high his heart's spirit had lifted. He now felt like he had a reason to live. It looked like the year that had started on a high note of his daughter's return, and was degraded by a few negative events, could be ending on an incredible high. The timing was nothing short of divine.

Frank spent a couple of hours looking for the perfect card to send to his found-again friend. Once he found it, it took him another hour to compose the perfect message he wanted to send. It read, "I'll go if I can take you. Call me, I lost your number. I miss you Hana Joi...... Frank." Almost giddy he enclosed a business card and whisked the correspondence to the post office, wishing to hurry a response. So dumbfounded he didn't even think to call the phone company information operator to check on a number for this confirmed address. He was blissful just knowing he might be hearing from Hana soon.

Yes.... that year ended with a flame of hope restored. The questions he had been forced to ponder during the affront to his dignity and reputation were now put aside for another day. The future seemed bright from the vantage point of caring. Top of the mountain stuff, only by Grace and sober still.

~~~~

We all can say, wow what a trip can be woven. A rollercoaster of emotion such as this would make any one of us question our journey's timing of events. The highs are relished, the lows influence darker outlook, and when run so close together in the weave, the mind can reach overload. The string we follow is no different.

CHAPTER 20

DEPRESSION

Now some horrible things happen on this planet. Some of those horrible events are caused by humans, to humans. Because of the actions of a few we don't say that all humans are bad, or do we? Have we made an assumption that all of humanity has a flaw, thus allowing the suspicion of harm from another to invade our daily life? Have we allowed this fear to fragment society, dividing us up into prejudged groupings pitting one against the other? Have we become so preoccupied with daily survival that we have allowed ourselves to be told how we must think about any given subject because the 'experts' say so? Have we allowed these perceived fears to reduce society to the enforcement of the 'the letter of the law' as opposed to the 'spirit' behind it? Have we allowed the lawmaking 'experts' to split the letter of the law so fine, so as to create a mechanism for the removal of rights from groups of individuals the 'experts' say we need to fear? Has our categorizing of the 'bad guys' allowed basic rights of human dignity to be removed so control can be exerted? Is not the 'spirit of the law' a design to promote peace and harmony? Can the 'letter of the law' and its design to control through fear ever produce the intended goal of harmony and a sustainable peaceful existence? Does prejudged categorizing promote forgiveness or simply condemn from the black and white perspective of the so-called 'experts'? Does condemnation promote peace or create backlash from finger pointing based on our prejudgments? Does prejudgment allow us to read a book by its cover, or should we read each book individually to determine content before we pass judgment? Should we judge? Have we sunk so far into an existence in the negative energy of fear that we cannot return to positive celebration of diversity that each book has to offer? Do we have to accept what we are told by the 'experts' about a book, or can we think for ourselves? If we see something is wrong can we still change it with the positive energy of what's right? Or are we stuck with the negative energy of fear, letting the 'experts' tell us it is 'in our best interest', purveying a sense of security? Can security ever be attained by fear, or does the fear for security just breed more insecurity? Have we been so thoroughly confused by information and disinformation from the 'experts' that we are allowing ourselves to be controlled and directed by fear, the 'experts' suggest? Are the 'experts' of yesterday the 'experts' of today? Are the 'experts' of today the 'experts' of tomorrow? Will humanity head down the road of 'one way only' paved in the fear mongered by 'experts'?

These and a myriad of other questions had been thrust back into his reality. The answers to these and other questions were not pleasant to him. He was now being forced into reevaluating the direction he and humanity had been coerced into following. Was this 'One Way' the 'Right Way'? A reawakening was about to begin.

As if divorced to alone isn't disheartening enough with feelings of failure, add in the opening of the failures of the past behind the door to 'What if' and a deep psychological upheaval is sure to be incurred. The moments of perspective from the top of the mountain needed to be cherished as lived, because the valleys filled with darkness that were to be forded as the journey moved forward were to be vast and encountered with increasing frequency.

~~~~

A tapestry is a completed picture; each string has its place. The one we follow struggled for a moment in the fray of taking a deeper look before a lift could be gifted.

CHAPTER 21

SURRENDER AND LEARNING TO GIVE IT AWAY

As a new year unfolded with excitement and anticipation, Frank's energy level was elevated beyond even his wildest imagination. With the thrill of new possibilities, adventure filled each avenue he had chosen to pursue. The greatest of which was yet to unfold. Creativity and imagination were unstoppable. Standing in his hot morning showers that started each day, his mind was flooded with creative concepts, which pushed his projects forward in the flamboyant confidence of a mad man.

A catalyst for his new found freedom was a financial security provided by provisions executed in his mother's will. He had never been privy to his mom and dad's financial status, having no idea that certain well-placed investments were to be dispersed to him and his brother at the time of her passing. The freedom from financial worry that was provided by the substantial amount of money received lifted the mental burden of the hand to mouth existence of his previous six years. Despite the urge to pamper himself in extravagances the copious amounts of money tempted, he opted instead to look for the more gracious ways to utilize the goodwill 'It' could perform. He remained on the small income provided by the business, utilizing reasonable portions of the new wealth to augment pay increases for his employees and new equipment as needed for the growth of the business. This strategy paid off as the growth of the business soon covered the wage increases and more part time help. He was even able to start thinking about one day buying a home to live in, rather than paying rent for the rest of his life. He really was beginning to wonder why we had all bought into the idea that owning a home had to be a 'dream'. But we had and he dreamed as well.

A whole new world had opened up to him, a world he noticed in which good and evil were closely intertwined. That concerned him. He had to remain vigilant against any negative appeals that extra wealth could manifest and the complacency it could encourage. A solemn promise was lifted up to his mother's spirit to do only good works with the gift she had left behind.

A positive start to the New Year made for a positive passing of another birthday. Shortly thereafter the phone call from Hana Joi came. The mid January timing was perfect. Frank just back from running route deliveries, Stevie had been cut loose to go home, or surf, and the shop was quiet. The ring of the phone shattered his daydreaming, or should I say planning and strategizing.

"Genesis Water Frank speaking," his common starting point.

"Hello Fraunk," the voice started and it was instant recognition of his dear friend's voice. The humorous convoluting of semi-French inflection given to his name was a dead giveaway as to who the caller was.

"Hana Lisa Joi!" Frank replied, startled.

"The one and only," Hana cooed matter-of-factly and the conversation was off and running.

Frank nailed the basics first, finding out that Hana had not moved, and in fact had the same phone number – just a different area code. He was stunned that so much time had gone by between contacts with her. The area code change recording had come and gone as it had been so long since making that first contact just before she married. This time Hana's conversation was not hesitant and it flowed easily from subject to subject.

He found out that Hana and Raul's relationship was having a rough go. Hana found out that Frank was divorced. Hana had a son Troy, eleven months older than Frank's daughter Elise. Hana owned her home on Bent Island, Frank still rented in Pismo Beach. Hana owned cats, he owned dogs. They both lived on the water, or at least very close. They both owned their own business. Frank's was a local enterprise, Hana mailed products globally that she manufactured. They both wanted to attend the twenty-fifth reunion and out of curiosity began to banter about the idea of going together. By the time they hung up Frank was in a daze of passion. His normally cautious heart began to soften its resistance with an eagerness to bask in the warmth of relationship returning.

Over the course of the next couple of months the phone call frequency with Hana increased. With each connection the details of their lives over the last twenty five years became more intimate. The recalling and reminiscing about their high school years elevated their curiosity about all the other friends they had had and what they might be up to now. Talk of what the reunion might reveal sparked earnest interest in his desire to attend. Frank's brain followed accordingly with the development of a plan to get away for a week to attend the mid-summer reunion events. Hana was willing to go with him; the warmth in his heart was driving him forward to make the trip happen. He'd have given anything to spend time with Hana. The planning was from a high place.

As usual he worked overtime to maximize the journey; and soon Elise was included in the plan. What an opportunity to show his daughter the nation's capital. With a little extra effort he was able to obtain two tickets for a White House tour from his local Congresswoman, Andrea Seastrand. By April he was in a frenzy with the mass of work to be completed in order to get out of town. The now ten day trip included a two-day visit to his brother's family in Houston, Texas, prior to arriving in Maryland. His fired up frenzy was being fueled by the growing glow of a heart hungry for meaningful connection. The glow had to be tempered though; Hana was a married woman, and he made sure that bond was to be respected. Nevertheless, his heart pounded with the anticipation of hugging the petit beauty he had adored so many years before.

For Frank, Mother's Day in May was a reflective journey through ever more precious memories of time spent with his mom. It had been a year since her passing and he still dealt with loss. The call to the florist in Pensacola, Florida, to place an order for a single rose to be placed at his mother's gravestone was followed by tears. Emotions crashing like pounding surf as he asked for a pink ribbon to bind the simple arrangement, he almost broke on the phone.

He shared his grief for the loss with no one, not even Hana. He spent that day at the Price House working on what he can't remember. A lone Sunday spent in the park with just himself, thoughts of Hana, his mom, and nature. The Price House and Park he was finding had a special positive energy, its remote location lent easily to healing. It was his refuge for spiritual uplifting. This place of refuge was to be needed again by the end of the month.

Have you ever walked into a closed sliding glass door? Walked into a pole on the sidewalk while you were looking sideways? How about backing your car into something you didn't know was there? That's what the brick wall felt like that Frank ran into at the end of the month. First the surprise startles you then the anger sets in. When your survival is at stake fear can numb you to the bone. That's what the registered letter from the Pismo Beach Police Department did for him. In the race of life he had forgotten all about the diggings of the DOJ into his past. The letter was an absolute reminder. An 'in your face' demand from Pismo PD for immediate contact regarding this matter hit him like a ton of bricks. He immediately picked up the phone and called Detective Bob. On the voicemail he stated he was sorry he had forgotten all about the issue and much to his surprise he had not yet received any of the requested material from the Orange County Courts records department. Hanging up, the numb of persecution he felt made his chest feel tight and he languished that night in the uncertainty of the situation. A very dark cloud had returned. 'What If' was again 'What Now'.

The following morning he called again, making sure he had enough personal time for an extended conversation before opening the shop for business. Detective Bob answered the phone. Frank explained that he was mystified that he had not received a response to his request. The signed blank check had not been cashed. He went on to explain that because there had been no response he hadn't been reminded to respond to the accusations arising the previous November. Detective Bob responded, somewhat annoyed, that he could have those documents within a day if he wanted. Frank suggested he do that as he himself didn't know how else to facilitate a response. After all, he had sent a blank signed check, how else could he entice their cooperation? Detective Bob responded that he'd make that call and would be in touch.

Twenty-four hours later they were on the phone together again. The detective informed him that he had all the paperwork in hand. The detective indicated he had not discovered the claims Frank had alluded to in the paperwork he had. He then stated that Frank needed to set a time to come down to the police station for a meeting to review what was received. The following day at three was agreed upon.

At 2:45pm the following day Frank was at the old red brick high school building that now housed City Hall and the Police Department headquarters. At the front desk Detective Bob was summoned, and after introduction the nightmare exploded into full color. Frank was led into a back room that contained several desks with one other officer present. The grind was started by the summation from the detective that no proof had been found in his investigation of the court documents to substantiate Frank's claim that the DOJ accusations were misdirected. Frank asked to see the records. He did his own search for those elusive words that could end the insidious claim that could wrap his world in the very darkest clouds of 'What Now'. His fevered reading of the few documents provided turned up some evidence that he had remembered receiving fifteen years prior. The Court Order of Dismissal had the statement signed by the judge that he thought should end this threat to his survival as a respected small businessman in this very small community. He showed it to the detective and read it out loud. The document stated,

"It is the order of this court that the plea of guilty or nolo contendere or the finding of guilt be set aside and the case dismissed; defendant hereafter being released from all penalties and disabilities resulting from said conviction, pursuant to Section 1203.4 Penal Code," signed by the judge of the superior court.

Detective Bob then pointed out another document that appeared to be a minute order from the court. Frank read it and believed it to be part of the requirement of probation, not of the final decree, also stating that other facts regarding 'expungement', 'dismissal' and the 'sealing' of the record were missing. Frank requested more time for research to find what he thought was missing those exclusive words demanded to be seen in black and white by the Police Department, those elusive words he remembered being spoken by the judge to his attorney, "Upon successful completion of probation the defendant shall not be required to register as a sex offender."

Detective Bob forcibly indicated that the police department had given him adequate time, after all it had been six months since the matter had been brought to his attention. The detective also indicated that he had all the documents in hand and there were no more. The detective then went on to say, if he did not have any other proof to provide the department, he needed him to register that day. Numb dumb, inched closer to explosive anger. Frank asked what the response might be if he refused to sign the document that would point an accusatory finger at him for the rest of his life.

"You will be arrested for failure to register as required," was the detective's terse response and that was terrorizing in scope.

Frank realized he was trapped. He either had to comply with finger pointing and mug shots, or find his name in the local newspaper's Police Beat column. This kind of publicity could kill a small business in a heartbeat, and he could imagine the ridicule that he and his family might face. On the other hand, if he signed the document, he would be agreeing to annual registration for the rest of his life. He pleaded for the detective to understand the quandary, after all it had been almost twenty years, there had to have been some sort of a mistake. It fell on deaf ears. He then asked what was to be done with the information should he decide to sign the paperwork as this was not something he particularly wanted broadcast. His daughter didn't know about this past and he wanted to keep it that way.

Detective Bob agreed that the situation sucked, but that he had no alternative. Without official documents with 'those words' his hands were tied. The detective tried to reassure him that the information was for department use only and only to be shared with the county sheriff's office. He encouraged Frank to sign the registration document as that was the only sure way to keep the matter as quiet as possible. Detective Bob went on to offer his support in getting this all reversed if Frank was to find proof to support his claim. He also offered to do the mug shot and fingerprinting, to make the process as quick and quiet as possible. "Gee... what a helpful thoughtful gesture," Frank thought in sarcastically rolling anger.

Gotta try to keep the heart rate down or die on the spot so he took a deep breath. Dazed by his dilemma he could only protest his indignation, venting frustration that the court's order was not good enough to stop the twisted process that was unfolding. Broken by the terror invoked as retaliation to dissent, under duress he signed the document.

Anger set in good and that energy prevailed, clouding his mind with the terror of pending doom and a diminished self esteem. The next several weeks were spent in a swirling river of solitary torment of 'What If' and 'What Now'. There was no one to talk to about this. It was solely his burden. He alone had to wrestle with the demons that the anger and indignation evoked. That night only cannabis allowed sleep to creep.

The wind had been sucked from his sails. The masts of self respect had been snapped off at their base, his ship of dreams was left to toss on an angry ocean of uncertainty. The tumultuous storm of torment took weeks to subside into a becalmed aimless drift. The attempts to recapture and sustain headway with the winds of motivation could only happen when the inner structure of self esteem had been stabilized. But the depression rendered was a darkness that concealed detection of any positive prevailing winds. Darkness gave way to a thick fog as his responsibilities restored feeling to the numb fingers that had been holding onto the rudderless tiller of his brain. It was a quiet time, only his daughter Elise sensed that something was wrong.

Awareness that the ship of life was always on the move, his daughter and responsibility began to clear the foggy quiet of 'no where'. Within a month or so the tack for progress had been reset and the rush of life's winds had Frank well heeled. Clarity, focus and direction returned. "Why waste time 'no where,' life had too much to offer on the journey that was positive and good," he thought. The 'If' was 'Now'. Could he let that 'Be'?

'What If' had blown into 'What Now' and those 'What' winds had no friends. All courses required adjustment and that burden was wearisome. The 'What' winds blew spasmodically, leaving only the debris of doom strewn about on the sea of tranquility he wanted to sail upon. His days of fine straight sailing was now going to be staggered by abrupt course corrections to avoid the reefs of grief the 'What' winds blew him toward. The search for truth was limited by bouts with those negative angry winds that provided little headway. Those ill winds became fewer and far between as he really didn't achieve any positive results from sailing those waters. Constantly on watch for disaster depletes your strength. He was growing weary and his need for a break was growing. The gracious calming wind out of the angry winds became Hana.

By mid July his giddy plan to get away to the East coast was well established. The plans of dreamy diversion from the everyday grind brought joy with anticipation, which was welcome relief. He and Hana now had all the plans firmed up for a five day long stay, except which hotel he and Elise were to be staying in. On one of his many phone calls with Hana he had mentioned that if she had enough room he'd love to stay with her. Hana 's husband Raul had moved back to his other house in Baltimore and he knew this was a little bold, but offered that he'd much rather give her the money for accommodations as opposed to some hotel. Hana thought about that for a few days, then agreed to provide accommodations for the two, three days before the journey was to begin. Better yet, the night before Frank and Elise's father/daughter trip to DC, Hana called to confirm that she and her son Troy would pick them up at the airport.

Frank was exploding with anticipation. He and Elise flew to Houston and spent two days with his brother's family. The visit was a blur, almost an inconvenient hesitation in momentum towards what was now a heart-pounding reunion. He recognized he might be falling into the memory of love he had known a long time ago. Recognition at the airport of his long separated friend was to be his first test of memory though, as he had not let Hana describe her self to him over the phone.

"How will you recognize me?" she asked at one point.

"I have a vision from your voice and I want to see how close its come," he told her.

He was lit with anticipation, hardly sleeping the night before the final leg to DC began.

Landing in Baltimore in early afternoon, Frank's feet moved at a fevered gait down the jet way leading to the crowd of people waiting to greet their designated travelers. Elise was in excited tow. Emerging from the jet way into the crowd he scanned the sea of faces from left to right. Wading into the crowd he slowed to a stop as his gaze lifted to faces toward the back of the crowd just behind the main surge. Sweeping right like a laser looking for its target his eyes locked onto a sparkling pair of deep sea blue eyes, radiating the twinkle of 'I know you' joyful recognition.

There she was, softly smiling as she returned the gaze of hello from those astounding blue eyes. He moved with purpose through the crowd toward her. She straightened from the casual lean she had taken against the column she stood next to. Her blond hair and soft complexion made her eyes that much more intense as he approached. Finally reaching the personal threshold of her space Frank confidently offered,

"Hana Joi."

"Hello Frank," Hana responded.

They embraced in the warmth of friendship they had known some twenty-five years earlier, picking up right where it had left off. The joy of that touch bringing peace to his soul that had yearned for this contact. The excitement of reaching a longed for destination, filled the air like electricity. They conversed profusely on the ride back to Hana's home. He couldn't believe he was in her presences.

Troy and Elise jumped all over Hana's suggestion to go to the pool after they had situated their belongings and had a bite to eat. The pool was a refreshing way for the kids to get to know one another, providing some time for Frank and Hana to get caught up. The change into swim suits was made, the short ride to the pool at the marina carried Frank back in time. The heady smell of humid Maryland summers stimulated the recall of familiar places from long ago. He still couldn't believe he was in her presence. The feel was unreal.

With the kids cut loose in the pool the adults settled in on the poolside lounge chairs for a good heart-to-heart. Frank may have been physically reclining in a chair, but his spirit was a thousand feet in the air. He wanted to know all about Hana's life over the past parted years and encouraged her to tell her story, his could wait. Hana looked at him with stern blue eyes and queried,

"Do you really want to know everything?"

"Yes." he said unequivocally, noting her serious yet indecisive tone.

"Okay," she said timidly from behind blue eyes that told of a trusting confidence one expects from a true friend.

Hana's recounting of her life's details they had not discussed over the phone, stunned Frank into his chair. The first astounding revelation was that from the time she was in junior high she had been sexually molested by one of her brothers. It went on for years and she had not been able to get her parents to intervene. Bam! There you go! Bombshell number one! "What do you think about that!" was read from deep blue eyes, cold with unfinished rage. Frank noted Hana's anger fueled by feelings of being let down by the ones who should have protected her. She had been unable to make it stop, and her anger and torment had yet to subside. He could only look into her eyes and in silence let her know he felt her pain. And he felt his own. His past tore his soul, he bled silently. Who was writing this script anyway? Why?

Frank couldn't believe it! He had a deep friendship with her for years and he never knew. Hana said no one ever knew outside of her family. Her torment through those years she kept carefully hidden with walls and drugs. The air of togetherness and confidence she had exuded the whole time he had known her was all a front. Hana's torment had been endured alone. It had been shared with only a few from the outside world, only as her personal therapy allowed. Then after the most outrageous of abuses had occurred, was Hana able to lash back in angry confrontation to make the cycle stop. Frank felt a heart-wrenching sympathy and apologized for not knowing. He wished that somehow he could have been the friend that could have made a difference.

Hana then revealed that part of her recovery was never to let this kind of abuse go unpunished. She had been made aware that an abuse case in her community was headed for a hand slap of justice, as reported in a local paper. Hana made it her mission to arouse community awareness, so that the victim in that case did not have to live the torment of shame she had. Hana was to be damned if this guy was to be let go with a sentencing that might serve to diminish his responsibility for the damage he had caused. Hana's poster campaign to heighten awareness worked, and the defendant received a harsh sentence. Hana only hoped she had helped as an advocate in justice for the victim.

Hana's fervor regarding this issue chilled Frank to the bone. Thoughts of Hana ever finding out about his past sickened him, as it could surely destroy this incredible relationship they enjoyed. He felt uneasy as Hana opened up her life for him to know. He felt as if he might be violating Hana's confidence if he did not reveal his past, yet his selfish desire to maintain their level of friendship kept him from full disclosure. The thought of telling her made him sick. He wanted desperately to hold on to what they had, but at the same time felt he was lying to Hana by not disclosing his secret. He was twisted with dilemma. His decision was to wait. Maybe he might never have to tell her if he could slam that door to 'What If' shut once again. Frank's euphoria of being with his special friend had been momentarily transformed into a depressed guilt-ridden shame of his own past. He listened intently to Hana's story and could only agree she had done the right thing. He remained quiet in his own introspection as Hana took a moment to gather her thoughts before continuing. Hana then turned more toward Frank leaning forward saying,

"Now I have something else to tell you and you can't tell anyone."

Frank assured her she could trust that anything she said was to be held in the strict confidence of a trusted friend. Hana paused for a moment, staring intensely into his eyes. She searched for and found that friend she could trust from the eyes of his returning gaze that emanated from soul. He couldn't imagine anything worse than what Hana had already revealed, and he sat up, leaning forward, to give Hana his undivided and secured attention. What he was about to be told changed his life's journey profoundly. Hana looked down, then gently back into Frank's eyes. She looked almost apologetic, as if what she was going to say might hurt. His return gaze reflected he was ready to be that friend she needed. Hana then revealed that three years earlier while having a routine annual physical exam from her doctor, she had been tested and diagnosed HIV positive.

Hana leaned back. She waited for his response. Frank sat back and took a moment to let the shock abate. He wanted desperately to respond, yet sat silent unable to speak. His mind turned to a Greater source as his own words were lost in the dumbing of disbelief. "Oh God let me say the right thing," he thought. In that moment he responded with words that came out of his mouth, yet had not come from his muddled brain. Where these words had come from he did not know, but he spoke them with absolute sincerity and Grace asking,

"Where do we go from here?"

Frank noticed a mixture of relief and disbelief on Hana's face. She took a moment then leaned forward to speak again. Her beautiful blue eyes telling the relief she felt as she began,

"Ya know Frank, you are one of the few people that I've told that hasn't broken down."

"Almost everyone else I've told I've had to console after telling them." She almost cried.

Hana, in her search for support and understanding from only the closest of friends and family, found that the eventuality of death from this disease crumbled the composure of the ones she had confided in. Their focus on the end blinded them to the need at the moment to be strong and supportive for Hana as she began her struggle for life. Not Frank and that was huge support.

In Hana's area, fear and ignorance about the 'homosexual disease' dominated to the point that the postman wouldn't deliver mail to those known to be afflicted. Local social innuendo dictated a distancing to downright shunning of those who were sick. Prevailing thought was that the affliction meant certain death and soon. The current belief suggested contact meant contracting the disease, so the uninformed made the ones who bore the illness pariahs in their own community. Hana so feared this backlash that she had become paralyzed to sharing her struggle with but a trusted few. He now had joined the ranks of the precious few that knew. It only took awhile for him to figure out that Hana too was haunted with his same demon of 'What If'.

Hana allowed Frank to enter her world of private torment, and with Grace his heart responded. As if someone had spoken directly to him his heart was told never abandon his dear friend's needs. Obliged to the Grace that had spoken to him, he promised to that Grace and himself that Hana's peace was to be his task. Hana struggled for an understanding of God or Grace, any gifting of his small understanding to be the most important friending he could impart. Only by example could this most important message be passed on. He knew he should take every opportunity to carefully suggest this Grace was guiding the pathway to his peace. They already had a treasured friendship, and this was going to take it to a whole new level. He didn't know it, but he too had started his own journey to life's greatest lesson as well. He was now going to learn how to give love away. The scripts Writer was writing a ride that had to be ridden to be believed. Hold on, the ride picks up speed.

The next four days comprised a whirlwind of activities. The reunion was the highlight of reminiscing. Old friends, faces and places came alive remembering the past and catching up to the present. From the old brought the new and Frank made a connection that proved to be tremendously important in the years to follow. By chance conversation he met and befriended a fellow Californian by the name of Mary Page-Brydum. Mary lived in Van Nuys with her family and the two decided to stay in touch. Once again Grace had charted a course of which Frank had no comprehension. Stepping stones to peace arrive in the most unusual ways. Gifts arrive from amazing places. The whole trip was a gift.

Frank's trip with the kids to downtown DC was another pleasant surprise. He noticed the kids acted much like siblings who lived apart and had a lot to catch up on. They whispered talk, showing they too had connected and that was special. The father/daughter tour through the White House was very special. The history was so thick you could smell it. Hana's quaint, humble house had the buzz of a family enjoying the fullness of life. Departure from the norm for Frank, he relished the feel of family with every moment. What a gift.

Frank wanted to hug and touch to show he wasn't afraid, yet he could feel Hana's hesitation. Hana did hug, but with a depth that had its limits. She wanted to feel that warm connection, yet held his affections at arms length. He understood this unspoken language, respecting her personal space while thanking his lucky stars that he could at least be part of Hana's life. Hana's desire to protect herself emotionally, and Frank physically, gave rise to a truth of love he had to recognize. That truth was, he should expect nothing in return for sharing love and compassion with his dear friend. He was beginning to comprehend that true real love had to be given away. Given away meant 'no strings'. This undoubtedly was to be the toughest, yet most rewarding revelation he was to learn to live.

On departure day he and Hana embraced deeply. A parting kiss on the cheek reaffirmed to Hana his intention to be there for her whenever she needed him and he respected her space. He was unafraid of staying close to help take on the challenges that the future held, conveying this message both spoken and unspoken. He sensed Hana's joy of having an ally and her bewilderment that someone could be so willing. He assured her that everything was to be okay, and then departed feeling intoxicated from the experience of growth through this new found love. The illumination of spirit lasted for months. The sadness of separation antagonized for months.

That year was punctuated with another unusually big event. ...Like he needed more. The ex-wife was having major conflicts with the daughter and one day a phone call revealed that Elise was coming to live with him. This was an outstanding turn in events for Frank; he welcomed the opportunity to raise his daughter. He was glad he had stayed in the same house. Elise could at least return to a more familiar surrounding. With her own bedroom and bathroom she was about as comfortable as a kid could be. They made a pretty good team as they plowed along through life. Funny how life events come full circle. Just over a year had passed since Dad had watched in anguish as Elise was taken out of his life, and now she was his life. Elise was job one. All other responsibilities were modified to include her wherever feasible, not always to her liking. They were cut from the same stone, so they butted heads from time to time, but that was to be expected. Still, she was back and that was full circle.

His level of contact with Hana had dramatically increased; her input regarding the understanding of Elise was absolutely priceless. Frank likewise provided Hana with valuable insights into raising Troy, the family feeling flourished. He had witnessed how Elise had taken to Hana, and Hana, the angel she was, took Elise under her motherly wing. The feeling of family he had felt while in DC felt so good that he wanted more.

Having Elise and Hana back in his life ignited the spread of positive joy to the other projects cranked out that year. The birth of the Baby Clams to Sam and Pam with a trip to LA for morning news had been spirited to success through the underlying enthusiasm that filled and fueled his energies. Elise was there; fortunately Hana could participate by phone.

The Price House project flourished as well in the same spirit. His obvious head-over- heels melancholy for Hana had Betsy from FOPH a bit worried she might lose Frank to this new-found love. He dispelled her worry by his hands-on progress fixing up the old house. Elise was there and Hana lived it by phone.

Genesis Water enjoyed a full 6% growth rate that year. Elise was there, Hana learned a lot about his small business over the phone. The phone was the umbilical cord for Frank and Hana's glowing relationship, but face-to-face, eye-to-eye was what he really wanted. So he hatched the plan to have Hana and Troy out for a visit. It was easier for them to come out than for him to travel back to them. That year Frank found a renewal of interest in holiday cheer. The plans to have Hana arrive the day after Christmas staying through the New Year elevated his spirit. It lifted him up to the joy of giving at a time of year he was not usually in his best of spirits. Giving Hana a week-long break from the stress of her daily struggles was a thrill for him to provide. He could live family again. Besides the fact that Hana could use a little time away, he could host face to face from his home. The uplifted spirit from the pending visit even inspired him to roll on a fresh coat of paint inside, plus a thorough cleaning of his humble abode. He had to at least try to appear to be a reasonable housekeeper. With Elise's help before she left with her mother to spend the holiday with her grandmother Pat, the place was looking pretty good ready for a special guest. He was giddy again. Don't we all get a bit giddy when love blooms? Frank was no different.

Frank was on cloud nine as he waited for Hana at the end of the skyway ramp. When she emerged they embraced, if there were a cloud eleven he was there. The three hour drive from the Los Angeles airport back to Pismo seemed to take just minutes. He turned over his bedroom and bathroom to Hana so she could settle in and feel at home. Hoping to sleep at her side that night was out, he detected he was still at arms length and that was okay. The couch would be fine, he was just happy to have her there. The kids wouldn't be joining them for a few days and he did his best to spoil her in the meantime. Two days of Frank's undivided respectful attentions had managed to put Hana into a blissfully settled state of mind. Despite the rainy gray skies that had set in the day she arrived, their cheerful enlightened conversations brightened any space they shared, lifting any doubt that their relationship was at the perfect place. Hana felt secure, trusting in her host's company, which was reflected in her conversations that delved far and deep into her hopes and fears. His too went deep, only to stop short of his greatest fear of full disclosure of his dreaded 'What If'. He did however take a huge leap into faith by sharing the gift of love, so long dormant

He had set up a day away from the shop so he and Hana could take a ride up the coast to Big Sur. They left mid morning in a steady light rain with the only goal of lunch in Big Sur and another pleasant peace filled day. He had an additional goal however. This goal was to tell Hana exactly how he felt about her from his heart. He had not had such a heartfelt emotion in a long time. He just had to let it all out. This was huge for him. He was going to divulge the full scope of his understanding of their relationship, honestly revealing the truth he knew about how he felt. He hadn't opened up to anyone like this in years. Open can be a scary spot. We've all been there.

His verbal journey started about an hour into their drive up Pacific Coast Highway. It took him that long just to muster up the courage to begin to explain what he REALLY felt. He wasn't sure how Hana might take his profuse outpouring of love. He was hoping that Grace could guide his words to her heart. He was REALLY stepping out of the box.

The rain fell a little harder as their car traversed the craggy shoreline. Frank started by asking Hana if she could recall an incident from their shared high school chorus class. This incident, a disagreement of some sort, was the first time he realized that Hana did have a deep seeded feeling for him. Her apology for the spat had been non-verbal, sticking with him ever since. Frank suggested to Hana that it might have been the start to this truly amazing relationship they shared. He was curious to know if she could recall the incident and the apology she extended.

Hana tried, but couldn't recall what had happened, or her response. She was now intrigued by what had transpired. She remembered he had asked her a few months prior about this same subject. He had not revealed at that time how she had responded, other than saying she had written the response down on a sheet of paper. Hana's curiosity was pushing now, she wanted to finally know what she had done that had left an obviously major impression embedded in his heart.

He obliged Hana's curiosity by telling her he was at a loss to remember precisely what they argued about. He did recall that whatever it was she had been on the losing end; the argument cut short of final resolution when the class was called to order. Unable to apologize verbally she had written the apology in the top right corner of her open binder so he could read it from where he sat one seat behind. As silence was called for by the instructor, she had looked directly into his eyes, turned, wrote the message then closed the notebook. That was his recall of the incident. Hana again couldn't remember. The message was short, just three words long. Written on paper freely with no expectation of return, the notebook closed with no glance back to acknowledge sending or receipt, or to elicit response to the message expressed. Frank's knowledge now of what had been going on for Hana then made it clear why the message was never verbalized and why he had been at 'arms length' ever since. He also understood that his reciprocation of deep feeling had to be 'given away' with no expectation of return. The message that had been written long ago and had been felt ever since simply said, "I love you."

The constant rain falling let up a bit. A moment of silence passed as Hana gazed out the cars window searching to remember. Frank turned, looked at her and said,

"I love you too, Hana Joi. I guess I always will."

This caught Hana by surprise and she responded in her surprise, "I don't know what to say Frank."

He reassured her that she didn't have to say anything. This is simply the way he felt and he was prepared to 'give this away' to her, free of any expectation of return. He then plowed forward, revealing that in looking back through his life he had realized she had been the model by which he had set a standard, to which all his other relationships had been judged. She seemed to have embodied all he had been searching for. He didn't know where it would lead, he was leaving that up to the Grace that had reunited them.

Reaching the café nestled amongst the huge pines of Big Sur, he was on a joyous high of truth and honesty. Even the car didn't seem to be planted on the ground. A fireside lunch only inflamed his euphoric mood. Not a care in the world, except for the condition of the road and hillsides that were prone to catastrophic slippage from saturating prolonged rain.

Hana on the other hand was concerned and confused on how to respond to Frank's outpouring. On the somewhat treacherous journey back down the mountain she was completely frank with him.   Hana confided she appreciated his honesty, but she did not feel the same way as him. She knew they had something special, yet felt she was not on the same level as him, unwilling to go there at this time. Frank affirmed he understood this, he had known all along that he was at arms length yet loved. It was okay with him to just bathe her in his affections, knowing the adoration was good for her heart, soul and health; his as well.

He didn't know how long he might have to enjoy Hana. The HIV virus that raged in her body could take her at any time. He wanted her to know just how he felt. He reaffirmed his commitment to be at her side in the battle she waged to beat the disease that still had no cure. He privately asked Grace to pour through his heart to help prolong Hana's quality of life. She had revealed her goal to live long enough to see her son graduate from high school, he asked Grace to grant those intentions.

His close attention to the road condition was his only real tap into reality. Feeling their connection deepen, the relationship rose again to another level. This was not a space of consciousness that he was accustomed to. For him it was a blissy yet intense twisting trip down emotions road. They finally slipped off the mountain, whisking their way home in a driving rain. Reaching home just after dark, Frank flipped on the local news to hear that a stretch of PCH south of Big Sur had slipped down the mountain and into the ocean. They had gotten through just in time. He hoped he had gotten through to Hana in time. No strings attached.

With the arrival of the kids, the last few days of the visit were filled with the warm feel of family. Kids this time did try a little rivalry of boy vs. girl. Having to trip around in between the rain drops put a damper on outside activities; kids grow restless inside. The intensity of rivalry continued to escalate providing smiles for the adults. That's what kids do.

The last night was spent in Santa Barbara, accompanied by the incessant rain that seemed to have been falling the entire visit. The sunshiny mild weather Frank had promised had failed to develop. The jokingly spoken mantra of this trip, "yeah right, there's sun in California in the winter". As Hana and Troy's plane lifted off from the Santa Barbara airport the next morning the sun did break through. Frank captured the spectacle on tape as he filmed the planes ascent into the sky of jagged blue and gray. When they talked that night by phone Frank informed Hana the sun did in fact come out. All Hana could say was, "Yeah, right!" They laughed.

It was a great trip, for that he was truly grateful. Hana was grateful too, feeling re-inspired and refreshed by her host's generosity from heart. The journey must go on and they were in it together. Frank was ecstatic Hana was accepting the hand at arms length. With cautions they stepped into the future not knowing where Grace scripted the tour. Caution or not the gift of the tour had started. A gift. No strings attached.

~~~~

We all have a wild journey from time to time. Trials are gifts to greater truth in living, opportunities to show our strings' true colors. If we pay attention our weavings stay on task, responsible and abundant. The gift returned teaches the greater lesson. Surrender to 'giving love away' and an Elegant Energy returns Light to bury whatever darkness lurks. Our string we follow learns to practice this art, and his journey is armored with enhanced truth.

CHAPTER 22

A SIMPLE RING

Imagine the experience of extreme high to extreme low all in a matter of seconds. Why was life sharing this with him he did not know? Made him wonder again just who was writing this script of the life he lived. The euphoria of Hana's stay was to be destroyed by the dementia brought on by the Pismo PD's phoned demand for an annual update of registration, required within 10 days of one's birthday. "How sick is that," he thought. Making a person degrade themselves posing for mug shots and finger prints on or about their birthday every year was a sick psychological assault on one's self-esteem at a time when one should be celebrating life. "Maybe that's their intention," was his speculation. "That could tend to make a person bitter." Besides he had just done the ritual a few months prior. How much of this abuse anyone could stand was up for speculation as well. His thoughts about it did not have a bright ending. He was sure he was not the only one to feel debilitating humiliation brought on by this annualized ritual. At least Hana had just left and didn't have to witness the ordeal.

The road out of this darkness was lined this new year by the demand of commitments. The darkness was repressed slowly and privately, helped along by the extension of love to Hana and his projects. The Price House was a healing ground providing the serenity of contact with the good spirit of peace. The house was becoming the surrogate for the girl he could not spend time with. The joy in Hana seemed to abound as he worked the farm's projects in the seclusion of the remote canyon setting. The house was given the time that would have been given to Hana had she been here. It was a beneficial trade off for both Frank and the park. He could be replenished in spirit; the park got a lot of work done.

Just when it seemed that his emotions were back on even keel the Universe threw another surprise his way. This one sparked a mixed emotion of pride along with the fear of 'What If' and 'What Now'. He was completely caught unaware when honored as the Pismo Beach Chamber of Commerce 'Citizen of the Year' at the annual Board of Director's Installation Banquet. His many efforts for the Chamber of Commerce were being honored. His selection was a well-kept secret. He should be proud, yet his gut wrenched from the fear of discovery of his past and the embarrassment it might bring to this group that he respected. His short humble comments from the podium were tempered by what he knew he had to do. This was early February, just a few short weeks after his humiliating updating nightmare. He knew if he could not get this enigma quashed, he must resign his board chair by re-election time at the end of the year. His gut feeling was that the supposed confidential information held at the Pismo PD was sure to leak out someday. His true desire was not to drag anyone else into the resulting bloodbath of possible disgrace. Bailing out was viewed as his only option.

The anger that was generated by the accusing finger of the registration ritual prompted him to again search for the relief from this requirement he had been promised years prior. He drafted and sent a letter along with a copy of the Court Order to the ACLU in early March. The response to that letter was again not exactly the feedback he'd liked. Some of the information was disturbing regarding a newly enacted statute called 'Megan's Law'. The letter contained the same message as relayed by the Pismo PD, that short of having written documentation stating "does not have to register," only a pardon from the Governor of the State of California could relieve him from the duty to register. This wearing negative energy was not the space he really wanted to live.

Eventually he drifted to the more enjoyable aspects of life. There was just way too much good stuff going on to let this humiliation run his life. Sure he could have quit all the projects and organizations that brought him notoriety. That could save him some worry, but that's not who he was. He loved these works. He had made long term commitments to do these things; he'd be damned if he was just going to cut and run. He was good at the things he did. That helped save his self-esteem from total annihilation from the blister of accusatory presumption of guilt associated with the registration requirement.

Sharing the joy he felt in his relationship with Hana was another good way for him to pull his mind out of funk. Two good friends, both women, had provided him with an outlet in which he could share the abundant joy he felt in Hana. One was his new friend from Van Nuys, Mary Brydum; the other was his next-door neighbor Joanne. Both ladies were married and raising girls his daughter's age. Their insights into relationships between men and women and raising girls gave him valuable insights in both areas.

Mary had been sincere when she had taken Frank's phone number at the reunion. She had vowed to stay in touch and held true to that promise. Mary's first phone call the previous fall really surprised him. So often someone asks for your number indicating they will call and they don't. Mary did. Her interest in how he and Hana were doing was sincere. Mary's strong yet humorous personality blended well with his and the friendship grew rapidly.

Mary's interest in the Pismo area drew an invite from Frank around Clam Festival time; Mary and her family came to visit. Frank and Elise got a chance to meet Mary's husband Steen and their two girls Kirsten and Erika.

The girls became fast friends and were off in their own world. Mary and Steen enjoyed the serenity of Pismo from the hotel room Frank had procured that was walking distance to the beach, many restaurants and the festival grounds. Frank was extremely busy with festival goings on, but did have time to catch a dinner or two with his new friends. His creation of the Clam family made for particularly humorous conversation especially when recounting the Los Angeles television interview, antics which had the group crying with laughter. His history tour talk and walk at the Price Anniversary House gave Mary and family an insight into the complete Pismo most visitors don't get. By the time they left to return to the Valley, Mary was hooked on Pismo.

Mary returned many times, eventually becoming a rock Frank leaned on at crucial times. He went far and deep into his past with Mary, his only confidant to the demons of 'What If' and 'What Now'. He was sure when you looked up the definition of 'true friend' in the dictionary Mary's picture was there.

Joanne was never told by Frank about his past. She became a listening post of another sort. Their Wednesday coffee hour was spent with Frank's pouring out of Hana and Joann's encouragement to him to love this lady she had heard so much about. They both poured out their trials and tribulations in trying to raise their girls. Common ground, the girls were the three baby clams. Joanne and Frank made a perfect team at a perfect time to lead the girls into the community service of playing the comical kid clams. It was a fantastic opportunity for the kids. Frank, with Joann's tremendously supportive participation, made the service of playing the baby clams a learning experience for the kids which was becoming a part of Pismo's history. Being next-door neighbors helped; he always felt a debt of gratitude to her. Without Joann's help he could not have launched and run the Clam program with as much success. Their Wednesday rendezvous at the coffee houses around town was the planning and strategy table that kept them one step ahead of the Clams and girls. The team effort to teach and guide did lend itself to a humorous analogy of being akin to 'animal trainers'. As the girls transitioned from grade school to middle school the 'animal trainers' needed all the humor they could muster.

Joanne also provided Frank with the inspiration to write in a journal from time to time, recording the adventures of love he had confided to her about Hana. Somehow she knew that these transcribed feelings could help him absorb his fascinating adventure called life. These exacting memories did provide him with a detailed personal account of important emotions encountered on his daily walk with Grace. His journal, even as brief as it was, demonstrated how important he regarded the spiritual element that guided his path. The journal also documented the incredible love and regard he held for Hana. The negative grind of the evil that followed him made its way onto the pages of the journal, but only a few times. Those entries showed the Grace by which Mary's friendship had been bestowed. The ever greater lapse of time between his entries indicated the ever increasing toll that 'What If' was taking on his joy of life. The year rolled on.

A flower was sent to Mom gravesite on Mother's day. The fireworks show on the 4th of July was even better than the previous show and Frank was finally proud of the Chamber's efforts. Frank, Jack and Lee put together a fabulous fundraiser for the Price House that garnered some big dollars and great publicity. The Price House was also undergoing a siding replacement, all donated by the good men from the Kiwanis Club of Greater Pismo. The Clams had 3 babies and did 4 parades. Hana was alive in Frank's heart and seemed to be holding her own against the HIV virus. He had made two new dear friends that encouraged him to love. And so he did.

By November plans were being finalized for Hana and Troy to visit again. It had been a tough year for Hana. He knew she could use another break. Her small business was giving her difficulties generating enough income, and that's always stressful. Frank helped out with bills from time to time plus buying a case or two of her Dream It products to sell from his store. He even went so far as to open up a joint checking account with Hana, sending her the checkbook to use in case of emergency. He literally wanted to make sure Hana had emergency back up to keep the heat on and the refrigerator stocked. He wished he could do more, yet he knew that this sharing was also stressful to her. He tried to let her know he was just passing on a blessing, no strings attached. Being human, though, he began to attach those strings of expectation unknowingly. Expectation is insidious.

Much like most of us on the planet, Frank's heart too wanted to feel the warmth of reciprocated love. He yearned to show Hana how much he cared with no strings attached, yet he had developed hopes for a return of affection. Exuberance overcame reason and he decided to give Hana a gift that was to be a symbol of his commitment. He just did not realize how unsettling the gesture might be perceived by its recipient. His selfish desire to step it up a level was leading him down a path that could have been a huge let down. Or he could learn. Expectation has an insidious creep.

There is nothing worse than a blind hopeless romantic. A ring as a gift was to require a ton of explanation. It seemed like such a good idea at the time. His soul just had to say it; he hoped Hana's soul could accept it. A petite design of simple elegance he hoped might meet with Hana's approval. A band meant to comfort. It took him a month to understand it had to be fully 'given away' if it was to be any comfort at all. As indicated in the past he wasn't the sharpest tack in the pack, taking awhile sometimes to stick to the best picture. Expectation had crept in and he tried to stay vigilant to its advance.

This time Hana and Troy arrived a few days after Christmas to stay a few days after the New Year. This time they intended to do Northern California back down to Pismo. A warm sunny arrival in San Jose followed by a beautiful day in San Francisco kicked off another glorious reunion. Their little family was together again. Frank was on cloud eleven or higher. The kids enjoyed the new sights, sounds and smells of the City by the Bay, and Hana seemed to be somewhere else. He could sense the unrest in her soul, making every attempt to keep his place by respecting her space. Hana still had a desire to avoid close physical contact, she still wasn't sure of his motives behind the kind things he had done for her. So at arms length he stayed, grateful for the occasional embrace. He was dying to give her the ring; he'd just have to wait for the correct time and place. Hopeless ...ya think? Romance pushed him forward anyway.

A drive down the coast route out of San Francisco to Santa Cruz was gorgeous, sunny and warm, not a bit of fog in sight. A two night stay with one of Hana's friends who had moved out from Maryland wrapped up the old year to ring in the new. Hana's friend had been her close confidant in Maryland and she had looked forward to their visit. Frank thought that their visit might have been what had diverted Hana's attention, taking the focus he wanted. That was his selfish side. The romantic was yearning for return.

New Years Eve was spent in downtown Santa Cruz enjoying the First Night celebrations. It was the most eclectic assemblage of entertainment that any of their group had ever seen. By the end of the night the four were charged with smiles full of peaceful energy. The following evening Hana and Frank left the kids at the house, going out together to enjoy some dinner and close conversation. He was excited Hana was somewhat more attentive to him. Love made him dumb to the core. Ego decided that this was going to be the opportunity to gift the gift he wished to convey the feelings he wanted to share. 'Dumb to the bone' thought the ring could also bring Hana back from the somewhere else she had been.

Arriving at a nice dinner house the two enjoyed a light meal with comfortable conversation. The time felt right. He excused himself to retrieve the gift box that had been well hidden in the trunk of the car. Returning, he presented Hana with a beautifully wrapped small box that held all he wanted to say. Hana watched the box apprehensively as he slowly slid it across the table to her.

"Happy New Year Hana Lisa." he said.

"Oh No!" was all Hana could say.

Hana looked up from the box deep into his eyes. His return gaze didn't do much to ease the reluctance she had to opening a gift that might carry a lot of weight. He tried to reassure her that it was a light load and to have some fun opening up the gaily wrapped four inch square box. She slowly brought her hands out of her lap to carefully grasp the box. For a moment she held it in her stare, afraid to unwrap what might be discovered, then mustered the courage to look anyway. After beginning to peel away its colorful foil wrap she gazed back into Frank's eyes with the 'what have you done' look. His eyes sparkled back 'have some fun' as she lifted the lid to look inside. Moving the tissue aside, Hana wouldn't find the prize, just another smaller box wrapped as gaily as the first. Removing the smaller box, Hana looked up vocalizing her feeling,

"How fun!"

Slipping the bow and paper off, she lifted the top only to find a still smaller box even more colorfully wrapped. This one had a small note attached that asked, "Getting scary now?"

"Yeah," Hana responded out loud with a look of hesitance to continue. Intrigue pushed her on.

Under this one's wrapping revealed a most gorgeous deep purple velvet box, just the size to fit something small and precious. Frank's heart quickened. Hana's almost stopped. Did she dare open it? Frank could see the fright in her eyes and prodded her onward.

"Go ahead it won't bite," was his feeble attempt at humor.

Hana smiled, looking down, then running her finger over the smooth velvet before beginning to lift the hinged lid on the delicate little box. Purple was Hana's favorite color, he saw the softening of heart through the sea blue eyes that drank in the deep colors warmth. When she rolled the top up and open, what she saw took her breath away. She looked back up at Frank and with the last air left in her lungs she gasped,

"Oh no Frank... I can't."

The simple band of gold a sixteenth of an inch wide held seven tiny diamonds embedded it its channel. The points of light the diamonds radiated were gentle and clean, dancing from the surrounding surface of smooth petite gold band. Hana wasn't ready for a serious committed relationship that such a gift might intend. The physical weight of the ring's precious metal was minute, mental weight could be tremendous. Hana closed the box, sliding it back towards Frank. He reached out, gently wrapping both his hands around Hana's hand and the box. He began to try to explain what he really didn't understand. He took a leap in faith trusting Grace to supply clarity.

The apologetic explanation for his selfish intent behind the giving was more or less personal realization for Frank. He had not realized that he had developed expectation she felt, apologizing for any duress he had caused. He promised to avoid placing any sort of expectation on their friendship in the future. He went on to explain with certainty that the Grace that guided his actions had been spoken from his heart. The ring was simply his way of physically showing Hana his love and unwavering support meaning no harm in the giving. It was meant to have no strings attached. Deep down he admitted feeling a tug of lust for reciprocation of love, then gingerly suggested a greater force was at work from his heart that led him to such a celebration of their friendship. The ring was that celebration. No strings. He encouraged another look.

Hana nodded approval in accepting the ring as a token of that friendship. That was safe she figured. She was a little confused by this strange force that had been guiding him, but she was willing to accept the goodwill intended by the Grace demonstrated in its gifting. She trusted that no expectation was intended by him or this Grace that so moved him. Maybe she might someday come to know this Grace which he seemed to interface with. He was already there in that hope.

Withdrawing his hands from hers, Hana again opened the box. She carefully removed the tiny ring to examine its simple beauty. Frank then said the ring was inscribed with what he really wanted for her and hoped that every time she put it on she'd feel its message. Hana raised the ring to reading distance and found the ever so small inscription on the inside of the band. Two small words said what his heart wished "Peace Hana." Hana smiled with contented relief of his true desires, slipping the ring on her finger she held it out to see how it looked. "It just might be okay," Hana's gaze suggested. Frank was happy she seemed to like it, plus it fit perfectly.

The last two days of the trip were spent in the Monterey and Carmel area. A planned beach scuba dive for Elise, Troy and Frank was done by Frank and Troy only. Elise had to sit this dive out as she had not fully completed her dive certification course. The choppy rough condition of the ocean with two young inexperienced divers was more than he wanted to handle. Good call on his part as the morning dive was punctuated with a near drowning witnessed by the three. Frank was to assist in the rescue of two disabled divers and the kids saw first hand how unforgiving the ocean can be.

The sun drenched seventeen mile drive along the coast with a whale watching boat trip done in short sleeves was testament to the weather's beauty. Hana now believed the sun did shine in California in the wintertime. The kids acted like kids stopping just short of physical injury, punctuating the family dynamic. By the time Hana and Troy departed for the return flight home they all believed the trip was just long enough. Of course living out of a suitcase for a week can get a little tiresome. The adults seemed happy, though a little confused. The sobering effects of unrequited love added restriction to the flow of love between the two adults who should have been madly in love. They were, they just didn't let go long enough to celebrate that gift of love arm in arm, cheek to cheek. Even the kids had picked up on the confusion Hana felt from the free love and affections extended by Frank. At least by the end of her trip his careful lavishing had restored Hana's more 'at ease' smile that they were all used too. All in all it had been a good trip in the sun for the part-time family of four and a glint of reflected sunlight could be occasionally seen from a simple band of gold that adorned the finger of a loved friend.

~~~~

We all are susceptible to expectations we place during our weave through the tapestry. 'Given away' has to be practiced, it is a gift in early life that changes as we bend to want. It is work to avoid expectation, the reward, happiness. Our string we follow almost stumbled with expectation, but did not fall and was gifted with happy again. That was a gift given away, no strings attached.

CHAPTER 23

ALLIES AND FRIENDS WITH DIVERSIONS OUT OF PAIN

The package of priorities that make up our lives was upside down, thrown askew as the New Year opened up. The selfish lack of fulfillment Frank was feeling regarding Hana's visit wasn't easy to overcome. Not so easy to overcome were the feelings of dishonor and disconnection, resurrected by the annual demonizing 'sex offender' registration ritual either. Again into the pit of despair he was thrown. Not once, but twice. By Grace all nightmares end or you are at least given the tools to fight the demons. Enticement to a 151 Rum runaway with the bottle was held at bay by the refuge of the Price House. The Price House managed to keep him from the meltdown of mind. The House held a meltdown at bay long enough for him to be given the refuge of sanity from his new friend Mary.

Mary and her girls had returned to Pismo a couple of times, staying with Frank and Elise. They loved their weekend getaways. Frank poured out Hana to Mary. Mary poured out Steen to Frank. The girls poured out girl talk and shopped for piercing the elders refused to fund. The friendships grew strong; Mary's solo visit in late January could not have come at a more critical time for him.

The disorienting emotional melting was spinning rationality out of control as his fear of 'What If' invaded relentlessly. All aspects of his life seemed to bare some negative impact if this accusation of disorder were made public. The worry was eating him alive. Presumed guilt on the public's part made him a target and that felt extremely uncomfortable. Basic survival mode was even difficult to perform on a daily basis. Elise sensed again something was wrong and so did Mary.

His beleaguered disheveled look was a dead giveaway that something was up, Mary was on it like white on rice. Her initial inquiry was to ask if what was bothering him had anything to do with Hana. His ambiguous answer of yes/no only prompted Mary forward like a hound on meat. Frank insisted that it wasn't something she wanted to hear, trying to fend off further inquiry though his heart cried out for a place to connect. He was at his breaking point. Mary knew it. She offered up compassion and silence to the private nightmare he held inside. Then he broke. The pressure was overwhelming. He had to confide in someone. She was the right person in the right place at the right time.

Frank asked her twice if she was sure she wanted to get into his stuff. Mary said she was willing and he gave it to her.... both barrels. Every sordid detail he could remember came pouring out. Every question answered. Trembling hands showed his trepidation as he unveiled his ugly past which now plagued his future. The pending doom from the dark clouds of 'What If' that followed him was felt in Mary's heart, he revealed he expected she might turn and walk away in disgust. His voice splintered, finally breaking as fears were laid bare for her to see. Mary held him as he sobbed, no longer able to continue. When he had regained his composure Mary asked a question that would make him think.

"So what do you think I should think about you and all of this," she asked.

He had never thought from this perspective before. He had always thought in the terms of what people 'would' think 'if' they knew. He had experienced that before! He had never thought much about what they 'should' think about him. What did he want Mary or anyone else to know regarding this incident in his life and who he was now? The answer caught him by surprise as much as the question had. It was responded to in his heart, then from his heart. Where the words came from he wasn't sure, but they came in an instant and he spoke the words that entered his mouth,

"It is something I did not who I am."

Mary agreed and then asked,

"What are 'we' going to do about it?" He was astounded. Not only was Mary not walking out she was enlisting to help. Her willingness to use her knowledge as a legal secretary to help him find his way was pure friendship, her compassion poured out in his direction. The warmth of this gesture was a manifestation of saving Grace. A compassionate human was coming to his aid. He felt for the first time as if life wasn't all coming to an end.

Their conversations were long and deep that weekend. The conversations regarding his unfulfilled selfish expectations in his relationship with Hana were also to be examined to resolve. Mary confirmed everything he had to offer Hana had to be truly given away because of his past and the real damage the disclosure might cause to their relationship. He came to understand that that disclosure of his past to Hana was to come only when Grace provided that time. Mary suggested he not worry so much about it, just love Hana for now. "Now is all you really have" Mary offered in her mentoring. It seems in his relentless rush of life he had forgotten that simple truth. I guess we all can forget that from time to time.

Feeling refreshed and renewed in having an all inclusive friend, Frank jumped back into his life. Had to, no one else was stepping up to take over any of the responsibilities of providing leadership and guidance to the projects that had become his life. Of course there was the occasional curve ball, this year was no different. The twist here was the fact that a forced move of his household did him some real good.

After renting for years, the owner of the home Frank lived in decided to sell. Frank was first on the list to make an offer. He did and the homeowner laughed. Frank had run some comps on the most recent sales in the neighborhood then made what he thought was a reasonable offer on the duplex in which he had lived for the previous seven years. Realtors called them twin homes in an effort to spruce up the image of the housing tract that had originally been built as affordable housing. Having a view of the ocean though had changed the affordability aspect, but you could still hear your neighbor urinate through the paper thin common wall. The common wall provided no barrier to sound. Some of those sounds occasionally had him looking for a place to poke out his minds eye, the visuals produced from the noises heard were pretty disgusting. To have the homeowner balk at his offer was bad enough, but to then have the rent raised and to be asked to show the house to potential buyers was the last straw.

Frank went into overdrive asking a realtor, client, and friend to find him a house to buy that could fit his meager budget. Within a week Cheryl had a list of homes that fit his parameters. Dad and daughter did a weekend drive-by to narrow down the potential homes they might like to look at. They narrowed the search to three.

Time was precious for both Frank and Cheryl, so a viewing was limited to one home prior to Cheryl's departure for vacation. The one picked was a gem. As soon as he walked through the door he knew he was home. The many windows in the home provided a warm light that illuminated every corner. With the overall ambiance of warm, cozy, bright and sunny, the home had the feel of his grandparents' home in Oakland. The house was situated on a small manageable piece of land, clean, older neighborhood with wide streets and a peek of an ocean view. Frank had an interview to do with a local television station scheduled, so his walk through was quick with few questions asked. He and Cheryl wrapped up in short order, and then withdrew to curbside for a quick discussion. Frank was informed that two offers had already been made and Cheryl wondered what he wanted to do. He told Cheryl to offer full asking price with one contingency: Elise would have to see the house and approve before he could commit.

That afternoon when Elise returned home from school Dad took her to the home so she too could see and offer her feedback. At first she seemed unimpressed, but once she saw the bathroom with its fancy makeup mirror he knew the home was theirs. On Wednesday, Cheryl phoned Frank to inform him the owners had accepted his offer. At noon that day he started the funding process. Cheryl phoned from the car on Thursday as she made her way to Laughlin, Nevada to inform him that his funding had been approved. Bam! Done!

Forty days later on May 1st Frank and Elise moved in. Just that quick life had changed from being a renter to now being a proud owner of a home that he could call his own. He had dreamed the dream, again pondering why a home had to be a dream? But this little dream was now his. He learned later that his little home had probably been built in 1953 the year he was born. Might be why it felt so right when he had first walked through its front door. Hana had lived the experience by phone, encouraging and enjoying his happiness. He wished she could have been there in person. Maybe one day she could. We are all able to dream. Now back to reality.

He had moved but a mile, but that mile had crossed the city of Pismo's boundary. He now resided in Grover Beach. Not usually a big deal unless you're a registered 'sex offender'. Once you have moved into a new jurisdiction you are required 'by law' to register in that new jurisdiction within ten days of arrival. Frank again leaned on Mary as he vented his anger and resentment to this protocol that did nothing but tarnish a clean reputation. This second episode on the edge of the abyss brought him down hard. He now had to hope the new police department staff would handle the information with as much dignity and confidentiality as the Pismo Police Department had.

By Grace, two things happened. One, Detective Mark of the Grover Police Department was as respectful as Frank could have hoped. The distasteful emotion associated with the procedure of mugging and blotting one's hands in black ink only stayed for as long as the smell of the jail cells stayed in his nostrils. Two, was Mary, thank God for Mary, who came up again, bringing back and sharing the sweet smell of life. Mary's encouragement fired him up with hope. A positive end to fear was the message he needed to hear, and Mary left him spent with that uplift.

Mary's second mission of mercy dealt with new topics in Frank's search for sanity under the label of 'sex offender'. What made things worse, he had been made aware by Detective Mark that the SLO Sheriff's Department now had a website that offered information on 'sex offenders' to the general public. The parameters of the program required: the inquiring party had to have a name and social security number of someone suspected of being an 'offender'. They could then retrieve information on that person if that person was in the system. Anyone inquiring could not just cruise through the files, they had to be granted access first. Never-the- less, this was again a threat to his privacy from something he had done and paid for years prior. It was not who he was now, but just being listed made it seem that way to him and probably whoever viewed the site. At best he was glad he didn't live in the city of Atascadero. There they were actually posting, publicly, pin-pointed locations on a city map of where 'sex offenders' lived.

Mary and Frank agreed that the Megan's law was valid; there were some extremely bad people out there. Knowing where the worst ones were was valuable for public safety. However, classifying all who had 'offended', labeling them all as one group, just seemed wrong. If these people, usually men, had let their morality slip once while in drunken sailor mode, do we persecute them for the rest of their lives? It was interesting to them that we didn't make other types of 'offenders' endure this invasion of privacy. Who wouldn't want to know that a murderer, drunken driver, kidnapper, robber or any other threat lived next door? Or was the 'sex offender' group just a test case for 'marked' living where rights and civil liberties are legally stripped away all in the interest of public safety? It smacked of Gestapo practice utilized by Germans against the Jewish in the 1930s and 40s. He wondered when the yellow star was to become a required accoutrement to the clothes worn by the labeled 'offender'.

Mary was able to convince him that it was now time to retain an attorney on his behalf. Begrudgingly he acknowledged that there were far too many twists and turns for the two to handle alone. He searched for and found his old attorney of record Mr. Bob Biggs, hoping to find suitable Council who was familiar with his case. Bob however, could be of no help as he now only practiced real estate law. Bob remembered Frank's case, but could not recall the actual agreement reached with the State. Furthermore, he had destroyed Frank's case records some ten years prior. Not good news. Frank then expanded his inquiries.

Pressing on, Frank was eventually informed of a Certificate of Rehabilitation that could be obtained to end his ordeal by an attorney with the ACLU. He called a local paralegal to investigate and was referred to a local attorney by the name of Jeff Tien. Jeff had done these types of certifications, agreeing to meet with him. This was better news.

By mid summer Jeff accepted his case and began his research. Unfortunately, Frank didn't qualify for the certification program as one of the prerequisites was 10 years continual registration. He had only three. Twenty years of being a good guy didn't count. Jeff, however, thought that other avenues might yield a way out of the scourge, stating he'd do more research and be in touch. The hopes of some light at the end of the tunnel were at least able to coax Frank back into life.

The Price House was in full swing by mid summer. He and Jack plotted together regarding the new redwood siding they had to push to complete. Jack and Frank had seen to all the prep work of priming for the practically flawless #2 grade redwood, but Frank had to gently nudge the Kiwanis a few times to get their crew together to come out. But when they came out they really had a lot of fun and a lot of hard work was accomplished. The day they finished Frank was able to get a television news crew to come out and cover the story. It was a good interview for him and the project, though he really wished they had covered more of the other volunteers.

As soon as the Kiwanis had finished their crafting, Mike Fairbrother jumped in and finished his, installing the new double hung windows and re-crafted front doors. The job Mike had accomplished in saving the badly damaged front doors was truly remarkable. Mike had originally wanted to scrap the old doors and rebuild with new ones, but Frank convinced him they needed to save as much of the original house as possible. Mike argued that new doors wouldn't look as rough and worn. "Hey man, that's the character of the house," Frank suggesting it was acceptable decor. As time went on they repeatedly chimed "it's the character of the house" every time they let a little nick or ding in the old house slide by as 'okay'. They had other quips that kept them smiling and enjoying the flow of creativity. Mike was an amazing craftsman and Frank felt very, very fortunate to have his service at hand.

Another carpenter that was befriended at Frank's shop came on board to assist in recreating the front porch once the siding, doors and windows where completed. This craftsman's name was Dana Valentine, and the job he and Mike tackled really exercised their artistic abilities.

The front porch was a bit of a mystery, it had virtually fallen off the home by 1950. The 1890s photo was scarce on details. Only one other photo was in existence that showed a dilapidated front porch prior to full collapse. Those two photos had to be examined under a magnifying glass to provide the details needed to recreate the gingerbread that adorned the home's front entrance. Their work was meticulous and the final product was gorgeous. Between the two craftsmen at least 200 hours of volunteer labor went into the work. The porch and its detail became the crowning facet of this jewel called the Price House. Without the volunteer labor given to the porch project, Frank was sure it might have cost thousands to complete.

Exterior woodworking was in its final stages of installation as the Price House board moved aggressively into painting. Porch railing infill was just being installed when the FOPH board selected Tony Esta to come on board to begin his painting magic. The board of directors knew how important it was to get a coat of protection on the newly installed redwood. They also speculated the visual effect of progress would inspire more public support. The flood of activity was intense, and by mid fall the entire house had been bathed in several coats of white primer. Colors came just after the turn of the year. Creative volunteer help was at fevered pitch, change was happening fast for the Anniversary House. Frank was glad he had pulled his camera equipment out of mothballs and started keeping a photographic record of those changes. From a crooked crumbling gray old house, to the straight solid lines, highlighted by the stark white primer coat, the gem of simple early American living stood out like a mansion in the middle of its undeveloped canyon setting. It really had people taking notice and asking questions about the status of the project. He found himself doing more interviews regarding the project, although he wished other folks in the organization had been asked to fulfill those tasks.

Newspapers, radio and television stations were also taking notice of the Clam family. A flurry, of before and after event interviews propelled Sam, Pam and family into household conversation. The agreement by the news outlets not to discuss who played the parts helped to develop the impression that they were real entities not just people in costumes. Frank had been amazed by how young and old some of those believers were. One encounter was memorable.

On the 4th of July appearance, Sam and Pam approached the entry gate to the pier when a little girl of about 5 or 6 came dashing out of the crowd, mother in tow. The little girl made a beeline for Pam who was all decked out with one of her many unique parasols and pink feather boa. Pam, just short of the entrance, heard her name being called by the little girl's mother. Stopping, Pam turned toward the little girl's mother who was now out of breath from the mad dash. The mother explained her daughter had been dying to meet Pam the Clam. Pam knelt down to say hello to her young fan. Pam verbally greeted the little one, extending her hand in friendship. The little girl didn't say a word, just bolted forward embracing Pam with a huge loving hug. Almost as if Pam was a long lost best friend, the little one embraced as much of the costume as her little arms could hold. Finally releasing and stepping back, the little gal launched into excited, engaging conversation with Pam. The little one spoke to the costume as if she had known Pam for years, not once taking a breath between topics. After the lengthy discourse of admiration from the little fan, Pam politely told her little admirer that she had to go and she would see her later after the show. With one last hug they parted and the entourage of Clams moved onto the pier for their appearance.

Half an hour later as they exited the pier, waded through the thick crowd gathered for fireworks, Pam was hailed again. Again it was the little girl's mother and this time she was carrying her little charger. Frank could see that the little girl was crying hard as her mother struggled her way through the crowd to reach Pam's location. Once together the mother put her daughter down and then explained the reason why her little one was crying so. She thought Pam was leaving and forgetting to say goodbye. Pam knelt again and the two hugged deeply. Pam explained that she wasn't leaving, she was in fact looking for her favorite little fan. Immediately the little girl stopped her choking sobs, grinned widely and hugged Pam as big as her little arms allowed. Pam held her while telling her she would be looking for her in a few months at the Clam Festival. They embraced again in farewell, waved goodbye blowing kisses as they parted. Frank was astounded at how real Pam 'the clam' had become to the tiny fan.

Not three minutes later Sam was stopped by a small pack of boys about 9 or 10 years old. The leader of the pack stepped forward, grabbed the front of Sam's costume, pulling down quite hard so he could peer into the costume's small eyehole. The netting material used by Sue to create the costume eyes was designed see out, not in. The young man had to put his eye right up to the material to see in, abruptly pushing away and exclaiming to his friends, "There really is someone in there." Frank was again amazed at how real their characters had become. They had done a good job making the characters come alive. Judy and Frank loved their jobs.

Frank took breaks from the rat race of all the projects whenever he could fit them in. Some planned, some popped up last minute at just the right time. That year's planned getaway was to travel back to see Hana and do some maintenance around her house. The unplanned getaway was a request to fly to Alaska and drive back with an old friend from Orange County. His friend Jan Kilgore had moved to Fairbanks, Alaska, to do church mission work and needed to return to Orange County for more schooling. Jan was looking for someone to assist in the drive and called her old buddy Frank. That was out of the blue.

Frank met Jan and her family in the mid 70s while living in Huntington Beach. He and Jan had become big brother, little sister. Over the many years Jan, her sisters Cheryl, Teri and Linda, had all gotten to know him, a couple of them intimately. They all considered him a part of the family. Even Dee, the Frazier girls' mom, grew to like Frank despite their rocky start. During his divorce the calls from the Frazier family inviting him to share in holiday get-togethers provided him with a sense of caring. Although he couldn't make it to most of the holiday events it was nice to have an invitation. It was also nice when Linda and her son Nick came up to Pismo for a getaway. Kids fought, the two single parents could 'carefully' play as adults.

The family always invited Frank to join the clan for their annual trip to San Felipe, Mexico and this was one diversion he did try to attend. He provided the water to ensure an amoeba free stay in Mexico for the 15 to 20 family and friends that went along. Those 15 to 20 folks supplied him with endless hours of entertainment. Mexican tequila provided unlimited laughter as he watched the effects take hold and twist the various members of the party clan. His status as designated driver on 'tequila night' reminded him with definite visuals of why he no longer drank. From topless dancing on a crowded dance floor to face down in strawberry margarita puke, the reminders were vivid. One particularly uproarious event became legend amongst the clan of partiers.

It happened at the end of one of those 'tequila night' runs that Frank was in charge of providing the transportation. At about two in the morning he had managed to round up and load the stuporous attendees into the van for transport home. The seven mile trip back to their beach campsite included a mandatory stop that evening at a Mexican Federally check point. That's when the fun really kicked into high gear for Frank.

As he slowed the van to the flagged stop on the deserted desert highway, he could only guess what the Federal`es might think of the packed van load of drunken revelers. Amongst the load of inebriated humans were two members that were sure to get the attention of authorities attending that check point. One was the short skirted, semiconscious Linda, sprawled out across one of the bench seats mumbling something about having too much to drink. The other was Jerry, Cheryl's husband, whose shirtless physique displayed his many tattoos and piercings which always drew concerned stares. He was a bit rough to the eye to say the least. This was the first time they had run into one of these roaming checkpoints. Frank knew they might be in for a grinding if the group didn't feign control, especially Jerry.

The crowd that had been obnoxiously loud quieted as the van stopped. Frank rolled down his window as the commandant with rifled sidekick approached. The commandant started his inquiry with rapid fire Spanish. Frank interrupted,

"No Spanish! Pequito Español! Inglés?"

The commandant, who was younger than Frank slowed and shifted to broken English.

"Señor where are you going?" he asked.

"Pete's Camp just up the road." Frank responded.

The commandant switched on his huge flashlight, beginning an interior search of the van load of faces as he rattled off more Spanish. Frank heard only one identifiable word, 'pistol`es'.

"Pistolas?" Frank responded inquisitively.

"Yes señor you know guns..... Pistolas," the officer responded returning the flashlight search to the back seat of the van. That's when he saw the shirtless Jerry, tats and piercings all on display.

The fevered increased pitch of the officer's Spanish drew the attention of the other half dozen soldiers that had been meandering around up until then. Frank knew the shit was about to hit the fan. The Spanish being spoken grew more intense as the officer's search focused down to the floor of the van at Jerry's feet, then up again into his face that looked much like a deer in headlights. The beam of light then danced wildly from front to back seats as the rag tag team of teenage gun-toting soldiers began to surround the van. Spanish orders flew as rifles were drawn down to defensive posturing. Frank sensed the situation was intensifying to out of control, leaned out the window saying with his own fervor,

"No pistolas, no pistolas.... too much tequila... just too much tequila at Rockadile's!"

That broke the intensity a bit and the group of gun slinging kids dressed in oversized army issue fatigues relaxed a touch. The commandant's flashlight then caught sight of the disabled blond sprawled across the bench seat mumbling incoherent discomforts. The officer drew closer to Frank, keeping the flashlight beam focused on the beautiful blond whose skirt was just short of exposure.

"And this one señor?" he questioned.

"Oh... way too much tequila!" Frank responded.

"She's fucking shit faced!" Jerry screeched from the back of the van.

"She is very beautiful señor," the officer offered as he pressed to the window for a better look. Frank saw his opportunity and took it.

"Yeah, she is. Would you like to buy her?" he blurted out knowing Linda was conscious enough to hear she was being offered for sale. The quiet, drunken crowd erupted into uproarious laughter as the skinny little man pressed even closer believing he was about to buy the incapacitated gringo woman.

"Ohhhh señor!" the little man whispered in lusting reverence.

The reality of what was happening finally hit Linda. Her drunken slobbering attempt at protest was priceless. Eyes still shut because everything was spinning; she tried to sit up as she slurred her defiance,

"What? Wait? I'm not going anywhere except home and to bed!" Linda wailed, then collapsed back down onto the seat to stop the spinning in her head.

The group exploded again in laughter. Even the commandant and sidekick smiled as they realized Frank's offer was only a joke at the blond gringo's expense. They were harmless gringos just having fun and the commandant had a moment of fun as well.

"Okay señor. You can go but the blond señorita must stay."

"What? What!" Linda responded in disbelief as she once again tried to sit up only to collapse back down to the level that didn't spin. The crammed van load roared again, as did the commandant and his compadres.

"Okay señor, you may pass."

"The señorita is very beautiful, maybe next time," he grinned as he waved them through.

"Gracias," Frank responded as he rolled the van forward to finish the trek.

Shouts of "more tequila" and thunderous laughter filled the warm desert air as the solitary vehicle sliced down the dark desert highway. They roared again to tears when the van of hooligans turned down the dirt road back to camp, Jerry yelling out at the top of his lungs,

"We almost sold Linda to the fucking Mexicans."

Not a dry eye in the bus except for Linda. She had finally passed out in bliss, unaware of the incident she was part of, which provided so much comedic entertainment. One of those most unforgettable moments! Legendary stuff.

So, saying yes to a trip to Alaska and driving back with one of the Frazier clan was sure to be fun. The timing was right between the business, projects and daughter. So in early September he left his rat race at home to enjoy an unforgettable race back down the Alcan Highway with Jan. The day-long flight and 6 day drive was to be epic. During the hours of endless driving, Jan learned all about Hana and his deep love for her. Frank learned all about Mark Sherman, the love in Jan's life.

Fairbanks to Pismo was a long way to drive. The time allotted forced a 586 mile per day average driving requirement to meet the deadline. The race covered so much ground daily that you could actually watch the flora change from region to region. The pristine vistas and endless miles of no one instilled a definite feeling of a remote wilderness journey. Because of the 'late in the season' start to their journey they sometimes drove for three hours or more never seeing another human being. A lot of fueling stops and restaurants along the way had already shut down for the season. Most folks in the small towns retreated south prior to winter snow setting in. September could have a blizzard at any time and that kept the pace out of the northern reaches brisk. Snow capped peaks and the icy faces of glaciers hinted at what was soon to come. You could get stuck out here and the cell phone might not work in most areas. If you were trapped in a blizzard you might die. It was remote, it was exciting. Just the recharge Frank needed as it would be balls out when he returned to keep everything on track so he could make the scheduled Thanksgiving trip back to see Hana. They made their destinations on time; the trip was a total success. Then back to work to ready for the next adventure.

All was going well until one day in mid October. His long time pet companion Blizzard did not greet him at the door when Frank returned home for lunch. He called out for the dog several times thinking she was fast asleep, not hearing the truck pull up. She always heard the truck. Receiving no response, he began a search around the house, when passing by the dining room window he spotted his unconditional loving, furry friend convulsing in the grass in the backyard. He rushed to her side. He spoke soft comforting words as he knelt to console the dog he dearly loved.

He had witnessed the tail end of a similar episode about a week earlier and knew it wasn't a good sign. Kneeling, trying to comfort, concerned tears formed in his eyes, his voice began to falter as the dog continued to convulse despite his touch and words. Slowly the convulsion subsided, but the poor animal could not get up. The gaze of her eyes seemed to be telling her master she knew it was time. He continued his comforting stroke as he called Steve at the shop, requesting his relief in shutting down store operations that night. Stevie knew something was up, answering in his trooper tone, "Yeah sure, no problem chief."

An hour later he sensed it was the end as Blizzard was still unable to lift her head up off the pillow he had placed her on. Her eyes could follow his movements, but that was all. He was in no shape to do what he knew he had to do. He called his friend Lenny to see if he could assist in the trip to the vet that Frank so dreaded. Lenny dropped what he was doing and came right over.

Frank carried his little white friend ever so carefully on her pillow to Lenny's waiting car. His eyes did not leave the gaze that the dog engaged with him. He petted her gently throughout the ride. He knew it might be her last car ride, his silent tears dropping onto her snow white fur as his composure crumbled the closer they got to the vet hospital. He spoke to her gently, telling her everything would be okay. He was actually trying to convince himself that the seizure would pass and the doc would have some sort of remedy for her malady....and everything would be okay.

They were seen immediately. The doctor's prognosis after examining the beloved pet was what Frank had feared. After almost 17 years of companionship he had to let go for the sake of his little friend. The doctor left the room to prepare the injection that was to end Blizzard's paralyzing misery, allowing Frank a few extra minutes to say goodbye. Blizzard was still on her pillow and struggled to raise her head as the doctor reentered. The dog seemed to sense her end was near, making two vain attempts to show her master she was okay. She whimpered slightly as the doctor inserted the syringe into her forearm. Frank held her head as her eyes closed and her muscles relaxed. His last words to his longtime, stalwart friend, "I love you Blizzard," and he laid her lifeless head gently back down onto the pillow that cradled her snow white form. The doctor again left, leaving Frank alone with his dog and sorrow; he put his head next to his friend's and cried.

Frank picked up the pillow that his lifeless friend laid on, carefully carrying it and its precious cargo out the side door of the vet office to the car. Tears cascaded profusely and he didn't look up from his friend the whole ride home. Lenny knew exactly what he was going through. He had gone through it himself a year before with his dog Sara. The two men needed to speak no words. When they arrived back at his house, Frank could barely compose a proper thank you to Lenny. Lenny offered from caring,

"Call me if you need anything," leaving Frank to his most personal grief.

Elise had waited for her dad's return, offering her sympathy and tears over their loss. She did what she could to help her dad prepare for Blizzards burial. Dad dug a small grave in the backyard, daughter picked out a pretty pillow case to put over the dog and the pillow she was to be buried on. At sundown they placed Blizzard in her final resting place, gently covering her with earth while lifting up a small prayer to the heavens to take care of their snow white little friend. He cried again that night while telling Hana what had happened that day. Hana did her best to console him with her loving understanding. The wound in his heart was huge. She held him in her heart from across the miles and her comfort gave him some peace. He did wish for a hug and Elise was glad to comply. The girls knew how he felt, their compassion over the next few days helped initiate the healing of his broken heart.

It had been 28 years since he had brought Blizzard's father Toroko home, and he had now buried the last of Toroko and Kimmie's offspring. He had buried both parents now their little girl and the pain was too much, he couldn't do it again, he was never to own a dog again.

The trip to see Hana a month later was good therapy. Frank gave Hana a water softener to replace her rental unit in an effort to cut her monthly bills. He also replaced her hot water heater at the same time to avoid costly repairs down the road. He got a ton of yard work done along with two trips to the dump to rid the grounds of aging debris. He cooked for Hana once and that was that. The rest of their meals Hana fixed or they enjoyed a meal out. The Thanksgiving meal fixed at mom's house was fabulous and he mingled with her family members he hadn't seen in 30 years.

Reminiscing with Stefen for the first time in years was interesting. Hana didn't attend the Thanksgiving meal. She wasn't feeling well and that was probably a good thing. Her anger with one of her brothers was still raging. She didn't need the stress of seeing her brother face-to-face. Frank brought a plate with all the fixings back for her to pick at, as she tried to recover from a bug that had grabbed her the night before. They joked the following day that her ill feelings had actually been caused by his cooking.

Hana seemed to be much more relaxed during his trip out. Because she was on home turf and not living out of a suitcase probably made the difference. He was still at arms length, yet the nightly bedtime hug with occasional kiss felt warm and sincere. Between his work on the house and Hana's new job, time together was spent engaging in deep conversation. Talking about her father's death that year, recent HIV blood work results, and the kids' growing pains typified the close loving flow they enjoyed. He had noticed from day one that Hana was wearing the ring he had given her. It appeared to be part of her daily attire which made him feel good. She was at peace with the wearing; he was at peace with the giving. Peace was its message. No strings attached.

The face-to-face with Hana made him feel even better, much like a drug to him. He returned home high. The fire in his heart was stoked again, its joy spilled out, felt by all the folks who were part of his life. Free flowing for all to enjoy, no strings attached. It was powerful stuff. He was back in the 'now' were he wanted to be and that was much like a drug called bliss. The 'now' of 'nothing attached' is freeing and when practiced it can be addicting. He was addicted to Hana and the loving friendship they shared that felt so much like the warmth of family. I guess he really wasn't any different than any of us who enjoy the bliss of the drug called love and the security found in its arms. And the 'What If' couldn't invade that fortress of bliss. That was Grace at its best.

~~~~

We all laugh and we all cry, it is part of the human experience as we weave our part into the tapestry. Grounding emotion we live in the moment of now, and then we move on. Our string we follow is no different. As the journey we follow unfolds, it is apparent the moments are profuse swings of emotion run closely together. As we have seen, the transition from one to another seems to be supported by an energy that diverts the low to high every time. Many may be asking why. He was. And to what end can be expected? Again, we should guard against expectation.

CHAPTER 24

MOTHER MARY

Holidays melted blandly into the dark dawn of the New Year. The birthday ritual with the police department for registration did a number on him as usual. He had become somewhat complacent about the task, trying to keep a more open, positive attitude about the process. After all, it only took about an hour of his time once a year. As of yet he had only seen a few regular customers disappear inexplicably from his business operations. Ramifications hadn't been as bad as he expected when the sheriff's department website was unveiled. Only one direct confrontation from an employee from a business next door, led him to suspect that a few folks had been getting an earful of the 'he said, she said' information hot off the grapevine.

Still, rumors in a small town can spread like a cancer; Frank knew it and the dark clouds were creeping back. To top it off Detective Mark brought to his attention that the morphing of Megan's Law was now requiring registrants to give DNA samples. This really set him off and he vented to the detective. The argument for invasion of privacy and the constitutionality of being forced to submit samples fell on sympathetic ears and Mark encouraged Frank to talk to his attorney in an effort to have the burden curtailed. Mark said he'd be in contact, leaving Frank with a different flame burning in his heart. That night he called Mary for advice. She always gave the support.

Within a few days Frank was at his attorney's office for more insights and discussions about his dilemma with the morphing Megan's Law. Nothing could be done at this point about 'compulsory' voluntary DNA sampling. The law had been found constitutional in its scope and was changing to include pre-statute convictions retroactively. Jeff encouraged Frank to try and secure a 'declaration' from his original attorney of record, stating the conditions as he could recall from the old case, hopefully including the words "not required to register."

Frank phoned Bob Biggs within a week to discuss the request. Jeff and Frank had talked about the fact that Bob should have filed a 'request for expungement' after receiving the final judgment from the court. This appears not to have been done and there were some questions in regards to whose responsibility that may have been. Jeff suggested it might have been Bob's responsibility, and that made Frank's request of Bob a ginger proposition. After all, if Frank got from Bob what he was asking for, Bob might possibly be admitting to an attorney/client failure. Frank knew at the end of the conversation with Bob he was not to get a disclosure that was to bolster his case. They did get a statement from Bob indicating that, in his opinion, "Frank had complied with the laws of the state to the best of his abilities and understanding". Blah, blah, blah.

Frank took Mary up on her offer to go to Orange County with him to go through his court record. This way they could make sure no stone had been left unturned. The trip down was a pleasure as Frank felt confident about this 'hands on' approach regarding his case. Now he could see for himself; besides it was good to see Mary and the kids. On the drive to Santa Ana from Van Nuys he let Mary know how much he appreciated her expertise and assistance that parted the dark clouds following him. He was so relaxed he even joked about the pair of handcuffs he had seen hanging on her bedroom wall. The trip was going to be productive, he could just feel it.

Arriving at the county buildings clustered in midtown Santa Anna, he and Mary entered the Superior Court Records Division. The line was short, the room was small, many of the divided cubicles already filled with attorneys and their clients examining files. It smelled musty and felt stuffy from lack of air movement. The glass enclosed record room was well lit, while the examination area was a little dim. The forty layers of paint on the walls provided the pallet for graffiti etchings that really gave the room the jailhouse feel. The stacks of criminal records behind the glass stretched from floor to ceiling, highlighting the impressive amount of business the courts had seen over the years. Mary's request for Frank's records had been filed the week before and their retrieval was prompt. Mary signed them out and the two found a cubical, sat down and went to work. The file folder was small compared to all the others they had seen sprawled out on the cubical desks under review. Mary's comment after quick review,

"This shouldn't take too long."

Opening the folder only revealed about 15 single sheets of documents and two manila envelopes. They split the pile in half, each taking an envelope as well. Mary wondered out loud what the envelopes were all about, they had no markings to identify their contents. "Kind of strange," she commented as she had never seen this in any files she had gone through at her office. They started with the loose items and did the envelopes last. They poured over the documents looking for anything that could bolster the statement made on the Court Order of Dismissal. A few pieces were found that might help, Mary jotted notes of the page numbers to request copies, then onto the envelopes. As they opened the envelopes to extract the contents Frank asked Mary, "If his record was supposed to be sealed, why was it so easy to get a hold of?" That got Mary thinking out loud, "maybe these envelopes weren't supposed to be opened." There was no seal or warning stating such, he pointed out, so they pushed on.

Frank's batch was stuff he had never seen. Police reports, interviews and such, nothing having any bearing on the court order. Mary's on the other hand did contain some valuable information. Psychiatric reports on MDSO findings could be very valuable in proving he should not be on any list accusing him of being a 'sex offender'. The reports stated just the opposite, the psychiatric finding by the two doctors indicated that Frank "was not a mentally disordered sex offender." Mary added those page numbers to the list. Other positive materials were added to the copy request form. Unfortunately the elusive words 'not required to register' had not been found. The documents were returned to their respective envelopes, put back in the file and returned to the deputy at the desk along with the copy requests. A few minutes later the deputy returned with some copies, but indicating he could not find the other page numbers listed. He asked where they had come from. Mary looked at the list and said, "Inside the envelopes."

All hell broke loose. The deputy went into a tirade about how those envelopes were sealed court documents and they had broken the law by opening them. He went on to threaten their arrest for breaking a court order. They both responding in their defense that the envelopes contained no seal or written warning 'not to open' of any kind, so how were they supposed to know? This stopped the verbal lambasting and threats dead in their tracks. The deputy looked for himself, reluctantly agreeing no warnings were posted, suggesting they leave before he changed his mind about having them arrested. He and Mary beat feet out the door, feeling the stares of the others in the room that had witnessed the tirade as they exited post haste.

"Man that was something else," Frank thought. Almost getting arrested for looking at a record of what he had lived. If he couldn't look at it, who could? It seemed kind of strange that the envelopes were unmarked with no attempt to identify their status. It made him wonder who else had been in those files. These and other questions Mary and he agreed had to be taken to his attorney Jeff.

Mary was now even more perplexed over the reason Frank was being pursued as some sort of dangerous individual. She had seen with her own eyes that he had been telling her the truth about his circumstances. Mary had seen the full package and had seen no justification for him to be crucified by labeling him a "dangerous sex offender." She again reaffirmed her support and assistance in helping him seek justice. Mary was truly a blessing.

All the rest of his activity that year paled in comparison to the emotional drain lived in this pursuit of justice. Hana, Price House, Clams, daughter, business, all were overshadowed by the dark clouds that infiltrated his 'American Dream'. DNA required, web site posting, birthday dance with the local police, former attorney losing the memory he had paid for. That can darken even your best day. But thank God for Mary. Through the Grace of her compassion he returned to Pismo reinvigorated in spite of the setback, jumping back into the tour he called life.

~~~~

We all need connection that supports our journey. Mother Mary was the gift to connect at the right place at the right time. Our string we follow truly has a gifted journey's weave.

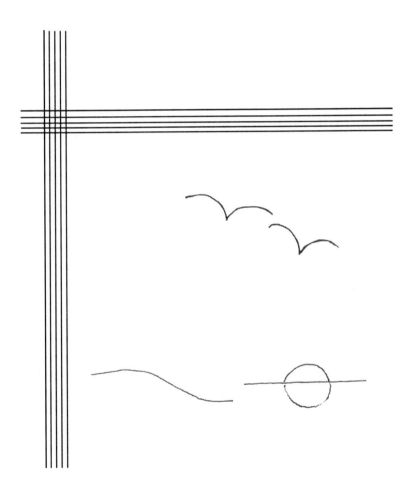

CHAPTER 25

THE KEY IS FREE

Frank felt as if he suffered whiplash as he returned to the breakneck pace of life at the place he called home. The effort to stay mentally balanced was augmented by a unique request from his surrogate sister Jan. Jan called in early spring to announce her engagement and pending wedding to Mark Sherman, the man of her dreams. Jan not only called to announce, but to ask a special favor of Frank as well. Jan's high regard for him made her decision to ask for his assistance a no-brainer. Jan told him that their plan to marry in July of that year in Fairbanks needed only one last detail to be fulfilled. She went on to explain that her father was afraid to fly and she needed someone to take his place at the wedding to give her away. Frank was her choice. He was honored to be asked to fulfill this important position and agreed to fill the post. He had a little practice in the 'giving away' department.

Unexpected journey, that's the way life worked, and Frank loved to fly by the seat of his pants. The plan he came up with was a stellar performance of maximum use of available time and resource. Soon tickets were bought and a game plan laid out for Hana, Troy and Elise to attend Jan and Mark's wilderness wedding in the wilds of Alaska. The thrill was on. Frank was drugged by the fact that he was not only seeing Hana again, but traveling to an exciting 'new to both' place. The family unit was to journey together again, and Hana too voiced her excitement over the phone.

The excitement over the call of the wild was fevered for Frank by the first of June. The whipping twists and turns of life were barely manageable with the time allotted. One turn was Elise's graduation from middle school. At the end of summer she would be starting high school and Dad realized he needed to have a father/daughter talk with her on the realities of the new life she was about to embark upon. Not all at once, but a little at a time he tried to impart his wisdom on what to avoid. ...Yeah right!

One afternoon just after her graduation, while he was having his lunch, he overheard Elise and one of her girlfriends, Alyssa, talking about friends they knew who had cars. Dad saw his opportunity to bring up the subject of the dangers of driving with someone you didn't know. The tragic stories of disastrous teenage driving riddled the headlines, and he didn't want to see Elise involved in such a catastrophe. He sat Elise down on the couch for a good heart-to-heart and Alyssa joined in. His bottom line to his daughter: if he had not approved of the driver in advance she was not to get into the car.

The lights were on. He only hoped someone was at home in his daughter's pretty little head. ...Yeah right!

Pretty she was. Elise was about 5'5" tall with long dark hair and olive complexion. Just a few days prior he had snapped a few photos on graduation day that showed her modeling potential. She had competed for a second time in the Miss Teen Pismo scholarship pageant, and did quite well. She had talked of modeling. The photos proved she had the look. A little work on the talent end and Dad figured she had a good shot at winning the pageant as well. She was going to be offered rides by the boys, he had no doubt. He just wanted to give her a reason to say no. She could blame it on her 'DAD' he said. This was his feeble effort to keep his kiddo as safe as possible. ...Yeah right!

Two weeks later Elise asked to spend the night at Alyssa's house. Dad agreed, dropped Elise off and spoke with Dave, Alyssa's father, to make sure all was on the up and up. Dave said no problem, he'd "Okayed the girls' plan" and indicated he and the wife were going to be home all night, and Elise was always welcome. Movies, popcorn and girl talk. He left feeling comfortable Elise was in good hands and returned to work.

Returning home a little after sunset Frank fixed something to eat. He was famished from his after hours work out at the Price House, removing and hauling plaster out of the house until he could not see from lack of light. By 10pm he was in bed getting the rest he needed for another big day on Friday. Really they were all big days and he was usually in bed by 9:30. On this night he was probably asleep before his head hit the pillow.

Deep sleep was disturbed back into a groggy semi consciousness by the incessant ringing of the phone. By the fourth ring he was almost coherent as the answering machine picked up to deliver its message. By the time the tone sounded for the party on the other end to leave a message, he was almost ready to listen. He couldn't imagine who was calling at this hour. His clock was reading 12:35am. Dazed, he laid in bed to listen to the caller's identity.

What he heard took a second to figure out. It was the ex-wife's voice and she was saying something about "Hoping he was not at home to hear her call." What? What she went on to say had him sharp, clear headed and on the move in a single heartbeat. Despite a confusing start the rest of the message was very clear. The stress in Linda's voice made the sense of urgency poignant. He dressed while listening, no time to talk. Linda continued,

"A witness or bystander or somebody called to let us know our daughter has been involved in a bad traffic accident. She was, or is, being taken to Arroyo Grande Hospital. I'll see you there."

Just that quick he was dressed and out the door as Linda ended her message. Into the truck and down the road to the hospital his mind speculating the status of his daughter's injuries the entire ride. All green lights greeted his speeding dash to be at his daughter's side. Pulling into the deserted emergency room parking lot, he spied Linda's car but no ambulance. He wondered how long Elise had been there and why he had not been notified sooner. Racing inside he found Linda, was informed Elise had not yet arrived and then heard the siren from the approaching emergency vehicle. Going back outside, he watched as the ambulance backed in to unload. The first one out was on a gurney. It was Elise and blood was everywhere. He only caught a glimpse as they rushed her through the doors and inside. He pushed back through the entrance doors and followed, fearing the worst.

He entered the exam cubicle, identifying himself as the patient's father, and the staff allowed him to stay. Most of the right side of Elise's face was covered in white gauze bandages as well as the top of her head. They were saturated with blood. Her left arm was in a splint and her shirt and arm had a substantial amount of blood on them. Things did not look good.

Elise was in a painfully conscious state while trying to answer the nurse's questions. Linda was ushered out by staff as she was unable to handle the scene, breaking down with tears like any mother. Frank stayed out of the way and watched the nurse remove Elise's facial bandages. Elise's left eye caught sight of Dad and she turned her head to say she was sorry. Dad told her not to talk, let the attendant do his work. The final layer of bandages came off; even the nurse had to grimace at what was revealed.

Elise's face was a horrific mess. Her right eye socket had been severely damaged with part of the eyebrow missing as well as missing tissue to the far right corner of the eye. The deep lacerations on her forehead and right side of her face turned Dads stomach. The right side of her face, from the top of the ear to almost the top of her mouth looked as if it had been splayed open by a very sharp filet knife. It was hideous, but at least she had not lost her eye.

Her left arm had been broken completely in two with bone protruding through the skin. The doctor came in and did his assessment, ordering up a barrage of tests and exams, and then left the room to look at the other victims. The nurse cleaned and redressed Elise's facial wounds, then removed the splint from her arm to clean that wound. Leaving the room the nurse made arrangements for a CT scan and x-rays; that's when Dad's anger briefly overtook him. He turned abruptly to Elise stating harshly,

"You've really screwed it up good this time. You'll never model now!"

He caught himself and stopped. Regaining composure he realized he was wrong. Not the right time or the right place to get into that now. All Elise could do is look into her dad's eyes with the look that said she was truly sorry. Dad looked back to say what Dads say,

"I'm sorry. I'm sure it will all be okay."

The nurse returned, asking Frank if he could help the orderly wheel Elise down for the CT scan and x-rays. He was glad to help. The nurse finished getting Elise prepped; Frank stepped out to update Linda. Linda was pale, white, visibly shaken. She in turn provided a status report on the other kids and their injuries along with the details about the crash. She reported that the accident had been a head-on collision. The other kids were walking wounded with bumps, bruises and a couple of broken ribs. Elise had sustained the worst injuries. Frank filled Linda in on their daughter's status without adding personal comment as to the long-range problems he envisioned.

Linda stayed behind to do admitting paperwork. Frank accompanied Elise for scans and x-rays that were to determine the extent of internal injuries. He reported back to Linda that Elise's injuries had not done any damage to the brain or skull, just massive facial lacerations with bruising. The eye and optic nerve were okay. Both the radius and ulna in her left arm had been broken and required plates and pins to fix. A plastic surgeon would have to put Elise's face back together. Both procedures were scheduled to take place at French Hospital in San Luis as Arroyo Grande Hospital didn't have a plastic surgeon on call.

At 4:15am the ambulance transported Elise to French Hospital with Mom and Dad following. The orthopedic and plastic surgeons immediately went to work. Four hours, seventy six stitches, two plates, and eight screws later Mom and Dad were able to see their daughter again in the recovery room. Physical recovery had now begun and wouldn't take long compared to the mental recovery that could take years. The nightmare of growing up through the teenage years was going to be complicated by a patchwork of scars Elise was going to have to bear. All this coming two weeks to the day after Dads 'riding in cars' conversation.

Frank's most immediate concern was to get Elise healthy enough to attend a wedding in Alaska. He needed to get his daughter out of town and away from the fixated recounting of accident details. The endless stream of well wishing friends who visited Elise only encouraged the retelling of the accident details like a broken record. She needed new scenery away from the place of broken dreams.

Sticking to recovery protocol prescribed by the doctors was fairly easy. The nightly cleaning of the sutured wounds did prompt Dad to step out of the box, however. Elise's plastic surgeon had been adamant in his instructions regarding the cleaning of the wounds. Hydrogen peroxide only, was his demand. No vitamin E, no Aloe Vera, nothing else to promote healing or reduce scarring, just hydrogen peroxide for cleaning and to help prevent infection. Four days into the program Dad altered the protocol, telling no one.

Frank's years of contact with Mother Ocean had taught him that skin abrasions, cuts and lacerations healed much faster when he had contact with the sea. So he went to the ocean, collected a bottle of Mother Nature's healing elixir, shot it with ozone (03) from the shop to kill any pathogens, then substituted it for the nightly peroxide applications. A week later when the doctor removed the bandages to inspect the progress of the wounds healing, he commented with quite genuine surprise,

"These are healing twice as fast as I expected."

Frank was the most pleased, but said nothing about Mother Nature's help.

Three weeks later Elise was given a reluctant 'okay' to travel to Alaska with Dad by the orthopedic surgeon. Dad promised not to let Elise hike on any glaciers after the doctor cautioned that any fall could result in damage beyond repair to Elise's arm. Her arm was not in a cast because the nine-inch incision that had been made to repair the break needed to heal. This was the only thing that concerned Dad as a rambunctious teenager is always prone to a fall.

Three days later they left on an adventure that was to be seared into the memory banks forever. It was going to be an amazing trek into a land where the sun almost never sets. Mid July in Fairbanks, Alaska has 22 hours of sunlight. The two hour's worth of sunset and sunrise only dims the illumination slightly. You can get a lot done with that much sunlight. They needed every minute of it in order to accomplish all the wedding plans they had been swept up and into.

What a fun feel for the fam of four from the lower forty eight to be in Fairbanks, enjoying being part of the happy couple's nuptials. The sights, sounds, and smells of this frontier town on the edge of civilization had energy flowing. Besides taking in the wilds that surrounded them, the bustle of preparation needed to pull off a wedding on the Chena River had each day lived to its fullest. Hana and Elise helped do the girl things. Frank and Troy did the macho things that guys do.

The night before the wedding, Mark the groom was in charge of loading, unloading and set up of the wedding reception area. No big deal if it had been an indoor event. Oh no, this would be 40 miles out of town on the banks of the Chena River, with enough equipment to outfit a small army. The plan to meet the girls at the remote location at 8pm was delayed, with the first cans of beer opened at noon by Mark and the other men there to help. By 6pm drunk was creeping. Troy and Frank could only watch. At about 10pm the two truck loads plus one trailer full of equipment rolled towards its intended rendezvous a full two hours late. Frank was sure the girls were fuming. He and Troy were the only two sober people in this otherwise well-lit caravan of wedding participants that was still 20 minutes away from their meeting point. That's when Frank spotted the moose.

The four visitors from the lower forty eight had been in Alaska for a full three days. They had driven several hundred miles and had not seen one moose. This was a first and Frank had Mark screeching the caravan to a stop so he could snap a photo of the 'first' moose, evidence to the girls that they had actually, finally, seen one. Troy posed as the great white hunter with moose in the background as proof to the girls they had seen the elusive creature. That's when the car loads of furious females pulled up, heading in the opposite direction. They had been waiting to help unload the tons of supplies and help set up, but now they had to return to town to get the girl things in order. Jan's brief but terse conversation with Mark was followed by Jan's request to see Frank. Jan knew Frank was sober, looked deep into his eyes and said,

"Please make sure everything turns out all right."

"Yes everything will be okay, I promise," was his required return.

At 1am Frank finally convinced Mark that the reception area should be set up in closer proximity to the mountain of supplies they had yet to unload. Just across the slough from where they were parked was much more convenient than loading, unloading and carrying the tonnage a hundred yards up the river. They reversed the process and at 2am when the sun set they had about half of the equipment back to the closer location. At 3:30am the sun was coming back up when the gang of exhausted men turned in for a couple of hours of rest. At 5:30am Frank was back up, fire started, coffee on, as Jan's haunting request, "Please make sure everything turns out okay." echoed in his brain. He just couldn't let her down on her wedding day. Frank finished the last couple of canoe loads of equipment himself. At about 7am the camp was alive as the others awoke and the frenzied set up began. At 9am the canoes were loaded back up and the hangover moved up river a mile to set up the girls changing tent at the intended riverside wedding site.

They were on time, and Frank was impressed with Troy's ability to keep up with the grinding pace. Not only could Troy play the guitar incredibly well, but he had a stamina that his mother could be proud of. The kid was alive with energy. That energy was rubbing off on Elise. The kids were having fun and now finally so were the adults.

The girls where on time at 10am to decorate the canoe for the wedding parties float back down the river to the reception site. The boys roared off to the Hot Springs Resort for a hot shower, change into their wedding duds, then back down to the wedding site in time for the late arrival of the bride. The boys looked good in their jackets, ties and jeans.

Jan arrived in her beautiful, long white flowing gown via limo. Frank greeted her at the limo door and assured her that all had been accomplished according to her instructions. The news made Jan absolutely beam. With delight he took her in arm, leading her down the pathway of tall pines at the waters edge. In a small clearing reminiscent of the surroundings he had married in he performed his honorable duty, giving his friend in matrimony at an altar only Mother Nature could have created. The wild pure setting was perfect. The vows were perfect, Frank held Hana in his heart. The ceremony really was uplifting for him, allowing a private reaffirmation to the Universe of his commitment to Hana through the vows that were exchanged by Mark and Jan. He felt joy being able to lavishly give his love away no strings attached. No utterance needed. The glint of refracted sunshine from a band of gold on the finger of Hana said all that needed saying.

After the kiss that sealed the ceremonial deal, the large group of friends, family and a handful of passerby tourists escorted the joyous couple down to their wedding canoe waiting at waters edge. The canoe that had been lovingly decorated by the girls with garlands of ivy, flowers and candles led the group of invited revelers on a mile long magical floating ride down the Chena River. The fleet of following floatation devices included canoes, kayaks, and rubber inflatable rafts in every shape and color one could imagine. The outlandish gayety of the colorful flotilla was in stark contrast to the serenity of the float down river, serving as reflection to the uniqueness of the event. Floating downstream, while watching the salmon swimming up stream, was a trip highlight the family of four from the lower forty eight would never forget.

Safe arrival by all at the slough reception site just off of the main waterway and the party was on. The many kids in attendance tested their rather hilariously limited canoeing skills in the calm waters of the slough. The adults stoked up the fire, threw two freshly caught 15 pound salmon on the barbecue and of course the bar was open. Gentle breezes blew, warm sunshine bathed the gathering, as Mark and Jan celebrated a first dance together on the canvas dance floor. Hana eventually gave in to Frank's repeated requests, taking a romantic canoe ride with him. The day seemed to go on forever.

At about 6pm Frank and Hana decided to take the kids and drive to Chena Hot Springs Resort to stay for the night. Securing a great two bedroom second story room, they carted their luggage in and prepped for dinner at the hotel restaurant. The kids had their own room with separate beds, Frank and Hana had their own room complete with balcony and separate beds. Dinner and dessert were great, capping off an incredible wedding event. Returning to their room for some much needed rest, Frank for the first time watched Hana fall blissfully asleep. He lifted up thanks to the Grace that had brought this surrogate family a most perfect day, before he too fell into his own blissful slumber.

The next morning the excitement continued. Frank was up first, quietly slipping through the sun retarding curtains and headed out onto the balcony to take in the view. He was astounded to find a herd of moose wandering amongst the cabin grounds. Wading through the pools of warm waters that surrounded the hot springs enclosure, the moose munched lazily on the grasses and mosses the pools had to offer. He watched for about half an hour before announcing his finding to the rest of the late arising crew. Elise and Troy were first, Hana was last announcing, "No way!" as she counted the seven or so huge animals that seemed to take small notice of the group's excitement. "The moose were loose!" was the joke of the day as they took in breakfast and a dip in the hot springs before returning to town.

Mark and Jan were off to honeymoon and the group's final full day was devoted to taking in the sights and shopping for keepsakes in the Fairbanks area. That evening Frank broke out the map of Alaska to get a fix on needed travel time back to Anchorage. Taking the Richardson Hwy back down to Anchorage he noticed might take them close enough to see the ice blue face of glaciers. Then he noticed something he had not noticed before. In the top left hand corner of the map was a slim body of water that separated two land masses. The main body of land which covered most of the map area was Alaska of course. The other small piece that showed just across the Bering Strait was Russia. That was a fascinating revelation to the four as they realized just how far out there they really were. It made the remoteness of their travel that much more astounding.

Up early the following morning the traveling foursome packed their rental Crown Victoria and headed south down the Richardson. No trip to Alaska was complete without a stop at the little town of North Pole, and they did. Saw the reindeer, did a lunch and then pressed on. Crossing the tundra with the huge vistas that displayed glaciers pouring out of ten-mile wide mountain valley mouths was awesome. Awesome too were the huge frost heave tundra bumps in the road that almost had the old Crown Vic airborne when hit at 80 miles per hour. The frost heaves were hard to see at times, when you missed slowing your approach your fanny would leave the bench seat and the asshole would pucker as you crossed to the downhill side. Made you lose your stomach. The feeling of weightlessness lasting until the car's full weight planted back on pavement. Really made for an E-ticket ride.

The wide expanse narrowed to a twisting turning valley ride about 3 hours out of Anchorage. That's when the fearsome foursome happened upon the Matanuska Glacier. This Glacier out of the four they had seen was almost next to the road, beckoning a stop. Time permitted, so stop they did. The ice blue and green face made a good backdrop for photos taken. Dad paid close attention to Elise's movements while trekking on the glacier. All he needed was to have to explain how his daughter had re-broken her arm while hiking on a glacier. They made it off the ice without a spill and to the airport with a comfortable cushion of time.

At the departure gate Frank received the warmest hug from Hana, a kiss and heartfelt thanks for a most amazing trip. He hugged back deeply and was surprised by the kiss. They hugged again knowing it would be the last for a while, grateful for the time they had together. Then spontaneous offering,

"I love you Hana Joi."

"I love you too Frank."

At that moment they were both really 'giving it away' and it really felt good. Hana's smile with eyes glowing let him know that this had been a very special adventure for her and Troy. He smiled back the same.

He and Elise reached home in Grover about the same time he figured Hana and Troy reached their home on Bent Island. He picked up the phone and called Hana's cell. Hana answered, and they talked as she drove across the Chesapeake Bay Bridge, the last leg on her journey home to the Island. They had only been apart for six hours or so. He told her he was already 'jonesing' for more. They laughed, agreeing they made a great traveling 'fam of four'. He promised they'd do it again. They also laughed with a degree of relief at how good they were going to sleep that night, now that they had returned to their portion of the planet that really got dark. They agonized a goodbye vowing to talk again soon. Frank hung up his phone lifting up thanks again to the Grace that had made this traveling partnership possible.

The euphoria lasted for weeks. The yearning to combine the households was to be discussed in fantasy as both knew it couldn't happen until both the kids had graduated from high school. Both children had a non custodial mother or father in their respective locations, both custodial parents knew the kids needed that contact. Picking up and moving by either was not an option, so they agreed to be satisfied with what they had until then. Besides, Hana had but one major goal she had relayed to him from the beginning, which was to stay alive long enough to see Troy graduate. He wanted to see that happen. Three more years for that to be fulfilled, he could wait.

A few months later Hana had one last bout with 'why' Frank shared his kindness so freely. She just couldn't figure out his willingness to love her, expecting nothing in return and why that meant so much to him. He tried to explain again, this time searching for clarity with a little more detail. He conceded that this experience of giving was even to him a changing landscape of emotional growth and spiritual theory. It was a learning experience for him into the true nature of real love. He was learning, and that was a good thing. He explained that 'giving it away' allowed him to love, allowing him to feel complete as a human being. After all giving was receiving. He explained that he could actually feel when love was pouring out of him to her. From one side of his being it was flowing out to her, on the other side he felt it as it flowed into him. He could really feel it.

That's where faith and theory kicked in together to become reality, he hoped to explain. Frank was sure that the origin of this positive loving energy was Grace. That was faith. The power of that Grace to heal was faith that supported his theory. Frank's theory was, 'the more he could be the conduit of this Grace letting it flow freely through him, the more Hana could heal'. The 'key' was 'free'. No stings attached.

Frank's somewhat abstract thought that Agape love could fight the onset of AIDS was a bit of a stretch for most folks. This was the first time he confided this thought to Hana. He pointed out that it appeared to be working, based on blood work results showing a reversal of the negative trend of higher viral load counts. Hana's happiness was key so any love given had to be given free. Hana finally hinted that maybe she was beginning to believe there really was a God. That made him happy; after all he confided, that was part of his job too. They laughed, but really the blood work results didn't lie. He promised to keep loving her hard!

He also told Hana that it was important to him to make sure Troy could grow up with as many positive memories of his life with his mom as possible. He had never confided this either. This revelation did make him a little emotional. He remembered his mom's passing, wishing he had done more with her. His voice reflected the pain he hoped Troy would never feel. She marveled at his compassionate motivation that worked from a place she had never known until now. From her own Grace she expressed her gratitude for the gift that he was.

Hana's heart began to feel the tingle of Grace that flowed her way. By the end of the conversation he felt the peace returning to her heart, feeling the smile on her face over the phone. He stopped his discussion of motivating factors just short of disclosing the amends he was making for his past. He knew one day he'd have to tell Hana of his sordid past. That darkness was not for now. He felt he was amending for that past through his giving to her, the explanation could wait. Today was not to be that day to dip into the dark with her. Hana was happy, at peace and that's where he wanted her to stay.

Frank followed up their heart-to-heart with a card. His creative brain came up with a unique way to make his point about what he had learned about love. A perfect card was selected. Inside the card he placed a dozen strands of string. The intent was that when Hana extracted the card and opened it up, the unattached string would fall all about. Inside he simply wrote, "No strings attached, love Frank." Hana got the point, called laughing at how well his card had conveyed his message. Later in joy he thanked the place from which that Grace inspired creativity had flowed. He was starting to remember to say thanks...a lot.

The remainder of that year's projects, events and business seemed to all flourish with the same creativity inspired by that Grace that he really didn't acknowledge near enough. He didn't really see how it all fit together, Quantum physics was years away. Yet he had an ability to move through bad events, forgetting the horrors they visited on him without a drink was just short of miraculous.

Even the turmoil caused by negative issues exhibited positive signs of light. He had an attorney and Mary to help in his plight with the Department of Justice. Elise had an attorney to help in her dealings with insurance companies. The ex wife was even being more civil.

And the good things just kept getting better. Many of his ideas for the Price House and Park that he had floated by the board had been approved for him to execute: fence perimeter expansion to include about two acres, re-establish John Price's apple and pear tree orchard to use as memorial tree sales for fundraising, find a suitable water supply for watering the trees and grounds, establish a temporary power pole to provide electricity with trench and conduit to supply underground power from pole to house.

On top of these many different directions he had a couple of personal projects he was working on alone for the Anniversary House. One was his search for the ornate fireplace mantle that had disappeared from the Price House in about 1972. Another was the refurbishing of the old windmill that stood majestically a hundred feet from the front porch to working condition. His biggest personal challenge was his work to procure a land lease from the Union Pacific Railroad.

All this and still more. Thank God for the volunteers. The Price House hosted its second annual ice cream social in November with an open house and a huge fundraising extravaganza. FOPH VP Jack Straw and his wife Lee made that event a tremendous success. Mac and Effie McDermott, longtime residents of Pismo, were ramrodding the adobe home site preservation. At the same time Effie had collected a canyon history, catapulting the historical park's scope way beyond just local history. Gabriel Iossi, another long time Pismo resident and primitive art specialist, joined Frank in a search for local Native Americans to bring the indigenous peoples history alive. This growing group of history buffs had a huge agenda. Strong hearts and backs were needed to make this all happen. Thank God for volunteers.

The Clam family also went through some changes that year. Three new kids had to be found as Devin, Kylee and Elise had outgrown the costumes. Except for Judy's granddaughter most replacements only participated once. A couple of times Frank had to find a stand in for Pam, but Judy was always there at Sam's side at festival time.

And Genesis Water had its best year yet. Gross sales for the year were just a few dollars shy of a hundred thousand. Banner year. Steve-a-Reno (Frank's nickname for Stevie) was the backbone to the rest of the team of four good-looking girls that helped make that year such a success. The loose, flexible crew interacted well together, Frank was grateful to have them working for him. The employees all received a handsome Christmas bonus. Well maybe the bonus wasn't that handsome, but at least there was a bonus. No strings attached.

Holidays celebrated by Dad and Daughter in their new home had a small plastic Christmas tree with one candle in the window, but that was as far as Frank let go with the Christmas thing. Small gifts for Hana , Troy and Elise, was about all he could surrender to the consumerism that infected the season. He just couldn't resolve the conflict he saw celebrating Jesus and greed at the same time. He knew how Jesus felt about the money changers, upsetting their tables was a statement! He had also read in the Bible that Jesus stated, "Celebrate my death, not my birth." This made the whole event an exercise in something people were told not to do by the very person they were supposed to be celebrating! Some historical theologians now even suggested Christ wasn't even born in December. Other evidence concludes that the 'birthday thing' may have been a ploy by early Christians to grow their ranks from the masses of people that celebrated the pagan ritual of winter solstice. By staging a celebration a few days after the winter pagan bash, the church elders figured they could beat the drum of repentance, enticing hung-over party goers into following Christian ways. Boy that truth can set you free!

The Grace of giving had really been lost long ago by the desire to receive. The whole event seemed to be a lie. Receiving was now the focus, true gifting lost to having. The feel-good feeling of the season was gone for him. "Besides, why celebrate gifting only once a year, life's a gift... celebrate!" his thoughts of that perfect world so far away. He kept his thoughts to himself hoping the masses would catch on to the deception soon themselves. Even the popularity of Santa Claus was a product of a marketing ploy to sell more goods by a retailer in the early 1900s. What is Santa now? "How sad, what are we really teaching our kids?" he mused.

~~~~

We are all here as a gift from the Universe to which some day we gift our return. How we weave between our coming and our going is the expression our children will weave by. If we gift we are gifted, if we take we are taken. Our string we follow may have made the wiser choice.

CHAPTER 26

REFUGE AWAY FROM 'WHAT IF'

Clicking off another birthday was no mental stress, but getting through the hour-long annual 'registration' humiliation was. Trying to stay positive, Frank phoned Detective Mark to make an appointment to satisfy the regulatory obligation he had been unable to delete. Secretly, he hoped Y2K would have taken care of what he had not been able to, but that didn't happen. Being passed off to a new detective in charge of registration updates made staying in positive light that much more difficult. Even the new detective, Cheryl, seemed to have some negative energy towards the duty she had been assigned to fulfill. He sensed the disdain she had for the job by the way she conducted her information gathering. She noted that DNA samples had not been taken, letting him know that the requirement was now mandatory; she'd be calling to collect them soon. She also announced she'd be stopping by his house to personally verify his stated residence.

Frank questioned the necessity to do such verification, cautioning his daughter had no idea about his past and he wanted to keep it that way. He was concerned that a personal visit by a police officer might have Elise asking questions about what was going on. The detective offered a remedy, suggesting that he tell his daughter that the officer's visit was about some 'other' investigation. It didn't dawn on him until later that he had been told to lie by a police officer. "How strange was that? Corrupted system or what?"

The DNA issue really agitated him. The now mandatory invasion into one's private genetic code had him seething to a point of seeing red. It wasn't a matter of him having something to hide; it was a matter of a government entity having his genetic code. The most private of personal information was now being extracted through threatened non-compliance, which could result in jail time if he didn't. Frank went back to his attorney's office in a heartbeat. Jeff had not been heard from in a few months, and he held out little hope of hearing any good news. He didn't. Jeff let him know that he had reached nothing but dead ends regarding his search for release from the duty to register. Only one other thing he could do besides petition for a pardon was to submit a 'change of plea' from the original 'no contest' he had entered years ago. By entering into a 'change of plea' of 'not guilty,' however, he would be opening up his case again for possible retrial. Frank was cautioned that if the District Attorney wanted to, he could refile charges against him and he'd have to stand trial. That was the gamble.

Frank was willing to do just about anything to relieve and remove the humiliation of the tag he was forced to wear, but he wasn't too keen on putting himself in harm's way. He was interested in finding out more, and he did. Jeff informed him that this course of action had to take place in the original jurisdiction in which the crime had occurred, that being Orange County. Jeff gave him the name and phone number of an attorney he thought might be able to help him. He thanked Jeff for his services, leaving somewhat dismayed at the overall results, yet encouraged to have any direction at all. Within a few days Frank called the number Jeff had given him. The phone call to Ann did rekindle real hope. Ann was kind and expressed interest in his case. She suggested they meet as soon as possible so she could see the documents he had collected, he could then decide whether or not he wanted to retain her. Frank accepted and a meeting was scheduled. Dark clouds were lightening up. At least he could hope.

Before that meeting was to take place the dark foreboding clouds of horror returned. Detective Cheryl jaunted around Frank's neighborhood crying wolf, handing out flyers that looked like wanted posters. That was just great! Now the cancer of rumor and innuendo could really start to grow. Detective Cheryl's phone call pushing Frank for DNA samples was just about enough to push him over the top and back into the bottle. He gained a reprieve of 30 days on the DNA sample request when he informed the detective he had retained a new lawyer and they were meeting soon. The detective did show some compassion, allowing him this one last effort to have himself removed from the registration roles. She did state that she really thought it was too bad that this one incident from so many years prior could destroy his life. That statement really said it all.

Frank met with Ann. The meeting persuaded him to retain Ann to represent him. Her statement that "he would probably be granted relief in the interest of justice" sealed the deal and he agreed to pay for her services, quite expensive services. But as I said before he was willing to do just about anything, even write a check for four thousand five hundred dollars. Even with new representation, he accepted the fact that there was not enough time to stay any further attempts by Detective Cheryl to obtain DNA samples. Still he remained confident that the nightmare might be over soon enough to keep the cancer from spreading. He could hope.

Frank, being a man of his word called the detective upon his return from Orange County. He made an appointment with her to give the samples requested. That was that and now back into the light of the everyday run for living.

The daily run always started with taking Elise to school. Her first year in high school was hanging on the edge of success; her adjustment to the new, often brutal surroundings wasn't going so well. The social aspect was out of control as Elise searched for acceptance in her new surroundings. The phone was ringing constantly and the school assignments were not getting done. By the end of the school year she squeaked by with a promotion to her sophomore year.

She had seemed to be angry and on edge all of the time, and Dad knew it was due in part to the scars she wore on her face. She had been told that it would be at least a year before anything could be done to mend the deformities that had been caused by the accident. That was a long time for a young girl to wait. She tried hard every morning to hide the scars ugly intrusions on her otherwise beautiful face. Dad tried to keep her spirits up by taking her to UCLA, beginning the process of selecting a doctor she felt comfortable enough with to help repair the damage. Her attorneys Jim Murphy and Tana Sinclair also helped by letting her know they were seeking compensation large enough so she could have the very best plastic surgeon available do the work.

Unfortunately, all of this was going to take time to work through the courts. It broke his heart to watch Elise struggle. One night as he lay in bed he heard Elise begin to weep as she showered. He could tell by her sobs that something was very wrong and when she had turned off the shower he called out to her to ask what was up. Her first response the typical,

"Nothing Dad."

Dad prodded knowing something was. The daughter finally responding,

"I hate my scars." She choked between sobs.

Getting up, Dad shared some words of encouragement, hugging her before she went to bed. He returned to his bed and lifted up a plea for peace for Elise to the Grace that had kept her alive. Thank God she was still alive. He offered up thanks for that little miracle quite often.

Another small miracle was the year for the Price House. The fence perimeter expansion Frank had dreamed about was completed in time to host an Arbor Day celebration for the city. The two-acre fencing enclosure had penciled out at almost $9,000, he got it done for about $600. He and Glen did 70% of the work and the California Conservation Corp did the rest. He also convinced the city to buy twelve apple trees to start the orchard's replanting, saving the Price House about $2000. He was also able to enlist the services of another volunteer, Sam Urton, who hauled in 100 yards of earth to finish off the grade plan around the Anniversary House. That saved FOPH another couple of grand. The adobe ruins were cleared of weeds and trees by Mac and Effie. Effie also secured a survey crew to mark their current four-acre plot. That saved FOPH another two to three thousand dollars. Saving money was the name of the game and he was getting really really good at that.

Unfortunately, Jack Straw lost his beloved wife of 50 years to cancer and that was hard on everyone. In June, just after her passing, Lee's contributions to the City of Pismo and the Price Historical Park were memorialized on a placard placed at the base of the first Jonathan Apple tree replanted in the orchard. She was sorely missed by all, and Jack's vitality for life slowly dimmed. Frank stayed close to Jack, making sure his buddy's sorrow could be shared, an even plane of emotion only reached after months of grieving and tending Lee's tree together.

July of that year was curve ball time again for Frank. This time the curve ball brought with it the horror of 'What If' turning **AGAIN** to 'What Now'. A phone call from the property management company regarding his lease renewal for his business space started off the chain of events. His buildings lease was up for renewal, and the property management representative inquired if Frank wanted to stay for another three years. Frank was in no financial position to move the state-licensed facility, so of course he wanted to stay. Despite the fact that the rent on the space was $500 more than his house payment, he didn't have an extra 20 grand to move the business to a cheaper location. The manager sent him an invoice for rent, and he paid it. Three days later one of the co-owners of the building called with the curve ball.

The owner/partner calling was an attorney in San Luis Obispo; his opening line was.

"I've decided not to renew your lease."

Frank was dumbfounded. He indicated that there must be some sort of confusion, he had just renewed and sent his check in a few days before. The attorney responded that there was no confusion, he was not going to renew the lease and had intercepted the check for return.

"Why? I've always paid the rent on time, what's the problem?" Frank questioned.

"I don't have to give you a reason." the attorney responded and hung up the phone.

That's when the light went on. Lawyer, website, sex offender... no lease.

Frank couldn't believe this was happening. He took a copy of the lease down to his daughter's attorney to see if this was in fact legal. Jim gave him the bad news; there was a clause that stated "No reason need be given for a lease termination." It took him weeks to stop reeling from the blow. Now he had to decide what he wanted to do.

He spun like a washer on spin cycle. Ten years of rent on time. Six years of plaza promotion coordinating. Five years as Chamber board representative for the plaza. All for what? Moving the business was not an option and he realized it. Moving the state licensed retail water and bottling facility could take months for approval. He did not have the cash to sustain himself or the employees while moving the business to a new location. All for what? To have rumor and innuendo force him to move again!

He felt bad for the kids who worked for him, especially Stevie who was now married with a young son. He was sad at the jobs lost for his other four employees. He was sad about all the customers who'd be lost, not to mention the loss of the old country store feel the place had developed over the years, where a customer was a friend and had a place to find a sympathetic ear. An honest, sincere business was being destroyed for what purpose? It wasn't right or just. The cancer was growing; there was nothing he could do about it.

It was hard telling Elise what was happening to Genesis Water. She was first to get the news. He tried to ease her worry telling her everything was going be okay, but he wasn't sure of that himself. It was really hard to tell the employees what he had to do. It was hard telling the customers, especially since the real reason had never been revealed even to him. It was hard disassembling something he had worked so hard to build. It was hard shutting the door for the last time. Life was dark, cold, shrinking. Isolation was not the life he wanted to live.

Hana was told the same reason he told the rest, "The owners must have a special friend who wanted his cherry business location next to the cleaners." He knew his dad thought something was fishy with the whole thing. He had to live a lie to cover up 'What If'. The world he was being forced to live in was very dark and cold; that's a residence that can make you sick.

Genesis Water closed the doors for good on October 1, 2000. With Grace he accepted the change he had not planned. Funny thing: no one moved in for over six months. The new occupants only stayed for six months, and then they were gone. The space remained empty for the following three years. Really kinda strange...or not, Karma has its own time.

However, October turned into a pretty good month. Clam festival was extra rewarding that year. Elise had been convinced by Dad and the festival's scholarship pageant coordinator, Lori Rye, to compete again in the pageant despite her scars. Elise was truly talented in social skills, she looked good in a business suit doing mock interviews with pageant judges, or strutting to the podium in her long evening gown. Her poise answering unrehearsed questions in front of the crowd even impressed Dad. Elise's social platform was seat belt awareness and her scars she bore made that theme hit home to whomever she spoke. At the end of the night Elise was crowned Miss Teen Pismo 2000, and Dad couldn't have been more proud. That locked the door to 'What If' for a while and life was a thrill again.

That year the festival started at 4am for Frank as he directed the festival ground setup. Setup completed, he donned his costume so Sam could march proudly behind the car carrying his crowned daughter. Instead of being a Clam that year, Elise was an escort for the happy Clam family as they toured around the festival grounds. Elise was beaming with pride and Dad beamed inside of Sam, lifting up thanks to the Grace that had provided relief for his daughters faltering self image.

Frank felt a little greedy by the first of the year in regards to his planned personal time. By the end of the year he had looked back to know that those getaways had given him the strength to weather the storms and curve balls thrown his way. Again, one of the getaways was a spur of the moment decision, the other afforded only a little more time for planning. Both worked out to be just what the Doctor ordered. "One day," he was to muse later, "I'll have to look that Doctor up to thank him personally for the favor."

The first of these getaways was one of those 'perfect timing' events. Linda, Alaska Jan's sister and the one he had almost sold in Mexico made numerous calls inviting him to the island of Maui for a visit. Linda was calling one last time to give him the opportunity for a 5-day visit. She and her husband Don were to be moving back to the mainland in early summer, so Frank's free place to stay would be history shortly. He bit the bullet, bought the plane ticket and spent five fabulous days in May on Maui. Surf, scuba dive and endless snorkeling in the blue waters of paradise really made it tough to get on the plane to return home. He commented to Linda before he left, as they cruised the island's incredible beauty, he found the surroundings and feel of Aloha was the absolute perfect place for him to write 'his book'. Maybe he fancied he could return some day and do just that.

The second of these getaways also had minimal advance notice. With the shop closing, he really didn't think along the lines of vacation, he was simply trying to survive. Mental survival was important as well, so last-second planning for mental therapy was jumped on. It had been over a year since he had last seen Hana. Biting the bullet again he purchased airfares for the two of them to go to Florida to spend Thanksgiving with Frank's dad and his brother's family. This was to be Hana's first encounter with Frank's family. He kept his fingers crossed that the family might like her as much as he did. His brother's wife Beth knew a lot about Hana, but the rest of the family was, for the most part, unaware of how he felt about her. They were soon to find out.

It was a perfect start to a perfect holiday weekend. Frank and Hana both arrived in Memphis, Tennessee, from their respective starting points to join up, then fly on to Fort Walton Beach together. By arrival time Frank was on cloud 19 again. He couldn't believe the affect Hana had on him. Her company, her voice, her deep blue eyes, just had a way of elevating his soul. He noticed right away that Hana wore her ring. It was a nice nonverbal 'I love you' that put the old smile back on the face that needed a smile.

On the ride back to the house from the airport, Frank's dad engaged Hana, truly making her feel welcomed. He also informed the couple of the accommodations that had been arranged in light of all the guests arriving from Houston. Bob and his family were to stay at Dad's house, Frank and Hana had separate rooms at Pauline's house. Pauline Riecher was Dad's best

friend plus traveling companion since Mom had passed. She was an exceptionally loving little Italian woman. Pauline's husband, who also had been a
career Air Force man, passed away a few years prior to Frank's mom getting
sick. Pauline had been a tremendous support to his dad while his mom was
ill; a God-send of encouragement to Jim after Elizabeth's passing. Pauline,
being a good Italian, took Hana under her wing, welcoming her as one of her
own. Pauline opened her home, providing two large separate bedrooms with
separate baths with all the amenities for the couple to enjoy. And enjoy they
did!

This was Frank and Hana's first getaway together without the kids. The
time spent together was an absolute dream. A day spent knocking around
with Frank's old surf partner Tim Mallambri was a real insight for Hana.
The two buddies talked lucidly about the old days of surfing and their old
womanizing ways. That was a real eye opener for Hana. The three relished
reminiscing about the by gone days of high school and the events of their lives
thereafter. Another day spent with Pauline and Jim sailing and lunching on
Jim's 30 foot sailboat, Misty, under perfect conditions made for a perfect day.
And of course there was the Thanksgiving feast with all the trimmings.

That day of feasting with the Lindsay clan was to be the day Hana
became an official member of the family. Hana had fit right in with the flow
of the family event, but a comment she made during the after dinner conversation cemented her position as an intuitive, spontaneous speaker of truth.
Hana's incredibly quick wit with lightening fast delivery made her the mouth-
piece for the tongue-tied. It was during a story being told by Jim about a sailing race, in which Jim's vessel Misty was being crewed by a handful of
novices. Jim's regular crew could not make the race for one reason or another
and Jim had to sail the race with an untrained crew of volunteers. Now Jim
had a certain amount of pride associated with his racing. After all he was
Commodore of the Blue Water Bay Yacht Club, therefore a good showing
was mandatory in his eyes. Throughout the majority of the race the crew, Jim
complained, had barely kept Misty out of last place as they rounded the final
buoy and headed for the finish line. The contender for next to last place was
on their heels and closing fast, Jim recounted. Jim knew they could beat their
rival by setting the spinnaker sail and shouted forward for the crew to do so.
Jim could see that the fledgling crew was having some difficulty setting the
sail and shouted,

"You better hurry." That's when Hana jumped in expounding,

"Yeah and I'll bet you said it with all the love you could muster."

That stopped Jim dead in his tracks as it took a second or two for the
comment to register. He stammered a verbal response with a confused perplexed look,

"Yeah… right." The listeners then launched into spontaneous laughter at the response. What Hana had said sailed right over Jim's head and he finished his tale of embarrassing loss on the high seas.

Hana had within a moment summed up and said what the others could not appropriately articulate. The captain of the boat was a little hard on the crew… ya think? Jim's reaction to the comment was priceless. He finally admitted that maybe he was a little over demanding of those that had gone along for the fun of it. Beth shot a look to Hana that said, "You go girl!" and Frank knew Hana had become a hero in Beth's eyes. Hana had given the Commodore some pause for thought and that was an amazing feat. From that point on Hana was viewed as Frank's better half.

It had been a fantastic extended weekend getaway without kids. The two had been able to share some real quality time together that bordered on romantic. Frank's playful hinting at intimacy kept Hana on her toes firing back her witty deflections. He knew he was still at 'arms length' yet he still wanted to let Hana know he wasn't afraid. He did tell her while staring into her sea blue eyes that he felt her arms were getting shorter. Hana leaned back holding his gaze and with a consoling air about her said… "Yeah?"

It was a grand time. They hugged deeply as they departed on separate flights home, not sure when they were to see each other again. Both returned home energized. Frank pushed forward with a huge breakthrough at the Price House. Hana gained a promotion at her new job with Star Guitar. It was a splendid way to end the year.

~~~~

We all seek refuge from the storms the weave presents. Connection counts. Our string we follow has some amazing connections. Apparently the Universe cares not of one's past. Now is really all that counts.

CHAPTER 27

MOVING A MOUNTAIN CAN'T KILL 'WHAT IF'

Rewind the tape, let's play it again. Frank wondered if this next year was to be the same as the last. It was guaranteed to start out same as the last; a birthday and a birthday ritual. This year he confronted his demon head on and booked his registration ritual to coincide with his birthday. It seemed the law had changed again, instead of ten days either side of the birthday to comply, it was now five. It turned out that the only day that could fit Cheryl's schedule was his birthday. Great! An 8am appointment booked at the police department to breakfast on ink and flash, the rest of the day to recover, and clean away the stink of ink.

Cleaning was done at the Price House, his favorite place to leave it all behind. After an early departure from the home office, where Genesis Water operated now, the park was the place to let creativity take over. The prize project at this point was the refurbishing of the old windmill. He had his fingers crossed that eventually he and a new volunteer, Scott Isher, could get the old girl up and pumping. It was the challenge of the project that transported his mind away from the angers aroused by the start of day. The only pain he was unable to shake was the anger that resonated from not hearing from his attorney in months.

The array of projects for the Price House, the business and his daughter's needs supplied the diversions needed to keep a sense of dignity. Now the cancerous growth of 'What If' uncertainty melted away on the back burner as his ambition stayed focused on the more positive. The plate of life had been heaped with healthy portions of more important tasks.

Staying afloat in his now severely reduced water business of course was job one. He tightened his cost of living belt again in an attempt to stop the hemorrhaging of money from his savings account. By Grace he was able to sell the water facility equipment to the same local water purveyor who had purchased his bottled water delivery operations. That sale also worked into a contract to locate, design and rebuild the water store operations for the new owner. The new owner went so far as to offer to buy the Genesis Water name and service customer base that he retained. That was something he'd have to think about.

The opportunity to get out of the water business entirely was enticing but working for someone else scared him a bit. After all, he had been working for himself for so long he wasn't sure he'd adjust well to punching someone else's time clock. Working corporate again just wasn't his cup of tea. Reduced responsibility, paid time off, benefit packages and bonuses were all big draws. Marching to someone else's drum with no real guarantees of sustained employment were the uncomfortable drawbacks to be weighed. He proceeded cautiously in regards to that decision. The 'What If' factor could certainly undermine the new potential employer's commitment. Then what? Was that a chance he was willing to take? Only time would tell. The deciding factor for that decision manifested a couple of months later, in the form of an event that took place on an early Tuesday morning in mid September.

By the end of March, a monumental success shifted the park project into yet higher gear. At the Price House on a warm sunny Sunday afternoon, a breeze blew that spun determined effort into pulse-pumping success. After a month of Sundays spent with Scott working on the windmill, Frank, Scott and Jack Straw stood ready to test the piece of history they had worked so hard on. If successful, a major component critical to turn of the century farm life would be brought back to life. Frank was given the honor of untethering the wheel that would bring forth the water.

The breeze was light to non-existent while he climbed the ladder to the top of the windmill. Untying the knots that held the eight foot wide wind blade in position only took a few seconds. Once released, the fan's vane turned the blades into the breeze, and a slow rotation of the mills fan began. The breeze picked up with a short burst as Frank descended. The mill creaked and clanged as rotating speed increased. This caused the sucker rods extending down some fifty feet to the pump to begin their movement up and down. By the time he reached the ground, the ever so precious resource needed to sustain life began to spit from the outflow side of the submerged plumbing. The past came to life, jubilant high fives celebrated all around.

The success of harnessing the wind's energy to bring water to the surface and fill the holding tank at the top of the hill was a real feat. It had saved the Friends of Price House at least $6,000 that had been bid by others some six years prior. That bid was for re-digging the well and converting to an electrically driven pumping method to supply the much-needed water for the farm. That would not have been historically accurate and was dismissed as a consideration by the FOPH board. Their effort was historically accurate and there was no electric bill to pay.

Their success also saved the City a big chunk of dollars. The City of Pismo's council members had directed their public works department to supply the Price House with water. After all, it was a city park. Frank's request for help from council members to supply this much needed commodity penciled out at about $45,000. This success saved the City a ton of money. Thanks in large part to Scott Isher; the two men were able to restore the historic windmill to operation, supplying the farm's life blood for only $500.

The twelve apple trees, fig tree and flower boxes around the house now had plenty of water. A win for the Price House was a win for Pismo.

The windmill also became a fascinating display of old-school farm techniques to the visitors Frank was beginning to field on the Park's open work days. The first and third Sundays of the month had been earmarked by Frank as open work days. Tourists were beginning to find out. The tourists supplied him a chance to break from work to practice his tour guide presentations. He began to gauge the quality of the tours he had given by the amount of money that was deposited in the FOPH donation can. Tours did take up valuable work time, but they brought in money that was good for the FOPH coffers.

The whole year was good for Price House. Whether it was a small or big package of tasks, the volunteers from the Price House managed to complete each one. The massive amount of time he devoted to the Park's projects was a direct result of the downsizing of his business. Whether it was designing, painting and erecting a front gate sign, or moving the two-story Meherin house out to the Park, it all took time and he had plenty of that.

Frank's time savings he had accrued by not having to attend to a burgeoning business was a lot like the money he had in his checking account, it went out as fast as it came in and was just enough to cover all the obligations. Out of the 60 plus hours a week he used to spend running the larger Genesis Water operation, he now was saving about 40 of those. He understood that, like spending money, for his time to be the most fruitful he had to follow the direction of Grace as to where that time was to be spent. His understanding with confidence that Grace will supply even if it was last minute was now allowing him to let the spirit of Grace direct the expenditure of his time. If it was a right project or task, he could feel it in his heart.

Ten thousand hours in a week of right projects, only 168 hours in a week of reality. He needed at least 56 of those hours just for sleeping to be at his best. The other 112 had to be divided amongst Elise, Hana, Genesis Water, Clam family and the Price House. For the most part, time for 'him' was slim to none. He could have been selfish and hoarded time, however he knew from experience it only leads to the edge of the abyss. If he didn't keep his mind occupied being creative, the dog of doom, The 'What if', destroyed any pleasure of being alive. But the label applied to his name was an insidious cancerous rot that reared its head, invading his thoughts, interrupting the creative output. The unsettling these thoughts brought with increasing frequency caused him to limit even further the projects that brought joy to life. Life kept shrinking.

Every time he put on the Sam the Clam costume 'What If' invaded. He began to plan the Clam family's retirement if he could not find a replacement. In Elise's life 'What If' invaded every time she had a friend over or had a function to attend. In Hana's life 'What If' invaded every time she recounted her progress in her personal recovery from abuse. 'What If' pounded his brain every time he did an interview for the Price House and Park. 'What If' even invaded the life expectancy of his business if he spent much time thinking about it. A toxic cloud of rejection was anticipated if the 'What If' cancer were to spread into the client base. He even saw signs that 'What If' was also affecting his health. A few times the pain in his chest, shortness of breath and dizzy numbness in his head, arm and legs reminded him that it could all end at any moment. He'd chew an aspirin while asking Grace to allow him a little more time. That did help to restore a normal heart rate. He redoubled his efforts to stay positive after these episodes. It just wasn't easy. Life was shrinking into a box.

It wasn't easy living with the invasions of 'What if,' but he just had so much to do and he wasn't a quitter. Foremost was his daughter. He wanted desperately to protect her from 'What If' as he prepared her for the challenges of 21st century life. The difficulty she was having in school was his biggest concern. He suspected Elise's difficulties were in part caused by her parent's fractured relationship along with the hideous scars she wore on her face. Time and time again Dad had to journey to the high school principal's office to deal with Elise's reprimands for aggressive behavior and failing grades. The social aspect of Elise's maturity seemed immense, almost overpowering. Could it be because she was an only child, or was it because of the facial scarring that she had to try so hard to fit in? Were her sliding academic grades due to his inability to articulate the importance of education? He never felt he was getting honest answers from her in regards to her studies. She flat out refused to show him proof of work completed. He felt he was fighting a losing battle in regards to education as Elise's mom discounted the importance of schooling. Elise was shutting down to educational success and Dad felt helpless in his efforts to impress and encourage its importance. He did not know that 'What If' had already invaded Elise's life.

After Elise's sophomore year ended Linda called Frank to arrange a meeting of considerable importance. He had grown accustomed to Linda's dramatic nature and really didn't expect anything major. He agreed to indulge the drama one more time. He was totally unprepared for the blindsiding information from Linda. The tale she told stunned him white and broke his heart at the core. Elise had found out about his past and his required registration as a 'sex offender'. The hole in his heart and numbness from anger made the details unimportant. The reality was 'What If' had turned into 'What Now' for Dad and Daughter's relationship.

This had been a bridge Frank hoped he'd never have to cross. His soul was tortured with what he knew he had to do. That afternoon when Elise came home from school Dad had to offer the explanation and apology his daughter deserved. The laborious explanation was received by Elise in total silence. Dad apologized for the fact that he had not been able to stop the hideous innuendo she now too had to bear. Her silence was killing him. He offered to answer any questions she had now or in the future. Elise's only response was she had none. It was to be years before it was to be brought up again. Elise did comment to her mom that she hoped her friends would never find out. She was now forced to live with 'What If' and that was an outrage for any kid to have to live through. Frank wondered again, "Was justice really being served or had it simply created another victim?"

The anger the incident with Elise had sparked translated into another call to his attorney in Orange County. Ann again indicating she was working on his case, but as yet had not found his avenue of escape. Somehow he expected that. His call did satisfy his need to vent. He also expressed his opinion that the tactics employed by 'Megan's Law' were really doing more harm than good. Ann agreed of course. Frank's call to Mary was the one to provide real solace with solid advice he needed to hear. So at Mary's urgings he kept a close eye on Elise. He looked for signs of impact from 'What If,' noticing only a distancing in their relationship. Conversations were short. Elise wasn't around much. He knew she was trying to avoid him, so he dumped himself back into his work. He had to, there was simply too much to be done. By Grace he had a full plate.

Most of that plate had been filled by the Historical Park and business. The retail end of Genesis Water had been sold and the new owner contracted Frank to locate a suitable site and rebuild the water facility. This worked out great as it again provided water pickup service locally for all the customers he felt he had left stranded. It also provided a huge chunk of necessary income. By Grace it had been provided, and like his time, by Grace it would be spent.

Grace also provided the answer to his dilemma of whether or not to sell the rest of Genesis Water and become an employee for the new owner. As requested, he had put together a proposal for that part of the buyout, after he had sealed the deal on the sale of the store equipment and facility rebuild. He was waiting to submit the proposal for their response while he weighed his concerns.

It was early September. He was contracted and working eight to ten hours a day rebuilding the store in its new location. At the same time he had started the disassembly of the Meherin House. The Meherin House was soon to be a new addition to the Price Park, causing work days to run to dark most of the time. Storage of his office equipment in the old red barn out at the Price House for the previous year worked out perfectly. As he emptied the barn of his sold business property he had stored, he'd fill it right back up with disassembled items from the Meherin House.

Close to mid September the new water store rebuild was almost done. Tuesday morning had started out just like the rest. Up at 6am, start a pot of coffee, click on the news to catch up, grab a cigar with a hot cup of coffee, head out to the back porch to wake up and plan the day. Returning back inside for another cup of coffee, he filled the cup to the brim and headed for the shower. On the way through the dining room he glanced at the television screen and noticed something unusual. The local news had been interrupted by the national news "special report." Frank held up to see exactly what was going on. The screen showed an image of a skyscraper in New York City burning. The newscast blah, blah, blah was short on facts as he watched a commercial jet fly into the view of the camera and straight into the second of the Twin Towers.

He immediately knew what was going on, picked up the phone and called Hana. He left her a message of warning, and then woke Elise for school. Dad monitored as daughter readied. He watched in disbelief as Tower One collapsed. As they left for school, the split-screen visual on the TV set was showing Tower Two in flames as well as the Pentagon in Washington D.C. Elise had not caught on to what going on, Dad filled her in gently as they rode to school. He told her he wanted to talk to her after school, encouraging her to be prompt at the pickup point. He returned home to monitor the developing situation.

Frank talked to Hana shortly thereafter. He was very afraid that D.C. might still be a target for the ultimate weapon of hate, advising her to be ready to go at a moment's notice. Hana was shaken by the day's beginnings. After all, she lived only an hour away from the Pentagon. She told Frank how eerie it was to have no planes in the sky except for the Air Force fighter jets that flew low level high speed sorties up and down the Chesapeake Bay. The world had changed big time that day. Hana could feel it and so could he.

This really didn't surprise Frank at all. The only surprise was that it hadn't happened sooner. He was glad he lived on the Central Coast away from the large target markets of Los Angeles and San Francisco, or any other big city for that matter. If this obviously well planned attack was to continue to escalate during the day, it might include a nuclear detonation and that was likely to take place in some large city. He watched as news footage covered the people jumping for their lives from the stricken tower two. His heart went out to the souls suffering. He watched as the second tower collapsed. His heart skipped a beat at the horrific sight. He then called his dad to remind him of their dinner conversation 30 years prior. He went to work and monitored the radio, waiting the rest of the day for a report of a nuclear incident.

Dad picked up his daughter from school and took her home for a long heart-to-heart discussion. He apologized for bringing her into a world that had been filled with so much hate. He tried to calm her fears and hugged her with all the love he had. In a world gone wrong Dad wanted Daughter to know right. A huge hug was right.

His sense of this type of attack happening he had known for thirty some years. If he could be right about that, then the caution he sensed in not leaving his well being up to someone else needed to be acted upon. The events of that day gave him the excuse he needed to bow out of any consideration of working for someone else. He told the new owners that the recent events had prompted him to hold on to the rest of Genesis Water, just in case the economy turned sour from continued upheavals in social order. No one really knew what was next.

Frank did. The new owners wanted to suck him up, buy him out, employ him for as long as they could take advantage of him then let him go. That's the corporate way. That's what he sensed and his answer was no! Besides, the 'What If' dogs of doom were howling at the door so he preferred to spend his time looking for personal peace, not waging the war of survival dependent on others. Besides the time saved not working for someone else could be spent on the projects he loved. Timing could not have been better.

A year earlier the FOPH board had started talking about the possibility of moving the Meherin House out to the Park. Frank, Jack, Les, and Dave, the old timers on the board, had known about this possibility for years. It was actually a directive that was spelled out in the City of Pismo's General Plan. The General Plan had identified the Meherin House as having historical significance stating, "If the Meherin House was given to the city, the city should consider moving it to the Price Historical Park." Well, it was given to the City; FOPH took on the responsibility for the move.

The Meherin House was closely tied to Price family history. John and Maria Price's daughter Mary Ann had married Michael Meherin. Mike and John along with other investors were responsible for the building of Pismo's first pier. The pier catapulted Pismo into the lucrative sea trade that transformed Pismo into a bustling seaport village. The contract with the W.W. Montague Co. out of San Francisco to build the pier was signed by all the players inside the Meherin House. Historically, it fit several ways. The architectural differences between the modest Price House mission prairie style and the Meherin's well-to-do captain's home made for great tour comments with comparisons. The 12 years separating the building of the Anniversary House and the Meherin House showed the differences in exterior design emphasis. Indoors, the bathroom and lots of large closets in the Meherin House were the biggest standouts. The plank house that had been attached to the rear of the Meherin House was used as a kitchen, bringing a whole new aspect of mid 1800s building practice in for display. The elegant interior of the Meherin House, with its ornate moldings, pocket doors and bay windows, really could add a nice touch out at the Park. Now all they had to do was move it.

The Meherin House had been offered to the city by the developer who had purchased the property, Mr. Rick Loughead. FOPH's 2nd vice president,

Effie McDermott, knew Rick, introduced the two, and a plan was set into motion. Rick and Frank worked well together. Rick's target date to have the house off the property was October 2001. Rick's help to make that happen saved the FOPH another huge chunk of money. Frank's biggest challenge getting the move accomplished was to convince the City that the FOPH was serious about making the move. He learned later that the scuttle-butt around City Hall was that Friends of Price House could never make it happen. After all, they were just a bunch of volunteers without much money.

Frank and Treasurer Dave Atson penciled the project out at about $31,000. That kind of money FOPH didn't have. Procuring that money was to be the first miracle to pull off. Rick came up with a plan to make that miracle happen. Rick asked the City to direct his in lieu park fees paid on his prospective development back to FOPH to help facilitate the move. The theory behind the redirecting was that Rick's development didn't have a park where those monies could be spent. Rather than the funds going into the Park and Recreations' general fund to be spent elsewhere in Pismo's park system, the funds could be better spent helping to develop the Historical Park that could serve the whole community and tourists alike. He and Rick fought hard through the Planning Commission, Parks and Recreation Commission and City Council meetings to gain the City's approval. It took months. The amount to be awarded was just over $30,000. The Friends of Price House had enough to cover the rest. Finally in August the approval was granted.

Frank was under the gun not only to meet the time frame, but to keep the budget in line with what was awarded. He had to move a two-story house approximately three miles by the way the crow flew. That translated to about seven miles on the ground. The contract alone with Eric Randt of Randt House and Building Moving was $17,500. That didn't leave much extra for hiring a crane, a police escort, permit fees, Cal Tran's fees, fence removal and reinstallation and so on. He'd really have to be on his game to keep it all under budget. The time he expended pleading for financial breaks from all the different players involved in the move paid off.

The coordinating of chaos into an orchestrated, well choreographed event took huge hours. The pre-disassembly of the house took even more. The removal of doors, windows and exterior trim, then transporting them to the Park for safe storage, took him a hundred hours alone. If it hadn't have been for his good friend and master carpenter, Mike Fairbrother, he probably couldn't have gotten it all done on time. Grace provided the right people at the right place at the right time. Not that he was truly aware from whence that force of timing came.

An inch and a half of rain had fallen the day before the scheduled total disassembly of the house. The City's building department had delayed disassembly by a month, which brought the move dangerously close to the start of the rainy season. Start of the rainy season was when Frank had wanted the move to be done. He was frustrated by the delay. The disassembly, move and reassembly of the house was scheduled to take a week. The middle of November was an iffy time to be trying to make it happen without getting wet. That coupled with the fact that the week-long project now had reassembly scheduled the day before Thanksgiving made any delays for rain not an option.

November was the start of the rainy season for the Central Coast. That's why his original schedule slated the move for October 1st. Unfortunately the city's delay put the house in jeopardy of being soaked. The house had to be cut into three pieces to make the move under the freeway overpass, and any rain at all could ruin the exposed interior. Sure enough a storm moved in. Eric called Frank on Sunday afternoon after over an inch of rain had fallen, informing him that he had canceled the crane scheduled for the following morning. Too much rain, Eric figured. If the ground was a muddy mess it might make disassembly impossible. Frank was also concerned, spending the day monitoring the Meherin House site, national weather service and marine forecast for the upcoming week to better weigh his options. By late Sunday afternoon as he stood on the porch of the Meherin House he could see the storm front's tail end with blue skies beyond. The FAA and marine forecasters predicted seven days of good weather before the next potential storm system was to arrive. Frank made a huge decision to proceed with the move.

He knew that if this finely tuned, collaborative effort was not done now, it probably would not get done until after March of the following year. That was not acceptable, he called Eric back and asked him to reschedule the crane; game on. If the forecasters were wrong, the house could suffer major damage, costing FOPH thousands in repairs. If the forecasters were right, they'd have just enough time to get it all done, and FOPH would then have a beautiful new attraction for the park. It was a huge risk, but Frank had to take it. He was going to be on pins and needles until 'job done'.

Monday morning he was on site to meet Eric at 7:30 after dropping Elise off at school. The massive crane needed to lift the separated house sections roared up Mattie Road at 8am. The $350 an hour crane was the largest crane in the tri-county area and it really made for an impressive sight as all the workers from City Hall, just down the block, arrived for work. Frank and Jack directed traffic and just smiled while waving to all the city employees driving by, jaws open. Reality that the Friends of Price House was really making the move of the Meherin House happen, really caught most of them by surprise. Really.

Frank captured some amazing photos of the roof section and second story being lifted into the air then placed onto their respective moving platforms. With disassembly complete Monday, Tuesday was spent shoring up the ground floor interior walls. Both days were bright, sunny and a perfect

72 degrees. The weather Gods were smiling thus far. By Grace was to be evident shortly.

Wednesday Frank's alarm went off at 5am. The 31 hour day run for the roses had begun. Showered and coffeed he delivered Elise to school at 7am. From there he went directly to Lee Wilson Electric Company for final approval from Cal Trans for Glen Ray to remove a pedestrian standard that was in the way of the move on a critical corner. If Cal Trans had to come out to do it, it would cost about $2,500. If Glen did it the cost was nothing. Lee Wilson Electric had arranged the contact, by Grace Cal Trans approved.

At 8am Frank was back at his house calling Tony Pola, his local NBC reporter contact to inform him the move was on. Tony told Frank he'd see what he could do to cover the story. At 8:30am he joined Eric on site at the Meherin House to help with last minute interior wall shoring and dolly placements that needed to be completed by 10pm that night. By 10pm they had to be ready to roll in order to complete the three-piece move. Highway Patrol rules; all oversized loads had to be off State highways by 6am.

Frank left the site to secure lunch for the group at about 11:30. As they enjoyed the nutrition break, he nervously questioned Eric about getting all of it done by kick off time when Pismo PD was scheduled to arrive to provide escort service. Eric responded with his customary bright white smile saying, "Sure no problem," with accompanied laugh. Frank wasn't so sure. There was more shoring to be done and the huge dollies that were to carry the first floor hadn't been placed. He was afraid if he didn't get some rest he wouldn't make it through the night, so he broke away at noon to return home to try and get a power nap. Arriving home at 12:15 he called the fencing company to make sure they had achieved their goal. With that confirmation he laid down at about 12:25 to try and get some rest.

At 12:35 the phone rang. It was Tony from the TV station, calling to inform him that a news crew was enroute to the Meherin House for an interview at 1:30. So much for the nap. He grabbed his favorite Hawaiian shirt for the interview, then headed back to the site and immediately back to work. The three were in the middle of some really physical activity, bracing and shoring interior walls with some chunky 8x8 timbers needed to strengthen the ceiling-less first floor when Tony and his camera man arrived.

Frank and Tony had some history. He and Tony had done a couple of interviews together in the past, one on the Anniversary House and one on the Clam family. He threatened Tony in a jokingly serious manner about making Tony 'Sam for a day,' referring to one of Tony's community segments that ran periodically on the evening newscasts. "Give Tony the Job" was a piece Tony produced, in which he went out into some business in the community and worked it for a day. The pieces were well done, showing a variety of skills and talents performed by the everyday guy or gal. But Tony took on positions which were sometimes challenging, displaying his humorous inability to perform the given task with any competence at all. They were fun segments to watch and often laugh with.

Tony could have made a great Sam the Clam; Frank suggested as they readied for the Meherin interview, teasing him about taking the idea to his station manager. Tony quaked at the thought of having to put on the suit, jokingly begging Frank not to plant the idea. They worked well together and always had a good time. Tony remarked that he always learned something new whenever they got together. Frank threw on his clean shirt and lickity split, they produced a piece that Frank was told later was outstanding. He didn't get to see the news that night. The three intrepid workers were going to be working straight through to the dinner hour, then dine on site with another round of subs and sodas, then back to work. At 9:30pm, a half hour before Pismo PD's two motorcycles and one cruiser escort were to arrive, a problem arose. One of the dolly's brakes that were to carry and stop the first floor didn't work. This wasn't a good thing.

Losing a third of the breaking system needed to control the huge piece of tonnage they needed to tow made for dicey speculation. The crane had measured 42,000 pounds when the second floor was lifted from the first. That's a lot of weight to control on the hilly terrain they had to traverse that night. He expressed concern to Eric as they frantically searched through millions of parts to see if they could find an appropriate way of making a second hydraulic connection. As they crawled out from under the house at 9:59 Eric shot one of those perfect white-toothed grins and said, "No problem. We just won't stop on Campana Drive." finishing with a laugh full of white. At 10pm sharp the police department pulled up and asked,

"Are you ready to roll?"

"You bet!" Eric smiled and within minutes Eric's white freightliner lurched out onto Mattie Road with the first piece to make the journey to the hills above the Price House. Once there, the pieces were left in a cow pasturing area and a return made for the next piece to be transported. The seven-mile journey was made at three to five miles per hour, the pull up the 5% grade of Campana Drive took fifteen minutes alone. Arriving at the top of Highland Drive, a barbed wire fence was opened 45 feet to allow the cargo to be pulled into the cow pasture for chocking and storage until Monday's pull down the hill. Eight hours to complete three pieces. Everything had to run like a well-oiled machine or they wouldn't make their 6am deadline. It was going to be tight. The adrenaline was flowing.

In the wee hours of the morning, the growling entourage of diesel engines topped with flashing yellow lights preceded by the red and blue flashing police department escort made quite a sight as it squeezed its way through downtown Pismo. Sometimes the clearance was only by inches and the lumbering multi-vehicle parade had to slow to a snail's pace. When approaching the railroad crossing, the adrenalin pumped the blood to full flow. The speed picked up to a break-neck seven miles per hour, hoping to cross the railroad tracks without encountering a speeding train, an intense two minutes. It was an exciting night. At 6:15am Frank's lead escort truck pulled up to and opened the cattle gate as Eric pulled through with the last piece. The ground floor with the precariously attached plank house kitchen was the last piece to arrive safely. They made it. The coffee they had been sucking down all night had done its job. At 8:30am they had extracted Eric's truck from the mud bog pasture, and Eric and his helper then rolled home to Santa Maria for some much needed rest. Frank took a couple more hours, making sure cattle fencing was secure, pedestrian signals reinstalled and moving equipment stowed away. By 11am he returned home and collapsed into bed. He slept until sunrise.

At 7am Thursday, Dad took Daughter back to school, checked the cattle fencing, and checked the weather for the hundredth time. At the top of the hill he readied his to-do list for Friday, Saturday and Sunday's prep work needed before the final pull down the hill and into the Park.

The weather held Friday but began to deteriorate on Saturday as Frank prepared the second story for reassembly. On Sunday a few rain drops fell as he finished cutting the 3 1/2 inches off the second story framing. That provided the space needed for the plates to be placed to reattach the first and second stories of the balloon framed home. He could only lift up hopes to the rain Gods to hold off until after Wednesday's scheduled reassembly. Nerves were starting to fray.

Monday, 7am, Frank and Eric started the pull of the three pieces down the hill about a quarter mile. The D4 Caterpillar had no problem moving the three pieces down to a preposition for Tuesday's final descent into the park. The last 100 yards was a VERY STEEP HILLSIDE, and he again questioned Eric's assurance that the final drop could be made without the weakened house falling apart. Eric again smiled bright white, saying with a laugh, "sure no problem." Frank was a little more than apprehensive to say the least.

Brent, from Specialty Crane Services, was out on Monday as well to inspect the dirt easement road down in to the Park. If it was too wet he might risk skating the huge million and a half dollar crane over the cliff and down the hill. That was not acceptable. Brent gave his okay. The following day Eric, with an assist from volunteer Roger Mande and his D7 Caterpillar supplying brakes, made the final drop into the Park.

The first piece to go was the ceiling-less first floor. Eric, who always smiled, wasn't smiling as he pulled the monster load over the top of the ridge that began the point of no return. The angle of descent was so steep you could see the floor of the home through its open top, from the road at the bottom of the hill. After a full twenty minutes of heart-pounding, snail-paced descent to the canyon floor, Eric finally smiled again. It was incredible. They had made it. The most vulnerable piece was still intact and they all breathed a cumulative sigh of relief. The rest was easy; by day's end they were ready for the crane to reassemble the 96-year old home the following morning.

At 8am Wednesday morning Frank arrived to meet the crane at the top of Highland Drive. He had just dropped his daughter off at her mother's house and was anxious to get reassembly underway as a storm front was due to pass through on Thursday, Thanksgiving Day. That surely meant rain, so the house had to be back together with a few sheets of plastic tarp placed over the exposed kitchen roof before the storm arrived. The weather nerve was shot.

By 3pm the reassembly of the Meherin House was complete. Frank had shot a ton of photos documenting the process as the clouds from the storm front began to fill the sky. Glen, Mike and Frank worked until dark getting the kitchen roof tarped over before calling it a day. That evening the rain started, lasting through Thanksgiving Day, dumping more than an inch plus of rain. By Grace they had made it and the Park's look was changed forever.

It took a couple of days for Frank to realize what he had accomplished. With the blessings of the City of Pismo, he had changed the skyline of Mattie Road in Shell Beach forever. A two-story house that had been somewhat of a landmark along the old road where Mattie's brothel had once operated was now gone. The Park had a new asset, and he felt proud of his hard labors. He tried not to let the board's praise go to his head. They had already shocked him by voting unanimously to name the park's amphitheatre after him, that honor he was still trying to live up to.

Now with the big job done Frank focused his attention to the planning of another family adventure. Hana had lived the events of the year with him via phone. Now it was a priority to see her again. The kids were getting older; one more trip together might be the last time they could cruise as the family of four. Hana agreed. This time however the group grew by one. Hana's mom was included in their planning. Since Hana's dad had died the year before, her mom had not been in the best of spirits. Both agreed the trip with them could do her good. Cabo San Lucas at Easter would do them all well. He planned hard with Hana for the fantastic fam of five frolic far south of the border that upcoming spring. The planning brought light to funk.

The funk of the holidays and uneasiness of the world since 9/11 seemed to go hand in hand that year. The religious dogmas that drove both events were destroying the abilities of the planet to live in any semblance of peace and harmony. He feared that things were only going to get worse. The world's religions were bound to collide from the ever-growing population on the planet and the Internet that connected them all.

The internet was becoming a tool of hate and he speculated a weapon of choice by terrorists in the years to come. The Net had already become a weapon of terror bringing doom in his life. With the New Year just days away he prepared himself for his updated web appearance courtesy of the Grover Beach Police Department. Trying to stay in a positive frame of mind was tedious. He hadn't heard from his attorney in months! What else was new? He had moved a mountain, but he couldn't remove the 'What If' that plagued his life.

~~~~

We all deal with drama of life. The dealing invokes creativity. The greater the drama the more creative we must become to overcome. Our string we follow is no different. If not for the gift of creation, we would all surely go mad within the box of drama that is dropped on our doorstep from time to time.

CHAPTER 28

SPINNING DREAMS INTO REALITY

The blistering pace of life from the previous year mellowed somewhat as the New Year unfolded. It seemed to be something new every year at update time, this year was no different. Detective Cheryl was a little more understanding of Frank's predicament yet insisted on photographing him in his work truck. The powers to be directed this protocol. Putting as much positive spin on it as he could, he smiled and waved as the photos were taken. Seventh time was the charm; he dismissed the degrading feelings of the photo session in fairly short order. He even went so far as to bid Cheryl farewell saying he'd see her at his house later that year, when she'd drop by to do her required personal residence verification. He was getting better at letting go of the bitter feelings he harbored for the distasteful requirements imposed. Too much life to live to waste time wallowing in the darkness of that abyss, he reconciled.

Much to his surprise he received a call from Ann, his attorney, which offered up some good news. Ann informed him that the "Certificate of Rehabilitation" program that had been curtailed a couple of years prior had started up again, so he might now qualify. All he had to do was spend another thousand dollars to see a psychiatrist whose opinions where highly respected by the local judges and get a favorable evaluation of his mental status. He could then file for the "Certificate of Rehabilitation," which could be used to remove his name from the web list of 'dangerous offenders.'

Frank's gut reaction was to say no. He pointed out to Ann that by receiving such a document amounted to an admission of having some sort of mental disorder to begin with. It didn't make sense to him to do that when in fact two psychiatric evaluations 20 years prior stated he "was not a mentally disordered sex offender." He had years of clear record to back up those findings. To him it didn't make sense to be admitting to something he wasn't. He'd already been coerced once into doing that. He wasn't going to do that again, besides the idea of having to pay for an opinion from someone who was practicing an 'art' incensed him. After all, he mused, psychiatry is not really considered a science, but an art. The whole process was a "catch 22" and he was damned if he did, damned if he didn't.

There had to be another way to get the 'State' to uphold the court's original ruling of "Case Dismissed." He didn't want to settle for less. He wanted the slate wiped clean as promised; nothing else was satisfactory at this stage.

Ann did not agree with his decision. Mary did. He did indicate to Ann he'd give it some thought, however. The prospect of relief was quite tantalizing. The enticement pulled hard to give in and do it. The cost to self respect and his principles was just too great. If you make a deal you stick to it. He had.

Drifting away from the battle and back to the planning of the Easter adventure with Hana was the best way to usher back some peace. He had plenty of other obligations to attend to, but the Cabo trip was going to be the most fun. The positive energy created in this planning flowed into all other irons he had in the fire. Still that flow hadn't as yet been seen fully for the Grace it was. That would come.

The Cabo planning was flawless. He and Elise were to meet Hana, Troy and mother Gina at LAX, then fly on to Cabo together. On the way down to LA, Dad and Daughter had a little extra excitement that kicked it up a notch. Dad decided that since he and Elise had a little extra time they might make a small side trip. Dad had another friend from high school who lived in Encino. Since it was on the way, they'd stop to say hello.

Now Pete was not just some old high school friend who might bore Elise to tears. No, Pete was much more ... so very much more. Peter Bergman was an Emmy-winning television star. He was a daytime drama series star whose character name is Jack Abbott. His classy character played to millions daily on the daytime drama "The Young and The Restless." Pete had played the role for years. The fan following numbered in the millions and Elise, her grandmother, her mother, Hana, and her mom where all part of that fan base.

Elise had heard a lot about Pete from her dad. She knew Dad had stopped by or called Pete at least once a year over the previous seven or so, to invite Pete and family up for the Clam Festival and a ride in the parade. Pete always kindly thanked Frank for the offer, but at that time of the year Pete's heart was into running the New York City Marathon. So to date, Elise had yet to meet the famous friend of her father. Elise had even stopped by Pete's house once with Dad on a returning freight run, but no one was home. By now Elise might be thinking Dad had made the whole story up. She had heard so much but never saw Pete. "What the hell," she'd indulge her dad one more time. "Probably no one home again," she thought to herself.

They pulled into the driveway of the beautiful ranch-style house, parked and got out. On the way to the front door they both looked for signs of life, but there where none. Frank knocked anyway. Elise was about to suggest they might as well go when unexpectedly the ornate wooden front doors' knob began to rotate, the latches' squeaking works proving life existed on the other side. The door began to move, Elise took a deep breath and one step backwards. She about choked when the fully opened doorway framed the tall, well-dressed TV legend! Pete immediately stepped out with hand extended in welcome saying,

"Well Frank, it's been a long time."

Elise's jaw dropped to the floor, and she struggled to catch her breath. Frank introduced his daughter, and Pete invited all inside. Elise couldn't believe what was happening. Pete introduced his wife Mariellen, indicating she was a bit under the weather, and the three moved to the sitting room. Elise was barely breathing.

Frank and Pete chatted, Frank explaining they were on their way to meet up with Hana Joi then on their way to Cabo for Easter.

"Oh, I remember Hana." Pete said with fondness.

"She was in our chorus class," he remembered. Pete went on to say that he, the wife and kids had also planned to go to Cabo at Easter, but might not be able since Mariellen wasn't feeling well. Elise was breathing, but had yet to speak. Dad did her bidding, indicating to Pete that Elise was a big fan, and then asking if she might have a press photo if he had any around. Dad had to ask, the proverbial cat had Elise's tongue firm in its grasp.

"Ah yes!" Pete affirmed, as he put his arm around Elise, leading her to his desk in the den. He not only signed one he signed enough for Hana, Gina, and Grandma Pat. His hospitality was warm and sincere. The two friends chatted casually as Dad and Daughter readied for departure. Elise's eyes beamed when Pete stopped for a photo with her in the front yard. The guy was a true gem of a person. Frank thanked him for his graciousness as they bid farewell. By Grace Pete had been there. Elise now believed.

That chance meeting for Elise turned her ambivalent attitude toward the trip around 180 degrees. Now she was excited! She had a story to tell and the pictures to prove it. That was just the start. A few hours later Elise and Troy discovered lead singer Chad Kroeger of the rock group Nickel Back sitting across the aisle from them on the plane ride to Cabo. The week in Cabo was off to a great start.

Arriving at the two-bedroom two-bath concrete condo with wall-to-wall Mexican tile, the family of five settled in and the kids took a quick dip in the pool. The second-story condo had a great view of Cabo San Jose and the Sea of Cortez from the massive balcony that faced east to drink in the morning sun. The spectacular sunrise each morning was dead center of the picturesque view, the light breeze wafting the palm fronds all day reminding Frank of his trip to Maui. The cavernous living rooms with dining room, spacious kitchen, two master suites with private baths, were perfectly comfortable for the five. After initial inspection of the digs, Hana and Frank did a high five on Hana's choice of accommodations.

Frank let the thought roll by that he could write his book there. Favorable weather, mellow surroundings and the cost was a whole lot less than Maui. That book thing was still stirring considerations, or maybe it was the thought of running away to some exotic place that was the real attraction. As of yet that intention was sitting still in the idle fantasy of his private day-dreaming. Daydreaming of someday making a difference in the world.

They did not sit still. Every day was jam packed. The weather was perfect. Not too warm, it never approached cold. Journeys to the hot springs at the end of a 13 mile long dirt road or Tecolate Beach with 5000 Latinos celebrating Easter weekend, they were often the only Caucasian faces in the crowd. Water taxi rides to the rock arches, snorkeling Neptune's rock, parasailing 700 feet above the Sea of Cortez, Jet Ski rides and a fishing trip on their own private boat. There was a lot of water contact. Adventure was the priority.

Toados Santos and the Hotel California was an interesting stop. Dinner in La Paz was interesting as well. Seems Elise impressed a couple of teenage Mexican boys who waited their table. The boys were awe struck by her beauty and showered Elise with interest. It was comical watching the two young men stumble all over themselves to gain her attention. Great entertainment and a nice ego boost for a young lady.

The after-dark drive back to Cabo San Jose gave definitive meaning to the song lyric "Dark desert highway" from the Eagles' song Hotel California. The twisting, turning road following the foot of the hills on a moonless night kept everyone on the edge of their seat. Inebriated drivers, cows, and donkeys were all on the road that night. You never knew what the headlights might reveal over the next rise or around the next bend. Despite the cool wind in their faces the 'pop out of the darkness' driving gave everyone a couple of hours of sweaty palms. Quite exciting! Then there was the clubbing. The adults opted for dessert on the water front while the kids clubbed at Coyote Ugly. They all did Cabo Wabo.

And then there was the shopping. Oh my goodness the shopping! It never ceased to amaze Frank at how much stuff the Mexicans had to sell. The incessant bark from the shopkeepers lining the streets and alleys became the mantra for this trip, "Hey señor, almost free!" The girls had a ball and the boys could only oblige.

Frank and Troy did have some fun of their own though. The guy thing of exploring took the two to some very different places. Commandeering the rental vehicle one day, the two men took off for the back roads to see the real Mexico while the girls rested. They managed to find a location to humorously recreate the 'Great White Hunter' photo they had taken in Alaska. The family famous photo was a bit different this time, however. Instead of a Moose in the background this one had a scraggily emaciated old cow. The end product was quite a hoot, ending up framed and hung next to the Alaskan photo Hana treasured.

The boys' three-hour tour took them through the poverty and plight of a third world. Shacks of cardboard and tin squatted next to two-room homes of adobe, yet they all displayed one unique feature. Despite the lacking, all the faces that turned to look as they passed by, doing their gringo sightseeing, had broad white smiles. This prompted Frank to pose a question to Troy and himself.

"Because of all the smiles were these folks really happy?" and...

"If they really are happy, the smiles seem to suggest so; does that mean you really don't need money and things to be happy?" Food for thought for that day.

Gina kept up with it all. Frank and Hana both were amazed at her stamina. For a lady in her 70s she had a lot of pep. Gina was having the time of her life on a journey with her daughter, grandson and extended 'almost' family. Her husband had passed away a year prior, so the trip away was a good jump start back into vibrancy of life. Frank and Hana were happy to have her along, she was a great addition.

Frank did get a bit emboldened once as he imagined Hana's loving embrace. He knew he was still at arm's length, but he gave it a shot anyway. Hana had let him in a little closer as they enjoyed some alone time on the balcony one evening. The balmy night air, romantic setting and quiet, personal conversation led him to the bursting point with bravado, looking deep into sea blue eyes, "Kiss me Hana Joi." Momentary silence in fixed gaze, then Hana responded with remorse, "No, Frank, I can't." "That's ok," he returned, "I just had to ask." His request reconfirmed he wasn't afraid. Hana knew.

The family of five left Cabo the same way as they had come. Well. The flight to LA was way too fast for Frank. They had come together again as uniquely close friends, they departed even closer. His sadness as they hugged farewell at the terminal in LA was far outweighed by the joy of the close personal contact he had reveled in. The warmth and love in Hana's hug and kiss had to sustain his addiction to this beauty with the blue piercing eyes. He wore a smile on his face for weeks. Little did he know they were to be together again that year. After all it was the playbook belonging to another energy that moved through Grace that he didn't always recognize. Anything's possible.

Back at the Hacienda Del Grover, life resumed at the expected whip lashing pace. Planning for the planting of the Meherin house on a permanent foundation was an ongoing order of business. Another part of the 'work order' at the Price House was to maintain a bodily presence on the grounds for security reasons. As long as someone was there, the less likely a teenage drinking party was to break out, or in, as it were. When Glen Ray went out of town, Frank took over security and slept in the Price House. Occasionally on these week-long stays some unexpected events occurred. A couple stand out.

Scary and humorous at the same time are an unusual mix for emotion. One of the nights at the Price House provided him with a taste of that rush. It was about 1am when he was awakened by voices coming from somewhere outside the building. Getting up he peered outside the upstairs bedroom window to see flashlight beams of light dancing across the orchard. The beams emanated from the right side of the building to which he had no view, so he put on his robe to go downstairs to have a look out the kitchen window. Searching carefully, so as not to be detected, he witnessed two males and two females at the side gate. The two males were trying to unfasten the makeshift fence attachment that secured the fence to its pole. They were in the process of breaking in and he had no phone. Glen's phone was in his trailer that was in plain sight of the intruders to be. He couldn't make it to the trailer undetected to call the police, so he needed a plan B.

What did he have to work with...nothing but maybe the element of surprise? He had heard the girls ask the boys if they where sure nobody lived there. "No, no, it's ok no one is living here," he heard one of the guys tell the girls in a confident tone. The only thing he could think of to use for the act of surprise was his black hooded terrycloth robe. The robe he wore to ward off the chill just might work to ward off the trespassers. He forgot all about the Daisy BB gun he used for gopher control. "Might have made a good prop as well for what was about to happen," he thought later in retrospect.

Unfortunately the "Black Hooded Death Figure" had to do; time for improvising had run out as the intruders were almost done unhooking the fence. Unfortunate too, was the fact that one of the males was 6' 4"ish and weighed about 250-plus lbs. That could be a problem for Frank and his 5' 10" 155 lb. frame if the illusion didn't work. For maximum affect he waited until all four were through the fence. He figured if he could surprise them after they entered they might freeze in place, knowing that the path of retreat could not facilitate all four exiting at once in their dash from 'Death'.

He opened, in absolute silence, the kitchen door that led out onto the back porch. With perfect stealth he made his way to the edge of the porch undetected. Standing statue like, as tall as possible, the 'Hooded Death' figure waited, hands in pockets. The intruders' trek toward the orchard had progressed about fifty feet, the girls asking all the way if the guys were sure no body lived there. The little guy again responded assuredly that they were alone.

Surprise happens! And works! The big guy spotted 'Death' first. The big guy's step faltered, his hands slammed to his chest just over his heart, two steps backward to frozen, then roared,

"OHHHH GODDDDD!"

Terror thundered from the depths of the big guy's lungs in the "I've seen death" voice you probably only hear from those who are sure they are about to meet their maker. The girls screamed and collapsed to the ground. The little guy struck a defensive pose, to defend against that which he as yet had not seen. Then he SAW and almost SHIT!

The little guy was the first to begin with a barrage of lame excuses directed at what he wasn't sure. His visual search had found the dark figure on the porch that he now directed his apologizes toward, hoping it was truly human and not the real deal. All the while the big guy stood frozen, still holding his chest, Frank broke his silence to ask if they were aware they were trespassing on 'City' property. His bold, deep tone of voice used 'City' to feign backup at hand.

"NO, NO, We Didn't Know!" pleaded the little guy while the girls huddled behind the incapacitated big guy, who was still holding his chest unsure of what was real about the apparition on the porch.

"I've phoned Pismo PD and they're on their way," Frank fired back realizing the group was inclined to believe just about anything at this point.

"Why are you here?" Death's dark figure demanded from its lofty position on the porch.

"We were just bored and didn't have anything to do!" cried one of the females, who was in tears of fear.

"That's great! Nothing better to do so you decided to break into the Price House?" the dark figure boomed in a judgmentally questioning tone. Seizing the momentum created by fear and confusion, Death offered up hope of escape from their pending doom.

"Well the way I see it you've got two choices!   Either stay and wait for the cops and tell your story to them, or leave right now!" he bellowed from deep within the black hood. They chose the latter, apologizing profusely for their errant entry as they bumbled their way back to the small opening that would gain them freedom from the demonic figure towering above them. The big guy was still holding his chest as they beat their retreat.

"Oh, by the way button up the fence on your way out!" Death demanded in a demonic last request.

"Sure, of course," they said in unison as they Keystone Copped their way through the tiny opening.

Frank barely contained the laughter growing within his belly.   He watched, stifling the bubbling laughter crawling up his throat, as they hurried their departure. Then he realized he had been standing on his tip toes the whole time in an effort to look large. Plan B had worked! He watched from the upstairs window as their dashing flashlights disappeared in a hurry across the open field back to Price Canyon Road. He laughed again as he phoned the incident into Pismo PD dispatch. Would have made a good scene in a movie, he thought, as he drifted back to sleep with the smile of the event still on his face. He still had the smile the next morning when he awoke.

The second event of some note happened that same year. A little later on an August evening at dusk, as Frank pulled up to the gate on Frady Lane to watch the house and grounds for Glen again, another adventure was offered up. His radar was triggered to high alert by the dozen or so cars parked at the gated entrance to the Park where the road turns to dirt. Not a soul in sight, "What's up now," he thought. "Do we have a bunch of party animals out in the fields to celebrate ...or what?" Where were the occupants that belonged to all these vehicles? He decided to roll out to the house, use the phone in the trailer to call PD and request assistance. He knew he was outnumbered on this one.

He did his customary 2 mph cruise, keeping his eyes open for clues as to what might be going on. As he came through the narrows between the rocks and the creek, he caught a glimpse of a darkly clad figure disappear behind one of the Coyote bushes that filled the field in front of him. Frank maintained his slow speed so as not to alert whoever it was in the field that he was aware of their location. He kept looking for signs of more people but saw none.

From Glen's trailer he called PD dispatch, gave them what little information he had, and they rolled a unit his way. He drove back to an elevated vantage point hidden from the intruders' view to wait for PD to arrive. Time ticked on, dusk began to turn to darkness, the sound of a gasoline electrical generator motor filled the canyon with its groaning disbursement of fired up energy. Then a huge beam of light hit the canyon's cliff face. "That should be easy for the cops to find," he thought while he waited. Ten more minutes passed, still no cops. "What the hell!" "Can't the cops find them?" he thought as the generator and light reported no change in the activity taking place. He returned to the trailer to phone dispatch again to find out why PD had not shut the party down.

The dispatch officer informed him she had been trying to get a hold of him. The officer that had rolled out had reported back that it was a movie crew on site. The officer had also been told by the movie director that the Friends of Price House had given them permission to use the Park. "What the hell!" No movie crew had approached the board asking for permission to use the Park to his knowledge. And he was still the president the last time he'd checked. He had an inquiry months earlier, but nothing had come of it. He thanked dispatch for the info, jumped in his truck, and headed back out to see what was really going on.

It really was a movie crew. As he pulled up on a secondary entrance road he could see at least 20 people and tons of equipment spread out all over the field. Getting out, he asked who was in charge and was directed to Shane Amaral, the director of the shoot. Shane explained that they were making a low-budget thriller and found the Park a perfect location to do the shoot.

Besides, "Suzy Desmond from the Price House gave us permission," Shane spoke confidently.

"Oh that's Suzy," Frank mumbled.

He explained to Shane that Suzy had been a board member and the former President of the Friends of Price House but hadn't been an active player in years. But that was just Suzy. Frank knew Suzy knew he wouldn't mind hosting a movie crew out at the Park. Suzy knew that Frank knew the Park would one day make money from movie crews wanting to use the pristine location. They had talked about it years before. He had not pursued the industry because the houses weren't done. It had not occurred to him that scary movie producers might be interested in the unfinished product. ...*Duuuh*!

Frank apologized for wrecking their first night's shoot. Had he known he wouldn't have called the cops. The cops had shut them down that night because they didn't have a city film permit, and it was his fault that the police had been summoned in the first place. He really felt bad and told Shane he'd do his best to see they got what they needed. Within a week the crew was back out with FOPH board approval and city credentials.

Since co-writers Shane and Michael Carver were using film students from Hancock College to man the different components needed to make a movie, it was easy for Frank to convince the board to let the crew use the Park for free. After all, the entire Park by design was a teaching tool. Shane and Michael were giving the students valuable hands-on training (teaching) so it made sense to cut them a break. Free; works for low budgets. The Park was a remote, secure location, so Police, Fire and the City Managers had no problem issuing the film permit. Besides, the Friends of Price House was happy to host.

Back underway, Frank attended the shoots until 11pm or so, making sure everything was on the up and up, not the staging ground for some ongoing party. It was legit, the group was all business. He found it fascinating to watch the movie-making process. He stayed back and out of the way marveling at all the stuff that had to be done between the director's shouts of "cut" and "action." Being on the set inevitably led to a request for help, a service he was happy to render. The crew of college kids also had jobs and not all of them could make all the shoot nights. One evening the crew was short of people, and Frank was invited to be the marker. You know, the clap sticks and slate used to mark a scene with the "Take One / Take Two" vocal while slapping the sticks together. Great fun to step onto the set and into another world, soon he was hooked. Soundman, fog man, blood man, props, even stunt driver, it was all a ball. He did a lot, enjoying every minute, even though those minutes often ran into the wee hours of the morning. Made it tough to get up and take care of his clients when he wrapped the night with the crew at 4am. Thank goodness they were only shooting three to four nights a week. Worth it to him as he saw potential in what the crew was putting together. Besides he had struck an agreement with Shane: if the movie made a little money then Shane would send a little money to FOPH ... if it made a lot... Shane would add a lot of zeros. Spirit mantra for the effort: "If Blair Witch Project could make millions ... then so could we." Couldn't hurt to try.

By mid September shooting was about done and the effort moved to the editing room. This gave Frank the break he needed for final preparation for the Meherin House permanent foundation project. He had been contacted several months earlier by another filmmaker who wanted to use the Meherin House, but he had to decline the offer as the house was suspended in the air on temporary cribbing making it much too dangerous to use. He encouraged Ben from Thunderhead Production to call back. The house might be down on its new foundation by the end of fall and safe for a movie shoot. He was eager to make some money for FOPH on the next cinematic endeavor. He hoped for that call.

One year to the day of its reassembly out at the Park the Meherin house was lowered down onto its new foundation. It was the day before Thanksgiving and the rains had held off long enough again to get the job done. He again lifted up thanks to the Grace that guided the work and held off the rains. Three days later Ben called back. Whose timing was that of?

By the end of the year the Meherin House had starred in its own movie and FOPH had put a couple grand of rental fees in the bank. This thriller did not garner as much of his time as the first, thankfully the Thunderhead crew was in and out in 45 days and their check was good. Boy, movies were going to be good income some day, he speculated. Cha Ching.

Squeezed in between the first movie and the house planting, Frank managed a quick getaway to be with Hana as she recovered from major surgery to fix some female issues. He arrived at her bedside just hours after she had been assigned a recovery room. Even though she was heavily sedated he could tell she was glad he was there. He stayed that night in the bed next to hers and awoke at her every rustling to make sure she was okay. He was happy to be at her side. A day and half later Hana was released to return home, under strict orders to do nothing. He was glad to be recovery support.

At her house Frank stayed busy rebuilding Hana's storage shed and catering to her every whim. Her recovery progressed well, and by week's end she was up and moving most of the day. One day as he toiled to finish the shed she called for him to take a break. She had prepared a plate of shelled Chesapeake Blue Point Crab for a lunch munch you'd pay big dollars for in any restaurant. The dozen or so morsels had been arranged on a bed of ice, and their flavor was out of this world. There was a lot of love in that preparation, and he glowed with the mental nutrition it provided as well. "Boy, If I could just stay here I'd have it made," he dreamed out loud. He liked dreaming. "Yeah?" Hana spoke from twinkling dreamy blue eyes.

He returned home knowing that by Grace they would go in their relationship. If it was meant to be it would happen. He was grateful for having one more chance to bask in the light of that love again, even though he was still 'at arms length'. He at least understood that the flow between the two was best left alone; his needy grasp could only serve to bung things up. Giving love away was working best. He kept the selfish hands of 'I want' firmly planted in his pockets, but he 'Dreamed On' to where the Universe might take them. He liked to dream. Don't we all?

~~~~

We all have the ability to weave our string with any color we wish to create. Our string we follow is no different. As he weaves through the tapestry of life, he is the creator of the color he wishes to be. Demon, hero, crew member, president, dad, actor, lover, friend ...he is all he wishes to mirror, gifting the richness of color to all he connects with on the journey.

CHAPTER 29

BY GRACE ALL ENDS ARE

Wins, losses and draws, those are the outcomes in the game of life. That New Year offered nothing different. Broken record or what? The downbeat loss of self worth associated with the registration game of course started the New Year. He was at least getting better at not beating himself up as badly over the insinuations. That was followed by a successful gathering of local Chumash volunteers willing to build the pre Spanish Native village at the Historical Park. In that aspect of the Park's growth plan it had been important to him to have the local natives tell their own story, not a white man's interpretation. He had been looking for just the right ones for several years, and he finally had been introduced to the right one, her name was Elizabeth Smith.

Elizabeth, also affectionately known as Grandmother Silver Bear, could trace her Chumash heritage back at least six generations, even though her last name didn't exactly sing with the linguistic ring of the Chumash language. Frank's introduction to Grandmother Silver Bear by the colorful FOPH volunteer Darrel Cotter was the connection that opened doors he had only dreamed of entering. The family Silver Bear brought to the Park that first meeting day in January was the perfect group to fuel the project. The right people at the right place at the right time. Whose game playbook of timing was this anyway?

Silver Bear's eldest son Jack, aka Lone Wolf, was a huge man in his mid 50s, bent over from years of hard labor, embellished with a built-in distrust for your run-of-the-mill white guy. Rightly so Frank figured. The Chumash who had lived in the canyon for ten thousand years had been disseminated almost to nonexistence by the coming of the white faces. The ones that survived had not been treated well ever since. Lone Wolf's skeptical reluctance was to be expected.

Lone Wolf's spiritual nature was the door to acceptance that Frank had to pass before any agreement to help could be offered. He sensed that Silver Bear and Lone Wolf both had to approve of participating before the rest of the clan could respond to the invitation. This approval process relied largely on Jack's summations. Most of the day was spent by Lone Wolf testing Frank's honesty and his understanding of the spiritual nature that guided the Chumash way of life. Jack's almost harassing questioning had the rest of the family tense and on guard; Frank fielded his prodding and took it all in stride.

By mid afternoon the group had strolled to the end of the Park that had been reserved for the building of the Chumash village. Frank was getting some excited feedback from Grandmother and the others, but Jack was still on the fence. At one point Frank found himself alone with Jack in the middle of the vast field. The sun was warm as the circling hawks cried out their greetings. He had been thwarted in his attempts to find the common ground with Jack. What could he say that might convince this very big man that the little white guy was sincere in his offerings? From out of nowhere he stopped and turned to look the huge Native in the eyes saying, "You know Jack; nothing will be done on this project if it doesn't meet with the approval of the Great Spirit."

That was it, or wasn't it. Without a word Jack turned and returned toward the group. He passed by his mother grouped with the others and walked into the thicket of willow that choked the creek's bank. Frank didn't know what to think. Maybe he had to pee or something, or maybe he was just fed up with the whole discussion, needing to take a break Native style. "Maybe I had offended by invoking the name of the Great Spirit," Frank thought. Nevertheless he figured he had lost the opportunity to connect. He returned to listen to the rest of the group's high-spirited dialogue on visions they had for a village they could call theirs if the Elders chose to participate in the co-creation.

About the time Grandmother raised the question, "Where is Jack?" Ho Chi Chio, as he is also called in the family circle, emerged from the tree-snarled creek. In his right hand he carried a long straight branch of willow an inch and a half in diameter, whittled to a point at one end. The shaft had been cleaned of leaves and small branches, the opposite end from the point had a couple of feathers attached. For a second Frank thought that Big Jack was going to skewer himself a white man, as the large man lumbered up and over the creek bank, eyes searching intently and finding Frank's.

No, this was something different. In his left hand Lone Wolf carried several small stones. Everyone watched inquisitively as Jack hobbled to a clearing under a large willow overhang. Bending down on one knee with noticeable discomfort, he arranged the stones in a small circle, and then raised himself with an assist from the spear's shaft. Turning to face the open field full with family, he gripped the shaft with both hands, shoulder width apart, and raised it and his face skyward as far as his tortured body allowed. Silence fell, all eyes were riveted on Jack as he stretched skyward in silent prayer. Hawks in the distant sky circled in silence as well. With a brush of breeze through the trees, Ho Chi Chio spoke as he looked to the heavens,

"With the Great Spirit and to the honor of the Chumash people I plant this spear."

"May the Great Spirit of all bless all we do."

With that said Jack plunged the spear into the earth within the circle of stones. Several in the clan chanted in unison the Chumash words of approval and rejoicing,

"Aho, Aho, Aho!" With that the seed was planted that was to grow a tribe and build a village.

The tribe that grew named itself the Sa' Pismu, in honor of the tribal village that had existed up the canyon for some seven to ten thousand years. Most of the ancient skills of the past had not been learned by the younger generations, all of the clan had to learn as they went. Volunteer Gabrial Iossi's knowledge of primitive arts and skills really paid off big. His wealth of primitive crafting techniques was passed on freely for all to learn and an apt (hut), smoke (sweat lodge), ceremonial grounds and fire ring were constructed the first year. The workdays for the Village and the Price House were the same, allowing Frank to be on site to monitor safety concerns for property that was to one day be City owned. He knew the owner of the land wouldn't mind, the only thing that bothered him was the fact that he had not informed the current owner he was already building a village on the site. He had at least let the tribe know from the very beginning that the village site was tentative. Yet he was confident the owner was going to approve; he was privy to the owner's future plans. Everything had happened so fast, now all he had to do was muster up the courage to tell him.

The owner was Rick Laughead, the same gentleman that had given the Meherin House to the FOPH. Rick had shown Frank a proposed development tract map in which the 2.5 acre parcel of land, from his proposed project adjacent to the Park, was to be offered to the City as part of the development's park fee requirements. It had been stipulated in the City adopted Historical Park Master Plan and Rick was willing to oblige. So no big deal, Frank pushed forward with the building of the village that had been directed of FOPH in the action items listed in the pages of the Historical Parks Master Plan. He was doing as directed and like any good president, he was doing it well. A year later he finally fessed up saying,

"Oh by the way Rick we are building a village on your land." Rick chuckled saying he had known all along.

Frank had done what had eluded others at the City. He had established a balanced relationship with a clan of Chumash peoples. City Council members began to ask his advice on how to work harmoniously with the Native Americans. He thought that a bit funny that they should be asking him for advice. He stressed honesty and respect.

"No different than the way you would like to be treated," he offered. The past is past, we made our mistakes, it is time now to move forward in mutual respect. That's how he found it easiest to create progress. Knowing Grace helped, but he couldn't explain that part to the City.

It was interesting to him as well when the City Planning Department referred a resident's request for house moving information to him. They must have been impressed with the flawless Meherin House move, he speculated. It was nice to feel like an asset to the community. Still, the dog of doom raised its ugly head to dull the shine of personal progress. He couldn't keep the thoughts of 'What if' out of his mind for long. By the end of summer the dog howled in his face again; this time it would take a bite, leaving behind a nasty gaping wound.

By Grace, before any of that happened, Frank's emotions were taken on a completely different ride. Late in February his ability to give 'it' away faced its ultimate test. Hana called with sadness in her voice. After detecting that an underlying torment was not passing as the two conversed, Frank asked what was bothering her. Hana carefully responded that she missed not being able to have a close intimate relationship. He understood the kind of a relationship that included intimate contact and why Hana had kept him at 'arms length'. She so dreaded the thought of passing on her affliction, yet needed to be held close and dear, the one thing she could not do with him. He knew what else she wanted to say and asked,

"Have you found someone?"

A pause of reluctant silence and Hana quietly responded,

"Yes."

Frank swallowed emotion; he wanted to know the who, what, when, where, and so he asked. Hana's relief poured forward into the open arms of her friend that did not judge or demand. His name was Jerry and amongst other common ground, they shared the same health issue. She met him in an online chat room for those of similar circumstance. Jerry's difficulty in dealing with his recent diagnoses was comforted by Hana's years of wisdom she gladly imparted. The attraction grew as the communication developed, and soon Jerry flew from Houston to Baltimore to meet Hana face-to-face. Jerry's charisma was powerful, sweeping Hana off her feet. The meeting confirmed attraction, from that grew a solid foundation for a relationship. Jerry needed Hana, Hana needed Jerry and the intimacy was safe. Frank understood; he was happy for Hana and told her so.

His heart sank a bit in despair, yet at the same time lifted in relief. Relief, that Hana was never to be told about his sordid past or current nightmare. However despair grew from the possibility of never again seeing the gorgeous blue eyes of this girl he so loved. Never again was a dark place to him. He had long been afraid that he couldn't take care of Hana well enough to keep her happy, but never again seeing her was a possibility that hurt. He was also afraid of his past. That dog of doom had always howled loudest whenever he entertained ideas of being a man and asking Hana to marry him. Maybe this was for the best, he thought. Hana could be happy and his dog of doom regarding her could be put to sleep for good. That made him happy…kinda.

Frank offered his heartfelt wishes of happiness for Hana and her new journey. Hana offered her heartfelt thanks and gratitude to him for all he had done and the support he had given to her and Troy. He thanked Hana for teaching him how to do these things 'no strings attached.' Hana commented with restored peace,

"You always say just the right things to brighten my day. Thank you Frank, I'll stay in touch."

Frank responded,

"You better!" then added,

"I love you Hana Joi, I always will." He hung up the phone and cried.

He had let the girl of his dreams go and it hurt. At least he stuck to the most important lesson he had ever learned about love. Give 'It' don't hold 'It'. That had been taught to him through Hana Joi and that made him feel good. A piece of her was always to remain a peace in his heart. He lifted up thanks to the Grace that had provided the time they had together. He also said thanks to Grace that had allowed Hana a life long enough for her to see her son Troy graduate from high school. Hana had reached her goal. Frank had reached his. Give 'It' away and enjoy the ride, 'no strings attached.' Some doors close and others open.

Hana remained in his thoughts on a daily basis as he immersed himself into life full of abundant pathways of diversion. That made the void left in his heart a little easier to bear. It also got more work done at the Price House. The house was the preferred place to escape. The remnant of Genesis Water was able to eke out a living for him and his daughter to survive on. The remnant of Dad and Daughter's bond had been reduced to the point that had Elise questioning the wisdom of Dad's parental advice. Elise was struggling with her 'What If'. By the start of her senior year she had dropped out of the regular High School program and entered a continuation school program. It broke his heart to watch his daughter miss the senior experience. The day the class of 2003 graduated, Elise was not there. Dad's emphasis on education had been lost to the cancerous 'What If' and Elise retreated into a small circle of friends. Her mother's voice was now speaking louder than his, and its directions did not reinforce the importance of academia. He was losing his daughter, and that hurt. Elise felt as though she really didn't know her dad, and that hurt her.

The wars and rumors of war that swirled around the globe left little to no room for sound bites of peace. The sense of conflict was everywhere. The voice of peace was barely a whisper and the idea of a Department of Peace was only a dream conversation for those who liked to think totally outside the box. The war on 'sex offenders' fueled by the media was propelled to new heights with an increasing ease of access to the volatile information provided by the Megan's Law and Sheriff's websites. No room was provided for the voice of defense for those caught up in the sticky strands of the web of terror. The war was at his front door and the dogs of doom howled in the darkness of dreams late at night. The cancer was spreading.

Even more abhorrent was the media-reported backlash by Floridians towards those tagged as 'offenders'. Florida laws were now being crafted to deny entry of 'offenders' to evacuation shelters during hurricane events. All in the name of public safety, fellow humans would be left to fend for themselves in the face of Mother Nature's furies. How sick is that. Compassion seemed to have a limit. Separating out 'offenders', from being considered members of the general public was a scary thing. Doesn't everyone who pays taxes as a member of the tribe deserve safety from the storm? The thought of how far tagging to separate might go was only leading him to one disturbing conclusion.

His routine provided plenty of time to think about his situation and how it might relate to the grand scheme of things on planet Earth. During these meditations he not only looked for similarities but for resolutions to his conflict, and conflicts that plagued the planet. The frustrations he encountered in finding answers to the mess he found himself embroiled in led him to focus on what he could do to create personal peace. It was in that small epiphany, again, that he found the clue to finding the real path. The path did begin within.

Now to some, complexity the mind creates to simple solutions creates thick clouds of foggy haze covering the path to be traveled. Like trying to drive an unfamiliar road through a tule fog. You can only see ten feet in front of you so you slow as you strive to reach the known destination safely, but it's a slow go. You pay attention to the complexities of the path not knowing what you will find around the next bend, yet you know what you will find at the end. The treacherous trek through the unfamiliar terrain keeps your travel forward slow and cautious. Your desire to make headway to reach your goal is hampered by the swirling fog that obscures the path. That makes the journey laborious, enjoyment curtailed by gloomy swirling unknown. By Grace the fog will occasionally break and the path will become clear. You take advantage of the Light of clarity to move forward as fast as possible before the fog returns to slow you down. You just want to get there, yet the complexity of the fog keeps you from enjoying the journey. Feelings of doom can do that to all of us.

Such was his journey. His mind knew what had to be done all inside; it was just a matter of taking the baby steps through the fog to reveal the uncharted course. Those brief interludes of Light revealing clear direction in which to proceed are blessings provided by Grace. He jumped on those opportunities whenever Light cleared the path. Sometimes he was actually surprised by the direction and added benefits that such opportunities afforded. One of those experiences took place in July.

After speaking to his dear friend Mary, Frank grabbed a few phone numbers and jumped into the car to drive to San Diego. The trip's original purpose was to visit with relatives who had come to the coast from Arizona to beat the heat of summer. The Warnocks were from his biological father's side of the family; it had been years since he had seen most of them. Unfortunately, their visit coincided with his brother's family getaway to their timeshare in Lake Tahoe. He wanted to see both and that logistically made for a marathon of a driving trip. Twelve hundred miles in five days made for a blindingly fast visit at each location. Long enough spent in San Diego though, to be struck in an Elegant Light, streaming from a hole in the fog.

A phone number in the pile of hastily collected contact numbers was actually meant to be a small side trip if possible, suggested while talking with Mary about her two daughters, Kirsten and Erika. Both were fine and doing well, Mary suggesting he call Kirsten while visiting San Diego as she was attending UCSD at the time. Frank had always held Kirsten in very high regard and promised Mary he'd give her a call. Over the past several years he and Kirsten had built a friendship facilitated by a couple of intense and sometimes funny events that cultivated a free flowing, trusting bond. One tends to bond to another human being when one's life is placed in the hands of the other.

Such was the case for him, when he agreed to Mary's request to give Kirsten her first LA freeway driving experience. The intensity of the hour-long exchange of trust was forever burned into their collective consciousness. Also burned into his was the near miss with the man in the yellow plastic car. Kirsten's intent to beat a red light at a freeway on ramp caused Frank considerable consternation of pending impact. Not only did he hope a cop wasn't witnessing the attempt, he also hoped the yellow Corvette's driver would look up in time to stop his creeping right-hand turn into Kirsten's purposed path. Halfway through the turn the light clicked yellow to red, and at that instant the eyes of the opposing driver finally noticed Kirsten's willful headway. The driver's eyes nearly popped out of his head as he jammed on his brakes, white knuckling his vehicle to a lurching stop. Kirsten breezed on through, never realizing Frank's heart had just skipped a couple of beats, and his fingers had left their impressions on the handhold that he had grasped in the intensity of the moment. Kirsten was oblivious to the intensity he experienced. The family laughed hard at his recounting of those few intense moments.

It wasn't her driving skills, but Kirsten's intelligence and kindness that inspired him. To him she was a Grace filled human, bathed in a mysterious Indigo luminescence indwelt with a higher understanding. Her Light easily danced through the fog in his brain, affording him opportunity to make progress in his goal of finding peace. Kirsten sought the same; her mysterious Light seemed to radiate uncommon understanding profusely. He found the time spent with her to be most enlightening, bringing joy and inspiration to the journey. That's why Kirsten's number rang for attention from somewhere in the pile of contacts.

By the time he had reached his La Jolla destination he had decided to give Kirsten a call first, just to see if she was even around. As he dialed her cell number into the pay phone, he was resigned to the thought that leaving a message early might mean a chance to see one another on his very short stay to see family. A brief visit was better than no visit. It had been at least a year since they had had a chance to connect. Connection he wanted.

Kirsten answered, much to his astonishment! The contact led to plans to get together the following morning, meet some of the clan from his family, and play the rest by ear. That evolved into an elation filled day spent snorkeling the La Jolla cove, coffee, cave exploring, and a dinner laced with the hot topic of Kirsten's writing desires. Her new direction in her course of study intrigued him. Kirsten's dream of effecting peaceful change through dynamic writing kept him transfixed, he was drawn to her like a moth to light. The opportunity to share in the peace she exuded lifted his spirit. He began to entertain thoughts that this young lady's intelligence might possibly help him do what up until now had only been a remote dream of his. The evening's energy brought him to the brink of a leap into hope. Dare hope? Dare ask?

Emboldened by the euphoria of connection, he asked Kirsten if she might be interested in helping unravel the confusion of a book that had been churning in his brain for years. If he could just get it all out, he felt that Kirsten's talent might turn the mess in his head into a coherent work. His imaginings of telling a story that could effect change was a goal they both shared. His heart had been opened in Light; while the path was clear, he ran. Would she help?

Enticed by the offer Kirsten responded with an emphatic "Yes." Then she asked for the one thing he was terrified to offer. Details! He could only muster a vague, mysterious confiding and if she was willing to help all the 'details' could be offered up later. The 'What if' dog of dooms roaring stopped him short of disclosure, but could not howl loud enough to drown out the joyful sound of hope when Kirsten had said "yes" she'd be "happy to help." Overwhelmed by her generosity he could barely let her go that night. They were out until early morning, hashing about details of a project they committed to co-create.

His spirit was elevated for weeks and he marveled at the youth he felt. His faith that this incredibly intelligent lady could accomplish what he couldn't was well founded. After all, you have to have something a little special if you can ace a class in Quantum Physics in the Fourth Dimension. You also have to be a little special if you're willing to take on helping another human in a struggle, not knowing the struggle's full complexity. When you define a 'giving human being' you define Kirsten. Kirsten's leap of faith to join him in his effort was Grace and he knew it. The same Grace that had taught him to 'give It away' had given him a new person to 'give It to'. That 'It' void needed to be filled and was. Doors close, doors open. The joy of giving 'It' was celebrated by him with reserve, alone but nevertheless celebrated. With thanks he passed the gift of love quietly on to this gift of Grace in human form.

His search for peace had presented him with two amazing gifts. One was a selfless ally of co-creation, a Light called Kirsten; the other was the willingness to love. That love was a gift, joyful, profound, confusing, unimagined and terrifying. If 'It' was to flourish 'What if' was a threat he must one day let go. He couldn't do it that day. He hated the thought of that day ever coming, but in order to accomplish the task of co-creation he knew that door had to be opened for his writing partner to see. At this point he still wasn't man enough to face the rejection it might release. Kirsten was willing to help this day; she might not when that day came. That thought tortured him. It was to be a long passage of time before he assembled and delivered the information Kirsten needed. The day of reckoning was in the hands of Grace that provided the gifts. He was content to wait knowing that if it was meant to be, it would be and that is peace. Hello....another gift! That makes three.

Back home the charm of life was being lived when the phone rang in Frank's office. He picked up and announced unexpectant of return,

"Genesis Water, Frank speaking."

"Hello Fraunk." The voice on the other end responded. That could be only one person on the planet and Frank retorted,

"My God it's Hana Joi!"

"It is," she responded matter-of-factly.

"It's about time kiddo, I haven't heard from you in months, what's up?" he inquired with excitement.

"Yeah it has been a long time... I'm sorry," Hana began.

In the course of the half hour conversation Hana invited Frank to a wedding taking place in August. The wedding was not to be hers much to his (silent) relief; the wedding was for Hana's brother's son, Shawn. The wedding was to be held in Soma just a couple hours south of his place. Hana and Jerry along with Troy would be flying to California to attend, and she invited him along. He was thrilled at the opportunity to see Hana and Troy, along with meeting the man that had filled the void in Hana's life, which he couldn't. He accepted the invitation with a giddy thrill resonating in his voice. After getting the hotel location particulars he closed the joyous conversation with his usual gifting,

"Remember Hana Joi, I love you," hung up and inked the date in on his calendar. He was thrilled. Blue eyes again... for a minute. Another gift.

A month later, Frank arrived at their hotel in Thousand Oaks, early as usual. His heart raced as he asked the front desk clerk to ring Hana and Jerry's room announcing his arrival. Waiting in the large plush lobby filled with fine appointments he could hardly contain his excitement. Scanning the columned corridors in anticipation didn't make Hana appear any sooner. When she did appear the whole room slipped into a surreal slow motion, she seemed to glide across the glass-like marble floor towards him. When they finally touched in heartfelt embrace, time returned to its normal beat and the party was on. They retired to the restaurant and waited for the boys to arrive. At least that was the way the romantic in him remembered those first few seconds in the years to come.

Hana's sea blue eyes warmed his soul throughout that day and the next. Jerry was a gentleman with Hana's well being appearing to be the focus in his life. Troy was growing up and loving the west coast vibe. The wedding and reception where tastefully well done. Happiness wafted in the gentle breeze, and Hana invited Frank to dance. He gladly accepted. He held Hana with ultimate respect as they talked while dancing, his heart pouring with joy. He told Hana he loved the fact that she had found happiness and was grateful they had this chance to see one another again. She agreed.

The group left the reception to return to the hotel after a side trip to the Pacific Ocean to dip their feet. Back at the hotel lobby farewells were imparted. It was a short visit but nevertheless a visit that sparked joy. He hugged Hana, whispering his reminder,

"Remember Hana Joi... I'll always love you."

"I know Fraunk; I'll always love you too," she returned in soft affectionate tone.

The charm of joy was with him on his ride back to Pismo. The two-day reconnection was another gift that he'd lift up thanks for, falling asleep that night fulfilled. What, another gift from the Universe? Did he really see 'It'?

Within days fullness cascaded to emptiness as cancer was spread into the lives of the Pismo Clam family. The new Chief of Police for Pismo found it necessary to inform the new Chamber CEO that a 'sex offender' was operating one of the Chamber's promotional campaigns. The context of that conversation left the CEO with some sense of urgency. Her request to meet with Frank was done spur of the moment when they ran into one another at the Chamber office. He said "sure" and they entered her office. He had immediately noticed her distressed demeanor and asked, "What's up?"

His gut told him what was up even before she began to speak. 'What if" was about to become 'What now.' As she started to reveal her intercourse with the Chief, a numb buzz of adrenaline muted his hearing of her nervously delivered discourse, leaking with the belief that danger existed. She went on to demand the return of the Clam family costumes immediately. The

Chamber wanted to avoid any embarrassment in the event his 'accused' identity became known, or as she put it, "...if something were to happen."

There it was. The cancer had arrived. Instead of Frank being the good guy he had been for the past ten years he had run the Clam program, he was now the bad guy under the unsavory tag of 'sex offender'. Weighted with the innuendo of 'dangerous' puts the element of fear into those that hear the 'official' side of the story, which can instantly turn one into the Bogeyman! In the numb of accusation he was dumb to a response. He felt he was a villain, the confusion of 'What now' kept clarity elusively scattered. The torture of his mind's misfiring continued, trying to get out of the box of accusation when Grace supplied clarity as a strange sensation of relief washed over him. He took a breath or two, looked the Exec straight in the eye and said what he felt, "Well that's a relief!"

With the request to step aside he savored the feeling of no longer having to run the razor's edge. An edge 'What if' had put him on every time he put on the costume of Sam. He reassured her he'd be prompt in the return of the characters, going on to suggest a retirement program for the Clam family at that year's festival. She resisted insisting that they could find replacements to fill the costumes. He was willing to bet they couldn't and told her so. She'd have about a month to find any willing takers, the Harvest Festival parade was coming up and she planned to have the whole clam family in that parade. He wished her success in her search and returned the costumes the next day.

A month later the Chamber Exec called Frank asking to meet again. He listened as she conveyed the founding of his suspicions. An intense month-long search to find someone to take on the role of Sam found no one even remotely interested. "Tough shoes to fill," Frank suggested. She agreed, and was now interested in discussing the retirement plan he had proposed. She communicated with greater ease, not as fearful of the monster she had first envisioned. They spoke at some length on how that might be handled. He left grateful that the dignity and respect he had brought to the Clam family was being returned. They were not to just fade away to nothingness. Another gift.

On festival day he started the early morning set up for his last time. He taught an intrepid newcomer the fine art he had honed over the years of set up and control of the festival grounds and vendors prior to festival start. This was his last time for everything at the festival and at that predawn hour with hot coffee in hand, it felt good. Emptiness was to come later. By nine he was at the Chamber office to begin the end of the Pismo Clams.

He had informed Judy, his stalwart partner since the Clams inception, the reason for their retirement was related to a medical advisory issued by his doctor. He hated to lie to her, but he didn't want his effervescent little friend to have to endure the pain of his cancer. Judy kept a door open for eventually returning if his 'condition' improved. She stayed happy in that moment. If she had known what that 'condition' truly was, the bright spot of her fond memories could have been tarnished. He could not do that to his little friend, keeping that horror from her.

At ten they boarded the car that had been selected for them to ride. The Clam kids were not part of the plan, and the two traveled the parade route alone, disconnected from the crowd, they could only wave their gloved hands. Shaking the hands and extending warm welcome to those supporters lining the route was the one thing they truly missed, as they rode their way into history.

After the parade Sam and Pam walked hand in hand to Judy's hotel for some farewell pictures. Then back to the Chamber office, shaking as many hands as they could along the way before disrobing from the characters one last time. They hugged before parting, thanking one another for the past ten years of priceless memories. With a last wave farewell they parted and that end was done.

For eleven years he had worn the suit as Sam. Never a problem. Never a complaint. One pair of grateful parents, their smiling autistic little girl in her wheelchair happier than she had ever been, extended their appreciation. One little girl in her wheelchair was the motivation for him. His courage to pick up the ball and run ultimately produced smiles and happiness for the little girl bound to a wheelchair. The tens of thousands of smiles since were thanks enough for him. He felt he had paid down some of the debt that had burdened his heart. A chapter of life now closed and it was time to move on.

Wins, losses, highs, lows, ups and downs, it was the flow of life. The Price House scored big that year. The electrical rewiring of the Anniversary House was well underway, along with the trenching for the underground power that was to supply the rest of the Park power and communication lines that had been designed to originate from a central location. That building was to be one of his more unique creations. The building had to fit the farm motif. He came up with an idea to build it to resemble the outhouse that had once been attached to the Anniversary House. The finished product he and Mike Fairbrother constructed was brilliant, almost exact in dimension to the original, sided with original 112 old redwood siding that had been removed from the Anniversary House some seven years prior. He was glad he had saved the siding, even though most folks thought he was crazy. The character of the wood made the building look like it had stood for many years and it saved a ton of money on the project. The little outhouse was a big hit at the annual Ice Cream social.

The Ice Cream Social was a huge hit, in and of itself, thanks to the dedicated FOPH volunteers. Almost twenty Price family descendants converged on Pismo to be in attendance. Stunning performances and displays put on by the Sa' Pismu. Former rocker Mary Ramsey and her husband Salvador sang

Chumash chants that held the crowd spellbound. Big Jack Smith delighted the attendees' taste buds with his famous fry bread, while the sweet tooth was tantalized with Rich Oung's homemade ice cream. Frank was MC for the festivities and presented awards to twenty or so very deserving volunteers. The event was a draw that filled the Vets Hall auditorium to capacity. The day long doings were topped off with a trip to the Park to unveil the Park's new star, the Sa' Pismu Village. The 'outhouse' shined as well.

The pile of cash contributed to the donation bucket far exceeded the costs to put on the annual 'free to all' thank you. By nightfall Frank locked the gate behind him, satisfied that once again FOPH had delivered another stellar community happening. Feedback received over the next few weeks proved the success of the effort. The Chumash were becoming the talk of the town. He lifted up thanks to the Grace that had provided that connection. He was also grateful for the Grace of the volunteers. He thanked them with 'free' ice cream, cookies and beverages. The karma in Grace rocked the Price House world and back onto the local six o'clock news. Good things really do go around. What you give does come back, and sometimes extra.

"Nightlife," the first movie filmed at the Price House, screamed back onto the stage of life as that extra. The kids had worked hard in post production and the first cut was in the can. To celebrate their success cast and crew planned a premiere showing at the Palm Theater in San Luis to blow their own horn. Frank was invited into the planning group loop a couple of weeks prior to showing, and he was astounded by the grand scope of the kids' dreaming. Limo for cast and crew, spotlight, movie promo posters and even a red carpet to walk, it had all the trappings of Hollywood. When he was shown the movie's promo poster he was ecstatic to find that the Price House was prominent in display. Then as he read down the listing of credits he was jolted when he found his name listed following the words CO-PRODUCED BY! Confused he asked,

"Hey Shane is there another Frank working on this project?"

"No... why?" Shane queried.

"What's this all about?" Frank asked, pointing to his name. Shane looked up from the poster and shared the group feeling,

"Man if it hadn't been for you and you're pushing the movie would probably have never been completed. Besides in this case Co-Producer just means unpaid help!" they all laughed. Frank was honored by the group's consensus nevertheless. He thanked those in attendance, pledging to do what he could to make the first showing a success.

"Good," Shane said, "you're in charge of publicity!"

Frank called his friend Tony at the local NBC affiliate and was able to put together some great news coverage. The 6pm news live remote from the red carpet at the Palms the night of the premiere was the spark that lit the fuse of excitement. He was able to get in a great plug for the FOPH board and City of Pismo's cooperation. As was his custom he jumped all over the opportunity to praise the kids for all their hard work into the wee hours of the morning. His invite to the general public to come down and join the fun of a first run was his final enticement. After the interviews and theater prep the group gathered at a bar in Grover Beach for the Limo ride back to the spot light. The group as a whole had sold all four hundred tickets they had printed for presale. The big question on everyone's mind was "how many will show?"

Silence replaced revelry and tensions peaked as the limo rounded the final corner in their ride to the red carpet. Would the sidewalk in front be filled with movie buffs or empty of the curious? The bright neon lights of the Palms' marquee illuminated a scene way beyond expectations. A bulging crowd spilling out into the street awaited the arrival of the 'stars'. Silence was shredded with the roar of elation that he was sure had been heard all the way back to Grover. The limo glided to a stop and the entourage emptied out onto the waiting carpeted gangway that provided a red path through the gauntlet of crowd. Flashbulbs popped and the crowd undulated forward to get a look at the 'stars of the night'. The electricity of the crowd was a great ego stroke for the kids to say the least. They drank in the adulations and autographs were signed as they made their way to the theater lobby. He loved watching the kids play their parts one more time.

For Frank the rope-lined carpet held another message he had not expected. Pressed against the velvet rope boarder and bracing against the push of the crowd stood his daughter. In her eyes he saw something he had not seen in almost two years. Pride! Elise beamed as she pointed out her dad to best friend Lauren. What a stoke it was for him to see his daughter once again sharing their bond with pride as she called to him to stop for a picture. That made the night for him. All the rest of the evening's hoopla paled in comparison. Elise was coming back to her dad and he was elated! ...*Let's see, at this point I've lost count in the gift department.*

The show drew applause, mostly out of courtesy as the final credits ran. Post production needed more work to really make the movie a keeper. Not bad all in all, but not what Frank could call good. It had been a good effort but... the overall consensus was to go back to post production for some heavy-duty work on the special effects. That part of their work had been rushed for the premiere and it showed. Energized by 'we can do it,' the rag tag team of movie makers headed back to post, their goal to make it into a film festival somewhere. Lofty ambition he thought but they might have a shot. You just never know what another year might bring.

The same can be said about the outcome of any phone call you answer. You just never know what journey you might be asked to take when you pick up that receiver. Frank picked up every time, he wasn't one to screen his calls through the answering machine. House phone or business line, if he was there the phone was answered. Except for the salesman all calls were important, some more than others, and then there were calls that were critical. It always amazed him that when those critical calls were made he was always there to answer them. He often pondered what force was coming together to make that happen. Coincidence?

It was another gorgeous warm fall day on the Central Coast. He had spent the morning under clients' kitchen sinks plying his trade, making the dollars needed to sustain his simple lifestyle. Lunch at home with a check on messages then out to the Price House for some farm labors. There was always a job to do on a farm, the peaceful surroundings reward enough for his volunteered time. That afternoon he was nudged home early, not something he usually did. He figured the gentle nudging that pecked at his brain to return was to handle the mountain of clothes that heaped out of his hamper. "Oh, and the lawn needs to be mowed!" his brain interjected. The duties that called were well underway when his business line rang. He picked up,

"Genesis Water, Frank speaking."

"Hello Fraunk," was the response that brought instant joy at its recognition.

"Hey Hana, what's up?" He glowed with just a hint of surprise.

It had only been a couple of months since he had seen Hana in LA. He had not expected to hear from her so soon.

"Is everything ok?" he asked instinctively.

"Well, no." Hana began. Frank's brain shot straight to the virus as being the trigger to her distress.

"No it is Jerry." Hana confided. She filled her friend in on the details of infidelity she had discovered and the mess the relationship had turned into. Hana had decided that sticking around was not good for her mental health, her decision to leave had been made. She was calling her friend to see if he could help. Of course he could!

The plan was simple. The one decision left for Hana was whether to drive east to Pennsylvania and family, or west to his house. His desire of course leaned to the latter. "You never know she might like to stay," he thought. Or was that more like a dream. The decision was hers, she could make her choice while he flew to meet her. Either way was a four-day drive, he rearranged his schedule appropriately. Forty-eight hours later Frank landed at Houston's Continental airport and was greeted by a pair of sea blue eyes that gleamed in relief at the sight of a trusted loyal friend. They collected his bag from the luggage turnstile then headed for Hana's car that was packed to the gills, ready to roll. He asked which direction they might be headed.

Still, Hana was undecided as to whether to roll east or west. Family comfort sounded good, but so did the comfort of this friend that was very close to being family. Frank stowed his bag in a small corner of the trunk she had saved for him. He closed the trunk lid reached into his pocket and extracted a quarter.

"I'll make this easy," he announced.

"I'll flip a coin. Heads we go west Tails we go east."

Hana nodded hesitantly grinning with game as Frank launched the coin skyward. The coin flicker flashed in rotation to its peak then down to the floor of the parking garage, hitting with a ting. As it spun in slow motion he could only hope for heads. It was tails.

"East it is." He announced with just a bit of disappointment he did not show. Then the power of woman spoke.

"No, we are going west!" Hana said with that power vested in woman. The power to change anything! Frank was astounded. The girl he so cherished was coming home with him. Who's writing this stuff?

Frank had made Hana an offer she couldn't refuse. Come to his house for clear open space and a chance to think. Discover what you really want to do, then do it. He'd take the couch she could take the bedroom. No strings attached. He meant that from the heart and Hana's heart knew it. She had responded to what spoke from her heart, thus started an incredible journey. They jumped into the car, pointed it westward, and rolled out letting life unfold as it may.

A few hours later just after dark they stopped at the Alamo in San Antonio for a break and a bite to eat. And the wino that got them for $10.00 in phony parking fees sourced riotous laughter as the road warriors pushed forward onto the blacktop rolling out in front of the headlamps that lit their trek. Like the day, conversations were long and uninterrupted. First night's rest came at 2am somewhere in mid Texas.

The next day's advance rested their radio flier in the desert wilds of New Mexico. They walked into the dry desert night to lie on their backs and allowed a billion stars to ground thoughts of personal significance. Tucson, Phoenix and the energy filled red bluffs of Sedona supplied visual backdrop to deep communications the two enjoyed while road tripping along. Their Phoenix landed the third night for play at the Flamingo Hotel and Casino in Laughlin, Nevada. The Pink Flamingo theme had long been a humorous collection of gifts Frank had given to Hana. Staying at the Flamingo was almost like staying at a personal theme park. Unfortunately lady luck didn't supply the million dollars they hoped to extract from the one armed bandits. The bandits instead got them, but still a great way to spend their last night on the road together.

The cruise continued the next morning. They checked off the town's enroute to pick up Frank's car he had left at Mary's house in Burbank. Santa Barbara at dusk and home in Grover after dark, Elise was there to greet the weary travelers. After a good night's rest Frank arose with the privilege of serving coffee to Hana in his own home. He felt that privilege as they sat on the back porch sipping fresh brew. The warm morning sun welcomed his houseguest. They talked at length about her options for life. He made sure she knew she could stay for as long as she needed. He hoped that would be a long time, despite the agonizing 'What if' that just wouldn't leave him alone.

They fell into the family routine almost immediately. Frank off to work in the mornings while Hana played on her computer. Hana tended the house, shopped and cooked, warming the 'beach house' with her feminine touches. He was on cloud nine hundred and something. He knew to relish her company while he could and only dream she might stay. That private hope scared him to death. The 'What if' dog of dooms howl, was never far away. If Hana did decide to stay he knew he'd eventually have to reveal his inner most secret. The thought left him weak with anxiety. His fondest dream was being destroyed by the fear of rejection the revelation might bring. He decided not to go to that level until he was clearer regarding Hana's intentions. The misery of the dilemma plagued him, and the thought of Grover PD showing up to do a spot check made him ill. That would be a horrible way to open that door. He wasn't man enough to bring up the subject. He was beginning to feel that he wasn't man enough to take on the care and comfort of this dear girl. The fear of that failure haunted his thoughts almost as much as his fear of 'What if.'

Within a couple of weeks Hana was thinking she should return to the family on the East Coast. She missed them and Frank perceived her yearnings. She had a burning desire to make her relationship work with Jerry and he knew that too. Hana was pressed by both desires. Right up to the day she left, Frank attached no strings by voicing his desires. He knew he had to let her go. The weakness of his own stresses kept him mute in voicing any objections to Hana's departure. He did let her know that the door was always open to her should she decide ever to return. He offered to go along and assist in the drive. Hana said she would be fine and thanked him for his gracious help. She kind of looked forward to the cross-country trip, a replay of her trip some 30 years earlier. They hugged closely. And with a parting kiss to the cheek Hana drove away. He watched as she disappeared through the mist of the morning or the eyes, he wasn't sure.

A sense of relief mingled with the sense of despair. The joy of three weeks spent with Hana crowded with the anger at the obstacles that kept him from commitment. Self worth only bolstered by the fact that he had remained true to his philosophies. He had 'given freely' to his dear friend and that had helped her through a very trying time. At least he had a few weeks to pamper her in his own home. They even spent a day working at the Price House together. He really had a lot to be happy about, just sad he had to say goodbye again. He was actually glad she was gone the following day when Cheryl from Grover PD stopped by to verify that the 'sex offender' was still living at his stated address. Made him ponder just who was in charge of the timing thing anyway? The ending of Hana's stay...Another gift.

He called Hana daily to check on her progress. By day four she was back in Houston to pick up her cat, spending a couple of days to communicate her feelings and listen to Jerry's explanations. Then back on the road to Maryland to see her son and close friend Joyce for a few days, recharge with purpose then on to Pennsylvania. He was on the phone every step of the way encouraging her effort, remaining grateful for the contact. Hana remained in Pennsylvania for a short time, and then returned to Maryland to work the boat show as she needed to get an income generating.

It wasn't long before Jerry came to Maryland. It wasn't long before Hana returned to Houston. It wasn't long and the phone grew silent again. It wasn't long before the Price House was back in the paper again. Frank was asked to submit recent photos of the Price House project to compliment an article written. The one chosen by the editor was a photo he had taken of Hana working in the Chumash village. He sent her a copy.

~~~~

We are all part of each others' journey. As our strings co-mingle we share a beautiful color only our connection can bring to the tapestry. The more we weave with others the more color we create. Then there are those strings we weave with, that create an Elegant color in our journey we cannot quite describe. Those are the chosen ones that bring our best to Light. Our string we follow knows that string, and its purity is the color of Love. Our string we follow is ascending into that color.

CHAPTER 30

DEPTH OF THE EXPANDING JOURNEY

Marching forward despite the depressions of the holiday, challenges the joy of living. The turn of the New Year played like the broken record it had become. Life kept skipping back to the repeated refrain prolonging the episodes of mental torture. The media didn't help. The war on the 'sex offenders' and the hunt for the 'predators' was top end nightly news and the morning's front page. One network even turned the hunt into a prime time show. The internet 'offenders' web site was now wide open, available for anyone to peruse. Local media encouraged parents to visit the site so they could know the 'predators' that lived in their vicinity. The media was whipping the public's emotions to frenzy. The reporting of "thousands of known 'offenders' living in the state" made it sound as if an 'offender' lived on every block.

He only imagined how the information was handled by anyone who visited the web site. What could people do, burn copies of the mug shots to keep in their wallets for quick reference? Maybe parents could take the family for a Sunday ride around town to point out all the houses where the 'predators' lived. 'Know your neighbor' was taking on a whole new meaning in twisted suspicions. The crush of the cancerous pointing finger drove him so low that at a point he began to welcome death. Life had its great highs of success, but the dark gloom of pending doom and lack of hope was making the peace of death preferred. Anger generated by his attorney's lack of real concern only compounded mental duress. He had not heard from her in months.

Lack of companionship was at an all time low. Hana was busy with her tangled relationship with Jerry. Kirsten's Light was busy with her new life in San Francisco. Mary had gone through a divorce with Steen and now had a new relationship with Joseph Bell. Mary had not visited in months. Frank missed the depth and comradery of these special people. The circle of friends from the Price House only supplied work-related contacts for the most part. Glen Ray and Frank did go deep at times into some very interesting subjects, but not on a regular basis and never to 'What if'. His relationship with his daughter was better, but five hours away. He found their bond reconstructing itself as Elise matured into her 19th year. That was good, but slow. Deep with Elise was still a ways off.

Deep was what he yearned for. Some way or someone to go deep with to receive insights into the mess in his head, that kept his spirit impounded in doom. Deep into the spiritual journey we all take from time to time. Most of his journey was taking place alone in the solitary confines of the Price House. Eventually his call to connect was answered; the Cavalry rode in on two Italian horses. One, his 'Italian stallion' friend Lenny, the other was a new connection made at the Sa' Pismu village, her name was Karen Epifano. Both had that driving Italian spirit that was full of life, spirit looking to live each day to its fullest. The two Italians had minds that questioned constantly in the search for truth and that's just what he was looking for.

He and Lenny were tight friends, yet Frank's rush through life had the tendency of separating the two for long periods. Funky head space and life rush obscured the obvious; it had been awhile since he had touched base with Lenny. So on a drizzly February afternoon he dropped in to see his old friend and his dog Murphy. As usual he found Lenny abuzz with a new ambitious project. Of course, that was Lenny; the little Italian always had a million things going on. Lenny's robust spirit for living constantly amazed him. This project however was a monster that caught Frank a bit off guard. The two spent a couple of hours planning, and then planting four stakes in the vacant property adjacent to Lenny's main residence. A mountain of groundwork had already been done to level the half-acre plot, and those four stakes represented the tentative placement of a 48'x 24' foundation pad. On that pad a two-story structure was to be built.

Lenny moved about with his signature scurry. The limp in his gait was a clear giveaway to the agony he put up with from his distorted legs. His maimed feet in their two-inch heal orthopedic shoes caused agony of their own. Lenny never complained as he shot a million questions regarding the different aspects of the project at Frank. There was a plan. Bold forethought by Lenny for his family's well being had prompted the plan for future security. Water, power, sewer, communication lines, fire hydrant, water tanks, propane tanks, and the trenches to connect it all to the future 'garage'. Frank's head swam in the complexities. He listened nervously as Lenny explained his idea to build a two-story 'garage' and maybe after completion convert some of it into living space he could rent out for income.   Lenny knew there was to come a day when he might need help with income; a rental property could provide money when he was crippled and could not. This was huge; a permit to build had already been issued, and Frank was relieved to be informed that Lenny had in fact hired a General Contractor.

He was absolutely blown away by Lenny's loving energy for family and friends. He wished for only a portion of the Grace and compassion that poured through Lenny's heart. The little Italian worked like a horse pumped by a heart of gold. The two had fun plotting the foundation footprint, Frank offered up his help in any way his friend might benefit. He owed at least that much to his friend that had always been there for him. Lenny had always stepped in to help take care of the business when Frank traveled. He owed Lenny big time.

Frank promised to stop by to meet the contractor Greg Hill. That led to stopping by every couple of days to lend a hand in foundation preparations. That led to stopping by every afternoon to help as framing got underway. Greg did laugh at, and joke about, Frank and his antique nail apron he sported. He wasn't a pretty sight, but did provide extra energy that helped move the project along. It was a toss up between Frank, and Greg's helper Jethro, as to who was the daily brunt of Greg's joking about looks or abilities. They became a tight crew and enjoyed each other's company. Greg ran the show and besides all Lenny did, he also kept the group well fed and watered in typical Italian fashion.

Right about this time Frank received a "Hello Fraunk" call from Hana. "It's about time!" he always scolded in jest as they started conversation. He loved hearing from her and getting caught up on how she was doing. Hana informed him that she was still on the fence regarding Jerry's commitment to their relationship, despite the fact that she had sold her home in Maryland and moved back in with him to demonstrate hers. She wasn't quite sure how that was going. Frank detected her resentment to unfulfilled expectations. On the positive side Hana had scored a great job with a major fabric importer headquartered in Houston. Even better she had just been added to the excellent health care plan the company carried. That was important peace of mind for Hana, knowing she could again monitor and manage her health considerations without going into debt. That part of the conversation led to an interesting comment made by Hana. She had remembered Frank had told her that he didn't carry health insurance. Casually fantasizing she suggested that if things didn't work out with Jerry,

"Hey if you marry me Frank you would have health insurance too."

The comment floored him. Was Hana actually revealing she'd even consider him as a potential life partner? The sincerity in her invitation shocked his senses. In seconds the ramifications of the comment spun extremes of realities through his brain. Euphoria of a dream fulfilling then the doubt of his inadequacy coupled with 'What if' flushed honesty from his heart and he blurted out,

"Well before that could happen I have some stuff from the past we would have to talk about first."

"OH MY GOD WHAT A STUPID, STUPID THING TO SAY!" flashed his next thought. He couldn't believe he had just said it! Now he was in trouble! He had just opened the door and Hana would walk right on through.

"Yeah...What kind of stuff?" she asked.

Oh shit! This was not where he wanted to go. Not now. Not ever. He began to back peddle as fast as he could. He begged for forgiveness at even bringing up the subject, it was not a conversation he wanted to have over the phone. That conversation he owed to her face-to-face.

"Please not here, not now," he pleaded, almost to bleeding.

Hana was not one to give up easily, but the distress she detected in his voice quelled her perseverance, she agreed to wait for another day. She knew the time would come. Unfortunately so did Frank.

That brush with honesty dampened further conversation; he thanked Hana for calling and bringing him up to date. He looked to get off the phone in a hurry before Hana changed her mind about waiting for details. At least he was in a space at that point where he could end with his reminder, although qualified,

"Despite everything Hana Joi I still love you."

"I love you too Frank," she responded, a bit unsettled by the unfinished business of a now-open door she had not known existed.

Hanging up, he sat stupefied at what he had just done. He knew Hana would not let this go. Fear gripped his heart as he prayed for the subject never to come up again. 'What If' had become 'What Then'. Only time would tell if 'What Then' was to ever be pushed to 'What Now' by any further inquiry on Hana's part. He was damn sure he'd never bring it up again. The only problem was the dog of doom howled daily in his ear reminding him of his momentary slip into the insanity of honesty. He dove head first into his work to escape the fear of the howl. He retreated to Lenny's for the immersion needed to calm the crazy brain. The timing by Grace he didn't recognize ticked anyway.

As the boys started the second floor framing, Jethro left for an extended trip to Hawai'i. The three left behind envied Jethro's good fortune and gave him hell the day he departed. Frank overheard Lenny tell Greg that he would pick up the work that Jethro had been doing, telling Greg not to hire a replacement. Lenny wanted save some dollars, but Frank knew it was more than his friend could handle. He privately committed himself for the long haul on the project, he was determined to give back some of what Lenny had given to him. Lenny had always been there for him, giving time and wisdom whenever needed. He now had a way to pay him back, and he adjusted his schedule accordingly.

The Price House was rocketing forward as usual too. Frank was busy preparing the interior walls for resurfacing. He had signed the $8,000.00 contract with a local company for a smooth finish resurfacing, matching the little existing original plaster that was left on the walls and ceilings. He was under the gun to get the wall lath reasonably level before the contract start date. The FOPH board was ecstatic that he might have the walls of the Anniversary House done by the next Ice Cream Social. So was he! It had been eight long years since he started, spending hundreds of hours removing and hauling thousands of pounds of damaged plaster out of the house. All that work was close to fruition and that harbored energy of accomplishment.

The Chumash village was rocketing forward as well. Medicine man Johnny Whitehorse had joined the group. Cheyenne, as he was affectionately known, was leading ceremonies of singing, drumming, dancing, and spiritual enrichment. The tribe was alive planning a really big show of their own for the social. The flurry of activities at the Park that spring bloomed, inspiring the City to celebrate another Arbor Day out at the House. Frank sought another dozen fruit trees to plant in the Orchard, and the City was gracious enough to supply, plant and help celebrate. Price family descendents put together a push to buy tree memorials that raised a lot of money at $500.00 a pop. He had been able to secure 12 memorial requests over the previous three years, which was a nice chunk of change for the Park.

Frank talked often about the Price House with Lenny and Greg while they toiled on 'the garage.' Towards year's end he solicited and received their help in the rebuilding of the front porch of the Meherin House. The Grace of generosity they supplied saved the Price House at least a grand or so on labor.

Lenny's generosity went far beyond; money began to show up on the front seat of Frank's truck. Lenny absolutely refused to take it back. Lenny was one in a billion and the three together where priceless. They called themselves the Bada Bing Crew, the three together knocked out a lot of work. Greg hired Frank for some of his other jobs as well. Greg liked his work, Frank liked the extra income. He appreciated the immersion he needed. He was appreciated by both Lenny and Greg, which lifted esteem. The three spent a great year together, the Bada Bing Crew working hard and bonding.

Working hard might be an understatement. One particular day worked Frank, like he hadn't been worked in years. A Saturday spent rolling trusses for the garage roof had his muscles aching when he showed up for the Sunday workday at the Chumash village. He was exhausted from the prior day's trapeze act of crawling around like a monkey in a jungle of 2x4s that made up the roofs structure. A relatively new volunteer Karen Epifano took notice.

Karen was a very nice looking, energetic Italian gal who was all about sustainable living practice as well as a Holistic Health Educator and Massage Practitioner. She enjoyed the group and what she was learning about the native practices that resonated sustainable living. Frank enjoyed her enthusiasm. He also enjoyed her wispy, cute frame and readily accepted her attentions. As tribe members began to filter in for the Sunday meet, Karen took notice of his depleted energies, asking what was up. He explained that he had worked the day before like he was a 20-year old, and today his body was reminding him that it wasn't. Karen offered up a massage for the stinging muscles in his back and neck, he greedily accepted.

As soon as Karen started he knew he was in the hands of experience. For the next twenty minutes he was treated to a magnificent rendering of the art of massage. Karen's strong hands, knowledge of muscle groups and perfect pressure guided him back to the pleasure of no pain. Her playful tug on his hair at the base of his neck at the end of the session led him to realize that more than just a therapy for his sore body had been received. A personal connection was being made, revitalizing feelings that had been asleep for a considerable period of time.

That was the start of a relationship that could tolerate busy. Karen was busy, yet she focused much attention on the Price House project. She sucked up the knowledge of the Chumash to incorporate into her own sustainable living theory. She hoped to create her dream project somewhere on the Central Coast, and her free spirit captivated Frank. By the end of summer Karen was one of the Park's regular assets. Her high energy and creativity imparted her character to the Park surroundings. The attractive little woman's presence surrounded Frank's brain with thoughts of closeness and loving as they worked. By the end of summer Glen was in a tizzy, feeling surrounded by the two's cavorting conspiracies.

Little did Frank know what kind of an impact Karen was having on Glen. Frank had been innocently toying with the notion of letting Karen stay in the Meherin House while she looked for property to buy for her project. Glen saw that as a threat. Glen knew Frank was frustrated with the amount of time he was off site. Frank wanted more of an on-site presence to deter people from doing stupid things, and Karen's added presence could help be that deterrent. Glen surmised other things. Karen's role as a catalyst for change at the Park went way beyond what advantages Frank was beginning to envision. A catalyst for change that could help protect the Park supplied through the Grace of Karen's presence is what he saw. A catalyst for deep honesty and revelation was the unexpected. Really free was birthing. Contractions soon to start.

Karen would be blindsiding him. A strange plan was being laid out to be lived. It took him a year before he realized the energy that moved the play had come from some Greater source. A Source who's diversity is manifested in the Ultra Violet and many other hues of light that are born when sunlight passes through rain. You can finally get deep when you ultimately step outside all the way. Karen was to be a major facilitator in his stepping way outside his box.

The great big ball of negative energy that ballooned between Karen and Glen did eventually burst into a positive energy. That energy created a new co-caretaker program that protected the Park and the valuable artifacts that where being entrusted to their care. The blindsiding came when Karen rid herself of a huge ball of negative energy she laid squarely in Frank's lap.

He had been working on interior wall prep at the Anniversary House when he stepped outside for a breath of fresh air and saw Karen walking up the lane. She had called earlier that day and asked (insisted) on meeting. Her tone on the phone had given him some cause for concern, she had been adamant about seeing him in person! Like any good Italian knew, face-to-face was the only way to see truth spoken. He could only imagine what matter demanded such attention. He could feel Karen's tensions as they greeted. The pit of his stomach said something was very wrong when he looked at the stress in her eyes and he inquired,

"What's up?"

"Yeah"… she drifted off in tone as she focused on his eyes and her thoughts. Then stated, "I've heard through a source in the group that you are a registered sex offender. Is that true?" she said demanding response.

Frank instantaneously felt sick to his stomach as the words spilled out of her mouth, then the numbing buzzes of lower level existence in the clutches of limiting flight or fight choices for survival. The fear gripped his chest, shortened his breath, forcing him to sit before the gray of blood draining from his head made him fall. His ears only reported what sounded like the rush produced by strong wind through Pine trees. The brutally demanding inquiry from the fiery little Italian had taken him down, so far down that his brain could barely compute an answer. A long pause followed. The numbing buzz had to wear off before he spoke.

"Well I guess I should tell you the whole story," he stammered.

His breathing slowed to somewhat normal, yet his hands shook as he began the journey of truth, deep revealing that leaves one naked. The next two hours were filled answering every question Karen posed. His wall of protective anonymity leveled, emotions that had been buried were slowly uncovered layer by layer. Karen got the honesty Mary had received. She now occupied a sacred place in his journey to be whole. By late afternoon he was physically and mentally drained as he fought desperately to keep from breaking down into a flood of emotional release. Karen knew intuitively of the pain and toll of the nakedness. She looked him in the eyes, hugged him and told him to let it go. The gates opened and he did. The torrent of emotional swirling was protected and soothed by Karen's warm, compassionate embrace of understanding. Her loving touch proved relief from rejection. Karen's healing acceptance instantly became the blanket of insulation against the cold dark clouds of doom. The need for fight or flight now gone, her demand had set him free. He noticed how light his heart felt from letting her in. He felt the weight lift from the shoulders. He felt someone close, just like he had felt with Mary. They parted at dusk and he quietly lifted up thanks to the energy of Grace traveling through this new friend in healing. Where the road led from here he didn't know; he was just glad to be on it with a friend who could help drive, a by-your-side-through-thick-or-thin friend which was now Karen too. Isn't that the concept of Angels he wondered? Gift number…? This was a record playing that wasn't broken. The experience left a profound feeling of change to come soon. So back to work he went, waiting for that ride to unfold.

The interior refinishing contract came off as planned for the Anniversary House. Frank spent two 12-hour days at the end of a paint gun, priming and painting the finished product. By the time the Ice Cream Social rolled around the interior looked magnificent. The House was a home again, the job that had been done was praised by all who attended.

Praise was also heaped on the Chumash at the other end of the Park. The outstanding efforts on the expanding village along with the program of ceremonial drumming, dancing and singing done in traditional costumes left folks in awe of what had been accomplished. Karen took photographs to document the event. Her presence alone was testament to the power of truth. That truth had been forced to Frank's defense by the cancerous innuendo of the "sex offender" tagging. It was something he had done, not who he was now. Based on results Karen had found that to be true.

The success of that year's Social triggered inquiry about another aspect of Park operations. One of the Meherin descendants, Sue Enny, called Frank to ask about school field trips. That was a goal that the Friends wanted to fulfill. All along in the development of the Park's plan it had been stated that the purpose of the Park "was to be a resource of learning for the community and tourist alike." School field trips the board envisioned could become a common occurrence. Providing history from where it happened was a terrific resource, which the schools could be encouraged to take full advantage. After all, the Park was practically in many of the local schools' backyards. No long bus trips for Chumash history. Best of all it was offered free, donations accepted. He jumped at the chance to provide that service. That's what Presidents do.

Sue thought to bring 20 or so students down for an hour or two to see the village. Belleview Santa Fe Charter School's 3rd and 4th graders were to be studying the native culture and the Sa' Pismu village was a great place to see real structures that the Chumash had utilized in their Pre-Spanish daily lives. Frank agreed, adding the Chumash may want to provide some exhibits. He might be lucky enough to have some of the Chumash attend; he'd check.

He immediately called Grandmother Smith. Within days the whole tribe was on board and the outing for the students was turning into a full-blown event. Tribal members excited to show off their culture expanded the field trip into a four-hour learning experience. Frank phoned Sue back a week later telling her to plan on packing the kids lunches; they were in for a treat. Sue was ecstatic. A date was put on the calendar with an alternate in case of rain. The wheels were in motion for the first school field trip hosted by Price House.

Two weeks to prepare and the day of the event was absolutely perfect. Bright, sunny and warm, as students, teachers and chaperones were dropped off at the Frady Lane gate. Now he had given a lot of private tours in the past, but this was by far the largest group to be served and he was grateful Karen was along to help. Once the drivers had deposited their cars out at the House and hiked back, the adventure began. First order of business, a head count then group photo at the entrance sign. The group then dropped down the dirt road, the hoard of shuffling feet raising the dust. They stopped briefly to admire the huge mural of early Chumash life painted on the Railroad's creek crossing bridge cement abutment by tribal member Jackie Rawhoof.

As the dust settled he and Karen pointed out the copious amounts of Poison Oak and Stinging Nettles that lined the road, encouraging all to stick to the path, hoping to maintain some sort of control over the energy that drives youth. He also reminded them that if they wished to see wildlife they should travel a bit more quietly. Yeah right! Traversing in a cloud of dust that reminded him of the 'Peanuts' cartoon character Pig Pen in motion, he narrated history of the Portola expeditions, Mission Friars and De Anza settlers who had all passed though Price Canyon. Karen narrated plant life identification. They both kept a close eye on the stragglers and those that wanted to race ahead.

Arriving at the backside of the village just beyond the dry wash and trees, the group was gathered for a head count. All present and accounted for, the mass was pushed forward by the over anxious as they strained for a glimpse of the 'Indians' just beyond the thicket of willow. He managed to stop the surge, pointing out the Red Hand print that glared from the piece of wood it had been impressed upon that hung from a tree limb above the small path leading through the creek bed's overgrowth. The vivid image brought a halt to spasmodic surging; ears were ready to hear what the ominous graphic meant. He and Karen explained that the symbol was used at this site to let the visitor know that they were about to enter sacred land and that their utmost respect should be shown at all times. This was sacred ground.

That was the ticket. The now quiet group of kids listened to instruction, rafting up two by two to file down the narrows and up the bank into the village. The smoke of the ceremonial fire wafted close to the ground as they began to emerge from the tree line, the drums of the Sa' Pismu beating welcome. The silent, awe-struck students were led to the edge of the ceremonial circle defined by a rock perimeter, filled with Chumash dressed in all manner of colorful attire. Frank again asked for respect of the land and its people, then introduced Cheyenne, the Sa' Pismu tribe's medicine man, and one of their spiritual leaders. The show then relinquished to Cheyenne.

Cheyenne took control of the transfixed crowd of youngsters. Skins and a bone breastplate with feathers adorned his dark-skinned body. Two long black ponytails flowing from under the Coyote fur bonnet atop his head made him an imposing figure. He approached the edge of the circle to face the mesmerized onlookers, raised his head and hands skyward, proclaiming,

"Oh Great Spirit welcome our guests, be here with us!"

"Help our friends know our ways."

"Let us all respect this place and enjoy our day together."

Followed by a welcome in native tongue, Cheyenne then motioned for all to enter the circle, offering the massive tree trunk along the west edge for them to sit. He performed a cleansing and blessing of the guests with the pungent smell of smoldering Grandfather Sage wafted with Eagle feathers. More words of welcome offered as the cadence of the beating drum echoed a special welcome of its own. Cheyenne had the attention of everyone.

Cheyenne introduced the rest of the tribe. Frank actually felt the oxygen get sucked out of the circle by all the little lungs that gulped for breath as the massive Ho Chi Chio stood for introduction. Frank later heard one of boys telling another that Ho Chi Chio was the "biggest damn Indian he had ever seen!" Cheyenne told a tale or two of Chumash lore, and then retired to drum for the Chumash chants sung by the women. The women's voices filled the air with mystifying harmonies sung in native tongue, followed by traditional dances celebrating native belief. The large group of youngsters sat spellbound. Not one broke total concentration at what was unfolding before them. They listened intently as the rules of the village were explained and the areas of different activities were pointed out. With that done Cheyenne turned to Frank for further instructions. Frank gave the boundaries of the village compound as boundaries for their explorations. He reiterated the special kindness of the Chumash peoples for allowing them this special visit, asked for and received resounding applause as a sign of their thanks. He reminded them of the respect expected then announced, "Go ahead have a ball."

Momentary hesitation was followed by uncontrolled chaos. The kids ejected from the circle, punctuated by squeals of delight as they found the unrestrained hands-on exploration almost unbelievable. The hardest thing for their racing little minds to do was to decide on what to see or do first. Grinding acorns with a real mortar and pestle or painting Chumash symbols on shells they could take home. Maybe try drumming or watch the women weave baskets, then try for themselves. One stop for all at some point: Ho Chi Chio's fry bread was the big delight. They roamed in droves through the Apt and Smokehouse, soaking up the experience; when a head count was called for prior to lunch, all heads were present and accounted for.

After the lunch bags were distributed the kids were again cut loose to dine anywhere in the village they wanted. Frank noticed something rather interesting during the lunch break. For the most part the girls ate in the Apt and the boys inhaled theirs in the Smokehouse. Funny how the old rules still seemed to apply. The half hour passed quickly with another head count called, then all headed off for some Price family history, with hands-on showing of FOPH's most treasured artifacts. Teachers couldn't believe Frank passed around the stone medicine bowls, grinding bowls, arrowhead, and John Price's watch bob for the kids to handle. He had no worries; he knew the kids were operating from respect. He had reminded them of that respect before entering the House. When the call was issued for the return of the artifacts, they were returned promptly, intact and with respect. It was pretty simple to him; if you issue respect it will be returned. It was returned abundantly, much to the astonishment of most of the adults.

The tours of the Price and Meherin Houses were followed by rambunctious, independent exploration of the farm grounds. When the head count was called for, all the heads were there. Then back to the village for closing ceremonies by Cheyenne and a closing prayer of thanks to the Great Spirit from Grandmother Smith. The kids thanked the tribe for having them and showing the teachings of the old ways. A final head count with perfect attendance. Teachers and chaperoning parents commented on how well the children had behaved on the four-hour trip, they hadn't lost one of them. They were so impressed that all adults in attendance agreed it was the best field trip that they had ever been on. The kids later wrote FOPH thank you letters confirming the same. No bumps, bruises, lacerations, Poison Oak or Stinging Nettles and all were on their way home with heads full of stories of the day they had spent with the Chumash. Karen and Frank agreed it was a smashing day for the Park.

The first school field trip to the Price Historical Park was a resounding success. Many of the kids returned on open Sundays with parents in tow. Parents commented they had no idea such a wonderful resource was sitting so close, yet felt so far away. Frank added the return tease, "Just wait till you see it when the Park is done." He was proud, but he knew the Chumash stole the show. At the next board meeting and in a story he crafted for the newsletter, he thanked the Chumash lavishly for their unselfish efforts.

Praising words of the event brought additional inquiries from other schools. The Price House was now an operating public service like it had been envisioned. All the volunteers could be proud of what they had created. The part Frank liked the most was the fact that it was all FREE, a novel concept that was working in the 21st century where everything had a price. The only price at the Park was in the name. "How cool was that," he thought.

Another very cool thing was happening for Frank. His daughter Elise was growing up! Right before his very eyes the wild teenager who didn't seem to listen was beginning to make some important decisions, the greatest of which, at least for him, was her deciding it was time to move out and try life on her own. Finally some peace and quiet with continuity of sleep maintained throughout the night. To imagine sleeping soundly again on Friday and Saturday nights seemed like a foreign, long-forgotten practice. Those two nights of the week in the past had produced the wee hour of the morning phone calls

that jolt you awake with the most unpleasant news. Like the one in which the
ex-wife explains,

"Well they'll have to stitch up the lesion in the abdomen and she's lost a
lot of blood, but she'll be okay." That was the partying and rough-housing
on the beach night 'till 2am at barely 17. Or the ex-wife announcing,

"Well she rolled the Jetta on the freeway, but she and Sabrina will be
okay." How that one happened still isn't quite clear. Or the call from a Hotel's
manager expounding into his answering machine,

"Well Mr. Lindsay I'm just calling to inform you that the room damages
in your daughters room will be charged to you." That was the one where
Elise rented a suite for her 18th birthday and had 150 of her closest friends
show up to party. Pismo PD had to break that one up. He never did figure out
how she managed to rent the room without a credit card or ID showing
acceptable age requirements. Or the ex-wife again saying,

"Well Elise was hit from the rear when the other car rolled, but she'll be
okay." In that episode she was lucky the CHP didn't cite her for racing. The
kid seemed to have a gift for walking away from some pretty serious stuff.
The scars she wore on her face from the first accident at 14 reminded him
daily to be grateful she was still alive. Some strange power was working overtime watching out for his little girl. He thanked Grace for the interventions.

Alive and at 19 set to do very well if wise choices prevailed, the attorney
she had been paired with for her accident case had procured for her more
money than her father had ever seen. So much money that the facial scars
Elise had worn for the past five years could be attended to by the very best
surgeon with a large amount of money left over. So much money that the
amount scared him, thinking it was way too much for a teenager to have. At
18 the settlement was all hers; the parents could only counsel caution. By
Grace some of that stuck.

Wisely Elise used some of the funds to have some facial scars worked on
and the droop in her right eye socket fixed. By Grace pediatric facial recon-
struction master Dr. Henry Kawamoto agreed to work his magic. Renowned
for his work at UCLA and the separation of the conjoined 'Guatemalan
Twins,' Elise was lucky to have his gracious gentle wisdom at work for her.
Dr. Kawamoto's hand restored Elise's beauty, which in turn began to heal her
esteem of self.

Wisely, she bought a new car, financing a small portion to build credit.
She secured a cash-backed credit card and began to learn the pros and cons
behind the money industry. The ever lingering urge to splurge was fortunately
held to small fits of gluttony. Reality dwindled as clothes and shoes swelled
the closet, self esteem swelled the head. Before long it was evident to the parents that education on proper investment was the only way to curtail the dis-
appearance of the sizable chunk of money still left from the settlement. The

options were endless. It was a long hard road on the learning curve. Information poured past so fast it blurred the sense of best option, even for the grownups. The final decision rested with the newcomer to the world of adult. In the end Elise decided to buy a house. Unfortunately for that to happen Dad knew his daughter might have to live a very long distance away. By Grace his little girl was growing up, moving out to move on with her book of life. For Dad that Grace was to take him closer to his own book by testing his capacity to be alone.

Elise wanted to get out of Podunk, small-town USA and get closer to the action offered in LA. She had family all over the basin and wanted to be closer to them. Linda and Elise spent a few months shopping for a home that could do the job of substantial investing. Shopping... and they were experts. When all was said and done they had found a brand new 3 bedroom 2 bath home in Victorville, CA. So much for getting out of small-town. At least Linda's sister Ann lived in the area. The location was high desert, just on the other side of the San Andreas Fault from the LA megalopolis. The huge down payment required put most of the cash in a safe place. Dad was impressed with Daughter's decision. With all the volatility in other investment possibilities they had considered, Elise had made a good choice. Housing seemed to always be going up in California. Dad didn't believe that trend was sustainable, but the price was decent at the time for this tangible asset.

The move was made in May. Frank did his usual Dad thing of planning, packing, driving the truck. Unloading all of his daughter's worldly possessions and putting stuff together was all part of being Dad. Then came the part he had not thought about. As Dad and Daughter drove down the Cajon pass to rendezvous with Dad's ride home, the fact that he would not be seeing his daughter for a while really hit hard. She had lived with him for nine years; now she wasn't. It may not have been pleasant at times, but at least there was daily contact. Now there was to be none. As they reached the bottom of the hill to meet up with Cindy and Sabrina, his ride back to Grover, he realized he was going to have to say goodbye to his baby girl, returning to an empty house! That had not crossed his mind until that moment.

The small talk turned serious as they parked, Dad adding "now all you have to do is get a job" to break the building tension with a little humor. Cindy and Sabrina pulled up and it was time to go. Elise's eyes filled with tears as she handed her dad a card, carefully penned and sealed the night before. Dad hugged the apple of his eye, telling her they were only a phone call apart, saying that was meant for solace, his as much as hers. He patted her gently on the back as they hugged, like they hadn't hugged in a long, long time. Dad kissed her on the forehead, telling her "everything will be fine," he'd see her as soon as he could. Elise knew that meant it wasn't to be for a considerable amount of time.

Closing the door to Cindy's car he looked back at Elise sitting in the driver's seat of hers, knowing it was going to be awhile before seeing her again as well. He waved. She waved and Cindy drove away. His eyes began to well; he couldn't let his daughter see. Silently the moisture collected and fell onto the envelope he clutched in his hands. He hadn't felt like this since the day she had left with her mother so many years before. It was an hour before he could open and read the card, the tears fell again. The emotion surprised him.

He didn't talk much on the four-hour ride home. Arriving at the house, he almost didn't want to go inside. He was already feeling the emptiness. He really didn't understand it. Silence greeted him as he walked through the door. No more "Hi Dad" or "Bye Dad." No more Sunday morning breakfasts. No more late night phone calls. Empty hole was a new emotion he had experienced in his rush of life. Welcome to the next level.

Half full, or half empty? Life's purpose seemed to be draining away. Life's bucket had a hole in the bottom and the fluids of purpose were leaking out. The invitation to Hana and Jerry's wedding only took the bucket's level down even further. The invitation was just another reminder of dwindling purpose. His personal vow to look after his close friend was now being passed to Jerry. He had fulfilled that purpose to the best of his ability and was rewarded with understanding the value of 'free' when you love. Frank called Hana and left a voice mail message of congratulations.

Hana returned the call a few days later and they talked in depth about the recovery of their relationship. The tone of confidence in her voice provided him an assurance in Jerry's ability to provide Hana peace. They talked about the kids. They talked about Hana's health. Hana revealed she had told Troy about her condition and Frank asked if it was okay if he told Elise. Hana approved. They talked of future communication, both vowing to stay in touch. He was grateful 'What if' never arose. He ended his communication with his customary closing,

"Remember Hana Joi I love you." In the back of his mind he hoped it wasn't the last time he'd be able to tell her that, yet he knew it could be awhile before he could tell her again. Hana responded before hanging up, "I know Fraunk."

He hung up the phone knowing life was getting a little smaller. A little less responsibility, a little safer from the storm the dark clouds of his past were sure to bring if Jerry had not taken his place. Hana's gentle prodding about that past had been fended off in that last conversation. He now hoped the question would fade into unimportance as her life moved forward. Life was moving forward and full for her, backward and empty for him. He longed to stop the slide.

Voids created by such changes are sometimes filled by unexpected opportunity. Opportunity he could definitely use. Elise had been mystified by Dad's relationship with Hana. He had never been able to reveal the whole story, sworn to secrecy by Hana in regards to the HIV issue, now he wasn't. Because Troy now knew, Elise could also. Now Dad could heart-to-heart with his daughter and tie a lot of loose ends together. His intention was to explain the tremendous value he had found in giving to someone in need, no strings attached.

A few months after her big move Elise came up for a visit, Dad took the opportunity to share his experience of the journey with Hana. The Grace part he wasn't sure she was ready to comprehend. Shoot, he didn't fully comprehend. Elise arrived with a whirlwind of plans to visit friends, Dad asked for a few of her precious minutes before she disappeared again. Dad offered to make a couple of Diet Cokes to sip while they talked.

"What's up now, Dad?" she questioned, expecting Dad-like invasions into her personal goings on.

"Well I'd like to talk to you about Hana," he offered.

"Why, is something wrong?" she questioned with concern.

"No, no, no, I just what to fill you in on a few details," suggesting they sit in the living room while they chat.

Bright sunlight streamed in the west-facing windows, warming the room and mood. Frank sat on the couch and Elise in the armchair, kitty-corner to his seating. Dad leaned forward, looking his daughter in the eye, ready to tell what he had needed to say for a long time.

"I want to fill you in on why I've done what I've done for Hana and Troy over the years. It's not exactly what it may have seemed at the time, there is a lot more to it and now I can tell you. Hana has told Troy and now I feel it is appropriate to inform you."

Over the next hour Dad unveiled Hana's journey with HIV and his commitment to never leave a friend in need. He told of learning valuable lessons regarding 'giving with no strings attached,' of how he was sorry about not lavishing his daughter with gifts of wealth she might have expected, how maybe the paltry existence they had lived really provided good lessons, reminding her that his gifts from her grandmother's passing were shared in beautiful trips that created memories all could embrace. What had been done for Hana and Troy had been done through Grace that somehow had spoken to his heart, saying "it was the right thing to do." How he loved Hana from the bottom of his heart, and she him, "It went way back." How he and Hana had decided not to interrupt the relationships the kids had with their other parents, opting not to move in together. Elise got it all. Except for the childhood traumas Hana had suffered. That was a subject he didn't go into. That dog of doom was his and hers to live with.

The daughter sat in transformation, many of the questions she had regarding the 'whys' had become clearer. The truth had given Elise a whole new insight into her dad's personality. Maybe he wasn't the miserly scrooge she had previously concluded, dad who didn't really date nor has much of a social life. He had saved it to give it away to help a friend, not really expecting anything in return. The daughter caught a glimpse of how really, really deep love can go. And from all places it had come through her dad. Grace that had begun to rebuild the father/daughter bond and now was lifted to a whole new place. Frank could see Elise's eyes soften with understanding compassion as Dad ended with the news of Hana's wedding to Jerry. Elise sensed Dad's void and hugged him hard before departing. Dad welcomed the renewed connection that filled the void Dad and Daughter had been missing the past few years. The timing was perfect, even if they only had a moment together to enjoy it before Elise returned south to her home.

Frank wasn't quite cognizant of all voids that needed to be filled. Some were just there and went unnoticed. Being thanked for your efforts always makes you feel good. That's why he enjoyed working with Lenny. He always left Lenny's knowing his effort was appreciated. He enjoyed, as everyone does, a really big heart-felt thanks. When the 'thanks' surprises you is when the 'thanks' are really sweet. Surprise usually means the person saying it really feels you have gone all out to make something happen. It usually means you loved what you were doing, not expecting return. 'Thanks' can then catch you by surprise 'Thanks' is a great stroke for the self. A self image that is stroked gently occasionally is healthy. Healthy mind and healthy body are hand in hand and healthy is good. Lenny's place was a healthy place as his 'thanks' kept Frank from growing too old too fast.

'Thanks for the help' did manifest in other ways. To say Frank was surprised when Shane called to inform him that Nightlife had been accepted into the New York Independent Film and Video Festival would have been understated feeling. His surprise included a heap of thanks that the kids had succeeded. He always felt they would. His participation had been part of their success and that was thanks he could feel.

The post crew had spent a year cleaning and reconstructing the rough cut. It was good enough to have been accepted into Festival contention. A showing was to be held at the Laemmle Cinema in Hollywood, and Shane invited him to attend. Shane was pumped about the polished product, Frank agreed enthusiastically he would be there. He called Elise to share the good news. The movie Dad had worked so hard on was actually going to be shown on a theater screen in Hollywood. Dad was excited. Elise wasn't quite as jacked up as Dad about seeing it again. She had really panned the first cut she had viewed at the 'Premier'. The lighting was bad, the special effects needed work, and there were scenes that just didn't work and so on .... She finally agreed to meet Dad at Mary's in Burbank and go when Dad offered to buy her ticket. On the night of the showing Elise showed up at Mary's with her friend Lauren, Dad discovered he had to buy two tickets. Of course he'd agree, he hadn't seen his daughter in a few months.

Elise was in a state of delight as the three traversed their way to the theater. She was real happy to see her Dad again, it had been awhile. Dad was happy even if it was only a few hours to visit. It had been a year since the three had attended the first showing, and they joked apprehensively about the quality of the version they were about to view. The chance for "Nightlife" to win anything was slim at best, they agreed, yet it deserved a second look just for fun. When they arrived there were but a few bodies milling about on the sidewalk in front of the theater. It was a much different scene from the mob-like crowd on 'Premier' night. They were early and Frank speculated the crowd might thicken closer to show time, or at least he entertained that hope. Ten minutes to show time the crowd had grown only minimally.

Many of the cast and crew did show. Nightlife was to be shown second in a block of three films. Even with the other two films' cast, crew and friends in attendance, only about a third of the theater filled. Looking at the bright side, Frank mused that a small crowd equaled better seats. They settled in for what they hoped wouldn't be an ordeal.

Lights dimmed and Dad shared popcorn with his daughter. First film up was a 15-minute short film called "The Next" and it was great! A power packed, fast moving, brain bending quality piece that garnered generous applause. The bar had been set and as "Nightlife" flickered onto the screen Frank was thinking, "This better be good." And it was! The lighting was great! The re-edit was great! The special effects worked! It was a whole new experience; even Elise jumped at a couple of intense scenes. The dream scene caught Frank by total surprise. Lauren too admitted to being entertained. Not perfect, yet still a hell of an effort.

Frank's surprise stoke came as the final scene faded to black and the credits started to roll. Written by, Directed by, Produced by appeared in a succession of acknowledgments as the audience gave up a hearty round of applause. The last one, Produced by riveted Frank back into his seat. On the blackened background of the immense screen, burned white lettering, at least three feet tall, listing the names of those that had helped produce the movie. His name was listed first! He had forgotten all about being considered a 'producer' by the kids. For him it was quite astounding to think, "Here he sat in a Hollywood theater and his name was on the screen as a producer. Only in your wildest dreams," he thought as he sat stunned. What a great way for the kids to say thanks; it really made him feel good. Elise was impressed too! As he drove back to Grover that night he felt the ego stir with a little pride. Now he had a good story to tell the grandkids some day, with a movie to prove it.

The fullness he received from the kids' respect gave him an uplifting bounce for days. Just enough uplift energy to get him through the emptiness of retiring the Clam Family the following weekend. Ten years of Clam Family participation was difficult to say goodbye to. Self esteem faded as life shrank a little further. The dog of doom was never far behind. Twenty years without a drink did prevail. Time at his empty house marched on.

Unexpectedly the void in household bustle filled in mid fall. Another friend in need was to break the silence of the humble abode on North 16th Street. The mundane existence Frank led in the house he only occupied exploded to life when Cindy and her daughter Sabrina moved in. Cindy had lived with him before when she and her boyfriend had broken up. That was the summer Elise had spent at her mother's house recouping from her scarring auto accident. Cindy and her daughter had again been forced to move out, after troubled times with the same boyfriend. Cindy came to Frank as a last resort, but she was desperate to find shelter from her storm. Frank was happy to be of help despite the "What if" that plagued; he looked forward to having the company. He offered his room to Cindy and he'd take the couch. Cindy took the couch.

The Beach House sprang back to life with daily hustle. Frank had to be up early to use the can before the two girls monopolized the one bathroom they all shared. It was the perfect filler for the void of family. Frequent dinners and conversations ended the days of his silent solitary supping accompanied by only the drone of the TV set. The two new dogs that came with the deal livened up the lives of the two cats. Though small dogs, they had a ball harassing the cats with spirited 2 on 1 chases into the street or up a tree. By late fall the three-pound Yorky (Tiger) and the six pound Silky (Lilly) ushered in a litter of puppies that had been conceived the moment the humans dropped their guarded vigilance against the nasty dance of procreation. Damn that Tiger was a fast little fuck!

The household dynamic was well established by the time the holidays rolled around. The blending of daily activities was working well. Frank taught Sabrina the fine art of parallel parking so she could pass her driving test. Cindy taught Frank a thing or two about cooking. It was a pretty tight little group complete with dogs and puppies. The dark void that could have been hanging around in Frank's head that year end wasn't. Cindy's talented yet stern hand in many things and her sense of humor made sure of that. She ruled with a gentle fist. That was a New Year to remember and is a whole story in itself. And the puppies simply stole everyone's heart. Puppies tend to do that to us all.

~~~~

We are all creating the depth at which we want the journey of our string to weave into the tapestry. The deeper we go the more connection made to the other string weaving with us, the more color co-created. The string we follow is no different. His voids encountered in the fabric of life forded by expanded connection, keeping his color from fading as portions of life shrank. This part of the chronicle details the depth we create from when we are unwilling to live less than full, and the abundant color created when we live to our fullest.

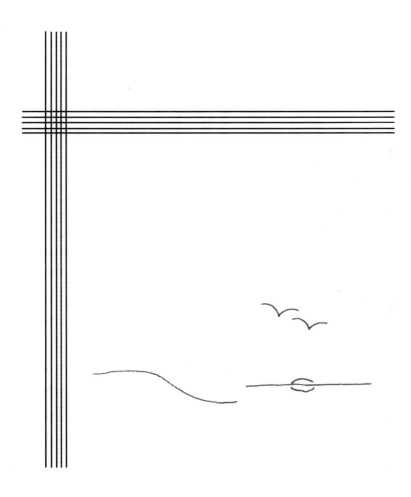

CHAPTER 31

REALLY REALLY FREE

Registration time was sobering after coming off the high of a New Year's celebration of fullness. Morphing Megan's Law now had new restrictions to sign off on. 'Sex offenders' now could not possess any pictures of children. What! Did that mean he was supposed to throw away all of his photos of his daughter? That thought just pissed him off! What next, banned from the beach? The slow erosion of rights was depressing. He tried to stay positive through the stink of ink and jail cells. The camera didn't work that year and Cheryl said she wasn't worried about it. At least that lightened the anger load a bit. He thought about calling his attorney, but figured 'what's the use'. That call might anger him more. No contact from Ann meant nothing had changed; that wasn't positive, so why bother. To him there was more important stuff to do than to be mired in the spin of the negative world. Thank God for other stuff, keeping the skip of the record from breaking the momentum of the spiritual journey.

The Friends of Price House scored big with some major funding from outgoing County Supervisor Peg Pinard. Peg had been a big fan of the Price House efforts during her tenure as County Supervisor. Every couple of years she'd call Frank, suggesting FOPH submit a grant fund request for any given project. Once reviewed and approved by the Board of Supervisors a few thousand dollars of grant funding was awarded from her discretionary funds. Her last funding in office she awarded FOPH with ten thousand dollars. That was a lot of money. The FOPH board knew just where to spend it.

Ever since the Meherin House had been moved to the park, roof replacement was high priority. Glen and Frank had managed to stop the roof leaks, but that was only a temporary fix. Frank didn't particularly care for crawling out onto the 10/12 pitched roof with rope and harness. He and Glen spent hours each year tending to the ravages Mother Nature inflicted on the aging roof shingles. He did get some great pictures of the Park from that perspective. However, the re-roofing was an activity that he was all too willing to pay some one else to do. Peg's award made that possible. He was all to glad too seek the bids; in between the winter rains.

Just like all the other projects he had done at the Park property, on time and under budget was the goal. A steady stream of contractors flowed to the Park site through February, by the March Board meeting Frank had a contract to sign. The price was fair and the guarantee would expire long after he did. The job was scheduled to start August 1st to avoid any chance of rain. Thanks to Peg, one of Glen and Frank's biggest headaches cured. The Meherin House was getting a new roof.

March started off with great energy, the flow of work followed suit, as well as a spot of good press. A 'check presentation' photograph was taken at the Price House and run in the local paper. The new county Supervisor, Jerry Lenthal, and neighboring Supervisor, Katcho Achadjian, handed off the 3ft long $10,000.00 check to FOPH Vice President Les Splear. Frank took the photo, opting to stay out of the lime light just in case. Karen represented the volunteer contingent of FOPH as well as adding some beauty to the picture.

This unfortunately was to be one of the last things Karen did with the Price House. She was leaving the area in May to return to Washington State to pursue her dream. After the PR shoot the two shared dinner and Frank shared he was sorry to see her go. She in her own way was sorry to be leaving, sharing she'd miss the laughter they had roared with together in their unique relationship. She'd miss the Price House experience they challenged and lived to laugh about.

Lenny's project was consistently moving forward challenging the mind too. Electrical, sewer, and grey water systems were almost complete, and drywall was scheduled for May. The daily visits to Lenny's gave him an opportunity to work mind and body as he tackled Lenny's unique visions. Hand trenching through Calichy rock worked the body. Creating cabinets out of dead spaces worked the mind. Layout for a concrete patio, sidewalks and carport worked both. He enjoyed the working friendship he and Lenny shared. The experience was like being on break time all the time, a very casual and creative atmosphere.

Genesis Water was flowing well. Word of mouth kept the account base slowly growing, equipment sales managed to keep him ahead of demands produced by the billing wave. An occasional call from Greg for concrete or framing side work helped start a small savings. Greg's friendship and praise of Frank's work was always a boost to self-esteem. The almost nightly media blitz in the 'hunt for the predator' continued to work in the opposite direction. Life was beginning to feel full again, yet tense at the same time. The media made sure of that.

Then Hana called. Frank answered the phone to hear,

"Hello Fraunk" and his pulse jumped.

Not because he was thrilled to hear from her, he was. No, it was the split-second fear of 'What If' crashing his brain. He could see his heart beat in his wrist. Had Hana found out? She was a master on the computer, had she been encouraged by the media to search the Megan's Law web site? It all ran through so fast it made him a little dizzy. He did his best to hide the fear, responding with a robust upbeat,

"Hana Lisa Joi it's about time. It's good to hear from you. What's up?"

He didn't know why he was so apprehensive about the call. Why when they spoke was his brain leading him straight to fear, as opposed to the pure joy of the contact? He tried to dispel the feeling, but the gut still wrenched.

"Oh just thought I'd call and catch up, it's been awhile," she responded, a bit evasive.

The response seemed to be genuine, yet had a hint of another agenda that needed its curiosities satisfied. He was tense. He tried to let that feeling go as they traversed only the surface of the catch up subjects, 'what have you been up to/how are the kids'. Then Hana shot from the hip.

"Ya know Fraunk I've been thinking about that thing in your past that you didn't want to talk about.... I'd really like to talk about it."

"I don't think that you could have done anything that could really shock me," she tried to offer in reassurance.

"I mean come on! What could you have done that is so bad.... kill someone?" she coyly coaxed, setting the bar of tolerance very high.

BANG!!!!! Brain on overload straight to grey numb. The bar of tolerance set at death, was to him one notch short of what was to be needed to afford forgiveness of his past. He much preferred to have curtailed conversation with Hana than go any further. He hated that knee-jerk response. He cursed the moment he had opened that door with her. Now he was in flight mode, not wishing to face the potential loss of his friend to a bar set at the next level. That was just going to have to wait and he responded abruptly,

"No, Hana, this is not a conversation I want to have over the phone! Please, I'd much rather it be face-to-face someday." His tone was stern.

With a last attempt at gentle persuasion Hana pried,

"Oh come on, I'm pretty understanding you know."

Frank had to deny her and end the phone contact abruptly.

"No Hana I can't. Not now ...Please!" he pleaded. He hated doing that.

"Okay." She relented again.

"We will do this sometime though!" she promised.

They parted with good-byes only. He again cursed that moment he had opened that insidious door. Sitting numb, pulse still racing, he knew he had dodged the inevitable bullet again. But the ability to continue that trend in the future was looking pretty dim.

Thus the dis-ease of grey skies produced a retraction into self and defense of all that was held important. He didn't want to lose Hana's friendship. He didn't feel he had much left to hold on to at times like these. He so wanted out of the crashing negative waves of bad energy. He so yearned for the calm, favorable breeze of peace.

It is said "The winds of Grace are always blowing... but it is you who must raise the sail." He thought he had set the main sail to embrace the fullness of the right winds. Being blown so far off his intended course made him wonder just what wind was filling the sail. The driving gale of what seems to be an evil wind leaves you lost, muddling about looking for answers. You are blown to the edge of destruction, you tack hard to avoid going over, and you see you are making no headway against the tide, yet you continue to try in a vain attempt knowing deep down the tide might win. You know at some point you will have to release the main sail and let it go. You'd just like to be sure that when you do let go, the wind will blow you to the right place. It seems that the ill wind never brings you close to the right place to release. The lunch time call from detective Cheryl put Frank right there, in the right place to release. April had started out well; it wasn't going to end well.

Cheryl was asking Frank to come down to the police station. She explained she had received an inquiry from Pismo PD in regards to his status as a 'sex offender'. Pismo was following up on an inquiry from a concerned citizen, who discovered Frank's profile on the Megan's Law web site, questioning his involvement at the Price House. This now had prompted an investigation. Cheryl had referred to it as an interview. They should meet right away, she insisted; the following morning was good. Frank said he'd be there.

Now began a journey of darkness and evil toward the edge of the abyss. The overnight hours marked with relentlessly rude dreams. Awakening repeatedly disturbed rest. Relentlessly the negative energy interrupted like the pull of addiction. The unknown drained him. He swallowed two aspirin before leaving the next morning, one for the headache, one for the heart, just in case. When he arrived he was a ball of inflamed nerves ready to explode.

Cheryl opened the steel security entry door and ushered him down the hall into a small, dank interview room. A Pismo PD officer was already seated, waiting. Cheryl shut the door, offered Frank a seat on the opposite side of the table, took hers and the odyssey began. Information flowed as follows: Pismo PD received a call from one of the Pismu tribal members. She had come across his picture plus credentials on the Megan's web site and questioned if he was safe to be around the Park. She knew he had been a guide for a school field trip and expressed her concerns. Because Pismo was not his city of registration the inquiries were referred to Grover. This triggered an investigation by Grover PD and an additional internal Pismo PD investigation to determine threat potential of having Frank involved with a 'City Project'. If somebody sued, might they be liable? The joint PD interview was being conducted to determine appropriate action. The tag of "Dangerous Sex Offender" had done its job.

The 'interview' lasted for an hour. Pismo PD ultimately demanded that Frank stay out of the Price House Park pending further investigation. A final determination would be delivered to the Price House Board of Directors at their next meeting in May. Cheryl suggested that he might want to call his attorney. Life was turned upside down. 'What If' was 'What Now' big time!

The threat from Pismo PD of posting his 'Wanted' poster at the park if he went out to the park almost made him vomit. Twenty six years after his failure he was nothing more than a criminal, the past fourteen years with the Price House meant nothing. Results didn't matter. Life hit a brick wall of evil wind that blew him at will toward the edge of the abyss. The depressing grey of shock had set in hard. 'What Now' kept being answered by 'I Don't Know'. It took days of soul searching for him to discover any answers. Those answers tore at the few strings of sanity he had left.

When looking for the best way to tackle a problem, he had found the solution that makes the most sense, tackle the one that was last on the list of preferred courses of action, last because it was the hardest. Working the solution tests you, and by Grace you can only hope you survive your task. He recognized his day of reckoning had come and the honorable way to deal with it, to inform the folks he called friends. It was only right that they not be blindsided by the cancer that was growing on him. He'd leave his future with the Price House, and the rest of his life for that matter, in the hands of the folks he didn't want to hurt. He knew not where those winds could blow. He was prepared for the worst. Alone was becoming preferred.

Frank began with Glen Ray, the former NASA-hydraulic-engineer-now-reverted-hippy and a sage of sorts to him. Their ten year friendship was tight. Glen was a board member, his thoughts were crucial to how Frank was to approach the rest of the board and Pismu tribal council. This was his walk into fire and Glen's reaction could be most insightful. He called Glen to select a time to meet.

Frank was early. While he waited for Glen he wandered around the Price House thinking about the projects he might not get done. If he was asked to step aside would any of it get done? Was Glen prepared to take over watering the trees, mowing the grass, not to mention all the woodworking projects underway? Glen already had a bevy of projects of his own to handle. Could he handle it all? This was a nightmare waiting to unfold. Pretty much all onsite activity by Frank had to be curtailed under the threat of 'posting' which could jeopardize FOPH's position of respect within the community, a position he had a big hand in building. Feeling the sick twisted road of life had him asking, "Who was writing this part"?

Up in smoke again, first his business, then the Clams and now the Price House. Life was being eaten away by the cancerous accusation of "Dangerous". The downsizing of life was coming to the point of looking for something to do so as not to dwell on loss. Dangerously close to the edge. Dangerously close to wanting a drink. Dangerously close to accepting the final end.

He heard the latch on the pedestrian gate, looked out the parlor window, and saw Glen riding down the wood chip path to the house. "Here we go," he thought, trying to shake the fog of fright from his brain. He met Glen at the trailer and they exchanged greetings. Glen could tell something was wrong and asked. Frank said it was going take a while to explain, suggesting Glen might want to grab something to drink.

They sat together at the table in front of Glen's trailer. The sun was warm, but a chill ran up, then down, Frank's spine as he started unveiling the dark past that was now coming back to haunt him. He laid out the event of his failure and time frame as it had unfolded, leaving out only the explicit details. Glen didn't ask. He laid out the charges filed by the State that he had pled "no contest," served his time in jail, and completed probation as stipulated, to his understanding all requirements for registration should have been dismissed; the fact that he couldn't find that stipulation in writing now brought on the problem that was going to infect the Price House. He explained the web site and the problems created when one of the tribe members began asking questions, then answered all of Glen's. Their conversation lasted well after the sun had set.

Glen's reaction throughout was totally unexpected. He read the Court's Order of Dismissal; appalled at how Frank was paying a price he should not have to pay. Glen's observations based, on his long-time contact with Frank. There had been nothing he could recall that even remotely suggested any truth to the current accusation. Glen offered to help any way he could, to defend and disarm untruths. He asked Frank if he needed money for an attorney. Glen's loyalty to Frank's character lifted his spirits. Glen expanded to suggest Frank meet with tribal council first. Frank agreed, and Glen said he'd make the calls to set a date and time. By this point Glen needed a glass of wine. Frank, too, but he didn't. They did share a pipe; intensity of the conversation demanded it.

Glen hugged Frank before they parted just to let him know he wasn't alone. Frank almost lost it as emotion swelled. He felt the same relief of burden he had felt when Karen had hugged him. The warmth of relief brought a tight throat and mist to his eyes as he left. By the time he reached home Glen had already called, leaving a message to say that like wild fire, word had spread and all the tribe was aware of the problem. Date and time had been set. Frank inked in Friday 12 noon on his calendar and tried not to think about drink. By Grace he went to bed sober.

Friday came, they always do. As he turned down Frady Lane he wondered who might show up, tense uncertainty rattled around in his brain. How was he to approach telling a group of his friends that because of his past they now had his participation in his passion in their hands? He felt numb in his hands as he reached the gate to the dirt road. Open gate meant someone was already there. No time to be alone with some time to collect his thoughts. How many pairs of eyes of potential contempt would be waiting for him as he arrived at the village? His heart beat a little faster as his truck idled slowly down the grass carpeted roadway. With the hazy daze numb buzz interrupted only by the throb of a headache coming on, he reached for a couple of aspirin.

The truck drove itself. He didn't notice the two fat Quail with brood that darted in front of his truck. Time raced in the slow motion drive down the tire worn paths, marking the roads' course in the sea of green. Nothing was clear, just fuzzy color drenched in sunlight. Reality checked in as he turned off the road into the village parking area. Six or seven cars were already parked. The two picnic tables were already full of tribe members. He parked facing away from the group, hoping to regain some composure before getting out. He noticed his hand quiver as he put his tobacco into the ashtray. He looked into the rear view mirror and saw all faces turned in his direction. The thought crossed his mind to just drive away.

He crossed his hands on the steering wheel, leaned forward, lowering his head to rest, trying to make the fog go away. A few deep breaths only made him dizzy. Raising his head, he focused again into the rear view mirror seeing Glen and Cheyenne approaching. "Here we go". "This ones yours," he said out loud to the Universe, popped the door open, and got out to meet his fate.

Glen and Frank shook hands of greeting. Cheyenne just looked at him with wise old eyes deep with sympathy and after a moment said, "Oh man," reached out and embraced him. He felt Cheyenne's sincerity in the strength of his embrace.

"Thanks for coming," Cheyenne welcomed.

"We look forward to hearing from you. Come on over." Cheyenne offered as he turned to lead the way.

No small talk, straight to business, that's best for focus, Frank tried to convince himself. As they joined the group he saw eyes of concern and eyes of anger. Grandmother Silver Bear was the only one with a smile for him. He bid hello quietly and took the seat appointed by Cheyenne. Cheyenne announced to the group he would wait a few more minutes before starting,

"More tribal members might show."

Those minutes seemed like an eternity. Frank said nothing and nothing was said to him. More cars unloaded, more members. He could only look deep into the new spring grass at his feet, wishing he could be anywhere else. Cheyenne finally stood to engage the group's attention, jolting him back to reality. The fear of 'What Now' settled somewhat as Cheyenne spoke a prayer to the Great Spirit for wisdom and understanding. Cheyenne fanned sage with Eagle feathers as he walked through the gathering, asking the Great Spirit for truthful intention in this time of trouble. He ended where Frank sat and asked him to stand. Cheyenne saged him and chanted Chumash words, stern, yet with compassion. Cheyenne turned to the group and spoke.

"Our brother has come to us with much trouble. He wishes to speak to us and ask for our council. Let us listen and give good council, Aho!" The gathering responding, "Aho!"

Frank raised his head, scanned all eyes, finding strength in those of Grandmother Silver Bear. He was grateful to find Glen's as well. He looked past the tribe to the stand of Willows that lined the creek, then back to Julie, the one who questioned. Julie's eyes had the stare that demanded his attention and that is where he began.

"It was almost thirty years ago when I was young, out of control, and I went way beyond the bounds of decency."

He spoke words of truth about the pain he had caused and his journey out of the abyss. He addressed each members gaze as he talked story and answered all questions. He apologized for the troubled spirit he had brought to the tribe from the cancer that followed him. He explained that 'it' was something he had done when he was intoxicated with youth and 'it' was not who he was now. He knew now that it was the tribe's decision on whether or not he stayed as a member of the tribe. He was emphatic that his last desire was to bring any embarrassment to the tribe or its efforts.

At Glen's suggestion Frank handed over the Court's Order of Dismissal for inspection. Some of the member's could identify with his dilemma of being told one thing, only to have something entirely different happen in dealings they too had had with the court system. The eyes that had been hardened with disgusted speculation now had softened. Other eyes had tears of compassion. That was something he had not expected to see.

Cheyenne approached, giving him two Eagle wings. He asked Frank to hold one in each hand, instructing him to raise them and his eyes to the sky. He placed his hand on Frank's shoulder and engaged the tribe.

"My people, this man has come to us with his burden and told us his truth that we feel in our hearts." Cheyenne again addressed Frank.

"Raise your hands, eyes, heart and mind with all your strength to the Great Spirit and let the burden go on the wings of the hawk."

"Oh God," was all he was to remember of the next couple of minutes as his being stretched skyward and his eyes thrust him deep into the blue of the sky. A rush of emotion enveloped him as a hawk flew into his focus of the journey. He broke. He felt the weight of his world lift from his soul. He felt light as his mind's focus came back down from the heavenly journey to its earthly attachment. The rich smell of sage fanned by Cheyenne filled his lungs with cleansing aroma. He lowered his head and hands, feeling for a place to sit as he could not see. The salt of tears blurred his vision, he shut his eyes to fend off the sting. The knees weak from the drain of emotion forced him to sit. The touch of caring hands brought him fully into the moment and he realized many had gathered around him. He opened his eyes and stood as beckoned by Cheyenne. Cheyenne embraced him with strength, expressed his sorrow for his burden and offered his support for Frank's continued leadership. Others embraced him as well.

Glen offered a petition of support. Glen had created a simple document for any to sign who agreed with its statement. Glen felt it was to be a valuable tool in Frank's quest for justice, as well as some peace from the storm. Its statement was clear, one line.

"We the undersigned do not feel that Franklin U. Lindsay is a danger to the children of our community." All of the attendees signed, even Julie. Glen was first and Karen was last. The signatures in between were all little rays of light that illuminated hope, book ended by good friends. A powerful display of support that lightened the enormous load he had been living alone.

Karen wanted to make sure her friend was okay. She knew the tremendous energy the day had taken; she felt the drain he experienced. She stayed close well into the early evening. She now had a better understanding of his response to a question she had asked weeks prior,

"What's the worst thing that can happen?"

"I'll be a target," he had responded.

That day he had been a target. The weapon that day was expressed by doubt, ridicule, hate and termination of participation in a love of his life. She had seen that day's weapon and now understood his greatest fear; the gun-toting vigilante was in fact the reality of the finality of ignorance. Karen hoped he never would have to pay that price.

Frank experienced the price of freedom is truth. As the days rolled away he was to bring that truth to dozens of close friends. Dreading each encounter one after another, he bared his truth, answered questions and apologized. Day to day he didn't know from where he might be summoned to testify next. He didn't want friends blindsided, so he flowed with the intent to protect those friends. When it was right he knew. He just hoped for the best, feeling a sense of relief with each friend he saved from the pain of ignorance.

The May FOPH board meeting was his next inferno to walk. Putting your participation in one of your life's passions in the hands of others is very humbling, especially when that passion is such a big part of your experience. Giving away any right to plead on your behalf is a stunning exercise in relinquishing self. Total surrender. Imagine saying, "you decide what you want to do with me; my desires are not part of the equation". That is literally what Frank said when he opened the FOPH monthly board meeting, introduced the Pismo Chief of Police, then sat back to watch what was to unfold.

The Chief immediately started to cast aspersions, attempting to discredit Frank's reputation. He passed around to the group the "Dangerous Sex Offender" 'wanted' poster that he threatened to post at the Park if Frank participated with the group. Dave Atson challenged, asking for clarification on participation, arguing successfully that board participation was not a violation of any current statute. The Chief tried again to shock the board into forcing Frank out by divulging the age of the victim. He used the word 'molested' freely. The Chief seemed to be looking to have a board action to remove Frank as president altogether; the board had a different view, and welcomed Frank to stay. The Chief left the meeting, demanding letters for his files regarding the extent of Frank's participation from both the Chumash council and FOPH board. The board had stood behind him and that was profound to Frank. His fire walk continued.

Finally mustering the courage to reveal your deepest darkest secrets to your closest of friends is Grace flowing. To tell his dear friend Lenny took a lot of flow. That endeavor had been bothering him for weeks. The right time had not presented itself. The daily emotional pounding he received by telling others left him weak, unwilling to bring up the subject when he arrived at Lenny's to work. The walk was taking its toll. Frank could tell that Lenny knew something was up. Lenny finally broke the ice when he asked if everything was okay. Frank knew it was time, asking Lenny if he had a few moments to hear something out.

"Sure I always have time!" Lenny joked as he hobbled to his chair to sit and listen.

"I've got something to tell you I've wanted to tell you for awhile. I just didn't have the heart," Frank prefaced.

Lenny interjected,

"Stop right there. Before you go any further let me just say I think I know what you want to say. Judy and I have known for years." he revealed.

All Frank could do is stare at Lenny in disbelief for a moment and then ask,

"You mean you know about my past?"

"Yes," Lenny responded

"How?" Frank queried.

"I had a friend at the police department tell me five years ago," Lenny confessed.

"How come you never said anything to me about it?" Frank pried.

"Because it didn't matter, I knew that isn't who you are! I've known you too long for that to be true," Lenny stated with conviction then added;

"Besides I know you answer to a higher calling. I know of no one else I could call at two in the morning to help me look for a lost dog in the rain. Not stopping until that dog was found is character that speaks for itself. I know you're not what they say you are. I know that in my heart buddy."

Frank felt the flush of emotion that starts deep, washes up and out of the body transforming heavy to light. Again the gift was overwhelming, a friend who had so much faith in him that he had been unaffected by the cancer of accusation. Lenny had never questioned his character, neither had Judy. They had fed him, given him work, supplied him with rest and never accepted the suspicions. The two were truly gifts of Grace, a blessing of hope that sustained his sanity, and he was grateful. And the walk continued to expand.

The gift of that truth also had to be revealed to the kids of some of these friends. He had to enlighten those young adults as well. These were kids who had grown up around him and knew him well. They deserved not to be blindsided by information that was contrary to their experience of who he was. These were extremely difficult encounters, yet again and again all returned the gift of understanding. Frank suspected at this point that there might be another force at work in the grand scheme of things here. There was just no other way to explain the fact that no one accepted "Dangerous Sex Offender."

By the end of May he was pretty beat up by the roller coaster of emotion. Laying out your deepest secret for others to judge you almost on a daily basis can really wear someone out. He was worked. He really needed a change of scenery for a few days to recharge. Lenny was game for taking Memorial Day weekend off, telling Frank to get out of town.

Several days of thought on the subject provided brief respites from the torments that taxed the brain during the long hours. The anger regarding the situation he was being forced to live flared like a boil. He needed to lance the boil, but how? It was slowly dawning on him that in order to stop the madness he lived, and he was sure others had been swept into the same madness; someone would have to tell the story. The question was how.

There was a trip, he thought in a moment of clarity, which might shed some Light on a solution, plus give him a few days away with a soul his heart was enthralled with. It had been a while since he had seen her and it was time to connect. One of the brightest people he knew on the planet lived in San Francisco and she had shown an interest in helping him write a book. What kind of a book she didn't know. Neither did he exactly, but he was starting to get a clue. She only knew by his sketchy details he had something interesting, and she was willing to investigate further when he was willing to share the details he had withheld. Those details, however, could jeopardize her co-creative support in the book quest. He was in the uncomfortable position of revealing the cancer that infected him to someone for whom he cared deeply. He wasn't sure he could let go again to someone who meant the world to him. If he lost her, Light of such rare qualities might never shine for him again. She was a path he had to walk if he ever hoped to be part of the change we all want to see in our world.

"What the hell give it a try," something in his tired mind was telling him to go. Almost like a calm little voice saying, "There might be answers to questions you've been seeking answers for." He picked up the phone, calling Mary for her thoughts. Mary laughed,

"Yeah... she'd be glad to see you and your truck.....haaaa!" Then continued, "She has the Really Really Free Market this weekend and I know your truck could be a big help getting stuff there. Give her a call and see," Mary prodded. So he did and Kirsten agreed!

Frank promised to fill her in on details for the book and that intrigued her. He also promised his truck for the Really Really Free Market because that intrigued him. The only spoiling in his thoughts of three days with Kirsten in San Francisco was the thought of having that damned conversation. How and When? What would be her reaction? Would she ask him to leave......forget the book? Damned the negative madness! What will be will be. Kirsten deserved the protection of knowledge. He felt he owed her at least that, but it still scared him to death. She was so very, very special to him.

He had all the confidence in the world in regards to Kirsten's ability to direct the mess of a book that boiled in his brain. He had watched her produce stunning grades her first two years at UCSD. Then moving to San Francisco to continue schooling, selling her car to live green, mixed with social activism for global responsibility impressed him. Kirsten was feisty yet settled. Worldly with feet well planted, and if anyone had a finger on the pulse of the planet he figured she did. Arrested once for "unlawful assembly" during a San Francisco Bio-Tech Convention protest, she had first-hand knowledge of Gestapo tactics used by police, as well as cover-up of detainee mishandling. If anyone could make his thoughts work he figured she could. Besides she was beautiful in his eyes which made being in her company a delight.

He arrived at Kirsten's apartment on South Van Ness in the SF Mission District Friday afternoon just as Kirsten arrived back from her work at Dante's on Pier 39. Delighted by the timing, she welcomed him to her humble home. She had graciously offered her couch for him sleep on. He accepted, trying to stay on budget, promising to buy her meals in exchange for the kindness. They jumped right into catching up. It had been a year and a half since his last trip to see her in San Diego and a lot had transpired. One piece of the past popped up to draw laughter, with Frank's request of Kirsten never to mention the sailing incident in Mission Bay that still embarrassed him. His miscalculation on tack put their rental sail boat in jeopardy of being pounded onto the rocks at the mouth of the channel. Had it not been for the dingy that appeared from out of nowhere, pulling them from the floundering luff he had mired them in, they surely would have gotten real wet. Kirsten agreed mum's the word.

Time slipped by to late, and hunger motivated them to walk around the corner to Kirsten's favorite Sushi spot to get a bite. The walk was serious for Frank as severe back spasms from overexertion at work and the five hour drive began to restrict fluid movement without pain. A bent hobble was the best he could muster. The pain signed of aging that said 'getting old' in big bold letters. He didn't want to get old almost as bad as he didn't want to have the conversation he knew he had to have. If he waited it might offend her, maybe even anger her. He knew he'd have to tell her at dinner. Her one room apartment in the old Victorian was small and she might feel uncomfortable with him staying. "She might ask me to leave," was one speculation. That made the walk up the block that much more painful.

Seated at a booth far from the bustling crowd, fun conversation turned more serious. He waited until after they had eaten before bringing up the book idea. Kirsten was up for hearing more. He warned her that at any time she may want to stop. He informed her that after hearing what he had to say she may want him to leave.

"That will be ok, I'll understand," he said with resignation resonating in the voice.

With that he bore his soul to a special human being, telling the story of then to now. Answering all questions, all the while feeling he was dealing a death blow to a very special friendship. It was an arduous conversation going well into the evening. Kirsten listened intently as she now began to understand the nightmare of a story that could be told. She asked intelligent deep questions. She read the "Dismissal." Kirsten's demeanor throughout seemed to be one of intense information retrieval and compassionate intrigue. She did not display any sign of judgment good or bad. She remained on neutral ground. After spewing the mess in his head he apologized for unloading such baggage in her lap. He admitted he knew that someday he'd have to tell her, he just didn't have the courage up until now. He apologized for waiting. He reiterated his understanding if she wanted him to leave. Kirsten looked intently into his tired eyes and after a moment of focused thought offered back an opinion that could only have come from someone that was on a whole different level.

"There might be an avenue to teach in such a book," She stated simply.

Frank had no clue how far Kirsten's mind had raced ahead of him. Just like the chess games where she had kicked his ass every time, she was already many moves ahead. She sensed his shame and diminished self esteem. She knew he expected he might be asked to leave and he was willing to risk it all anyway, even if it meant he'd have to drive home that night. She saw surrender and defeat in his face. Her Grace created freedom from weighted anticipation of rejection and manifested as Kirsten added,

"And no, Frank, I don't want you to leave."

Kirsten's trust lifted him high out of the blanketing dark clouds of uncertainty. Slowly the shaking in his hands subsided. Their conversations then delved into the opportunity to transcend conventional thinking. She was still on board to help with the book and already miles ahead of him. He now was beginning to recharge with the power of purpose. By some strange power of the Universe he had been led to this incredible human, who through her Grace would teach him new ways of creating peace. The dimensions of his walk now expanded exponentially.

The walk home in the wee hours of the morning was much less painful. The back was about the same, but the brain was calmed by thankfulness for Kirsten's unwavering support. The following day was to be spent with Kirsten teaching him the new joy of Really Really Free. Frank had no idea of the scope of the journey Kirsten was about to launch him onto. What he did know that night, life felt good again and his heart was warmed with gratitude for his extraordinary friend.

The fog filtered dawn sunlight peeking through the east facing bay window in Kirsten's room woke Frank early. Quietly, so as not to disturb his host, he crawled off the couch cushions he had arranged on the floor. His back was still in bad shape despite the comfortably hard surface he had chosen to sleep on. Gathering fresh clothes, keys and tobacco he opened the door silently as he glanced back at Kirsten asleep in her bed with her cat Shiloh curled close. The cat was only slightly disturbed by his rustlings, Kirsten remained blissfully asleep. He was astounded by her beauty even as she slept and then gently shut the door to begin his mission for caffeine.

The streets of the Mission District were deserted in the early morning sun. Even South Van Ness had only an occasional vehicle glide by in the quiet of the new day. He hobbled to the truck, the lower back pain unaffected by the aspirin he had taken. The pace was slow as he cruised to find an open java house. A few blocks away he found Muddy Waters and scored a robust house blend. He found Soy Milk and unbleached sugar for the coffee and fruit for breakfast at a corner market that had just begun to awake for business. He had to choose wisely as Kirsten was a vegan; he wasn't sure if pastry was on her list of things she could eat.

Returning straight away he took advantage of a shower in the shared bathroom facilities. The other occupants behind the other four doors in the hallway weren't up yet and Frank was in and out in short order. The hot shower helped the back feel better. The coffee and tobacco on the back porch gave the mind a jolt of awakening. His sense of relief from his burden to Kirsten brightened every minute he enjoyed from his third story porch top perch overlooking an older San Francisco. His mind celebrated the fact he had not lost a dear friend, his heart celebrated the closeness he felt in their bond. It was going to be a very good day he was sure. He was aglow with Peace.

He wandered back to the room with a third cup of coffee just as sleep-in beauty awoke. Sharing coffee and fruit they readied for the day at the 'market'. Running late for the noon arrival, Kirsten dressed while Frank loaded the truck with the array of items donated for the 'cause'. Boxes of clothes, shoes, stuff. Artwork, microwave oven, guitar amplifier, you name it Kirsten had probably collected it for the once-a-month event. The twenty-two stairs between the truck and hall cubby that held the booty let Frank know he wasn't getting any younger. The 800 milligrams of Ibuprofen was doing nothing. Damn back made him feel old, he surely would have given just about anything for a Vicodin and a back brace. He struggled to be useful.

Truck loaded to the gills then off for the few block jaunt to Delores Park and set up. Kirsten commented on the fog, Frank guaranteed her sun by noon or so. Kirsten had her doubts. Three other organizers for the Really Really Free Market greeted their arrival. Franks back was grateful for their help as they set about unloading the treasures and laying out the gatherings design. Within an hour many other vehicle loads of people with treasure had been unloaded and spread out on blankets to form a giant circle. The plot of ground they occupied was just a small portion of the immense park that occupied two city blocks of beautiful open space. The fog danced and wafted with breezes that opened blue holes in the grey sky as visitors drifted into the park. Frank kept his fingers crossed his prognostications for sun would pan out.

The "Really Really Free Market" sign that hung between two palm trees was the only clue to what was truly going on. The scene looked a lot like a giant yard sale from a distance. Visitors from all walks began to filter in from around the park's edges of old Victorian neighborhoods, as the sun began to filter through the billowing, retreating banks of fog. The grassy sloping knoll filled with warm streaming sun and the vibrancy of a warm family gathering drew curious attentions from the passersby. Yes the sun appeared as prognosticated as if Frank had some sort of inside info into such occurrences; he and Kirsten high fived at its radiant arrival.

As the curious stopped to investigate Frank noticed a delightfully fun occurrence take place. Transformation after transformation of reality occurring to those unaware at first glance, that this was something way different from their expectations. The casual observer arrived with hands in pocket protecting wealth, intent to see if there was anything worthy of their sacred dollar. They browsed with scrutiny, not expecting to find anything they really needed, only to find something they thought they might like to have. They would bend down, pick the item up, examine it and then ask the person attending the blanket of gifts,

"How much?"

"Free," comes the response.

The observer would then look at the attendee in disbelief, the gears of comprehension not quite meshing and stammer,

"Really?"

"Really," the one attending the blanket responds.

A transformation then descends into the one who had just been gifted. A broad smile would lighten their face and the walls of separation begin to melt into willing participant. Humble acceptance of the gift was followed by a measure of joy displayed in delighted eyes eager to experience more. The gift of that joy, however perceived, was then passed on to others as they flowed into the peaceful spirit abounding from this unique community of people. Food arrived and was shared, the talents of jugglers, dancers and music shared for entertainment, yoga and massage shared for mind and body meditations. Festive colorful energy ran like a river into a pool of magic harmony 'Really Really Free' had created. This was amazing to witness. Brightening someone's day with no strings attached was an awesome way to share in co-creating peace, he marveled at what he was seeing.

The real power of what Kirsten and her group were creating was evidenced in comments Frank overheard by a very excited first-timer. The lady in her mid thirties had asked Frank for more information about how this event started, and he directed her to Kirsten. The bottom line on the barrage of comments and questions she hurled rapid fire at Kirsten manifested when she stated,

"This is the most amazing thing I've seen in my two week visit to San Francisco; how do I start one?" Then going on to say,

"I'm visiting from Wisconsin and as soon as I return home I'm starting my own Really Really Free Market," a frenzy of excitement filling her tone.

Unbelievable, he thought. One small seed at a time was being planted by Kirsten's group. A seed implanting the joy of giving, no strings attached. Other layers of teaching existed as well, but he'd have to ponder for months before discovering the vast scope of gifts the 'Market' bestowed. Kirsten was that many moves ahead, planting small seeds of peace in such a powerfully simple way. She was blowing him away, living out her chess moves of life designed to checkmate the evil that stands in the way of transition to sustainable human harmony in peace. Kirsten was tapped into another level of consciousness; he wished he was twenty years younger so he could have time to catch up. His respect and admiration for her essence of Grace grew again exponentially.

At the end of the day they loaded Frank's truck with the little that was left over. Kirsten even had a plan for that. The excess was taken to a local thrift store that then donated profits to Aids research. A full circle of giving impacting many lives on the planet, so simply provided by a Grace that flowed through this incredible human he called friend. Her energy for living peace was inspiring. Frank knew he was in the company of a very unique person, her spirit lifted his to a level he had never experienced.

The last thirty six hours spent in the City delighted the senses. Kirsten worked a shift at Dante's, Frank worked to negotiate City traffic for delivery and pick up service provided for Kirsten to the Wharf. In-between he took in the sights, sounds and smells of old memories, creating new ones accented with the pain of horrible lower back spasms endured while negotiating steep sidewalks. The sunny days warmed to shirt sleeve weather and the color of the City was vibrant. Every minute with Kirsten was precious to him and he apologized for monopolizing her time when he finally met Kirsten's boyfriend, Jake. Jake was gracious,

"No problem, I knew how much she wanted to see you." That made Frank feel a bit special.

Not wanting to overstay his welcome Frank readied to leave early Monday. He drove Kirsten over to Jake's apartment, so the two could finally spend some time together. On the way he felt his brain losing control as his heart welled with gratitude for Kirsten's company. He was flowing with warmth that had only been experienced with Hana and that surprised him. That was a very, very special place and as they approached the point of their parting Frank desperately looked for words to articulate what he felt. The mere thought of trying to covey this on the spur of the moment was crazy, but the heart pushed the brain and stupid spilled out of the mouth. Pulling to the corner to park he opened up with the best he had spur of the moment, last chance dancing from his brain he spoke,

"Well we have covered a lot of ground Kirsten."

"You are amazing!" he gushed.

"The Really Really Free Market was amazing. I still haven't absorbed the full extent of what it has to offer," he admitted.

"But I haven't got around to the good stuff," he blundered.

"Oh yeah what's that?" she asked inquisitively.

"I'm crazy about you; I just wish I was twenty years younger," his heart mouthed.

That reply drew silence and a flustered look from Kirsten. "Man that was STUPID!" was his first thought. He opened his door to meet her curbside for farewell, kicking the shadows on the sidewalk for the brashness of his blubbering. He sensed Kirsten's silent questioning and apologized for any misunderstanding.

"That's okay," she consoled. They bid goodbye amid respectful embrace with declarations of missing one another until they chanced together again. He kicked again at the shadows while walking back to his truck. He sat and watched as Kirsten walked to Jake's building, never looking back.

The ride back to Grover was a mix of looking forward and looking back that churned with uncertainty. He had a hard time staying happy in the moment. The euphoria of the weekend drenched with the sinking feeling he may have confused Kirsten with the intent of his blubbering. He was only a human who wanted to love and he voiced that which should have been given away in silence. Kirsten had grown into his heart; he should have been satisfied by that Grace. He had learned a lot that weekend, but nothing about keeping his big mouth shut!

Out of one walk into the fire, and into another. He hadn't been home a moment and the business phone rang; he picked up to hear fear.

"Hello Frank." It was Hana Joi and he shuddered at the point in her voice.

"Hello Hana," he said in a surrendered tone knowing this was 'THE' call.

"How have you been?" Hana queried secondarily.

"I've had better days, how are you?" He replied trying to refocus on her well being.

It had only been weeks since they had talked last when usually it was months and in this case he knew that wasn't a good sign. Diversion didn't work. Hana redirected and came to her point,

"You know Frank I think it's time we talked. You need to tell me what is so bad that you think you can't talk to me about it. Don't you trust me? I've told you everything, it's time you to tell me everything too."

No was not an option! Abrupt silence made that clear.

"You're right Hana we need to talk, and it's just that being honest with you scares me to death." The moment of silence that followed certainly made that truth clear.

"What I'm going to tell you Hana may make you hang up the phone and never talk to me again. That is my greatest fear, but I wouldn't blame you, I'll understand." He took a deep breath, then added,

"Are you sure you want to do this over the phone?" trying one last-ditch effort for reprieve. No time for silence to make any statement, Hana fired an instant adamant demand,

"Yes Frank I'm ready, and I want to know now!"

The next hour was the nightmare of shame recounting the past; again to a treasured friend he did not want to lose. The questions went far beyond where he had gone before with anyone. Hana demanded it. He owed it.

Hana did show some understanding of why he had been reluctant to share this part of his past with her. She remembered her ranting to him on death to all molesters. She could only imagine the pain he had felt listening to her anger and living his shame in silence. He asked for pardon and forgiveness, offering sincere apologies for his silence. He hadn't been 100% truthful, but now he was. At least that felt good to let go of what he had been holding back, but still he was frightened of what was to come. Heart, soul and being had been handed to Hana, now she could choose what to do with them.

The Grace of compassion was her road so chosen. Hana thanked him for his honesty even if it was only ten years late. Her humor lightened the load. She then acknowledged to having found deeper understanding of his spiritual nature. He was trying to respond to a higher calling in all things, although she gently reminded him he had put this off for ten years. She now knew that his

Grace-driven desire for redemption of his past was in part being paid forward through her and Troy. Gaining an insight to the truth, that the Grace she had struggled to understand and almost abandoned had come to her anyway. Through this dear friend with a horrible past, she gained a greater faith in the Grace of the Universe he had spoken of at times. She had a deeper perspective when reflecting on his frequently used comment,

"Miracles happen every day Hana Joi."

Hana returned that miracle of Love that night. Frank bid goodbye with his reminding statement of fact,

"Remember Hana Joi, I love you."

"I love you too Frank." Hana returned from the heart.

They both knew that no strings could be attached to the Grace that had been created to flow between them that night. They parted on a higher level of connection than ever before, not knowing when, but that they would speak again.

Frank hung up the phone, drained from the strain, yet feeling the energy of being out from under this burden. The freedoms from guilt, after rendering truths to so many, especially Kirsten and Hana, provided peace to his soul. Not knowing when he might talk to them again was a small but dark cloud that tightened his throat. He gazed out the dining room window thinking now it was on to the future unknown, tomorrow's another day. He retired early that evening in the quiet of the house he called home.

The terror continued soon enough. Frank's self-imposed ban on going out to the Park under threat of posting by the Chief was exceedingly difficult. The Park had been his refuge from the storm and now it was a tool of terror. The total ban was ridiculous. Ninety nine percent of the time he was there, there was no one out at the Park to be a threat to. It seemed to be a ploy by the PD to force him to quit and he knew it. The denial of any access plan he presented was a blatant attempt to force the board to change horses in the middle of the stream.

Frustration brought him to the point of surrender. He was willing to spend another thousand dollars to receive a report of 'rehabilitation' in order to get his name off the 'list' before any more doors closed. He was a day away from the scheduled appointment with the psychiatrist in Orange County when his attorney finally returned his call. Her news was not good. The "Certification of Rehabilitation" avenue to remove 'rehabilitated' individuals from the Megan's Law list had ended early. The DOJ had just pulled the plug on the last program left where those accused could plead their case. That was it. If you where on the 'list' at this point in time you were on for life. No redemption, no rehabilitation that was the message. Closed by interpretation was the letter of the law, the spirit of justice lost in hysteria. Reactions to hysteria didn't seem to be the America he had been taught to believe in.

The course of following an ever-constricting letter of the law was creating problems for him and now society in general. Adhering to the dogma from prominent psychologists that "sex offenders can never be rehabilitated" DOJ closed the door to justice. All based on an art form of probabilities, Psychiatry. The media had bought into it, so seemed the justice system had as well. The human factor throwing in the monkey wrench that makes one hundred percent accurate behavioral analysis unattainable, when by Grace is included in the equation. The mysterious power that transforms is immediate sometimes; sometimes it takes years, but because it does happen that destroys the math. The math of theirs that says one hundred percent never change.

On the other hand no one seemed to notice evil follows a very predictable path of destruction. The harsher the punishments become that subscribe to the premise of 'no ability to rehabilitate', the more people were dying. These punishments now taking on the qualities of revenge are less than just in their intent. For those affected by the disease of Testosterone Intoxication that stimulate the deviant behaviors now were not leaving victims alive. To avoid discovery, prosecution and punishment with no end attainable, monstrous consequences are to be expected. It is human nature, when backed into a corner that threatens survival; the lower levels of fight or flight make people do unimaginable things. To survive the evil of revenge the current course of actions by society against offenders was trending was leading to some very bad outcomes. No witness, no prosecution.

For him the only relief to his dilemma was a pardon from the governor; according to his attorney that was not likely to happen. Politics and image associated with that office were for all intent and purpose leaving that door shut. So much for justice and fair play.

In the bigger picture the direction the DOJ was heading with 'offender' registration was becoming clearer. What at first seemed to be a good idea was now appearing to be a more elaborate effort for control of society in general. Newspapers, magazines, television and radio were playing into the plot without even knowing it. Or did they? After all just a few media conglomerates owned vast holdings across the globe. Those giants had considerable debt to the world banks. One protects the other in the 'good old boy' system. Were the giants working together to gain the ultimate control of money and the debt it could inflict? Infected by debt with no end sucks up hope and spews out drones; this is otherwise known as control. So how could they do it? Frank's mind had raced with Kirsten's on this subject; together they had postulated plausible theory.

It was apparent to them both that the current laws for controlling 'offenders' were really pretty ineffective by 21st century standards. Jails, posters, fliers and websites weren't stopping the bodies. Total control and monitoring of the severely afflicted are better accomplished with 21st century tools. Implantation of GPS chips, RFD micro chips, could do a much more effective job. 24-7-365 eyes. Cost less while creating more jobs. Also it creates a more secure feeling for the public, easier to sell than having the Star of David tattooed to the 'offenders' forehead. Sounds like a win/win for society. Seems like a good idea until you look a little further.

Expect to see a morphing of Megan's law to include mandatory 'chipping' of 'sex offenders' in your future. You see, if you take the scourge of society and use them as the excuse to force chip implantation, you could probably get the law to pass, no problem. It's simple. The Bogeyman of the 21st century needs to be chipped so we know were he is in our dream. Then he can't scare us because he can't hide in the shadows and surprise us. We need to know, so let's do it we say. Take a moment and think about what that sets us up for. Once started down that road the negative energy from whence it originated expands that road for 'public safety'. Now that we have approved the idea of 'mandatory chipping' as okay what about other 'criminals'. First we start with the really bad ones like murderers, kidnappers, terrorists, arsonists and strong arm thieves. Then it might be okay to include drunk drivers, burglars, gang members, con artists and the data base grows. So we are down to shoplifters, juvenile delinquents and all other enemies of our safety. The data base grows. In the ultimate grab for this sense of security we then make it okay to 'chip' our babies.

"What better way to keep your kids safe, parents, than a Rincon GPS tracking chip with the built in 'Quick Locater' feature? Just press the button and follow the bleeping. You'll never lose your kid again! All this for just three easy payments of $49.95," reads the advertisement that pops up on your computer screen. And the data base continues to expand.

Then comes the happy day when you too receive your very own 'chip' and you feel all safe and warm. Then annual updates begin, maybe at our local Police department. Updates include height, weight, hair color, scars, tattoos, dental work, tickets, and so on. Then we transfer our financial package for tracking our dollar dance, just because it will make our life so much easier. **GOTCHA!** Now we have relinquished all control to those that infect with debt and probably most of our rights as we know them today. Right now we have the power to say NO, then.... we won't.

This is all plausible they agreed, yet would it be this, or the outright failure of the economic system that would be the great catalyst, a great catalyst for the paradigm shift of collective consciousness, needed for the survival of the planet. Or might it be something else? Kirsten and Frank could go on and on. Whatever the light switch may be, they agreed if not found and illuminated, we're done.

Without Kirsten's Light, Frank's refuge from all his solitary contemplation was the Park, which now he could not frequent for retreat. So when a writer called wanting to do a story on the Price family, his self imposed ban put him between a rock and a hard place. She wanted to do the interview at the Park to satisfy her requirement for getting a feel for what she was going to write about. Jean Ubbard, the FOPH historian, was ill and that left him next in line to expound on Price family history. The writer's deadline for the story was fast approaching; he had to make a decision quickly.

Good publicity from the article for the Price House dangled like a carrot in front of the horse. He thought about it, figuring the tour/interview wouldn't take long. He could book the visit for a time when no one else could be out at the Park. He could also drop off a couple of the completed Memorial Tree commemorative rocks that had been purchased by descendants. Sitting in his front yard is not what the descendants had paid for. His Memorial Tree idea had really taken off, and he still had four more to chisel and deliver. Coupled with the August 1st re-roof of the Meherin House, he knew at some point he'd have to break the ban or get permission to go out.

His meeting again with the Chief regarding access to the park was flat out denied. Not enough manpower to baby-sit and the financial liability exposure was the excuse. So Frank stepped out of the box and booked the interview anyway. Besides, the sweetest part of the carrot was the drug of serenity that an hour at the Park could provide his tired head. He should have known that a serene escape was not possible under pretext of slipping in and out of the Park undetected. The Park serenity addiction pulled for a fix anyway.

The result of that short visit was a phone message left on the Genesis office line by Pismo PD requesting a return call. Frank returned the call, only to be grilled by an inquiring detective wanting to confirm information placing him on the Park property. Frank isn't a liar and he didn't. Yes he did visit, the trip was brief, he dropped off rocks, met with a writer, and they encountered no one else. The dick's response was to threaten 'posting'. For the first time in ten years, Frank angered and flared in retaliation. You know if you keep poking someone with a sharp stick, at some point they are going to probably poke you back. Frank poked just a little,

"Well you do what you think you have to, seems there may be more important things to attend to," he retorted.

The strain in his voice evidenced chronic threat had exacted a toll. He aired his opinion of bullshit surrounding the whole exercise to protect the public's safety. Two days later Glen Ray called, furious, informing Frank that three Pismo PD dicks had showed up earlier in the day to hang his 'wanted poster'. Didn't seem to be any lack of manpower for that task he thought as he listened to Glen's hectic message. Glen's disgust and outrage about where the cops had posted the fliers implied deep concern and need for Franks input. 'What Now' reverberated as the all too familiar quickening of the pulse reminded him he was poked again. This poke pierced the heart in its deliberate attempt to wield a death blow to his involvement with the Price House. He downed a couple of aspirin, picked up the phone and dialed Glen's number.

Glen picked up and immediately went off! Frank calmed him somewhat by reiterating the City's incessant desire was to protect their back pocket. It was simply a money-driven exercise to avoid liability in a sue-happy society. It wasn't that they were out to get him so much, they were bent on protecting their money bags. Glen calmed, so did Frank, and he agreed to come out and see for himself the locations chosen to post the full color warning fliers. Why not, he hadn't been threatened with arrest for going out...yet. Damage done and he left to do damage control.

Pulling up to the gate on Frady Lane brought the blood pressure up again. There at the gate entrance, the sign for the Park he had made was posted with a letter sized 'wanted poster'. Sandwiched between the Plexiglas that covered the sign's surface, a crooked flier with its bold red letters proclaiming 'Dangerous Sex Offender' with his photograph. That was obscene he thought! The audacity the City had, assuming that they had the right to post their propaganda on a private sign on private property. The city didn't own the sign or the land it was planted on and that incensed him.

Pulling up in front of the Anniversary House to see another poster planted in the flower bed at the front steps just made the blood boil. Glen walked him to a third location were PD had stapled a poster to the oak rain barrel at the back porch steps. Full colored, red lettered and disgusting Frank agreed, "but there is nothing we can do about it," he said in defeat. The House was City property and they could do whatever they wanted. The front sign, however, may be a different story he offered. The hanging of fliers of any sort on some one else's property without their consent may be illegal Frank speculated. Funny thing, that poster at the front gate disappeared within the first 24 hours.

The two discussed their options while Frank took photos of each posting. He was relieved to find no postings within the House. The comedy in the drama was the discovery that Frank's name had been misspelled. That was unbelievable. Here, an agency of government, who by 'authority' professed to be offering known truth, didn't even have the name spelled correctly. How good was the rest of the information if they couldn't even get the name right? After a closer look he noticed the hair color was wrong too. They had a good laugh at the inept display and how easily it was concealed with well placed trash cans.

Frank's life through the previous month had been a lot like the sailing adventure with Kirsten that almost ended dashed against the rocks. In that adventure he had the presence of mind to call out, "Can we get a little help here?" With blind faith he knew somebody would respond. At the darkest moment when fear grips your soul, you see the rocks just a few feet away from your little boat's fragile hull, and you scan the empty horizon for assistance. Confident that Grace will provide what you need, you run to the front of your boat. Out of the barren roll of ocean swell, lo and behold a dingy appears with angels of mercy, when hailed extends you a line and pulls you from certain doom. To this day he acknowledges that miracle. The dingy had appeared from out of nowhere. A moment before, reality was the empty nothingness of never-ending ocean with no hope in sight. Then it was there. His only explanation was Grace.

Frank was now calling out again, "can I get a little help here." His passion for the Price House was slowly being turned into an illegal act, life was on the rocks and in danger of sinking ever further into nonexistence. He was sure he was to be asked to leave command of FOPH at the July board meeting, this latest round of crap sure to be the last straw. The doom of gloom weighed heavily and he figured he should submit his resignation. The 'Man' had won and it was now time to fade into the sunset.

That's when the dingy with Angels appeared again from out of the nothingness of nowhere. Actually it was a whole ocean liner this time with a fine golden lifeline extended to benefit untold numbers and a crew of attending Angels that likewise couldn't be counted. Frank's floundering sailboat of life was about to be rescued again by Grace. Pulling him away from rocks that roared with doom was the power of purpose guided by Grace. It all began with a call from his old friend Linda Rawson, the one he had almost sold to the Mexican Commandant, her question to change his direction forever,

"Hey Frank, do you want to go to Maui and write your book?"

~~~~~~

This part of the story is so unique and revealing of character I will let it be told from his words. What follows is a series of excerpts from Frank's personal journal. The excerpts are exact; I did, however, rearrange some of the chronology of their entry to better preserve a 'then' to 'now' timeline of what transpired.

~~~~~~

Wednesday 10-12-5 ...Hello old friend. I've wandered across the street from my new living arrangement to watch a glorious sunset from the shore of Maui. I have to remind myself from time to time just where I am. South east shore Maalaea Bay, Kihei, Maui. I should feel I'm the luckiest man alive and at times I do. Since we last wrote my life has been torn apart by implementation of law that has done nothing in my case except destroy a productive human life. ... An attorney who has done nothing since being paid a large sum of money three years ago has at least inspired me to try and wage war with words on this despicable act of continuing punishment. I've come to Maui to write a book. By the Grace of God I go.

...At the end of June my friend Linda Rawson called to ask if I wanted to go to Maui and write my book. If I'd be her roommate she'd cook and input what I wrote into the computer. My first reaction was to tell her that it would be great, but I figured I had too many responsibilities to up and run off to Maui for a year. She had four days to make up her mind as she had the promise of a job and a deadline to let them know. My mind raced! ...

Friday 10-21-5 ...So Linda asked and my mind raced off. Working daily with Lenny we would always highlight the interesting stuff we would encounter when we were apart. So the next day or maybe it was even that day I say to Lenny, guess what kind of an offer I got today. Lenny knows of Linda so I tell him what she offered and he looks me directly in the eye and says, "Go you deserve it. I'll take care of your business." I couldn't believe what he was saying. Like I thought he was serious! Soon after I had put up all the other reasons why I couldn't, he said it again and really meant it. My mind raced weighing feasibility of arranging the other two big hurdles, Price House and money. The Price House had a contract for a reroof of the Meherin House the first of August and maybe I could shut down the rest of my end. Money might be a loan from Dad. So before I left Lenny's that night I asked if he was really serious about his offer and again he said "yes" and I got it. Truly a one in a billion friend. So the next day I called Linda back and told her that I needed to know what day she needed to know by. Four days is all I had.

That night I received an invite to go to my brother's house in Huntington for their fond farewell party. That event would take place on 4th (of) July weekend the following week. Saying yes I'd be there, I then called Dad to see what he was up to and mentioned Bob's the following week. Dad said he would like to go, and next thing I know he's got a flight out to arrive the following Saturday. I didn't say anything about Linda's offer over the phone, I would inform and ask in a week, face to face.

I began to let Price House personnel know what was up. Most were stunned. ...I knew I would have to piece my part out to several people. I took my caretakers advice and began writing a book of instructions regarding what was in my head.

Before I called Linda back that Saturday I checked and double checked to see if Lenny was still on board with the plan and he said he was. So I called Linda and told her YES. I figured I couldn't pass up this opportunity. Money would come, if not from Dad then from the house. I could take a second mortgage if worse came to worse.

I'm at the beach right now and its getting too dark to write. Gorgeous sunset again.

One last comment. I haven't heard from Hana. Did speak to her sister and finally wrote Stefen. I've left Hana a couple of messages—she'll call. Soon I hope!

Tuesday 11-15-5

Well with Lenny firm and a commitment to Linda made, plans for a vehicle began. Linda and I decided to take the Lexus over and share one vehicle. Plan was to come down to Roberts's house for the 4th of July, pick up Linda on the return and drive back to Pismo. She would then return with car and documents for shipping. Car would arrive shortly after she arrived on the island. So off to see Robert, Beth and family. Arrived on Saturday, July 2nd at about noon. Dad was due in at 1:00 p.m. but his plane was late and wouldn't be arriving until about 3:00 p.m.. Robert was at the beach so I chatted with Beth and Michaela for awhile. Robert arrived home and one of the first questions was "So what are you up to?" No one had been informed of my attempt at this venture so I filled him in. He listened intently as I explained what I was trying to do and especially to the part about asking Dad for a loan. When I was done my brother blew me away! He said "Well you know how Dad is." I said "yeah." He continued "If Dad doesn't do it come and talk to me." I was astounded but now I had a plan "C." I didn't bring up my plan with Dad until the following morning.

Early a.m. coffee on the back porch and I laid out the plan. To Dad I'm sure it was just another wild plan of mine and he voiced his opinion on the prospects of success. He had had a few friends that had attempted to write books and they were never published. After the usual grilling, Dad asked if I had a plan "B." I told him "yes." Dad asked what that was and I told him I had another investor that might be interested in funding the project. Dad asked who that was. At first I was reluctant to tell him but he pressed. So I told him that it was his son. He sat there stunned for a moment and then said he would consider my request and talk to his attorney. Three weeks later I signed a promissory note and the project was funded.

Lenny was ready and on September the 7th I turned over all the necessary info to the FOPH and they were as ready as they could be…. The house had been packed up providing Cindy and Sabrina with some room to breathe…. Elise had come up to spend time with (her) Dad and on Thursday the 8th. Elise and I drove to Burbank to spend the night with Mary and Joe. Friday morning Elise took me to LAX…. Elise was sad that Dad was going and I was sad to be leaving her behind. Six hours later I was in Maui and the writing journey began….

Wednesday 10-12-5…Switching subjects for now. Hana Joi, a love of my life …a short time after my last writing. …I called her as Hurricane Rita was 24hrs out, to see if she was in a safe place and out of harms way only to find her in distress. Hana had left Jerry's (in Houston) that morning with all her worldly possessions packed in a (rental) truck and car in tow. She had reached Lake Charles Louisiana where the truck broke down. The Hurricane was supposed to come on shore at about Houston but now had taken a right hand turn and was heading for Lake Charles. She was forced to lock and abandon the truck and flee in her car to try and get out of harms way. When I reached her by phone she was just out of Louisiana and into mid Mississippi. Her goal was to reach Mobile Alabama to take refuge and wait out the storm and return, when safe, to rescue her truck and possessions. I tried to comfort her the best I could. I did bid her safe journey and closed with I love you Hana Joi, call me any time. She did that night. Reaching Mobile, finding accommodations and food, she called to catch up.

During our talk.... Hana was extremely distressed at having to leave all of her possessions right in the middle of ground zero. Where the truck was, with 22 years of picture memories of her son, was in the exact spot Hurricane Rita's eye wall would come on shore. I tried to reassure her that because the truck was on interstate 10, was about as high up as you could get and would probably remain above the storm surge waters pushed in as the hurricane came on shore. Because the truck had the extra weight I was willing to bet that the winds could not push it over. I silently asked God to protect Hana on her journey home. ...

Hana's cell phone was turned off by Jerry as spite kicked in. Repeated calls, over the next few days, were met with the same recording of "no longer in service." I waited a few more days and then called Hana's sister Ann. Ann informed me that Hana had returned to her truck after the storm had passed.... The area where the truck had been left had been completely devastated and water covered the neighborhoods on either side of the freeway rendering them uninhabitable.... Able to gain access to the restricted area ...she rounded the curve on the deserted freeway to find the truck high and dry...Three men appeared from out of nowhere and helped her restart the truck and load the car onto the trailer and two days later she arrived safe and sound in Pennsylvania. So where did these guys come from? ... The Grace in assistance may not be clear to Hana. It is to me. ...Angels, Hana.

Tuesday 11-15-5 Ann had provided Hana with a cell phone. ... I waited a few days before I called. I left a message for her and waited another week before leaving another. ... Another week went by ... Ann called...said that no one had heard from Hana and she hoped she was with me. I wished she was but she wasn't...The lack of a return call was telling...Another week or so went by and I called again and this time left a message voicing my concern.

Last Friday night Hana finally called. Boy it was good to hear her voice! ... I closed letting her know, I love you Hana Joi. ...Thank you Lord.

~~~~~~

Jumping back out of the pages of his journal, I'm sure you can now understand that there was something extraordinary happening to a man who at times felt he was the lowest of the low. An amazing power, he didn't quiet understand from out of nowhere had given him a new path in life. He was determined to show up daily to live the Aloha he had been handed. His spirit journey on the Island of Maui was the most difficult thing he had ever done. The long days of remembering, tendering, reliving, then writing out the details, took courage to fulfill the compulsion that burned.

Frank had called Kirsten shortly before he left on his journey and she reassured him that she was still on board to help with the book. He offered her a free place to stay if she could come over for a visit. .

Kirsten received a letter from him shortly after he arrived on Maui. He told of his joy of having made progress after an excruciating struggle to start. The first words finally came when he had started to bleed. But as he put it, "Grace had provided once again." She knew his passion; she could only imagine his pain. His proposal scripted in the letter astounded Kirsten by what he was asking her to do. He wanted to turn his completed work over to her for first review. Kirsten's decision on what to do with it was to be final. If she said proceed, final edit was to be her creation. His confidence in her discernment seemed to be unshakable. He left participation up to her. She was in.

Kirsten didn't hear from him again until Christmas. He sent her a card and he received one from her. In his brief note she detected struggle, she hoped her card might bring him a ray of hope. It did and he called. Kirsten always gifted Light and her grounded understanding of the process he was living brought clarity of direction for their work. He could have talked for hours, he missed her terribly.

~~~~

We are all told that nothing is ever really free on the weave into the tapestry of life. From the Garden of Heart, however, the string we follow found the Light of Gifting from Universal Grace was a gift that is REALLY REALLY FREE. Spirit freed by gifted purpose. Here today ...gone to Maui. From hell to paradise gifted by the Light of Heart that is the hand of Universal Grace. "Can we get a little help here?" answered by "Can we give a little help here."

CHAPTER 32

DIDN'T SEE THAT COMING

The holidays this year were an amazing, wonderfully different experience. I received a card from Kirsten and the "I love you & miss you!" really really made my day. I called her to give her an update on the book's progress that had slowed to a snail's pace. It didn't take her long to center my direction forward. My job at Spices restaurant was taking up time I should have been spending on the book, but I had hit a brick wall, not feeling the direction. Comradery of human contact combined with the isolation of the writing experience enriched perspective. The book's concepts kept expanding way beyond my original scope. At Kirsten's direction, during my free time from work, I jotted down an outline of visions resulting from my mental wonderings. Grace knows the way, and by the end of January that path became clear, Kirsten's insights again inspired the deeper look.

Unfortunately while talking with her I discovered I had inadvertently given her boyfriend Jake a new name. I was so fucking embarrassed to find out I had addressed the card I had sent to: Kirsten and Stan. Where the fuck did Stan come from. I felt like an absolute idiot. Am I losing my mind? Kirsten eased my embarrassment somewhat when she reminded me that I've been doing that forever. Her high school boyfriend Blake, I called Blaine for years. I'm such an idiot! At least Kirsten could laugh about it. At the end of our conversation I correctly invited her and "Jake" over for a visit. Something came over me as we readied to part, my mouth blurted out what my heart felt and I said, "I love you kiddo." Silly me.... I think I do.

I've also come to love this island. The spirit of Aloha grows within me every day and the path to peace becomes more discernable. Mind, body, heart and soul have been uplifted. Every day I see subtle effects that this Aloha spirit has. Even the mandated registration as an 'offender' shows the Grace of this gift. The process when I arrived was simple and done with dignity. I don't have to go in on my birthday for an annual humiliation. I simply respond to letters sent to my residence every ninety days. No police officers have been out to distribute fliers to my neighbors or come to my door to see if I really live there. That blessing sets my mind at ease. I thank this Aloha daily.

The sounds of tropical birds awaken me every morning with the song of Aloha. The lush habitat that surrounds our home seems to have millions of voices that greet the new day. It makes for a sweet way to remind me daily as I arise, of were I am.

By Grace the struggle I face trying to articulate the passion of the soul is mellowed by interludes of watching the birds doing their thing. Feeding, playing, courting, mating, building nests and raising their young, then teaching them to fly. It's quite a trip to watch. The mated pair of orange beaked finches living under the tile roof at the corner of my lanai are my companions. They eye me inquisitively as they frolic through the branches of the Plumeria tree hanging gracefully over our space. They are great entertainment and a nice break from the blocks to creative flow. This is the birds' gift of Aloha, quieting the entwined minds story wanderings.

Grace has also provided for Elise. Her job is treating her well and her spirits are lifted from our almost nightly conversations. I had to make a bold move, lending her a large sum of money to get her out from under the oppression of credit card debt. The stress of payments that did little to lower principal was dragging her down. My heart told me it was the right thing to do. It was. The tone of her excited voice reassures me that the thoughts of debt despair don't plague her daily. Besides it's what 'Dads' do even though it will cut my time here on Maui by a couple of months. Another lesson in Aloha, even shorter time on Maui is all good.

Linda and I have tried to stay as low impact as possible while we stay on this beautiful little piece of the planet. Sharing the car became difficult so Linda and I bought a moped. The two-wheeler is dangerously fun with the wind in your face, enticingly green at 80 miles per gallon. Gas inching ever closer to $5.00 a gallon despite the gas cap here on the islands. Boy we are hooked! My hope is that this dependence one day will be a trigger for the collective consciousness to kick in. We may have time to turn it around, rather than waiting then watching as the house of cards falls down around us. Abrupt changes are ahead if we can't get our heads out of the sands of Mesopotamia. Living smaller makes you a much harder target than living large in the SUV. Living responsibly, that's Aloha.

There is so much to this living in Aloha thing. There is warmth felt in the 'welcome' of Aloha. There is a peace of safe passage felt in the 'farewell' of Aloha. Abundance felt in the 'love' of Aloha, no strings attached. It is the passion to give that is the true extension of Aloha gifted 'Kahiau'. Kahiau: 'to give lavishly and generously from the heart, without expectation of return' that's Aloha. The gifting is done from an awareness that all deserve dignity and respect which allows one to extend lavishly and generously. That compassion of Aloha resides in the collective human experience; we need to learn to set it free. Can we do that?

"Can." as the Hawai'ians say. We did once. You may recall if you were living in the moment of 9/11. For a few days after that disturbing event, most folks turned on the Aloha that lives in all of us. We drove our cars for awhile with dignity and respect for one another. We felt we were all one in the same boat for a moment. Think real hard and you will probably remember at least one incident of this amazing Grace. You may have even participated. Can we do it again and begin to live Aloha more fully each day we are alive? Can!

So I tried to call Hana to bid her Aloha at the first of the year, but I could only leave messages. I had not heard from her in a long while. My fears for her wellness intensified and I took a chance on the computer. This was a stretch as I am not one bit computer literate, I barely know the basics. I managed to get an e-mail sent to her last known address, it didn't get returned "unable to locate". A couple of weeks went by and I had heard nothing, so I sent another. Still nothing and I began to feel one of my greatest fears, rejection. I refused to address my other great fear, death. Yes there can be dark days in paradise. Had Hana decided to cut all ties? Another week slipped by and in desperation I sent one last message. I figured no response would mean she just didn't want to be bothered, or worse.

"Is anyone out there?" is all the electronic messenger asked.

Finally, March 15, 06 a response.

Subject: Wednesday

From: Hana Joi

Hey Frank: Ya I'm out here. How are things going on the book?

K

Thank God. She was alive. I was so relieved just knowing that she lived and breathed. I fired back at the speed of internet,

"Great to hear from you Hana, I hope all is well. Fill me in when you have time. Book's the hardest thing I've ever done. Love always, Frank."

I always tell Hana I love her. It's part of the therapy, hers as well as mine. Given away ... no strings attached. That's Aloha.

Having been on one of the most remote places on the planet, I've been able to clear the hustle and bustle, and slow to Aloha. The protection from distraction the distance provides has helped tremendously in my focus. But oh my God that ocean beckons. There is something about swimming with sea turtles and hearing whales call when you dive below the surface. Coral reefs, teeming with the abundance of sea life in vivid color make each visit a treat. I try to get in only a few times a week and I've stayed away from surfboards. Only twice have I ventured out for the bliss of a board, carving its signature into the face of a perfect wave. Each trip reaffirmed the addiction, if I fall back in I'll fall right off the planet. My work will never get done and you would never have the opportunity to read it. Besides I'm not 25 any more, I'm a little slower.... go figure. Doing a little body surfing at sunset, with drums in the background at Little Beach, is spiritual expression in the rhythmic surf cascading in perfect little barrels, making for a good substitute to boarding adventures. Warm liquid blue is church for this old mind, body and soul.

The remoteness of Maui does little to isolate one from the media however. The hunt for the predator is alive and well on local cable. Nightly national news and daily talk shows cover the hunt to nauseous proportion. They cover the horrors inflicted upon the victims, inciting the wrath and revenge in punishments. Hunt them down, put them in jail and throw away the keys! The word 'rehabilitation' is never used; the perpetrator is only judged as having a "problem" that can't be fixed. The drug-induced addiction, the real cause, is never brought into the discussions. Thus communication from a responsible perspective is denied. The fact that all men hunt for mates makes them all by their very nature predators. Some become addicted.

The man hunts with intent to capture. The degree at which the sexual hunt is carried out depends on the uniqueness of the euphoric chemical load sent coursing through the brain at time of orgasm and the testosterone level pushing to re-satisfy. Gratifying the need to re-satisfy is different in all men, some can moderate and some can't. Gratification addicts like heroin addicts, needing more and bigger doses to satisfy, lead some men to socially unacceptable levels of pursuit for gratification. Soon the addicted mind will make justification for stepping out of bounds of the norm. It's a sickness of dizzying proportion, the nightly news will attest to that.

The lack of aware responsible communication that the sickness is treatable is leading to more dead bodies. Ever-stiffening intolerance, imposing obscene penalties with little to no treatment, may be creating monsters of gigantic proportion. With life-long humiliations required and the constant threat to survival through diminished opportunity, we may be setting ourselves up for terrorists we have created. We have already seen offenders leave notes of intent to "Take as many people out as possible" before committing suicide by cop or otherwise.

The monster we create is our own affliction of our own creation. The lives lost are a direct reflection of our inability to embrace the idea of compassion, redemption or forgiveness. **The rage of intolerance blinds the path to peaceful resolution.** We rain terror as a tactic to facilitate change. In the case of the sexually addicted, they are legislated into a box with no avenue out through redemption or forgiveness; we are simply backing the animal into a corner. Being in the corner is not a happy place. The adrenaline to change the darkness of the corner into the light of freedom from outside of the box can produce unsavory outcomes. When death becomes an option, things get even worse. Collateral damage is to be expected.

Intolerance of fellow humans leads to violent outbursts and compassionate communication is lost. We as a society, to maintain some sort of order, enact laws of intolerance rather than laws of compassion. The knee-jerk reaction to affect immediate change now borders on revenge as opposed to compassion. Time allotted for aware communication, leading to cooperation in co-creation of responsible rehabilitation, not afforded. The letter of the law has become revenge; the spirit of the law is compassion. Communication to cooperation is grown from compassion. Compassion in all we do guides us to co-creation of a more peaceful end. Communication to cooperation to co-creation, that's Aloha.

Across the board we have to try, or our children are going to die. My composure strains when the innocent die. No end justifies any means that allows harm to come to those caught in the crossfire of ideologies. The addiction humans have to being 'right' takes us down the slippery slope into the abyss of intolerance. Ideologically driven intolerance rains only terror. The compassion of forgiveness lost to the rage of intolerant 'rightness'. Intolerance lacks the knowledge of understanding that forgiving is rehabilitation. It is one of the steps to responsible living. Like any other addiction, the addiction to being 'right' can also be put into recovery mode through forgiving. Unfortunately right now the 'sexually' addicted are being treated, or not, by the 'rightly' addicted, and people are dying. This same road has led to Iraq and like in Iraq innocent people are dying! If I may be so bold to pass judgment, I submit to you that this is 'not a path to peace'.

I'll never forget my 'shock and awe' of Baghdad served from the platter of real time reporting. The embedded reporter's story was on a MASH unit on the front line, the first stopping point for the maimed. Amid morning shift change the reporter's story was directed to a surge of helicopters, swarming like mosquitoes laden with heavy loads of blood. The blood the helicopters carried was that of the innocent. As the reporter spoke of the compassion of the doctors, the videographer scanned the lineup of victims being triaged in front of the MASH tent. The camera angle was knee level and maybe 75 feet away from the 20 or so civilian victims lying in front of the tent. Sorting for treatment was at a frenzy to find those most in need.

The camera angle supplied graphic interpretation of the scene's intensity. The view of the victims was often interrupted by the blur created by the legs of attendants scurrying past. The camera's panning of the chaos stopped when the lens focused on a little 5-or-6 year old Iraqi girl being examined by the nurses. The nurses gently lifted the little girl to a semi-sitting position and her eyes caught the cameras lens as it zoomed close-up. I will never forget that stare. Looking deeply into the lens, her large brown eyes stared back asking "why." This made me ashamed of the 'rightness' that had been allowed to create such havoc.

The little girl's eyes continued to lock onto the camera as they became more distant, looking through the lens and a thousand yards beyond. She was gently reclined and her eyes closed, wincing from pain. The heroic efforts of compassion storied on with the wins and losses experienced in the blood covered operating theater. The photo story closed as the little Iraqi girl's body bag was zipped closed by defeated hands that cried with remorse as they tendered in reverent touch. I was ashamed I had let it happen. I was angered from the powerlessness I felt to prevent such atrocity. I'm ashamed that the atrocity continues. I am now trying to make amends. I will work for peace. That's the Aloha I wish to share.

By Grace if I can save just one, my job will have been successful. Stopping the march that is led by the 'right' is a key. The cornering of the animal has to stop. The hope for peaceful resolution has to be present for the animal to calm. To that end, understanding with compassion is essential. To manifest this understanding to every human will calm the animal we all can become when cornered, preventing collateral damage. To acknowledge addictions as treatable sickness, that with powerful treatments can be overcome, manifests understanding for the diverse paths the human mind can take. Its part of the Universal consciousness of knowing we are all different yet the same.

The power in the treatment is in the compassion of the giving. Being able to empathize with sickness, we can extend our hand in help to those who suffer. We help the mind, body and soul become whole and calm by removing the walls of division that prevent cooperative recovery, keeping the animal trapped in its corner of doom. Compassion from empathy inspires the willingness to give. Giving is the hand that is offered in peace. When truly given, no strings attached, compassion is the tie that binds and healing begins. It's that Grace, through which the sick are healed, allowing the animal to venture out of dark corners and into Light.

So, compassion is there in the Universal consciousness; little stimulation is needed to fire its use. It's the giving that needs a little push to be rekindled. The strangle-hold addiction to money has on us is a cold cloth that dampens the flame of the giving nature we all have within. So hard to part with that, which has taken so much to produce. The harder to produce the more we tend to expect return for the effort. **Return is expectation that isn't part of true giving.** Expecting nothing in return is a hard concept to accept yet, when practiced, reaps reward beyond the wildest dreams. All we need is to awaken the limitlessness of true giving, no strings attached. I'm slow; paint me a picture, I'll eventually get it. Hana showed me how to lose the selfishness of expectation found in 'me'. Kirsten lifted the project from 'me' to 'we'. The key is "Free".

So now I begin to sort through the volumes of accumulated information that made up the journey I call mine, intent now to share freely the tool I was shown by this incredible creature of Grace and Peace on that warm Memorial Day weekend in Dolores Park a year previous. The deep layers of significance under the simplicity of presentation just now being uncovered in this simple teaching of Peace co-created. Subtle are all the wonders to be discovered in Really Really Free. My passion is to pass on the how and why. Kirsten's hand will tell this tale to Peace; my hand extended hoping you can follow. Simple, she just knew it had to be.

~~~~~~~~

Imagine: If the Really Really Free Market came to your community.

Imagine: If you let your mind calm from the relentless reasoning rancor of rational mind.

Imagine: Knowing with clarity change starts here, now... step outside of your box.

Imagine: You stop long enough to see for yourself what might be Really Really Free?

Imagine: Really Free, Really!

Imagine: You stop and you find a want or a need to feed your hunger.

Imagine: Surrounded by gifting souls your hunger is fed to full.

Imagine: You feel the joy of abundance in enough.

Imagine: Might you share that uplifting for an hour or two.

Imagine: The smile of peaceful fullness spread broadly across your face?

Imagine: Maybe you find a big gift and you share its joy for a few days, a week or more.

Imagine: Your happiness is contagious.

Imagine: Your joy flowing to others around you and they are uplifted in their own experience. And those that you affect in turn affect others. The wave of warmth that you had created that had affected so many, all from the simple act of Really Really Free. Soothing energy abounding ... might you return? Maybe returning one day to gift back with joy? It does not take long before a whole community might look forward to the day of the Really Really Free Market. Needs being met, no strings attached; breaking free from the grip of money for a moment and the treatment for the addiction begins.

Imagine: "All you have to do is just show up".... Kirsten's favorite quip.

Imagine: "We're all in this together".... Kirsten's favorite quote.

Believe: Together We Can!

~~~~~~~

Frank did. And by Grace the box within which he had lived was turned upside down. He began this journey with the intention of ending his nightmare. His was not to be the only nightmare that may end. Like him, the others afflicted by tagging and targeting might have balance and equity restored to their journey as he stepped out with life on line. He was willing to risk, in an effort to avoid collateral damage, which can be inflicted by the cornered animal that has had enough from the other end of the karma pendulum. Spiritual growth from the gifts of Grace created his preference for a balanced living of life to the fullest. Preferring death to life was now the door to close.

Liberated from the bondages of financial concerns, even if for only a brief moment of time, allowed deep focused meditations that culminated in an explosion of scope. Living in isolation on the island for awhile helped. His lanai was his solitary sanctuary where he learned to give over the journey's process to the Grace he knew would provide. Then it was time for human contact.

Not that Linda his roommate, wasn't good company, he just felt the need to get out and explore his island sanctuary. He wanted a little variety after months of solitary reflection. He knew there were lessons waiting to be uncovered and he wanted a small job. Both desires were fulfilled by an amazing little place appropriately named Spices. From amongst the youth of the world that ran the island came inspiration that managed to soften the blow when the creative direction was uncertain. The extra money didn't hurt either. Running room service to the Maui Coast Hotel offered him exercise, human contact, tips, and a little tour guiding to eager new arrivals.

The revolving door at Spices' breakfast shift was a welcome mat, offering limited starter income for the worldwide runaways that sought out the island for refuge. Working with these beautifully free humans provided proof that even they knew what he was trying to articulate in his wording adventure. So young, yet knowing that something was amiss on the road humanity was traversing, they too searched for a better way as did he. Frank marveled at the drama that played out to fill the slow time and he had a ball experimenting with mentoring the "give 'It' away" thing.

The breakfast club that started the daily revenue engine began at 6:00am. The many different colors that make up each unique personality blended into a rainbow in which you could see both ends. The islands are renowned for those double ended rainbows. Straight, gay, young, old, happy, sad, it was all on menu at Spiceville, managed under the caring eye of breakfast management, 'the soon to be famous' Tony Stokes. They all had monster personalities like the comic book characters of Tony's writings, and most worked second jobs in order to survive in paradise.

One stood out in Frank's heart. He called her "Bama." Christa Zurick was a particularly fond memory of an incredible young adult who actually practiced the art of giving. Born and raised in Alabama and just a few months on the island, her adorable accent thick with down home could strike a smile in anyone's heart. Her tip outs were always most generous and she gave of her art as a favor to him. Nineteen years old with long blond hair, blue eyes and Scandinavian features that take your breath away, you might figure she would direct her energies elsewhere. Her journey through life was just beginning, yet she chose to 'give away' what she had been paid for in the past. Her art on the cart that motored the room service deliveries was Christa's permanent mark left on Maui. She was an example of youth really giving, leaving him with another glimmer of hope for our future.

Frank's reverence for his life on the island opened doors and windows of inspirations for him and those around him. Creatively he was taking giant steps. Spiritual steps were bigger. The warmth of Aloha was beginning to flow through more of the reality of his daily life and he reverently shared his visions with those around him. Most visions anyway. Some of those visions he didn't even understand himself. Like the thought that popped up early in his journey as he gazed at the palm trees from the lanai. Deep in thought about some detail or aspect of his current writing block, up pops "Oh, one day you'll be working in a canyon with Hawai'ians!" Where did that come from! Just popped into his brain as if it was pending reality then fading away back to the task at hand, leaving an intriguing impression of having some truth behind the thought. A sense, if you will. He couldn't explain the strange incantation other than some sort of funny side tripping his brain needed for rest, diversion or whatever. Answer to come eventually.

His intentions to explain to himself so he could explain to others had him living a process of expanding human. Each day had become opportunity for reverent celebration for the gifts the Universe delivered, explainable or not. What had become most clear was the fact that this life he lived was not a journey in an outrageous string of random events, falling together as an incredible string of coincidence. With only two months remaining on the island he had come to know... only by Grace had this journey been directed.

Frank was to have two important visitations before leaving his paradise. The first was to be from his dad and daughter and the second would be from Kirsten. We return to Frank's own wordings to pick up the flavor of the moment that was lived in Aloha through the flow of Grace.

~~~~~~~

"Both visits will give me a chance to venture from the 20 mile radius I have lived within. Adventure will abound as we find all the best places together. Some I know, a lot will be totally new. Dad and Elise will help me choose the very best adventures to share with Kirsten. It's the Grace of Kirsten's visit that really has my heart pounding. The year's work will be given from the heart. My excitement is to see if Kirsten thinks the journey is worth continuing. My euphoria is the honor of being her island host.

My mind races so hard I must take a break. Reality checks in at this moment. I must take leave from my lanai of peaceful blissful thoughts and writings to sign my name to the 'offender registration verification' I received in the mail yesterday, then deliver it to the post office for deposit. I have ten days to comply, but the sooner I mail it the sooner I can forget it. Afterwards I think I'll muster up the courage to go ask Jody if I can buy her a drink and tell her an interesting story. That would be a nice way to end this beautiful day of Grace."......Amazing! That's Aloha!

~~~~~~~

He signed, sealed, stamped and mailed his latest registration update and it was all but forgotten a moped mile down the road. In fact his brain barely noticed the bump of south swell that rolled through the cove in Kihei, as he zipped by on his "Hardley". His mission to ask Jody out for some real human contact had him in high gear before he lost his courage. He was allowing himself to change focus from the book for awhile. Courage only waffled a bit as he pulled up in front of the chiropractor's office where Jody worked. It had taken him eight months to shift to personal interests finally.

Frank had encountered Jody soon after arriving on Maui. The fire in her eyes and long curly blond hair had caught his attention. The little gal had a lot of spunk and seemed to know everyone. She was a perfect candidate to help establish a Really Really Free Market on Maui. Their connection had just never seemed to happen and that was probably a good thing as the work on the book may have never survived a relationship. His adaptation to the flow of Aloha facilitated asking Jody to join him in mutual communication, so he asked and she accepted his phone number for responding. He returned to his regular routine and waited for the phone to ring. A few days later it did and the female voice was not the voice he expected to hear.

His friend Effie McDermott from Pismo was the caller, bearing the reality check that spoiled his flow in Aloha momentarily. He was to be returning to the mainland soon and Effie was friend enough to call and warn him of the escalating negative energy around his position as President of FOPH. He knew that energy did not emanate from the Board but from the City. Frank understood the PR nightmare brewing and with some regret informed Effie he would be submitting a letter of resignation to the board by their next meeting. With Effie's approval he recommended her as a replacement for his position. The sights of the gun had been leveled, the trigger pulled and another small piece of his former life perished. The letter was written and sent. Then thoughts raised other issues.

This little nightmare preceding his return raised the hair on the back of the dog of doom. The thoughts of returning from his current paradise to the state most likely to introduce forced {required} chipping was not a pleasant thought that brought a few dark days to Hawai'i. Returning to the ever tightening noose of governmental restriction of personal freedoms with no recourse avenue afforded, tightened the muscles in his chest. Thoughts of what could happen ran dark. The 'hunt for the predator' being orchestrated by the same government that told us there had been a 'lone gunman in Dallas' was now making the 'sex offender' a hunted animal. The media played right along saturating the airways with the noble cause. The ratings grabbing stories followed by the suggestion that parents should check out the Megan's law website to see how safe your neighbor might be.... or not.

Awareness is one thing, but what about finger pointing at those that may be trying to recover from any addiction. Being told by the 'experts' that you can never recover from your addiction, or attain forgiveness, and you must be watched 24-7-365 for the rest of your life sounded counterproductive to the point of being possibly dangerous. His imagination took him to the depths of what a truly vengeful personality might do if it decided to lash out from this cornering in doom. He also probed the perspective of the vengeful vigilante delivering street justice to 'sex offenders' found easily on the list posted. "We reap what we teach" he thought and if we are teaching 'war' then what should we expect? That really makes the 'war' on terrorism a 'war' with us.

He also pondered the plight of the victims. Were they too forced to remember and relive their own terrors every time they saw a story or read a headline about sex offenders? Did kids in general fear abduction or feel that the stranger on the street might be 'one of them'? Is that teaching 'love' or 'fear' thy neighbor. What kind of a public mind set evolves from that kind of intent? Should we live in fear? Not a pretty place to return to and it made him queasy to think about it. Finding that input to be antagonist and counterproductive even in thought, he moved on and back to Aloha.

He wanted to turn the blight of his and the plight of others into something positive. He was not returning home who he was but what he had done years prior in the eyes of the ignorant. Unfortunately he knew if he were to succeed in raising awareness of the issues for this most disdained of humans and of chipping in general, he could be making himself the target that would surely usher an end just as assuredly as a lead projectile to the temple. No matter what choice he makes, he will be damned if he does and he will be damned if he does nothing, the outcome is the same. Another "catch 22" it appeared, except there was the variable of Grace.

Driven by the Grace of giving he was willing to step out and try any path Grace provided, even if it meant his family was to be exposed to the cancerous innuendo of his web projected guilt of continued perpetration. He became resigned to that end knowing the family was to be strong enough to weather that storm. For him, though, he still felt the sights of the gun with the eye of intolerance training for the kill.

From the wisdom of having had the experience, a simple man toiled for the words to unlock the compassion hidden away by our fears deep within our subconscious. If we still have government resistant to the compassionate use of marijuana, was there any hope for real change? Would the natural Universal laws written in the heart open the road to Peace before the laws of man bury the truth under the 'one way' 'right road' to 'gotcha'? Or was it to be just one cataclysmic event that shrinks the planet into global chaos before Peace ignites.

The image of the brown-haired, almond-eyed Iraqi girl lying on the dusty ground of the desert floor, life slowly fading away through her distant draining stare into the lens of the camera was burnt into his mind. Anybody would have stopped that horror if they could have. Anybody! It was wrong for anyone to justify the lack of compassion that allowed such a death to occur. That is not responsible living to think that such a death as this would not cause anguish to anger. What should be expected in return? Only those addicted to the rush of war created this atrocity and call it collateral damage. Is there any recovery program for this addiction? Shame on us.

The music of life played loudly as usual; now however Frank was beginning to hear the lyrics a little more clearly. He listened closely to the words being sung, his fog of confusion dissipating knowing the Light of Grace shows you what is good for you.

"So hate me today so you can finally see what's good for you," words from a song created by a tortured heart that knew what had to happen before the real healing of change could begin. Lyrics created from the wisdom and pain of the experience. When you hear music that speaks to you, being sung with your passion, your soul is lifted to Grace. The song "Hate Me Today" by Blue October, also spoke of Hana to Frank and he longed to hear her voice, look into her dream blue eyes and heart-to-heart.

An e-mail had to do. He sat in front of the computer he feared. This tool of the 21st Century had the power to do good and evil. The vibe Frank picked up on was mostly evil. He knew his computer knew they were potential adversaries and at the same time potential partners for peace. His computer tolerates his use as he sits to type a note of journeys end and extend a peace to Hana through the apology of a song that had spoken to him. By the time he hit the send key the peace of Aloha had been gifted to him again, though he had just released a special love of his life.

The release was the closing of one door to open another when he asked himself, "What do you want to do with the rest of our life now Frank?" The answer really came quite quickly, "Create peace wherever I can." Clear intent to bring a reawakening of compassion and give it a voice through the hate boiled in fear of the unknown. It is being realized that hate only breeds hate and never serves truth. Truth does no harm. The truth, that what is happening right now to sex offenders is not right, is awakening; yet he knew he would have to be hated anyway so "you can finally see what's good for you."

The young girl whose body had been assaulted by the bullet of a gun used in hatred to further a cause was no more justified than molestation performed in any other manner. The shooters and their supporters are no more than child molesters. So hate them today "So you'll finally see what's good for you." He knew he was to be hated to death and he was at peace with that. He saw clearly that the shrinkage in his life was from the closing of doors that sheltered him from pain was in fact a gift from Grace that suggested other doors are to be opened for real freedom. That same Grace was now opening a new favored door to pursue the truth, held deep within the loving layers of the Really Really Free Market. Journey on.

Knowing clearly the last part of his journey was to be spent teaching peace through giving, while working his way to the last journey, gifted peace itself. He felt he was living up to the name he had been given by the Chumash, "Dreams with Eagles" and he knew Grace supplied whatever was needed for that flight as long as the dream was true. He intended to dream to heights that compliment the limitless good that can be accomplished by responsible human existence. Killing a child is not responsible. We can rise above this. Just show up and Grace will show us how.

He had finally begun freeing himself from the fear of 'what if.' He knew 'what to do now'. It was time to live for the day and enjoy his final days on his island paradise of Maui. Visitors were to be arriving soon and his feelings flowed with an excitement that the end of his stay was to be as thrilling as it was when he had arrived.

It had been a long journey the past eleven years. The spiritual journey over the past ten months had been an even more intense sojourn that touched soul. The endless days spent on the lanai, struggling with the ups and downs of detailing his past and the unknown future, readied him for the here and now. In his here and now he knew but one thing and that is "by Grace we all go and that Grace is gifted, no strings attached." Here, now, he was living proof!

He took a break from his writing and his restaurant job to partake in some much anticipated diversion. Elise and his dad arrived for a week's stay, their company uplifting his heart although the pace challenged the serenity of living in the Aloha to which he had become accustomed. The touristas toured and ate. They snorkeled and ate. They scuba'd reefs and ate. They talked and ate. It was good to be with family, but boy they ate a lot. Keeping up with the demands for adventure on the exquisite island wore him out! He wasn't used to the pace of life being kicked up three notches. Tourist pace is exhausting; you have to slow to Aloha.

Questions from family regarding his writing also put a strain on his security level of consciousness. He offered up the first chapter. They approved and asked for more, but that's as far as he was willing to go. He still felt sensitive about the unfinished work and its contents. The fear of 'what if' that still lingered with the family would soon enough be 'Well Now You Know' and he was not looking forward to that day. It wasn't to be that day or that week, period! He knew his daughter would understand and gain insights to her dad, but the rest of the family might be a little shocked. He wasn't even sure at this point how or where the writing was going to end. He knew he was still living the details of that end.

When the family left, he had just two weeks to finish his book before the arrival of his next guest. He had to claim an ending and be ready to present the work of the previous ten months. It was that damned ending that pushed him into the abyss of old addictions, looking for the way to make the point clear about the sickness and where it can lead. Kirsten was to be the one that would know if the previous ten months of work had been fruitful. He needed to be clear and ready. The fall into the sickness showed him into the edge of insanity, fog slowed progress.

The clarity he sought remained just out of his grasp at the time of Kirsten's arrival. It had been a year since Frank had seen Kirsten, he yearned for the 'here now' they lived when together. By Grace she had stayed by his side during times of anguish, now by Grace she was here at his side to visit. Her evaluation of the work was to let him know if they were going to move forward or not.

He was on pins and needles as he awaited Kirsten's arrival at the airport in Kahului. He wasn't sure how to go about laying out the detail of the work. He just knew in his heart that it was to come as it should. He also knew that the peace of the island was to be gifted to Kirsten during her stay. By Grace he had been gifted the opportunity to serve to that end. So with joy in his heart and leis of aromatic blossoms in hand, he waited to greet this heaven-sent visitor and start their journey of 'here now' on Maui. Frank did ask Grace for one additional favor, however; that was to keep his emotions appropriate. That was gifted and then some.

Kirsten emerged from the arrival gate looking radiant, smiling just like everyone else who arrives for the first time in paradise. Aloha huge hug and draping in flowery aroma was the greeting received after the five-hour flight from San Francisco. Then the two moving as one were out the door on their way to meet Maui. The adventure waited. First stop home to settle in, some rest for Kirsten and of course a quick read of chapter one at Frank's insistence.

He could hardly contain himself as he waited for her to arise. It 'ALL' raced by in the rational mind, the conjecture can take you to the beginnings of doubt. Was the beginning the one it was supposed to have? Were the stories told the right ones? Did it flow? What could he do about explaining the rest? Could he even explain it? STOP! Knowing he had to quiet his mind he stepped out for a walk. Months of toil reliving fear, now awaited an initial response and on the walk to the mailbox he hoped to center his mind to what was really important. The palm fronds wafting gently together in trade winds, laced with pungent floral scent, naturally calms the relentless mind so one can relish the moment. And that moment was superb. After all, his dear friend Kirsten was here now and so was he. That was joy. And Grace was everywhere! That's Aloha and that's important.

Returning to the apartment he found Kirsten's rest had been interrupted by the damned phone. He apologized, she insisted all was good, the rest was revitalizing and she would be down from the loft soon. As she descended the stairs his quieted mind exploded. The quest for feedback spewed out, even before he had caught his breath that had been stolen by her mere presence. The need to know pushed,

"So what did you think?"

Her gentle smile was encouraging. He took a breath and bit the tongue that wanted to pry further. After a pause that seemed to go on forever, brief and to the point she stated,

"What I've read looks good. Only a few minor changes, nothing major."

With that the flow began. Both the flow about the book's how, where, why and the flow into the spirit of the island was like lava that flows to the sea. Like lava traversing a path picked by gravity. Its fluid motion of twists and turns smooth and unimpeded as it rolls on its trek, solidifying as a pillowy mass when it reaches the cool embrace of the sea. And like molten lava their adventures unfolded. The writing discussions flowed with fluid exchange of ideas, solid to the core in its intent and direction. And the island flowed its very best of visually spiritual sceneries and Aloha was felt from its core.

From the top of Haleakala at sunrise or the road to Hana for sunset, Aloha whispered continuously throughout. From sacred shrines discovered in the Iao Valley to a one day private beach at Ho'okipa, the island gifted a special splendor to each day's adventure. The two encouraged one another to try new things as they drank in the reality of 'here now' on Maui. Kirsten testing her boundaries in her first scuba dive with turtles at forty feet at Ulua Beach. Frank inadvertently experiencing altered consciousness, while attempting to keep up with an intense level three yoga class held in a studio in the middle of a sugar cane field in Paia. Both soaked up colors snorkeling La Pe'rouse, Fish Bowl at Ahihi or anywhere else they cared to stop. They enjoyed big vistas of Blue Ocean spotted by the Big Island, Moloka'i, Lanai, Kaho'olawe and little Molokini. Sunsets, full moon risings and every morning they awoke to the song of the birds that greeted their new day. Every night they slept deep while being wafted by the Trade's easy breeze. Maui had taken them in and showed them the best, and their spirits soared when they talked of planting seeds of Peace.

On the last night of Kirsten's visit the drums at Little Beach resonated in the background as they enjoyed a light dinner on the beach at sunset. Fire dancers became images burned onto the memory stick of Kirsten's camera as she moved through the crowd in search of that best shot. The full moon illuminating a swim in the warm clear ocean topped the night perfectly and they returned home to sleep deep again.

The morning of departure was anything but sad. The work that lay ahead of them excited them and the lazy breakfast slowed time. Frank sought advice on the ending of the story they wanted to tell. He wasn't clear and wanted to refresh from the comments Kirsten had made at the top of the volcano, in which she suggested he take the main character in a direction he had never imagined. "Make him a hero." so confused him. Kirsten's wisdom was known when she pulled from her bag a book she thought he should read. She gifted the book with her knowing smile that told him he could find what he needed from within. Frank accepted the gift knowing if handed a book by Kirsten Brydum he had better read it.

The ride to the airport was quiet and reflective. He gazed at Kirsten sitting in the passenger seat looking out at the final scenes passing, he knew at that moment that one day he would be working for this incredible human. That revelation he kept to himself as it was one of those unexplainable visions he encountered from time to time. Frank was curious and asked how Kirsten felt about her journey in Maui. She confessed she felt she had come to a most wonderful place on the planet and was given a backstage pass. He was pleased that her experience had been so rich, he silently thanked the island for gifting that treasure.

At the airport the farewell of love was from the heart. The gift of hope and excitement for the project Kirsten left with Frank was the Grace of her own special Aloha. He had gifted the same and he hoped she had felt it as deeply as he. His sadness at seeing his dear friend go quieted the heart that had not felt this full in a long time. As they sat together before heading for the security check in he turned to Kirsten and spoke his heart,

"I love you Kirsten Brydum."

"I know Frank, I love you too," her heartwarming response. They embraced deeply; he kissed her forehead with the all of Aloha. He watched as she passed through the security check, ascended the escalator and disappeared down the hallway never looking back. That was Kirsten...always moving forward. Never look back.

Her spirit lingered, burning.

Now it was back to work to get ready to go and grow. He picked up the book Kirsten had left and gave it no rest until it was done. Energy flowed, all the 'have to' tasks to leave Maui now upleveled to 'want to', fear of return upleveled to 'preference'. He could either be afraid of the killer or not. He chose not.

He looked closely at the emotional addictions that locked him behind the fear of 'what if' and 'what now'. Accusatory assaults on the ego's security that triggered attacks of unhappiness in the past are now mellowed by indifference and simply regarded as 'what is'. The journey to be lived was to be exactly what it is supposed to be. Kirsten's gift unveiled the magnitude of the last year of service that had taken ten years to create. To touch others with peace was a gift only gifted through Grace and she was amazing.

His last eighteen days on the island were full, rich and joyous happiness. Packing and shipping boxes and his car. Wrapping up work at Spiceville, the book's (maybe) ending and settling his roommate's psyche. Selling his beloved 'Hardley', paying final bills, changing addresses. Registration update for the State of Hawai'i and a courtesy call to detective Cheryl in Grover Beach all flowed with the Grace of Aloha, and he was rewarded with gifts that went way beyond what is needed for sustenance. He also had musings answered.

What had been noted in the beginning of the journey as a seemingly random thought played out to its fullest the Saturday before he left Maui, a full day spent working with native Hawai'ian's, restoring an ancient Taro village deep in a valley of the West Maui Mountains. Gifted with the sharing of island heart and soul by an island elder elicited appreciations only one could receive when standing in the visual wonderland of an ancient village, deep in a lush green valley located far behind the coffee fields of Ka'anapali. Remote, primitive, spiritual and totally unexpected.

Or being gifted a glimpse of a Universal truth evidenced once again by a younger human. It was but one stanza from a poem. It was the source of the evidence that confirmed to Frank that these wisdoms are known to exist in every heart at all ages. The poet's name was Shaylean Mandeville, and she was his charge for training in room service on his last day at Spiceville.

Shay was born and raised on the island, well educated in her ripe old age of seventeen. Between training runs, regular conversations led to talk of his writing and Shay showed interest. All the regular questions of 'what's it about' brought a response of "unconditional giving as a way to peace," and she strained in fascination to know more. His still feeble attempt to clearly explain did stumble across something about 'giving love away no strings attached', to which Shay responded so matter-of-factly,

"Oh everyone knows that. I've even written about it in a poem."

At the end of that shift Shay produced her poem "What I am..." and a stanza of perfection floored him.

Love was not put
In the heart to stay,
For love isn't love
Till you give it away.

Shay was another gift of the island and her gift was simply knowing this Universal truth. Kirsten was right, Frank thought, there is hope for an awakening of real truth on the planet. The designs of evil for a one-world system of chipped, robotic, disposable-if-need-be humans, was definitely going to meet some resistance.

His lovable roommate Linda held a going away party for him a week prior to his leaving. He had not gone out much in the previous ten months, yet twenty or so people showed up to bid him farewell. He had touched some hearts on the island, the folks who had come were genuinely sorry to see him go. Especially missed would be his Designated Driver service that was highly sought after around holidays. A service he gladly supplied... free.

He began a second reading of the book Kirsten gifted, managed to get in a couple of 'yoga for beginners' classes and one surf session that made him feel 21 again. Well maybe 25. Hana did e-mail an extensive update and an offer to help input his work into the computer for him. Frank fired back a message of enthusiasm for her offer and suggested she call. She did. What did bemuse him was the fact that Jody never did.

Twenty four hours before departure Frank was humming up Kihei Rd. on the Hardley for the last time, shirt open and blowing in the breeze. The mass of Haleakala to the east had released another day of beautiful sunshine, bathing the greens of upcountry in light that struck the ground in rays beamed from openings in the puffy cotton clouds shrouding Haleakala. A visual he will never forget. The cool blue of ocean to the west enticed one last snorkel at the ancient fishpond of Ko'ie'ie Loko La', across the street from his home. He watched his last Maui sunset from this place while listening to the ancient horns blown to celebrate the end of another day.

The song of the birds awoke him at 5:00am. He cleaned his space in the loft he had occupied for the past year, zipped his suitcase shut and inventoried his to-do list one last time. All items done to completion, except the one to bring peace to his distressed roommate.

His suggestions that offered pathways through the dark forest of rational mind had not been understood by Linda. Hormonal overload that short cir-cuited her ability to change led to a freefall into depression of mental turmoil. He felt he had failed his friend. Curbside at the airport he summed up his heart's torment, telling Linda, "I've loved you hard over the past year kid. I wish I had been better with guiding you out of your quandaries."

Her eyes welled as she reached out for one last hug. She could say noth-ing. They held one another tight and Linda sobbed from a deep place in her heart. He consoled his friend, whispering encouragement, returning deep con-nection in the strength of the embrace. She held on for a minute as the tears flowed, then released, with a quick glance and no words she turned and walked to her vehicle. She pulled from the curb and drove away; Frank watched and simply asked for Grace to follow his friend.

The Aloha Airliner's jet engines roared to life pushing the aircraft ever faster down the runway and into flight eastbound. Frank's last glimpse of Maui from the plane window was of Paia, Ho'okipa and the coastline road to Hana. Excited about the life ahead, a bit sad he had to depart his island refuge, he qui-eted his mind from the pasting and futuring, settling back to enjoy a few moments of addiction to love. A fire burned in his heart to experience the sen-sations of being in love with someone. He was and he enjoyed the feelings engaged. He just had to remind himself that love is to be 'given away, no strings attached;' after all he didn't know when he might see Kirsten again.

He then turned his mind to the myriad of layers of teaching buried deep in the experience of the Really Really Free Market. Its instruction of peace and harmony through giving was to be directed by Grace. He looked forward to flowing from that space, Kirsten referred to it as "creating peace using share tactics." The book project was already flowing with Grace from her generosities. He knew he'd be working with her to see her work succeed, planting the seeds for a quantum leap forward into Peace on earth in our time. At least these two people were bold enough to suggest it was possible and could be counted on just to show up for the effort. No 'us' vs. 'them,' just 'we' moving forward.

Kirsten lived from a space that knows there is a spiritual reference point in all things; he had become her student. She suggested man's rational mind that operates from the lower levels of flight or fight consciousness kept the planet divided and blind to what the God Spirit really is. God is all things, really is very simple. Kirsten's Light nudged him gently to wrap his brain around the obvious. The Power we call God, Kali, Krishna, Allah, Christ, Buddha, Jehovah, The Great Spirit, It is all things and It is manifest in all things both called good and evil directed by choice that is a product of Man. Man chooses to do good or to do evil. So where does God's Grace really come from? Who is God? I am. You are. We are all part of that Grace.

The experience is ours to choose and the results of each choice shall determine the road we continue to travel. The inexplicable joy received through the Grace of unconditional love far outweighs the emptiness that is bought, sold and traded with strings of ego attached. It is Love. It is God. Giving It away is the Power that is in all of us. Releasing the ties that bind us to the evil of possession and ego is just one of the many lessons expressed in the experiment of Really Really Free. He experienced peace knowing that the Grace in all of us is what he was gifted and now responsible to teach. He promised himself by Grace It will be done.

Frank chuckled to himself at the thought of how appropriate the name of the airline that now transported him to his mainland journey. Aloha is Grace Kahiau, a joy he was destined to share to the far corners. The airline was perfectly named for transport to his first corner. He was not so sure how far, far was to be, but he knew he was going to enjoy the journeys there.

Peace took him to a quiet place in his mind despite the roaring drone of the airliner's jet engines that became the lullaby which brought sleep in spite of the upright position of the travel accommodations. As he drifted off he couldn't help but wonder what the future might hold. His last conscious thoughts of seeing Kirsten again brought him one last rush of joy in the Love that inspired his life. That's Aloha… that's Grace.

~~~~

We are all part of the co-creation of Grace. The string we are and the string we follow.

We're all Grace.
That's Aloha.

CHAPTER 33

IF WE JUST SHOW UP

He wasn't sure if it was the roar of the jet engines, the sharp pain in his neck from sleeping upright, or the extreme dream that woke him from a drooling, heavy slumber. Returning to consciousness was difficult because of the disorientation experienced moving from dream state to now in an unfamiliar surrounding ever so quickly. The sharp pain in the neck was the first issue to address as his mind oriented to the interior of the plane returning him to his mainland home and life. The theme of returning reverberated in Frank's brain as he rubbed the crick of pain in his neck acquired while sleeping chin in chest, then opened his eyes and wiped the drool from the corner of his mouth.

Returning was going to be interesting, was the first conclusion as he pondered ahead into the potential of life unfolding. As the moments of consciousness began to tally, his relentless mind forged forward with speculation of answers to the questions he was just now formulating. He just couldn't help himself stay in the moment, he wanted to know the outcome of the journey before it was lived. The rush of life was starting with a billion possibilities; it took a moment or two before he finally slowed to now and only the near future. The near being the daughter greeting him at the airport and the only thing he knew for sure beyond that was that Grace supplied the rest. All he had to do was show up. Easier said than done. The Aloha flow was already under siege by a brain that felt a shiver of doom.

Just showing up is a process of living an aware responsible life. He arrived home aware, responsible and ready to live. But it's difficult trying to remain on the upper levels when dealing with attack all the time. The new 'offender' registration detective in Grover was bearable, but that responsibility was to do nothing but tear at old wounds. The assault on the Aloha he wanted to continue to live was developing, the continued ban on his participation at the Park only to twist the blade a little further.

The business was in good shape, however, delivering the dollars needed to exist, barely. The thanks he owed his friend Lenny for insuring the health of the business while he was away was a debt he felt obligated to pay immediately. It was priority one on the list of the things to do. It wasn't long before the Bada Bing Crew was pouring more concrete sidewalks, driveways and patio pads at Lenny's. The Grace of grateful for his ability to exist, along with Lenny's smiling face, helped put his smile back occasionally.

Grateful to hateful in seconds though was just a news report away in the blindsiding of society's paranoid knee jerk law making. Moving forward with his eye on peaceful existence was shattered by the choking restrictions proposed by lawmakers, offering safety from the Bogeyman of the 21st century. The State was now offering Proposition 83 to the voters in the upcoming November elections. That Prop made it mandatory for all 'sex offenders' to be saddled with a GPS ankle monitor and restrictions making it illegal for them to live within 2000 ft. of any school or park. A City of Grover ordinance sought to go even further, making the exclusionary distance 2500 ft and to include daycare facilities. Basically, in Grover Beach, no matter where you lived was within 2500 ft of a park, school or daycare center. That was an interesting twist, laws enacted to cleanse a city of people tagged as undesirable on a blanket basis. He angered at the implications. Might he be forced to sell his house and move? Knowing anything was possible, he decided to fire off another letter to his attorney he hadn't heard from in a year, requesting her input on the impact to him in the event of the passing of these pending laws. Once again the paid help did not respond.

The only place on the planet he could escape the constant thought of eventually being forced out of his own home was the oasis of 454 South Van Ness, San Francisco. Membership in the tribe of Kirsten Brydum and her roommate Alex Friend, creating the energy of 'Really Really Free,' was a weekend adventure into higher levels. A step back into the zealous pursuit of truth in youth that explodes into an enriched creativity abounding to glorious heights of awareness, to produce the illusive reality of utopian peace for all mankind. Anarchist ideology stretching the imagination to include possibilities of Peace Parks built with the abundance of 'Free' in the middle of the hate, which has been lived for centuries. Peace parks built for the mothers and children who are done with war. Levels that dared to dream that one day a Department of Peace might co-exist with the Department of Defense. Levels so high that on one particular Sunday in late fall, the trio's energies attained a level that stopped time for the day in the kitchen on South Van Ness, fondly known as "The Bombshelter."

This does not understate his relief felt from the lack of attack in the company of an understanding soul, or the value of the face-to-face contact with Kirsten that was afforded his soul. He adored her, loving the experience she brought to his world, and felt privileged to be included in hers. Her quiet teaching, coupled with Alex's more robust gregarious recital of poetic life lessons, served well for mental health. He was humbled by the Grace that provided him a place to sleep at the foot of her bed and the wisdoms she imparted.

His trips to San Francisco where few at first, becoming many and so very important to sanity. Between those trips to see Kirsten, he read books she gifted to keep up with the sacred growth encouraged in the exercise of pol-ishing his own written work. The spiritual growth she gifted was daily inten-sification to clarify, that which yearned to be quantified and articulated. He relished teachings from the diversity of the Universe, of which he now was more acutely aware.

It was that diversity which kept the tagging nagging from destroying the movement forward in purposed intent. Intent of pure creation to peace guided by Grace floated the boat of change he preferred to sail. He was get-ting better at 'now,' not letting vintage actions of the past dictate who he was in the present. But he struggled with the uncertainty of where the journey leads. Would he have to move or be fitted with an ankle monitor? The depres-sions gloom was lifted by the brilliance of the special friends at the 'Bomb-shelter' on South Van Ness. Each and every one of those trips to San Francisco were so very, very special.

The year end melted into another zero 'something'. He pushed to finish his written effort by isolating himself at his house on the weekends. Input into the computer was tedious. Editing and rewrite needed hours, and during the week he couldn't change hats fast enough to get anything done before retir-ing for the evening. So weekends it was. And despite the constant work, he still had not found the ending for the book suggested by Kirsten almost a year prior. But he tarried on, not only on his writing but on his reading as well, feeling the drive to fill the mind with creativities that might shed light on the path to unfold. He felt as if an unfolding or 'something' was imminent, the call from Hana started the 'something' unfolding.

It was a joy to hear from her it had been a long while again. Hana was in the doom of failed relationship, yearning to continue her faithful struggle to be the best she could be. He could hear frustration in her voice. Frank encouraged her to follow her heart regarding staying or going and again offering his home to her. Unfortunately he couldn't do much more than that. He did inform Hana that if she chose the latter, the future for them might get a bit weird because of the laws that targeted his current living arraignments. That was not appealing to Hana he suspected, which is probably why com-munications eventually flickered into silence and her cell number ceased to operate. His heart was heavy for her, praying she could find the happiness she was trying to nurture with Jerry. He wished it wouldn't be too long before he'd hear from her again.

Time marched on and the unfolding of 'something' was hinting. Awaken-ing to a life led in the wake of Grace, the mind feels the grasp of connection which is entwined in the flow of a life that seeks. Observations heighten when you 'just show up'. Perspective changes. He began to live, expecting at any moment... 'Something'! Kinda rattled the nerves, but he awoke every morning determined to live as much light and as little dark as responsible. He was 'just showing up' daily no matter how hard it was to hold the head high while head down ducking attack and looking for the hints marking the journey's path.

He kept his promise to his friend Jan, traveling north to visit in lieu of payment he had offered for her help with the book's computer input. That had been on the list of things to do as well. The trip to Fairbanks at the end of February taught the danger of incessant cold, awe of spectacle in the Aurora Borealis, and bliss of the ride behind the team of dogs that pulled his sled. With that trip he checked off one of his last promises on the short list. Short list... getting shorter. No signs to unveil any future for a list that was about done. A life slowing that needed 'something'.

Signs of direction had already been given in pieces that were yet to fall together to reveal the journey's direction. Somehow Frank was able to hold on to sanity while waiting. Floundering for purpose is a real energy suck. He still had no end for the book that seemed to be constantly expanding. He had been shrinking away in his house, waiting for the other shoe to drop regarding the new 'sex offender' laws. No notice to move, no monitor strapped to the ankle, no word from his attorney....yet. No park to work at, no projects at Lenny's and no group to work with that didn't require a background check. Mary and Joe moved to Portland, Karen moved to Seattle, Cindy moved to Orange County, Hana hadn't called.

He kept his sanity by thanking the Grace that had created Kirsten and his daughter. Elise's frequent evening phone calls offered diversion from the evenings spent alone. Kirsten's words of encouragement sustained the momentum of the spiritual pursuit. He was to discover that Kirsten's few words where important pieces of the 'something' he was feeling. Kirsten was movement forward always. That is probably an understatement to say Kirsten was always simply moving forward. She was the movement. The movement of understanding post consumer society. Kirsten was quietly building a following of souls through the truth she lived. She was growing a *glocal* consciousness of responsible living, empowering all she engaged to join in the co-creative process of a Collective Autonomy. She was out to change things big time and Frank felt gifted to be so close to her Elegant Energy. He remembers Kirsten coming to him at the back door of the Bomb-shelter as he stood on the stoop sipping coffee, slipping her arms around him for a hug and asking with her warm loving smile,

"What are you feeling right now?"

"I feel like I am the luckiest man on the planet!" his heart responded. He was. She was 'something'.

Encouragement was also found in special places that also gifted glimmers to hope. A special young lady that worked at the grocery he frequented illuminated once again the fact that the young are all over the idea of change. Victoria was an investing fan of the Really Really Free Market concept and their conversations had gone into some depth. One afternoon Victoria produced a poem she had written that she thought embodied the general themes; he was again astounded by the perceptiveness of youth. Frank loves to promote, so we have satisfied the wish and her poem follows:

Societies Social Blunder

This time we cannot change
We walk amongst each other.
The thoughts of another are caged
without any expression whatsoever.
We hide from ourselves.
These bodies house the keys of our worth.
We locked the keys in our car.
Crying at night for I see the world
through these idealistic eyes.
Hoping for change
and wanting to be that change.
I run into these walls and yet I am convinced
I will get through somehow.
Bruises cover my heart.
I am disappointed with my kind.
We were meant to do so much more.
Not for ourselves.
I would like to meet a stranger and spend the day with them   .
We would love each other and spend a glimpse of our lives sharing.
The stingy second-hand of the clock grabs hold of us
spinning us round and round.
We are no longer human.
Human nature would not turn their back on another.
Mirages of money and material hang over us
like a dog salivating over flesh.
Convinced that once we obtain it
we will have success and feel complete.
You tell me that is not a mirage.
It is as though we have no choice.
We locked ourselves in this mess.
Forced to expend our money and have someone fix it.
We felt the need to have this protection,
so much in fact that we can't reach our serenity.
Drowning I sink.
Coughing is a good sign.

The noise means we have not totally lost our breath.
Silence will lead us to our death.
Smile at the person walking by.

Victoria Carranza
7.11.7   12:45am

She got it and that stoked the fires of hope. Otherwise Aloha ran pretty thin when the mind didn't divert from the energy drain of constantly contemplating his circumstance. His writing dealt with that and his mind dealt with some aspect of the writing most of his waking hours. It was a beating drum that didn't afford much tranquility.

At least when he had the opportunity to work with his friend Greg, he could divert his attentions to contending with the physicality of construction work. He could also observe the problems his friend encountered while trying to live in the higher levels of consciousness they both strove for. Tough for Greg when you've been raised in a religious box built by fear from his father, that was a Baptist preacher. Fertile ground to inspire Frank to compare his journey, looking for the commonalities that tie the string in the theory together. And when you least expect it. Total overwhelm. 'SOMETHING' happens.

That third Sunday in June 0Something started like any other. Frank arose looking forward to his coffee and morning read, followed with writing and brunch. The day was a little special. It was Father's Day; he wondered when he might hear from his daughter. That was to happen fairly early; the call was made from Nice, France. Elise was on vacation in Europe and Dad was proud of the daughter's spunk to travel and explore alone. His brother's transfer to London, England did help to establish a family base close to the intended destinations. Nevertheless it was a big step and their conversation reflected proudly of the journey's sights, sounds and smells already encountered. He loved his daughter's strong heart. She was a real chip off the old block.

Wrapping up the Father's Day well wishes and thanks, Dad returned to the reading he felt compelled to finish that morning before continuing on to his own written endeavor. The coffee was smooth and so was the reading that talked of recognizing the call of the 'Sacred Task' and 'The Journey Home.' The last lines he read asked, "Now, knowing what you're supposed to do, when will you do it?" "When?" In a flood of revelation that rolled over him at the very second he read the words from the book, the list of things to do in the life file folder filled to overflow. Each thought felt like the file folder icons on your computer screen as they pitch documents from one to another. Each time a document lands in its recipient folder another directive was revealed and placed on the life list of 'to-do'.

His response went down something like this:

"Oh. Oh. Ohhhh! Oh no. No, no. No, Noooooo! **NO, NO WAY! NO, NO NOT ME!**"

The list went down something like this:

Learn more about Quantum Physics and the spirituality entwined.

Live your intent of heart, revealed on the lanai in Hawai'i... make Peace your house.

Finish your book. Remember ..."It's an important work." ...Kirsten had confirmed.

Do Burning Man. ...Kirsten is right.

You have built one park from the heart; now build one more.

A place for the mothers and children of Peace, built on the borders of hate.

Remember... Kirsten affirmed "You should do this."

Share with them in 'Really Really Free.'

Encourage the planting of seeds for the Peace, to all who listen with open heart.

Two years.

No, is not an option.

Here, now, the end is this.

... Worry not, you will receive the land for free!

Okay overwhelming is an understatement. And the "NO, NO, NO, NO NOT ME" echoed again in empty defiance. Like he really thought he could tell the Universe he would not participate in that which the Universe directed. Bullet fast, short and sweet, taking all of ten seconds and the list of things to do in life overflowed. The 'something' he had felt coming had arrived and the unfolding started. A few more NO, NO, NO's trailed off verbally and he shook his head as if to shake off confusion.

Sitting straight up, he pulled off his glasses and rubbed his eyes as if that might make the directives more clear. Clear was: study Quantum Physics, spirituality, and live the intent of peace. Finish the book; attend Burning Man. Build another Park, to be called Peace, between Israel and its enemies, for the mothers and children who are done with war. Share with them the 'Really Really Free Market' and the abundance of peace it can bring. You have two years; this is the end of the book you have been waiting for. And ...you'll get the land free!

He swallowed hard. The addition of the parts to be completed was huge in scope, the amount of time allotted for completion scant. This all just seemed so ridiculous. To think he should follow inclinations brought on by the fatigue of mental trauma, injected with rich caffeine of a morning brew that is more mud than it is coffee. Add to that some inspired reading from writings with power and 'something' is going to pop. Or... was this some of that, that can't be explained. Calm ensued as review after review of the directives had been run through his head, now suggesting this had in fact been a communication of Grace. A moral point so perfect, timing perfect, the blending of talent to job energy perfect, making the author more than man. Besides the end for the book Kirsten had suggested at the top of Haleakala, he had struggled for a year to find had just been handed to him. That blew him away! 'No' to a request from Grace... Not an option!

The lethargy of no progress melted away in the frenzy of purpose. Egocentricity reduced to nonexistence with every lecture into the reductions of Particle Physics. Then further down the rabbit hole with Quantum. The spiritually abundant landscape of the 'Really Really Free Market' kept the flow going, and by the end of August his stage had been set for Burning Man. Mind wide open, it had to be. He wasn't sure of the why for being drawn to the event, but he was sure that a gift was to be received while there.

So he packed appropriately and arrived at 454 South Van Ness to pick up his other gift. That gift, Kirsten. To him Kirsten was the bar to be measured to, he was honored to be her ride. He flat out loved her. The company of this veteran burner sharing the journey was one of those dream wishes come true. Along with their inseparable comrade Alex, the intrepid trio lived the event theme of Green, rolling themselves to their given space on the Playa with the four cylinders of Frank's little pick up. The tight package of three friends burning all expectation, living diversity and celebrating the abundance of 'Free' with 40,000 of their closest friends was energy of exceptional proportion.

His virgin visit to the epic of the burning of the man was an odyssey into living the 'Really Really Free Market' on a 'Really Really' large scale. A nine square mile footprint on a dry lake bed called the Playa, located in the high desert outside Reno, Nevada. The town created for eight days each year, briefly becoming the third largest city in Nevada, affectionately called Black Rock City. The city has just about anything you would find in any small town. Hardware store, newspaper, radio station, boutique, pancake house, bars, auto mechanic, nightclubs, airport. The city also has a lot of things you probably won't find anywhere else on the planet. The funny thing is you can't trade money for anything in Black Rock City except ice! It is a barter, trade and gifting society that suggests the planet can function from a position of abundance and sharing. Money is no god. Way outside of the box and it thrilled Frank to be in attendance of the future. Every time he explored, the confirmation of elevated spirit oozed from the throngs exploring their own celebration of 'Really Free'. Some of the free spirits took his breath away, so did the art that was spread out for miles on the desert floor. Spirituality was aflutter in all directions and the Temple that stood half a mile from the Man had a constant visitation from those that left the message of Peace and harmony for our planet.

Harmonic responsible coexistence of 40,000 celebrating the gift of free, then leaving no trace at the event's close that humans had even been there was indefinable. Elements of life lived to fullness. What an event! Frank studied the layers to uncover the whys that had drawn him. After seven hours of digitally capturing Playa art on Saturday, day six, he was still wondering why he was really there. His burning question of whether or not the people of the planet will 'get it' in time to avoid disaster had been partially answered. At least the 40,000 or so in attendance did seem to indicate that at least 40,000 or so did 'get it'. That's a long way from 7 billion however. The bigger unanswered question, can a light switch be thrown so that all, at once, can make the paradigm shift needed to save this place we call home? Still no answer to that.

There was, however, some light shed on the motivation that might trigger throwing the light switch. The 'feel good about gifting' the 'Really Really Free Market' exudes was definitely a key to moving the masses. When a gift given fulfills a need that brings comfort, that 'feel good' walks with Grace and that is a place we all like to be. He had his own moment with this Grace while deep in the outskirts of the Playa at an art piece that supplied shade from the torching of the sun. A dust storm had just blown through, and a small building (art) had supplied refuge to several people fortunate enough to escape inside its walls, sheltered from the storm.

Those not so fortunate straggled over afterwards to gain relief from the heat and Frank noticed a little Japanese girl who looked as though she had been crying. Her male friend accompanying her was talking to her with some concern. He thought at first that they might be having a quarrel. He listened, discovering that the girl's eyes had been severely impacted by the dust and she could barely see. Frank remembered that somewhere in the bottom of his backpack he had some Visine, found it and gave it to the young lady. She flushed her eyes back to tolerable and came to Frank to return the unused portion. He gifted it to her for later use. Through the couple's verbal appreciation for his kindness and their gratitude he felt, along with the joy he felt in the gifting, are motivators that can throw the switch for a permanent shift in the way we interact with one another. That's one of the real lessons of Really Really Free. Compassionate gifting...no strings attached, co-creating harmony.

Saturday night they burned the Man, despite the Monday night attempt to do the same by an overzealous reveler. The drummers and fire dancers that numbered into the hundreds performing at the base of the Man before the burn conjured up memories that took Frank straight back to Maui. He could almost smell the island in the gentle warm desert breeze that cooled the crowd of thousands. When the Man was lit in his neon green and his arms rose, the energy rose to deafening. The spectacle of the burn rose spiritual to release.

And when the Man fell, the old was let go and the new was welcomed like a good friend. Afterwards the billion stars in the desert sky illuminated the walk by thousands deep into the Playa to blow up and burn the oil derrick of the Crude Awakenings art piece. Social comment interacting through dramatic art, the night was awe invoking.

Sunday and his last bicycle ride deep into the Playa gave Frank pause to reflect on the wow of the moments he had experienced and the meaning thereof. It had been a solitary spirit journey for him for the most part. He rarely saw Kirsten and Alex. The young-uns camped down amongst the party of the Ghetto Fabulous Posse, a group of 40 or so from the Mission District of San Francisco mixed with family from all over. The 800 block of Borealis was just too close to the action for Frank and he sought the quiet of the burbs at 815 Kelp Forrest. His 50 something couldn't keep up with the 20 something crowd.

He also wanted to provide plenty of space for Kirsten to flourish with her new love Tyson. They had just become an item and Tyson's art project assembled and showing on the Playa gave Kirsten the opportunity to introduce Frank to him. Frank was impressed. Sad he had to step back; glad his bubbly little ball of genius inspiration was thriving with happy. They were a perfect couple. This was one of the growth steps Kirsten was right about when she suggested years prior that Frank should attend the Burning of Man. Again by Grace, learning the value of 'Really Really Free' is really really full of abundance. Trying to hold on... only ruins the flow. No strings, no expectations and BAM!!!! More good stuff.

Temple burn on Sunday night was the not so subtle hint from the Universe that the Light can come on for all, at once. The hint, physically played out on the Playa, was an in-your-face occurrence that spoke softly to the spirit of hope. The smaller East Indian temple that housed the singing bowls was the backdrop for the message, the 10 or so bowls making a most wonderful harmonic sound as they where rung by those who chose to play. That noise to be emulated by the Temple burn assemblage was to be a distinct physical example that Universal spontaneity from the heart can be achieved.

Just after dark a random cheer, arose from a portion of the crowd a hundred yards away, and it sparked a spontaneous chirping cheer from those who sat immediately to the left of the original boisterous mass. In a somewhat sluggish almost hesitant fashion, the cheer continued to flow its noise to the left around the circle of several thousand attendees. The noise level of the wave-like cheer rose and fell in pitch and volume as it worked its way to the point of origin. By the time the noise reached its beginnings the Light went on. The fluidity of the verbal waves pitch, speed and volume synced, and the wave hurled left around the circle a dozen times in a perfect harmonic, much like the singing bowls produced, then came to a stop where it had begun. A thunderous round of applause ensued. Every race, every creed, every desire was represented around the Temple and they all synced to produce a common goal. That's when he knew the work to be done in the middle of hate was for real, to sync a common goal residing in the core of the heart and soul of everyone on the planet. Peace. Well, maybe it took a few hours before all of that set in. What was obvious, Kirsten had been right again. She's Amazing.

His work now was for the Light switch he had been shown to truly exist. Just maybe the 'Really Really Free Market' at a Peace Park in Israel was possibly a switch to turn on the Light that could shine on the path that leads away from chaos. Now that's something to show up for. Couldn't hurt to try, he figured.

As they returned to San Francisco, Frank laid out his revelations and understandings to Kirsten for the first time. He shared the course of actions he would undertake to investigate further pursuit of such a project. He speculated that if he could make contacts that supported the efforts, a visit might be part of the protocol and offered his desire for Kirsten to accompany him. To him she was the catalyst that could draw the dreamer from their sleep and into action. She accepted with her customary bubbly effervescence, "YES", that hinted of knowing that those contacts were to be made. To Kirsten there was no if, only when. He also revealed this was the last chapter of the book. Kirsten smiled her impish pixy smile with a twinkle in her eye saying,

"I knew that."

By November he had arranged a dinner meeting with Cheryl Hancock, who ran a Christian ministry in Israel. Cheryl had lived in Israel for seven years, and if anyone could give him an honest answer to "Am I crazy" he figured it was her. She took time to listen to Frank's proposal in order to afford feedback as to the viability of such a plan. After thirty minutes of intense information offered up by Frank about the vision of Peace delivered by Grace, Cheryl offered up her summation. She started slow so as not to misinterpret feelings she was experiencing regarding Divine timing.

Cheryl revealed her responsibility to a request she had been shouldering for the past year was now lifted by the fulfillment of her promise to help. It had been a year prior, a couple had come to her with their plan to build Peace in the region and Cheryl noticed the plans seemed similar in scope. The couple had asked Cheryl for her help and she had promised to look into finding them someone. Someone that could help direct their landholdings for a Peace Park, to honor the daughter they had lost in a suicide bombing in Tel Aviv. Here that help was being handed to her. She could now check off one of her items on the list of 'things to do because I promised' and she said that felt good. The two then set out a rough outline on how to proceed, parting late in the evening with the promise to move forward rapidly. Frank was simply blown away with how fast progress had been made. The Universe was right

...land for free. This project was beginning to feel as if it was falling together like Hawai'i had. He was so excited he called Kirsten with the good news that night. Kirsten said,

"I had no doubt you'd make that contact."

The journey was picking up speed, so in mid-November he applied for a passport. Checking another promise off his list, he flew to Seattle to enjoy Thanksgiving on Whidbey Island with Karen, having the actual dinner feast at her Iranian friend's home. Whose timing was that? Machmoud and Fadia provided fertile ground to test float the Peace Park idea on the culture from the region to which the journey was to be made. The resounding favor they found in the project lent energy to sustain a growing confidence that what he was attempting was good stuff.

By the beginning of December, Cheryl had Frank e-mailing Rabbi Michael, who was the cousin to the landowners in Israel. Frank's passport had arrived in just two weeks and 'yes, Gina' it did have a chip. And on his birthday he ended his book. The new journey was coming together just as the Hawai'ian adventure had. That year began with little to no roughage noticed in the passing of the annual registration ritual of pictures and prints. Spiritually life soared.

Crazy as it seemed, 'Something' was driving the theme bus of 'if it is good it will happen'. "Holy crap" is all he could think as he watched, understanding that 'Something' could be created from nothing when it is tapped from the flow of the Universe ... that's Grace. By the end of January the invitation to meet with the landowners in Jerusalem had been extended. So Kirsten and Frank penciled in June of 08 to journey together to the land they felt would be the place from which Light might shine to the rest of the world. If we can do it here we can do it anywhere, the message to be sent. They were determined to 'just show up' and share the gifts they had to give. They really made a dynamic team. Amazingly, the landholders had agreed to share their land in the experiment of a Peace Park celebrated by the bounty of Really Really Free. The concept of 'we together just showing up' can be the shift for global paradigm change.

Like Kirsten emphasizes with her favorite quote,

"We're all in this together."

Kirsten furthers with Grace requesting, "All we want you to do is just show up and use your share tactics." Speaking from knowing she offers, "There really is enough." Suggesting as she taps her heart, "Change starts here." She then gifts from her wisdom, "We all tap from the same Source so Really Really enjoy sharing your Light."

Frank is... Now, Really Really Free. Sharing his Light of Peace... that's Grace. Aloha.

~~~~

We are all the Source of Light and Grace in the tapestry of life we weave with one another, co-creating the brilliance of a joyful perfect world we all wish to gift to the strings that follow in our path. That brilliance is Peace, harvested from the Garden of Heart by the Elegant Energy of Grace we all are. Truth: We're all in this together. Believe: Together we can. Imagine:

PEACE

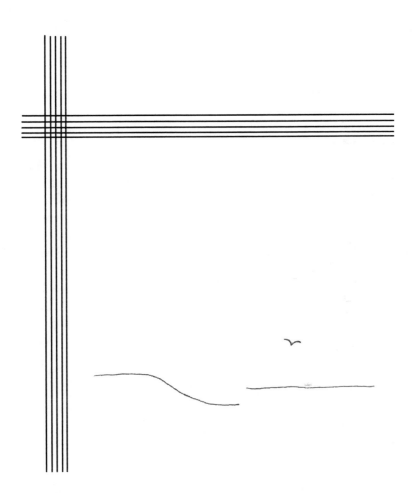

EPILOGUE

. . . So the winter months blended into the spring, with the whirl of life keeping Kirsten and me ramping up the energy. Kirsten was expanding her community creation events of Access Café, Really Really Free Market's, and Free Yoga classes along with her jobs. Her work as a waitress at Weird Fish Vegan Restaurant in the Mission District paid the rent, Spiritual activism work at New College helped pay tuition as she wrapped up her last semester for graduation in June. Add to that a consuming drive forward to create an intensely deep Senior Thesis entitled "Spiritual Anarchism." Plus she was planning to squeeze in a trip to Israel in between graduation, and her Collective Autonomy Tour which was already envisioned for mid summer through early fall.

The CollAut Tour was a brainstorm of Kirsten's to venture out to the Midwest, Eastern seaboard, and Southern states to observe what other community activists had found as solutions for food, housing, health care, education and market/resource exchange for those without. The information gathered she could then post on the internet to the collectiveautonomy.net web site, so all could have FREE access to the prolific amounts of information needed to facilitate a transition into a post consumer society. The CAN web site was just another gift of her brilliant spirit. She lived daily to serve the greater good. Kirsten was always building bridges of abundance through the power of information. Her intense energy to be the mission of change was astonishing. Made me tired just thinking about the overflowing plate of life she generously shared. I, on the other hand, only added a fairly clean manuscript of our work for her to edit, plus a lighting fast trek to Israel to talk with the folks that wanted to hear about our ideas for building a Peace Park on their land. I felt guilty about heaping more onto her plate, reassuring her that the books edit could wait for the train rides from place to place while on her CollAut Tour journey.

A growing number of us felt the current economic environment was destined to be tested soon by the pressures of inflation and greed. The first blatant signs of that pressure manifested in May, as I began to research plane fare pricing for our trip to Israel. Pricing jumped so high from the effects of one-hundred-dollar-a-barrel oil; we decided to put the Israel trip off until after her return in fall. I notified our hosts of our revised plans for the trip, then geared up for June's Really Really Free Market and Kirsten's graduation. Kirsten's call at the end of May to ask if I could take care of Shiloh, her cat, for the months while she traveled was put on my return list for that last weekend of

June. I couldn't refuse when Kirsten said, "You're the only one on the planet I can trust to take care of him."

The last weekend of June in San Francisco was a rare treat of sunshine for the gathering of friends and family from far and wide. The Bombshelter was full to overflow. Shiloh and I shared space on Kirsten's floor. Kirsten and I shared details of upcoming travel, and a new love that has inspired her journey. John Viola, a defense attorney from the City, was an amazing glow growing in Kirsten's heart. I marveled at the story she told of the chance encounter years earlier, and the crush she felt, that had now bloomed into a glorious relationship after another chance encounter that facilitated connection just two months prior. The courting was done through chess matches held in the most unusual locations. Her accomplished life now polished to brilliance by profound love that was infectious. I was glad to see her so happy. John was away for the weekend so I wouldn't have a chance to meet him until she returned in early October.

Before things got too hectic into the weekend, I took Kirsten and her roommate, Alex, out for a dinner to celebrate their academic accomplishments. The three of us enjoyed our own special connection of creative energy one more time. Heart, to heart, to heart, for life. The events of the weekend unfolded as scripted by the Universe. I toasted her academic success, served for the Really Really Free Market, and hugged her deeply with "I love you" as I bid her safe travel on her journey to champion change. Kirsten gifted "I love you too," then bid Shiloh and me farewell as emotion tugged. Kirsten turned and walked back to the Bombshelter with Alex, never looking back. That was Kirsten, **now** was always moving forward.

The summer fell into fall as I read the e-mail commentary sent by my dear friend as she toured and I awaited her return. Communiqué #1 dated August 10th 08, chronicling a romantic four days spent in Brooklyn, New York, with John, then on to West Philly. Bicycling to urban farms, benefit for Critical Resistance, cruising a free store, attending a single act play about the drama of our globalized food system, and garnering valuable insights on housing activism. Signing off with; "You're all in my thoughts. Misses and Kisses," Kirsten.

Communiqué #2 was logged mid month in Detroit, Michigan. "I arrived in Detroit at 7:30 am, with no contacts or place to stay after an overnight greyhound from Buffalo. This was the much-anticipated first moment of total estrangement. Since my last update I've been through Rhode Island, Boston, back to Brooklyn, and westward to Buffalo." Her investigations included anarchist-owned housing collectives, donation-based communal diners, interfacing with the Detroit Agriculture Network that transforms empty lots into a local food system, and then participating at the Northeast Anarchist Network meeting. Kirsten loved the train rides between destinations and was becoming more fluid "traveling as a lonesome stranger" carrying her house on her back, arranging needs as she went. From there it was on to Chicago, Milwaukee and Minneapolis. Signing off with; "Hope you are happy and enjoying the last bits of summer, wherever you may be. Sending you love from four states," Kirsten.

Communiqué #3: August 31, 2008 titled "Approaching Occupied Territory," relived Kirsten's voluntary walk into the police repression surrounding the Twin Cities and the Republican National Convention. Her intention was to be witness to one of the most poignant demonstrations in the States since the WTO shutdown in Seattle 1999, and to volunteer in the Food not Bombs kitchen to feed thousands of people in the streets. She did lament a bit more on the wasteland of Detroit, a city built to accommodate 2 million with a population today of only around 80,000. "An early morning 'traffic report' cut to a shot of barren highways. Public squares stood empty, their fountains presenting for no one. Trees grew out of disheveled warehouses. Weeds overtook vacant lots where abandoned homes had been bulldozed. And roofless houses, like a charred skeleton, littered the broken city."

"Sure, there's some romanticizing of a place like this: a post-industrial workless wonderland free for the taking, ripe with opportunities to create a pirate utopia. But in reality, the scene was sad. Some people do still live in Detroit, and the few that I met from the activist scene were bitter and burned out. It's hard to create the world you wish to see when there are no resources, few comrades to inspire, and no spare energy. Instead most turned to alcohol to blur the scene of their economy slowly disappearing."

Milwaukee's small activist community of Riverwest was a more vibrant encounter however. Riverwest's Neighborhood Association had created generous gardens, a food co-op, a local newspaper and a farmers market. I could tell this little nook of activism uplifted Kirsten. She signed off with; "So, now I'm short on time. This update is incomplete but I wanted to get it off before things pick up around here. 'Till next time, all my love." Kirsten

Communiqué #4 dated September 9 2008; "Processing Riot Police & Falling in Love with the No-Coast." This was a huge critique of events lived while in St. Paul for the RNC. The second largest police deployment in our nation's history met non-violent protesters with teargas, concussion bombs, rubber bullets and mass arrests. Her work as a cook for Food not Bombs to help feed the throngs of people was cut short by police intimidations. Disillusioned by police violence, National Guard soldiers, ineffectual permitted marches and surveillance cameras, Kirsten moved on to Madison, Wisconsin. There she found an age-confluence of social activism that had developed a local currency that, for her, opened space for a deeper understanding of the US currency system and logistics needed for possible alternatives. She scored a loaner bicycle and visited Madison's famous Farmers Market, spent a day in the Peace Park helping out Food not Bombs with a friend and sometimes travel partner Marika. She eluded rain storms, curling up on floors gifted, eating couscous and tahini out of her backpack. Wooed hosts with tea ceremonies, conquered public transportation systems, washed her clothes in bathtubs, thanked new friends for unexpected generosity and sometimes daydreamed about a sweetheart in the City by the Bay. Then on to St. Louis to visit with friends that could show her more counter institutions to fit into her little red notebook. She was so busy that I dared not contact her to ask how the edit of the book was coming. Kirsten signed off with; "Constant Love," Kirsten.

Communiqué #5 delivered in late September, told of St. Louis' varied and inspiring housing opportunities available amongst the abandoned, dilapidated North Side industrial wasteland along the Mississippi river. Then visiting Cement Land where people were living in abandoned train cars and cabooses. She visited New Roots urban farm co-op, and the Red Brick Land Trust that takes properties permanently off the market, putting them under the community's protection. Kirsten then boarded the Missouri Mule for a five hour train ride to Kansas City, arriving to a friend of a friend that welcomed her into a family of fellow activists that fed her. She shared floor space alongside six others, enjoying insightful political theory conversations and green, verses red anarchy debates that persisted until morning. They passed the remnants of hurricane together, spending days inside an apartment, singing songs and laughing, content with their secluded world. From there she trained back to Chicago, to catch a ride on to North Carolina. The to-good-to-be-true Craigslist ride took a strange turn and Kirsten was left stranded in downtown Indianapolis. She found shelter that night in a surprisingly comfortable hostel, and the next day connected with a back-up rideshare. "All in all, I was delayed a day, but the reward was found in traveling into the night, weaving through the looming shadow mountains with a feminist sociologist, a giant dog and a veggie oil Jetta."

Kirsten landed in Asheville, North Carolina, a small town nestled into the Appalachian Mountains. Kirsten comments, "Oh, I'm starting to feel a little tired. I have less energy to get out and fill my days as completely as I can. I'm cozy on a porch in Asheville. I'm quite content to take it easy in this sweet spot." Eventually she ventured out to find a fledgling Local Exchange Trading System (LETS) supporting a local alternative economy, and a worker-owned infoshop project called the Firestorm Café & Books that encouraged the local barter system. Kirsten enjoyed catching her breath in the Smoky Mountains, "with luscious greenery and wild sunsets." From Asheville it was on to Greensboro for a day, then on to Carrboro, North Carolina. Carrboro was the Really Really Free Market capitol of the country, and Kirsten was in seventh heaven. From there it was on to the Deep South for one last stop before the journey home. This was Kirsten's last entry on September 25, 2008:

"Right now I'm rolling into New Orleans. I really don't know what to expect. An old friend of a new friend offered to pick me up from the station and get me to the house of another friend of a friend. I am overwhelmingly grateful to the strangers I have met along the way who have been willing to go out of their way to welcome me to their cities. The sun is setting on the bayou-licked lands and I am truly fortunate. I have rounded this beautiful Southeast corner on the Crescent line today and from now on I am westward bound. Getting closer," Kirsten.

A day and a half later, Kirsten made her final journey home. She was bicycling back to her accommodations just outside the French Quarter when she was abducted, sexually abused, robbed and shot to death in the early morning hours of September 27, 2008. Darkness stole Light. The violence Kirsten abhorred extinguished her Elegant Energy of Grace. Raging bullets from an angry gun that knew not what they had done, took the Light of a saint from us all. She Loved everyone, and all life had to offer. Kirsten was the brilliance of Grace, lived and gifted daily. She was a precious soul of golden string, woven into the strings of so many other journeying souls. She gifted all the gift of abundance. Kirsten's intensions championed change for the greater good. I am sure as Kirsten transitioned into Greater Light, she was always moving forward, never looking back... no regrets, no fear. On that night we all lost one of the gifted children.

Two days later the family and I were to find that we are all just one phone call from our knees. Confusion of grief staggered my stride of life; I struggled to make sense of the loss I felt in my heart and soul. So deep the pain, I felt as if it was the end to all that we had walked in kindred spirit. Kirsten knew my darkness and Loved me anyway. Now she was gone, and I was lost in intense sorrow. Light from friends, family and the spirit of Kirsten's favorite quote, "We're all in this together" kept me breathing and moving forward, looking for the path that I should now walk. The message that resonated: I was to do that which Kirsten and I had set our intentions to create. Finish the work on our book, and follow through with our dream of a Peace Park that we wished to shine as a Light of hope for all of us that are done with war being written in our books of life.

It took two months before I could even open the book to work. Three months after Kirsten's passing I boarded an plane for Israel. Some of Kirsten's ashes now rest in that land we wish to guide to Peace. Kirsten is in my heart and the hearts of many others. And Her Light is the switch compelling our movement forward **NOW** to be the change. The end to division may finally be at hand. The Divine Feminine abounds when we **KNOW** "We're all in this together."

PEACE

Kirsten and I were bonded souls, equal partners in the creation of this work for change. We agreed from day one that profits from the sale of this work would be shared equally, and in so keeping, half of all proceeds from this book's sale will be donated to the Kirsten Initiative. The Kirsten Initiative provides funding for the creation of Really Really Free Market's, Access Café's, and Peace Park's in Isreal, and around the world where requested. After all, we all answer this question exactly the same; "From your heart, what do you really want to see for you, your family, the planet and its people?" Peace has been the answer received from all we asked. What better way to tell our leaders exactly what we want them to truly work toward. If We Work for Peace, so will they.

If you would like to learn more about this beautiful human and her work, simply Google Kirsten Brydum.

Mission Statement

The Kirsten Initiative assists projects which embrace interdependence by sharing abundantly the resources within the community and that together we are the source of heartfelt energy, co-creating a strong, sustainable, peaceful, and spiritual community in which we all flourish in balance knowing
"We're all in this together."

On April 22, 2010 Frank was savagely attacked with a hammer by a young man who entered Frank's home with intent to commit robbery and cause great bodily harm to a sex offender whom he had targeted from information found on the Megan's Law web site. By grace Frank survived.

Mahalo Nui Loa for your support.
May you be surrounded with Lei Aloha.
Peace to you in all you do.

Finished 1.5.8 2105 hours
Edit 2.17.8
Edit 1.26.9
Edit 3.8.9
Edit 4.5.9
Edit 5.7.9
Edit 5.23.9
Epilogue 6.6.9
Edit 10.28.9
Emailed to publisher 12.28.9
First Press Pass 5.8.10
Approved to Print 6.10.10

LaVergne, TN USA
09 July 2010
188999LV00005B/3/P